Kvetching and
Shpritzing

Dear Ed:

After you read my paper
on "Catskill Comedy," you praised
my skills as writer as well as
speaker. Such a kudo from a
distinguished academic spurred
the completion of this book.

I hope you will not suffer
disappointment. Racine famously
observed that "Life is a comedy
for those who think; a tragedy
for those who feel." We experience
both in abundance; therefor we
need the jokes. Enjoy!

Joe Dorinson   12/1/2015

KVETCHING AND SHPRITZING

Jewish Humor in American Popular Culture

Joseph Dorinson

Foreword by Joseph Boskin

McFarland & Company, Inc., Publishers
Jefferson, North Carolina

ALSO OF INTEREST: *Edited by* Joseph Dorinson *and* William Pencak: *Paul Robeson: Essays on His Life and Legacy* (McFarland, 2002; paperback 2004)

All photographs are from the documentary *When Comedy Went to School,* courtesy of Catskill Films, LLC.

LIBRARY OF CONGRESS CATALOGUING-IN-PUBLICATION DATA

Dorinson, Joseph, 1936–
    Kvetching and shpritzing : Jewish humor in American popular culture / Joseph Dorinson ; foreword by Joseph Boskin.
        p.   cm.
    Includes bibliographical references and index.

    ISBN 978-0-7864-9482-8 (softcover : acid free paper) ∞
    ISBN 978-1-4766-2056-5 (ebook)

    1. Jewish wit and humor—History and criticism. 2. Jewish comedians—United States—Biography. 3. Jewish entertainers—United States—Biography. 4. Jews in popular culture—United States. I. Title.

PN6149.J4D68 2015
809.7'935203924—dc23   2015033251

BRITISH LIBRARY CATALOGUING DATA ARE AVAILABLE

Front cover: Comedian Jackie Mason, 1969 (Klein & Jacino/Photofest)

Printed in the United States of America

McFarland & Company, Inc., Publishers
    Box 611, Jefferson, North Carolina 28640
    www.mcfarlandpub.com

Table of Contents

Acknowledgments

My roommates in college and at summer camp, Bob Boikess and Ira Goldenberg, continually imparted a mother lode of joke lore before and after the Internet was invented by Al Gore. A superb mimic, Ira, who died in 2010, artfully turned *tsores* (trouble) into comic observation. He taught me how to use levity to fend off an aggressive antagonist with humorous acupuncture, deftly needling a powerful opponent with impunity. I miss him fiercely. Bob Boikess, on the other hand, has compiled a voluminous collection of jokes, second only to "Uncle" Milton Berle, which he imparts orally with excellent timing and uncanny accuracy. Prolific author, also a Camp Kinderland alum, Henry Kellerman who shared many insights about psychoanalysis, film, and Yiddishkeit also deserves *koved* along with credit.

Words of gratitude go out to pioneers in our field no longer among the living though their vital contributions to humor studies endure. Sig Altman, Sarah Blacher Cohen, and Sam Janus spring to mind. Altman made me aware of certain recurrent themes in Jewish comedy. His death (at an early age) left a void in the ranks of humor scholars. Janus, a former colleague at Newark State College (now Kean University) wrote important articles on Jewish comedians, detailing their disproportionate representation (80 percent) among the ranks of first-rate comedians while Jewish-Americans only numbered 3 percent of the nation's population. My indebtedness to Professor Sarah Blacher Cohen, a masterful editor, a luminous author, a fine actress and a heroic woman who confronted pain and disability each day with admirable courage, is manifest throughout this book.

Alive and well, veteran columnist Steve Lipman wrote an excellent book on Holocaust humor that continues to inspire readers. Steve, whom I met in 1986 at a conference on Jewish humor at the New School for Social Research in Manhattan, solicited an article on Joan Rivers, which was published in *The Jewish Week*. Friends Tom Friedmann and Ira Epstein continue to amaze me with their multiple skills as they stitch media sources into their wonderful lectures on humor: illustrating that superior scholarship need not be deadly dull or confined to an ivory tower. Their cogent analyses invariably generated ripples of laughter along with pithy observations. Colleagues in many Elder Hostel programs, I joined them because I was both older and hostile. Now identified by a new rubric, Rhodes Scholars, these programs exposed me to their expertise from which I derived much benefit. More recently, Lawrence Richards, screenwriter, producer, movie maven, and friend, put me into his fine documentary film, *When Comedy Went to School,* wherein, contrary to most Jewish husbands, I had a speaking part. I also benefitted from author Lawrence J. Epstein's two excellent books, especially *The Haunted Smile,* that provide a template for this vital subject. He also played a prominent part as "talking head" in the Richards's documentary, co-directed expertly by Mevlut Akaya and Ron Frank.

I am indebted to many friends and relatives, too numerous to mention in a brief preface, but a few must be praised for their unqualified loyalty and gentle prodding to complete this labor of love. As Willie Loman's wife, Linda, insisted: "Attention must be paid." Thus, in gratitude I pay homage to childhood friends from the old neighborhood: "Cousin Vinny" Chiarello, Mike Gosset, Gerry Londin, Ivan Hametz, Irv Brazinsky, and Howie Weinberg. Boys of the "hood," in Brooklyn's Williamsburg Housing Projects, we gathered at Menashe's Candy Store to exchange jokes and comic observations about everything that we found funny, from teachers to parents and cops. More recently acquired friends also lent their support. Bob Gruber continues to send me clippings pertaining to all of my passions, from sports to humor. Dave Symons and Warren Lewis, two Brooklyn College alums—one a retired New York City lawyer; the other, a CPA, indeed my accountant—offer wise counsel in times of *tsores* (trouble) and companionship in better days. On April 15, Warren keeps my integrity intact when I send what I owe to Uncle Sam.

At LIU Brooklyn, I was enriched by such colleagues as Joram Warmund (co-director of a memorable conference honoring Jackie Robinson), Dennis Carpenter, Gary Marotta, Michael Hittman (with whom I co-taught an interdisciplinary course in humor), Sid Horowitz, Stan Mersand (former student; current friend), and our "Boss," the late Tom Stirton, who hired me though I brought a black eye (from an errant elbow in a basketball game) to a pivotal job interview. Over lunch in the faculty cafeteria, we bantered in a kind of "can you top this?" jousting or jesting contest, often spiced with Jewish humor. My students at LIU Brooklyn, starting in 1966, tested me in a variety of ways that sharpened my pedagogical skills and stimulated a latent desire to publish rather than to perish. I received solid support from Provost Gale Haynes, Dean David Cohen, and Media Arts Professors Stu Fischelson, Steve Molton, and Norman Steinberg, co-author of *Blazing Saddles* and *My Favorite Year*: two films teeming with Jewish humor.

Columbia College, where I learned how to learn as well as to teach, strengthened friendship's bonds and produced enduring connections with Bernie Nussbaum, Ernie Brod, Barry Dickman, Arnie Abrams, and their spouses. Close to home in Brooklyn and Florida, Stan and Gloria Kanter gave me encouragement when most needed. Add my youthful cousins, Mal Dorinson, 97 (now), Jeffry Mandel (the best man at my wedding), Betty Eldman (who died on September 6, 2015; one month shy of her 95th birthday), Ethan Sincoff, Dan Silagi, Ruth Smith, Sandy Hirsch, and Diane Laden and their bountiful families to the mix and you have all the ingredients for a good life, perhaps a good book as well.

A major hurdle in this literary adventure was my absence of computer skills. Hence, I needed all the technical support that I could muster from the excellent LIU staff under the aegis of Delicia Gaines. This stellar group encompasses Marfua Sadia, Alisa Yalan-Murphy, Kan Lun Fang, Stuart Alleyne, Garth Trotman, Keerthi Korthiwada, Md. Bodruddoza Rafique, Ian Williams, Monique Jackson-Howard. All provided assistance at critical points in pulling the narrative together.

To my parents, Peter and Rita Dorinson, who crossed the Rivers Jordan, Styx, and Sambatyon in 1962 and 1976, respectively, to their *rueh plotz* (eternal resting place), I owe life and laughter. My dad was a wonderful raconteur

Kvetching and Shpritzing **author Joe Dorinson pretending he's a sit down comedian as he offers insights on Jewish humor, his magnificent obsession.**

whose humorous stories captivated my older cousins and me. He shared many adventures as a teenaged runaway, hobo, "doughboy" soldier in World War I, IWW "Wobbly," activist, and adventurer. My contrarian mother aspired to high culture with serious pursuit. Her extraordinary demands on our nuclear family compelled me into a comic mode as a coping mechanism. In 1962, for example, she called me one Sunday morning to warn against the danger of impotence through erotic excess, not unlike the mother of Alexander Portnoy. She complained: "Joseph, you will run out of juice!" "Not to worry," I replied, "I drink four glasses of orange juice, daily." Listening to this irrational discourse, my roommates chortled with stifled mirth.

Sadly, my parents did not live long enough to witness the assent of their only child from underachievement. My wife, Eileen, and children, Hilary, Paula, and Robert (plus grandchildren Leila, Hailey, Rebecca and Brodie), however, contributed. They "paid their dues" while I labored in libraries, conferenced in distant cities, and wrote articles in isolation. I owe them more than can be measured quantitatively. My wife, Eileen, prodded me to clean up my desks and consoled me in difficult times. Unable to drive to lectures due to a series of surgeries, I depended on her motor skills as she played the loyal chauffeuse. With a keen, critical eye, Eileen urged me to put away yellowed notes during my lectures and to offer eye-to-eye oral discourse. Consequently, my presentations have improved measurably.

In the last analysis, a *geshrei* (or outcry in Yiddish): *Me ken laybn ober meh lost nisht!* (They don't let you live!) can be defiantly countered with this formula: *leybn und lachn* or life and laughter—with lots of love on the side. Enjoy what follows.

Foreword by Joseph Boskin

Professor Joe Dorinson is an historical messenger, and this work is a singular offering in the study of humor, a paean of imaginative scholarship. He ranks among the seminal figures in this society, as well as others, who focus on the subjects of popular culture, social change, ethnic conflict and gender issues.

I have always marveled at Professor Dorinson's wide-ranging intellectual pursuits and his constant output. His variegated pieces have always reached out beyond traditional boundaries, and his analyses—illustrated by numerous articles, scholarly papers, and focused monographs—have been outstanding in their insight and contribution. This vast breadth of work attests not only to extraordinary energy which many us find daunting, but also to an innovative mind enlarged by a sweep of interdisciplinary fields.

Thus, after publishing many articles on this topic, he has now produced a volume that not only is a welcome addition but one that vastly advances our comprehension of the subject's complexities and intricacies. And, to his credit, his latest foray is bereft of academic jargon; it is written in accessible prose that packs a powerful punch. Succinctly stated, his thesis is that Jewish humor provides a people millennially poised on the margins of society with a carefully constructed defensive perimeter as well as a weapon for counterattack. In so doing, they have elevated and broadened the scope of human laughter.

At this juncture, a disclosure on my part regarding his extensive productivity: I first met Professor Dorinson in 1982 at an International Conference on Humor & Culture in Washington, D.C., and was instantly drawn to his intellectual presence and personal qualities. A rewarding consequence of that encounter has been an ongoing relationship in which we have delivered joint papers at a variety of conferences, co-authored a major article and collaborated on mutual research and publications.

1

In this new work, Professor Dorinson operates as a cross-over artist selecting crucial facets of Jewish lore in history, language, literature, music, biography, theater, media, comedy clubs, and folk stories. A most ambitious task to be sure; yet he meets the challenge with kudos for his sweep of sources. Canvassing a vast array of primary and secondary materials, he persuasively demonstrates how Jews—as well as their African American counterparts—developed a keen sense of survival through transformative humor operating outside the mainstream but on the cutting edge of American culture. Inter-racial cross-fertilization is a powerful aspect of this narrative.

Harry Golden, a Jewish sage heralded for publishing a newspaper in North Carolina for decades in the mid-twentieth century, exhorted his readers to "Enjoy! Enjoy!" Professor Dorinson would second that emotion by inviting his readers to share his joy in "Kvetching and Shpritzing."

This volume is an intellectual and illuminating journey.

Joseph Boskin is an emeritus professor of American social and ethnic history at Boston University.

Preface

This book began many years ago. As a youngster, I played the class clown. Operating on the premise of anything for a laugh, I drove many teachers crazy while entertaining my classmates with crossed eyes, unsolicited commentary, and imitation of surly supervisors. Laughter proved helpful in coping with many traumatic experiences that plagued my formative years. With psychological assistance or shrinkage, I came to terms with my demons through painful self critical analysis—and humor. Eventually, I discovered that my coping mechanism was deeply embedded in Jewish culture both here and abroad.

European immigrants, my parents had a turbulent marriage. As their only child, I carried a burden of guilt if I did not measure up to their great expectations and shared their joy when I achieved something of value like entry into Stuyvesant High School, admission to Columbia College, and various awards that I garnered along the way. Since they put a premium on secular Jewish values, they *shepped much nachas* (derived enormous pleasure) when I graduated from after-school programs that promoted Yiddish culture along with the Yiddish language. Indeed, a secular bar-mitzvah present from my shule teacher known as *Chaverta* Rifka Wiener was Nathan Ausubel's book, *A Treasury of Jewish Folklore*. That tome contained a trove of Jewish humor, particularly the antics of Chelmites whose misadventures satirized wise fools and flawed sages. These topsy-turvy stories served as my introduction to Jewish humor and spurred on my endless fascination with this subject.

After years of graduate school and plagued by writer's block, I returned to explore the roots of Jewish humor and its sundry branches to identify Lenny Bruce as a "Jewish Humorist in Babylon." I delivered a paper on Lenny at a 1974 Popular Culture Conference in Milwaukee, Wisconsin. On my panel were two very distinguished scholars: critic Leslie Fiedler and sociologist Ruel Denney, co-author of *The Lonely Crowd*, as well as a young literature professor Sheldon Hershinow, who discoursed on writer Bernard Malamud. In the middle of my presentation, facing the exalted critic, I quoted a line that I culled from Leslie Fiedler's essay first published in *Ramparts Magazine* designed to curry his favor with this citation. To which, he retorted in fluent Yiddish, *"Es vet dir gurtnisht helfn"* (Nothing will help you!), evoking loud laughter. I countered with shrugged shoulders, uplifted hands, and words in equally cogent Yiddish: *"Shver tzu zein a Yid!* (It's hard to be a Jew) to even louder laughter. At the end of our session both Professors Denney and Fiedler praised my paper. Thus the idea of this book germinated from that brief but memorable encounter. My article on Lenny Bruce was later published in a left-wing publication, *Jewish Currents*, in 1981.

That same year, I fleshed out a more comprehensive study of Jewish Humor for delivery at a conference of psychohistory, a fledgling and somewhat controversial field. A successful delivery yielded another published article. My writer's block began to tumble. One year later, I presented another paper on "Jews and Blacks: The Gold Dust Twins of Comedy." In the audience, to my good fortune, was the preeminent scholar of African American humor, Boston University Professor Joseph Boskin, whose brilliant article on "Mr. Bones" had appeared in the *New York Times Magazine* on May 1, 1966. That protean article stirred my intellectual juices and inspired me to plunge into further research and writing. Professor Boskin and I began a long and fruitful friendship that led to two major publications on ethnic humor and many heady subsequent exchanges on our shared passion: the study of humor. In a course on humor that I introduced to my students at Long Island University Brooklyn in 1986, Boskin's books have become required reading staples each semester that it is offered. Indeed, Prof. Boskin encouraged me to put my ideas into a book of my very own. So, if my effort fails, he will incur some of the blame. If, on the other hand, my efforts prove successful, his encouragement and mentorship will earn eternal gratitude and one free dinner, a reward which eluded many famous folks according to the late comedian Red Buttons. I consider Joe Boskin my mentor as well as a dear friend. Therefore, he gets a dinner!

Unable to attend a major conference in Israel on Jewish humor in 1986, Professor Boskin functioned not unlike the designated hitter in American League baseball as my designated speaker. Evidently, he performed admirably because conference chair Avner Ziv, the late Israeli scholar, selected my study for inclusion in his book. This helped me gain international recognition when my article on Lenny Bruce, Mel Brooks, and Woody Allen appeared in his ground-breaking collection of *Jewish Humor*, which he edited and published in 1986 in both Hebrew and English. His next book distilled the best presentations of an international conference on Jewish humor held at the New School of Social Research in 1986. Although I failed to score a publication, my disappointment was tempered somewhat because I met so many fine scholars engaged in humor research from all over the globe. At these conferences, I befriended Lawrence Mintz, Arthur P. Dudden, Sarah B. Cohen, Emil Draitser, Don and Alleen Nilsen, Christie Davies, Paul Lewis, George Patton, and Hyram Davis among the best and brightest in our field. That dynamic duo, Don and Alleen Nilsen, merit special mention and high praise for their remarkable PowerPoints on all facets of American humor that immeasurably enrich my classes at LIU Brooklyn. They recently retired from Arizona State University, but continue to aid fledgling scholars and *alter cockers* like this author as well.

In the chapters that follow, I try to demonstrate the impact of Jewish humor on American popular culture, as well as the reverse. The introductory chapter provides an overview with salient themes regarding acculturation and identity. In subsequent chapters, I focus on folklore and joke lore, vaudeville, the Catskills as a school for comedy, Borscht Belt alumni, political comedy, dialecticians, literary humor, situation comedies, blacks and Jews, and a lyricist. All rest on a simple thesis of survival, subversion, and escape. Put in a framework developed by Gordon Allport, the humorous response of people in trouble can be classified by a "triple A" paradigm: acceptance, aggression, and avoidance. Jewish humor, in its infinitely rich and complex flowering, stems from these basic roots.

Though scholarly in form, this book is designed for a broad audience. Therefore, purists and *fineshmeckers* are advised to put aside their blue pencils until we complete this journey. To be sure, "Deconstructionists" will suffer disappointment in the absence of current academic jargon and their fashionable purveyors; but our effort to engage a host of new readers precludes such indulgences. I promise not to use and abuse such catch-phrase concepts as "negotiate," "constructed identities" *und azoi veiter* (and the like). The only time that I employ "negotiate" and "construction" is when I am seeking a salary hike or when dealing with a contractor for home repairs. Moreover, I will try to limit a current favorite, "resonate," unless the reference is to a favorite breakfast food that is eaten with raisins and almonds from a Yiddish folksong, *Rozhinkes mit Mandlen*. That's my *raison d'être*. Our goal is to entertain as well as to inform. Raised as a non-believer, I found spiritual nurturing in Jewish humor. Of particular inspiration were the many humorists, from Sholem Aleichem to Lenny Bruce, Mel Brooks to Woody Allen, Sophie Tucker to Belle Barth, who, armed with Jewish wit, boxed verbally with God.

Minus divine intervention, our craft is a lonely experience: one that makes huge demands on family, time, patience, and fortitude. Yet, as author Philip Roth responded to his acerbic critics, I, too, did the best that I could. Hopefully, this book will justify my Sisyphean labors. If not, I will just have to roll the rock up to the summit until I can successfully rock and roll both ways to success. Not all writers are endowed with natural rhythm.

Jewish Humor

Mechanism for Defense,
Weapon for Cultural Affirmation

A recent Pew survey of Jews in America indicates that humor ranks above Jewish religious worship, community membership, and food among categories of cultural identification. This astonishing result from a survey of 3,500 Jewish-Americans serves as a fitting introduction to and a proper paradigm for Jewish humor, a force which is alive and well, indeed resurgent, in America.[1] As a staple item in her acidic as opposed to Chasidic repertoire, Joan Rivers, the late Jewish comedienne, referred to Nancy Kissinger as "a horse" who wears saddles by Gucci and "neighs" at Henry's romantic, if not operatic, overtures. Rivers's observations are both devastatingly accurate and palpably cruel.[2] At a Long Island University commencement ceremony, several years prior, Rabbi Joseph Potasnik told a joke first, and then delivered the invocation. Thus, Jewish humor continues to stand up in comic relief and run around in academic circles.

Where is this curious phenomenon rooted? The Bible is allegedly devoid of humor. Granted that there are a few scattered references to laughter in Genesis, Kings, and Prophets, but these are provoked by disbelief such as the birth of a son to a ninety-year-old Sarah or spurred by mordant mockery of idol worship by her husband, Abraham. Psalms, I, indeed blesses those who avoid the company of jesters for they shall presumably inherit the ozone-layered wind. If the Old Testament welcomes strangers, it appears inhospitable to laughter. The New Testament, however, banishes levity (for Levites only?) altogether. Christianity's most successful proselytizer Saul (later Saint Paul of Tarsus) equated "foolish talking and jestings" with "fornication, uncleanliness, and covetousness" in Ephesians (5:3–4). The Resurrection story, fraught with pain and passion, yields no belly laughs though born-again Christians in the comic mind of "sick" Lenny Bruce sparked satire. Before his untimely death, Bruce pontificated that "tragedy plus time equals satire." His ardent admirers, this author among them, believe that Lenny also died for our sins. Arguably, religion and comedy are antithetical. Only the Book of Esther, probably derived from a pagan text, provides an exception to the rule.[3]

Modern Jewish humor has two roots. The dominant bloom issued from Eastern Europe, where exiled Jews living in the margins of Christian culture found a comic voice. During medieval wedding ceremonies, *badchonim* or *marshalliks* enjoyed license—well before the advent of Howard Cosell—"to tell it like it is." At wedding banquets, while guests broke bread, rabbis cracked jokes (as one modern rabbi did at my daughter's *simcha*). On other occasions, rabbis engaged on *sihat hullin*—"light talk" or banter—as they expounded on the law. Rabbi Dovidl of Dinov, for example, defended this tradition on the grounds that all humorous stories contained God's truth.[4] It is hard to conceive of priests, imams, and ministers making it as comedians after the fashion, say, of ex-rabbi Jackie Mason. Today, in fact, many mohels (like Jackie Mason's brother) furnish humor during the removal of foreskins.

Before coming to America, a tradition of folk humor sprouted in Europe, primarily in the eastern part, featuring arcane characters and droll types, namely *schnorrers*, *schlemiels*, *schlimazels*, *luftmentshn*, *kunyilemels*, and their kin. Some, like Hershl Ostropolier, were real people. Born in the Ukraine around 1750 to impoverished parents, Hershl had neither trade nor calling. A lively wit, however, attracted the attention of a melancholy Hassidic rabbi named Boruch of Miedziboz, who hired Hershl as his personal court jester. This arrogant as well as ignorant rabbi ruled by "divine right." And the utterly dependent Ostropolier played the fool, a role aped by future Jewish wits.[5]

Other forms of humor flowered among the folk. Chelm stories parodied the Jewish preoccupation with scholarship and *pilpul* bereft of common sense. These tales poked fun at sages fixed on millennial concerns at the expense of mundane reality wherein matter ultimately trumps mind. One earthy source yielded rabbi-priest stories that cultivated verbal jousts, to wit[6]:

> PRIEST: When will you give up those silly dietary laws?
> RABBI: At your wedding, excellency.
> PRIEST: Have you ever sinned?
> RABBI: I once had a ham sandwich.
> RABBI: Did you ever sin, Father?
> PRIEST: I once had a woman.
> RABBI: Beats a ham sandwich, no?

In the 19th century, Eastern-European Yiddish writers incorporated humor into their portraits of impoverished *landsleit* or fellow travelers. Mining the folk tradition for its rich vein of humor, Mendeleh Moicher Sforim wrote mordant satire and extolled *dos kleine mentsheleh* (little person) as did Y.L. Peretz. With more affection and less acid, Sholem Aleichem etched memorable portraits of Tevyeh, the hairy dairyman, and Motl, the cantor's son. The humor found in this literature—Peretz's Bontsche Shveig (the Silent) provides a poignant case in point—functions as a cultural line of defense. It mocked the pretension of self-absorption and the habit among Jews of avoidance, i.e., the repression of painful facts to make life more endurable. With wit sufficiently sharp and arms long enough, humorists taught Jews how to box with God just as the Biblical Jacob wrestled with the Almighty on top of a ladder. The ensuing laughter helped to create a delicate balance between piety and complaint. Confronted with a dominant adversarial culture increasingly oppressive from the 11th century on wherever they resided, historian Abram L. Sachar pointed out, Jews in Christian Europe experienced "one long succession of indignities and brutalities, culminating in wholesale massacres and expulsions."[7]

In Western Europe, spearheaded by enlightened rulers or despots in Austria and France, Joseph and Napoleon respectively, Jewish emancipation created another comedic front, namely, the humor of marginality. Caught between two worlds—"One dead and the other powerless to be born"—Jews responded with irony. Sig Altman chronicled the transformation from *badchen* humor to cabaret comedy and pinpointed certain recurrent themes from hypochondria to anti-Semitism, real as well as imagined. He explored latent if not blatant anti-militarism in the form of Ikey stories, a prototypical Jewish chocolate soldier. In this current of Western European Jewish life, conversion to Christianity beckoned as a possible passport to a better life. The attempt to swim in mainstream European society often resulted in failure as demonstrated in the confession of Moritz Saphir: "When I was a Jew, God could see me but I could not see Him. When I became a Catholic, I could see God but God could not see me. Now, I am a Protestant. He can't see me and I can't see Him."[8]

Among Jewish converts who failed to find fulfillment in his new religion, Heinrich Heine ranks at the top. Born in Düsseldorf in 1797, Heine made his mark as a Romantic poet but he also emerged as the sharpest wit as a Christian with a Jewish sensibility. In her recent book, author Ruth Wisse deftly captures Heine's ambivalence in his arresting self-identification as "a renegade Jew and a phony Christian" who characterized his conversion with a painful confession that it was his "ticket of admission into European culture."[9] Looking back in angry repentance at this Faustian bargain gone wrong, Heine employed lacerating wit as both shield and rapier. Witness these *bon mots* wrenched from context:

- Aristocracy is composed of asses—asses that talk about horses.
- Hugo is the perfect egoist or rather the perfect Hugoist.
- Vanity is one of his [Musset's] four Achilles' heels.
- All women love him [a minor poet]—all except the Muses.
- My constitution grows worse—even worse than the Constitution of Prussia.
- She is truly like the Venus di Milo. She is incredibly old, she has no teeth, and her body is covered with yellow spots.
- In the days of Napoleon when coffee was made out of acorns and princes out of nothing at all.

Bilious to a fault, Heine evokes Thomas Hobbes's argument that a sense of superiority dominates humor in his one-liners from above. Speaking through a surrogate, Heine created a character named Hirsch Hyazinth. "I was sitting next to Solomon Rothschild," Hirsch boasted, "and he treated me just as an equal, quite famillionaire." Quoting this gem of condensation wit, Sigmund Freud appreciated Heine's uncensored malice and unhappy laughter. Both aggressor as well as victim, Heine left a legacy, succinctly stated: "The pertinence of irony refracted through a prism of multiple meetings."[10]

Eventually this strain of humor so heavily salted with self-denigration siphoned off the wellsprings of Jewish identity. A different kind of humor was needed to bridge old and new, European and American cultures. Once rare, now plentiful, scholars of humor, drawn from all disciplines—psychology, sociology, literature, anthropology, history, philosophy, and biology—continue to debate the functions of humor. Of the many theories advanced, including instinct, evolution, superiority, incongruity, surprise, release, mechanical behavior et al., a synthesis formulated by Lawrence Mintz is most helpful in Jewish humor analysis.

The Mintz model provides a template of four categories: critical humor directed by one group, usually the dominant, against the other, often the subordinate; self-deprecating humor in which the target group maintains that its members can identify their flaws more accurately than its traducers; realistic humor which examines the problems of all groups, as in the observational humor of Jerry Seinfeld; and critical humor directed against the majority culture by members of a previously disparaged group. Thus, the humor wheel comes full circle. In the first category, critical hostility is granted license and oppression, justified. But it can also serve softer aims, such as the deflection of hostility and the substitution of ritual in lieu of real punishment. Critical humor tends to strengthen the morale and identity of the group on attack, although the prime motive is to elicit conformity or at least reduce tension by airing the source of that tension. At this juncture, analysts of Jewish humor diverge. An extreme view is that Jews suffer from psychic masochism while others see that self-criticism serves as an internal regulating mechanism to acculturate "greenhorns," or outsiders. In this mode, victims transform faults into virtues, thereby gaining ironic victories.

Realistic humor explores the incongruities of dual culture status. It concerns the knotty questions of intermarriage-conversion, immigrant adjustment and, in religion, the Reform-Orthodox-Conservative trinity of choices. That avuncular teacher who morphed into a comedian, Sam Levenson, whose strongly nostalgic and mildly pointed jokes aptly fit this model. His gentle humor evoked warm responses, especially from the elderly, Christian as well as Jews.[11]

Professor Mintz completes the cycle in category four—critical humor against the majority with a curious twist or karate chop, verbally. A mirror image of category one, it also reflects revenge, assertions of superiority, affirmations of cultural pluralism, attacks on the establishment, and occasional apologies for assimilation. Mintz finds examples of this kind of humor in Lenny Bruce, Don Rickles, Alan King, Dick Gregory, and Richard Pryor, among others, the majority of whom are Jewish.[12]

If this seems both complex and confusing, the problem inheres in our subject. As E.B. White warned us: "Humor can be dissected as a frog can, but the thing dies in the process." To explain the connection between Jewish humor and American life, another critic observed, takes genius and *chutzpah*.[13]

With these admonitions in mind, let us continue our journey through American Jewish humor with exegetical rather than ex-cathedral commentary coupled with specific illustrations. Writer Abe Burrows confessed: "Humor is a way to keep from killing yourself ... it removes anxiety. Other kids threw rocks, I made jokes."[14] Making jokes, another scholar after the fashion of Mel Brooks, is a way of keeping the *Malechamoves* (Angel of Death) away. *Unzer shtick* (our thing), it helps to define our place in an increasingly amorphous, anxiety-provoking America. A distillation of the eastern European *shtetl* experience, fusing poverty, pain, and putdowns, Jews entered American culture laughing at *tsores* (trouble). Critic Leslie Fiedler charted this process with bittersweet irony. Prior to World War I, Jewish women as well as men flocked to vaudeville shows, which often pandered to blatant stereotypes and exploited self-hatred. Later, they even "blackened up" to express their *pastiched neshuma* (multi-layered soul). For example, take Al Jolson, Eddie Cantor, George Jessel, and Sophie Tucker—please.[15]

Radio fostered a blander style of humor. Veterans of vaudeville, Jewish comedians like Eddie Cantor, George Jessel, Henny Youngman, Ed Wynn, and Fanny Brice flocked into this hot new medium. Arguably, the most successful of this group, Benny Kubelsky, originally an orthodox Jew, emerged as Jack Benny. Joining his program, wife Sadie Marks, sporting a new name and new nose, surfaced as Mary Livingstone. To be sure, Dennis Day, Messrs. Kitsel and Schlepperman as well as Eddie "Rochester" Anderson provided comic relief ethnically, but the victim, more often than not of their verbal barbs was the miserly, vain, slightly pompous main man himself. Yet Benny's image was waspish at best, as Edgar Bergen recalled. Perhaps the persona's preoccupation with money hinted at Jewish roots subliminally. Later in his highly successful career, the perennially thirty-nine-year-old miser came out of the cultural closet to poke fun at his own tribe. When, for example, General Motors recalled 72,000 Cadillacs on the eve of Yom Kippur, Benny, hand on chin, quipped: "I've never seen so many Jews walking to synagogue in my life."[16]

Still, the best analysis of the Jewish joke is found in the seminal work of the good doctor, Sigmund Freud. In his diagnosis, Jewish humor exemplified the "tendency wit" of skepticism, democratic thought (deflation), social principles, and self-criticism. A study by Freudian disciple Theodore Reik expressed love for Jewish humor's intimacy, dialectical process, and release of unmerry laughter at a moment of subjective truth or profound insight. Other scholars of lesser *yichus* (status) have labeled this phenomenon "psychic masochism" while folklorists and sociologists have provided evidence to the contrary. The rabbi has been rediscovered as a "trickster." Thus, it is the identity crisis spurred by cultural marginality, not self-hatred that drives the comic engine.[17]

A period of *sha-sha* (silence), actual de-Semitization in response to Hitlerian fascism finally dissipated in the 1950s. Jewish jokes were back in demand. On the new medium of television, comedians like Milton Berle, Sid Caesar, and Jack E. Leonard were sending messages and *shpritzing* (spraying) in Yiddish. They also massaged their ethnic *landsleit* (fellow travelers) with *Yiddishkeit*, i.e., Yiddish words and sensibility. Mort Sahl and Lenny Bruce, strongly tinctured with Jewish iodine, cleaned up old acts and injected fresh doses of comic wisdom. Both stood out as authentic performers, pop culture *mayvns* (experts), preacher-teachers, and medical exorcists. Both departed dramatically from the constricting formulae of their predecessors who avoided cultural conflict and political engagement. As children of the Depression, war movies, comic books, and radio, they mined a vast store of funny stuff; Sahl took the high ground vacated by Will Rogers minus bumpkin mask, while Bruce blitzed all hustlers across the social spectrum, especially men of religious cloth.

Like other Jewish comics, Bruce aspired to higher things. Unlike them, however, Lenny regarded his role as that of a moralist. Dubbed the leader of America's social and cultural revolution, Lenny used dirty words and ethnic phrases to shock white Christians and fellow Jews into self-awareness. A latter day Jonathan Edwards, he located our demons and invited us to expel them. Unfortunately, Bruce could not purge his own *dybbuk* (ghostly demon). Earlier in his career, he had maintained a delicate balance; he could express contempt, yet escape punishment. Haunted by his own corruption—drugs, deceit, vocation, and *shund* (vulgarity)—Lenny was forced into a "glass enclosure" from which there was no escape.[18] A chronic optimist in the tradition, say, of Sholem Aleichem's Menachem Mendel, arguably an extension of himself, Bruce tried to break loose and lead his followers to some mythical promised land free of cultural constraints and societal taboos. "A disease of America," in critic Kenneth Tynan's apt rubric, Lenny Bruce, marginal comic and double alien, plunged the ultimate needle inward and self-destructed on a toilet in 1966.[19]

Most Jews, and some comedians, are resilient. Perhaps Woody Allen is two or three in one. Representing *dos kleine mentschele*, cum laude graduate from Chelm University for schlemiels in his comic persona, Woody Allen, né Alan Stewart Kongsberg, confronts the cosmos. Born of a neurotic *ménage à trois* embracing Sigmund Freud, Frantz Kafka, and Sholem Aleichem, he embodies the comic anti-hero. In one of his earlier bits, he is hired as a token Jew. Desperately trying to look the part, he read memos from right to left but is finally fired for taking off too many Jewish holidays. According to movie critic and his super-fan Richard Schickel, Woody's style—verbal as well as visual—combines understatement and parody. For a little guy, he packs a devastating punch. At the end of the film *The Front* (1976), he refuses to answer questions put to him by the less-than-grand House Un-American Activities inquisitors. Speaking for the actual victims of the "Red Scare," he concludes his testimony, as the soundtrack plays "Young at Heart," in a retaliatory mode: "You can all go fuck yourselves!"

Like the Brothers Marx, Woody is something of a nihilist if not a revolutionary. He loves to puncture the powerful and to deflate the pompous. In the absence of genuine heroes, political stability, group ideals or his favorite Manhattan that works for all, poor as well as rich, we gravitate to Mr. Allen. Earlier, in his standup career before he became an acclaimed *auteur*, he spoke to and for us in the following one-liners[20]:

- Not only is there no God, but try getting a plumber on weekends.
- My only regret is that I am not someone else.

- I don't mind dying. I just don't want to be there when it happens.
- I don't believe in an afterlife, although I am bringing an extra pair of underwear.
- When we played softball, I'd steal second, then feel guilty and go back to first.
- I went to a school for emotionally disturbed teachers.
- I went with a girl who had a child by a future marriage.
- Sent to an interdenominational summer camp, I was sadistically beaten by boys of every race, color, and creed.

The above was of early Allen vintage. Later, more meditative, Allen conceded that he is a survivor ... eclectic ... skeptical. He agrees with Mort Sahl, whom he regards as a mentor, that "the issue is always fascism."[21] As opposed to exploitation and thought control, he prefers freedom and celebrates life. When asked how being Jewish influences his work, Woody replied[22]:

> It's not on my mind; it's no part of my artistic consciousness, There are certain cultural differences between Jews and non-Jews, I guess, but I think they're largely superficial. Of course, any character I play would be Jewish just because I'm Jewish. I'm also metropolitan oriented. I wouldn't play a farmer or an Irish fisherman. So I write about metropolitan characters who happen to be Jewish.

Many of his heroes—either musicians or athletes—are black.[23]

Penetrating surfaces, Woody Allen as filmmaker who wants to plumb our interiors. In this mood, he finds the Marx Brothers less lovable. You laugh with them but do not feel the pain. He prefers to identify with victims who use aggression economically, like Chaplin, Keaton (Buster, not Diane), and Hope.[24]

Critic Albert Goldman offered a key piece to the cultural puzzle that is Woody Allen in particular and American Jewish humor as a whole. Assimilation, he argued before his departure to an early grave, is no more viable in modern America than it was for Heinrich Heine in the 19th century. Though comfortably affluent, many American Jews now reject total assimilation. Caught between two cultures, they flit from conformity to alienation. Faced with Emile Durkheim's concept of *anomie* or a society *sans* norms, some find comfort in orthodoxy wherein they submissively follow rabbinical rule, while others seek mastery of their environment as they run around in secular circles. Jewish comedians of the immediate post-World War II generation mixed contempt and pride. The implicit phrase in all Jewish humor—*shver tzu zein a yid* (hard to be a Jew)—is a doppelgänger. On an overt level, this phrase emitted with a *krechtz* (heavy groan), evokes pity. Contrapuntally, a different theme is heard which states that, despite attendant misery, it is a badge of honor to be a Jew. Freud's felicitous leitmotif "the clear sense of an inner identity" informs the Jewish comic and leads, as a way of transcending the pain, to loud, nervous, almost hysterical laughter.[25]

Laughter, however, is not enough. Groucho Marx yearned for education. More than anything he prized his correspondence with T.S. Eliot (Tom in their correspondence), his pieces in the *New Yorker*, and praise from George Bernard Shaw, who called him the world's greatest living actor. If Groucho wanted to be a writer, Lenny Bruce wanted to be a lawyer. And Woody Allen, critic Pauline Kael contended, wanted to be the American Ingmar Bergman. Throughout his film career, during which he turns out nearly one film a year, Woody seems to transcend his role as Jewish comedian. As a non-threatening schlemiel, he wins without aggression and he conforms—in Kael's psycho-analysis—"to their idea what a Jew should be."[26]

Perhaps indifferent to E.B. White's warning cited above, critic Kael "mur-dered to dissect." Clearly in conflict with his tribal roots, Woody Allen protests too much. In whatever mask he wears each year, he remains a Jewish comic even if he no longer stands up. In that erect pose, Professor Mintz insists, the comedian serves two universal functions. As a licensed spokesman, he (or she, in this enlightened age) is permitted to say dangerous things. Secondly, "he can represent, through caricature, those negative traits we wish to ridicule … and renounce through laughter."[27]

Many questions remain unanswered; some unasked. Why are there so many Jewish comedians? Why not? Historically, the Jewish people have expe-rienced so much *tsores* (trouble) and, in Lenny Bruce's argot, have paid a lot of dues. The humor that they generated was derived from pain. Although conditions in America improved measurably, the tradition crossed over the Atlantic Ocean in their cultural baggage. Mort Sahl's monologues owe more to *badchonim* from Russia than to native American Will Rogers. Lenny Bruce's fierce sense of moral outrage distills prophetic wisdom from Mount Sinai. The self-parody in Woody Allen, a poorly disguised plea for love, often func-tioned as a mechanism for Jewish survival. Observational comedians like Mel Brooks, Alan King, and Jerry Seinfeld emit a primal *kvetch* against suf-fering and death, yet trumpet life and joy. "If your enemy is laughing," jokes Mel Brooks, "how can he bludgeon you to death?" As a coping mechanism for "high anxiety," he advises that "every small Jew should have a tall *goy* for a friend." In another tart observation, the 2000-year-old-man pontificates: "Death is more of an enemy than a German soldier."[28]

Scholar Salcia Landmann erred in asserting that "Jewish humor is more profound, more varied and … richer than that of other people." To a people allegedly chosen—and demonstrably reviled—such hyperbole is doing what comes naturally. Hysteria rather than cool often pours out of highly salted comedic strain as expressed in Neil Simon's *Prisoner of Second Avenue*—Mel Edison. Manic to a fault, the humors in the veins of Jewish humor run mostly towards melancholy. When super salesman Jack Roy returned, bereft of respect, as Rodney Dangerfield, success beckoned in the form of beautiful women, fine food, loud laughter, beer commercials, and big bucks. "So tell me," he asked in a letter, "why am I so depressed?"[29]

If success engenders depression, how does one deal with failure? Is laughter through tears via Sholem Aleichem a viable option? Critic Robert Alter observed that "Jewish humor typically drains the charge of cosmic significance from suffering by grounding it in a world of practical realities. If you want to forget your troubles put on a shoe that's too tight!"[30] Another shtetl residue invites literal escape, as in these words: "My son lost his wife, who left him with three small children, his house burned down and his business gone bankrupt—but he writes a Hebrew that is a pleasure to read."[31] Modern humorists play it both ways. The late satirist Art Buchwald treated "the facetious importantly and the important facetiously." On a topless pyramid or, more accurately, view from the bottom, the Jewish comic perspective throughout history seeks to restore balance. Although not usually a weapon for open combat, it has revolutionary potential—as Hitler must have realized when he banned cabaret humor in Germany, so heavily spiced with Jewish flavor. Indeed, a host of Jewish comedians, artists, and writers—Mort Sahl, David Frye, Phillip Roth, David Steinberg, Joey Bishop, Robert Klein, David Levine, Herbert Block, and Jackie Mason helped to dethrone, or at least disrobe, that man who would be Emperor of Watergate: Richard Milhous Nixon.

Jewish comedians have traveled far from the *shtetl chuppa* (wedding canopy in eastern Europe) and Berlin cabaret. They no longer have to "black up" like Cantor, or blend like Benny, or hide like Bishop. A funny thing happened on the way to a Tony Award. Triumphantly, a "top banana" Phil Silvers erupted into a guttural, slightly vulgar acceptance speech in Yiddish *sans souci*, i.e., without apologies. Buddy Hackett used *mama loshen* (the mother tongue) in order to sell Tuscan yogurt pops. Evidently, Yiddish-flavored humor plays in Peoria just as it pays on Madison Avenue. The proverbial wandering Jew has finally arrived in America, to almost full acceptance. So why do we still *kvetch*—whine and complain? Because *tsores ba leitn*—that host of real as well as imagined trouble continues to rain on our parade. Because in "making it" we've become smug, insensitive, and neo-conservative like Norman Podhoretz and Eric Cantor, unlike Norman Siegel and Eddie Cantor.

Besides his anti-Semitic effusions, author Thomas Wolfe was wrong. We *can* indeed go home again. To be sure, neither a Polly Adler house nor a rip-off nursing home will suffice. Home on this trip refers to that many-mansioned abode wherein one can find Jewish humor furnished in a variety of styles, spanning the antique buffoonery of *badchonim*, the classic irony of Heinrich Heine, the nouveau nihilism of the Marx Brothers, the neo-talmudism of Jackie Mason, the *yente* grandeur of Joan Rivers and the various *shtick* of Jewish comedians, as well as comediennes of more recent fashion. This vital tradition that travels through a grim past, a scary present, and a future punctuated by shock (if not *shlock*) serves as both defense mechanism and cutting edge of tribal affirmation—in short, a lifeline.[32]

ONE

God, Jokes and Money
A Subversive Look at Jewish Humor

Jewish humor is a mechanism for defense as well as a weapon for cultural affirmation. It also functions as a deeply subversive force. Germane to this study are the salient tendencies first delineated by Sigmund Freud. The good doctor observed that a collection of jokes under the rubric of Jewish wit had a tendency toward democratic deflation, revolt against religion, articulation of social principles and self-criticism.[1] In this chapter, I will relate a number of jokes dealing with God, religion, and money. My thesis is that jokes of this genre related by Jews have enabled a people living on the margins of several cultures to cope with the adversity of minority-group status, to establish a coherent identity, and, when necessary, to take the offensive against the enemy. I will try to avoid scholastic jargon without sacrificing scholarly rigor and, hopefully, what follows will provide enjoyment as well as add to our pool of knowledge.

Leo Rosten relates a number of folk sayings about God, etched in acid.[2]

- If God lived on earth, men would knock out all his windows.
- God may love the poor, but He helps the rich.
- Dear God: You help total strangers—so why not me?
- Oh, Lord: help me. If you don't, I'll ask my uncle in New York.

One joke, found in many anthologies with quite a few variations on the same theme, provides fuel for the burning bush. It involves a dilatory tailor and his dissatisfied customer.[3]

> A tailor promised to alter a suit for a wealthy client.
> Instead of two weeks, it took two years. The client complained.
> "You needed two years to finish my suit while God created the world in only six days!"
> "Nu," the tailor replied: "Look at the world and look at this magnificent suit."

This joke has elicited a compelling essay which posits a skeptical stance vis-à-vis God. Jewish jokes stretch our tolerance for ambiguity.[4] One finds echoes of this kind of humor in the Tevye stories by Sholem Aleichem. "With your help, God, I nearly starved to death." Tevye tries to transcend his *tsores* (trouble) with a quotation, usually garbled, from the literature of theology: Bible or Talmud. An ironic shrug, a cleansing laugh, a restored sense of dignity helps Tevye survive as he dances on the tightrope between piety and protest.[5]

A more recent version of skepticism is evoked in the following joke.[6]

> Chaim Mintz went off alone one day to scale Mount Carmel. As he dug his boot onto a ledge, it gave way and he fell 150 feet—managing, by a miracle, to grab a branch from a gnarled tree. "Help! Help!" he cried.
> A great voice far above intoned. "My son, do you have full faith in me?"
> "Yes! Yes!"
> "Do you trust Me without reservation?"
> "Oh, yes, Lord!"
> "Then let go of the branch."
> "What?"
> "I said, 'Let go of that branch!'"
> A pause: then Mintz said, "Excuse me, but—is there anyone else up there?"

Irreverence toward the divine is found in the comic antics of Woody Allen, who considers God a tremendous underachiever. Woody juxtaposes the inability to secure a plumber during weekends with the death of God. If Jesus was a carpenter, Woody wonders, what did he charge for bookshelves?[7] The virtuous man, he knows, will "dwell in the house of God for six months with an option to buy." In the film, *Love and Death* (1975), Woody, as Boris, asks: "If God is testing us, why doesn't He give us a written?" Allen concludes that Jews celebrate Yom Kippur to honor a God who broke all of His promises to His people.

Religious confrontations appear in a series of Jew-Christian jokes.

- Jesus was Jewish. There is irrefutable proof. At the age of thirty, he was still living at home. He followed in his father's business. And his mother went around proclaiming that her son was a God, her son was a God.
- An old Jewish man was struck by a car in front of a church. A priest ran out to administer last rites. "Do you accept the father, the son, and the holy ghost?" the priest asked ritualistically. The man looks up at the assembled crowd and replies plaintively: "I'm dying and he asks me riddles!"[8]
- This same man is taken to a Catholic hospital for an emergency

operation. A nun in the admitting room asks him what relative would be responsible for the bill. He reasoned that his only living relative is a sister who converted and became a nun, an old maid who could not be responsible for the bill.

"I'll have you know," the nun replied testily "that we are not old maids. We are married to our Lord, Jesus Christ."

"Oh, in that case," the Jewish man exclaimed, "send the bill to my brother-in-law!"

- "Rabbi," cried the little Jew, "a terrible thing has happened. My son wants to marry a Gentile girl."

  "Your son!" replied the rabbi. "Look at me and my son. Here I am the leader of the community. Everyone looks up to me as an example and my son not only wants to marry a *shiksa* but he also wants to be baptized."

  After a long silence, the little Jew said: "Everyone comes to you with their problems but what do you when you have such a terrible problem. To whom do you turn?"

  "What can I do? I turn to God."

  "And? What did God tell you?"

  "God said to me. '*Your* son! ... Look at *mine*!'"[9]

On one level this last joke constitutes a mini-rebellion against God; on another, the joke reflects a wonderful capacity to live in ambiguity between truth and myth in defiance of authoritarian figures. Lacking power, Jewish jesters identified with the rabbi as trickster. Witness these jokes.[10]

- The priest baptizes his new Cadillac with a bucket of water so the rabbi cuts two inches off the tailpipe.
- The priest and rabbi survive a plane crash. The priest observes the rabbi making the sign of the cross.

  "Aha!" he exclaims, "in time of need you turned to the true faith."

  "What are you talking about?" replies the rabbi: "I was just checking my wallet, cigarettes, spectacles, testicles."

As Lenny Bruce observed, rabbis have a healthier attitude toward the body. There is no merit badge for abstinence in Jewish culture; hence rabbis "are big *shtuppers.*"[11]

Bruce used stereotypes to either destroy or transcend them. Unfortunately, even his caustic wit could not dissolve the most tenacious one of "filthy lucre." Money has been associated with Jewish figures, indeed equated with God. A preoccupation with *parnusseh* (earning a livelihood) most certainly courses through the Jewish experience. Listen to this sage from Chelm.

> "If I were Rothschild, I would be richer than Rothschild," quipped a scholar.
> "How could you be richer than Rothschild?" asked a skeptic.
> "I would have his money and do a little teaching on the side."[12]

Teaching on the side provides a clue to the character of Jewish humor. Thus, a comic figure of Jewish folklore deals with a primary need. True, man does not live by bread alone; but he—and she, in this enlightened age—does need bread for survival. Therefore, we are obliged to examine the juxtaposition of Jews, jokes, and "bread," i.e., money, leaving aside for the moment the Nietszchian possibility that God is dead or at best living in Argentina.[13] Despite the stereotypes hurled at Jews by anti–Semites, poverty rather than wealth characterized the life of European Jewry.

To cope with their dismal conditions, Jews developed a tradition of folk humor, featuring arcane characters and droll types, namely, *schnorrers, schlemiels, schlimazels, luftmentschn* and their kin. Some, like the trickster Hershl Ostropolier, was real. Born in the Ukraine around 1750 to impoverished parents, Hershl had neither trade nor calling. He gained *parnuseh* (livelihood) by entertaining a melancholy Hasidic rabbi whose arrogance matched his ignorance. The rabbi often rebuked his court jester for spending so little time at prayer. Hershl retorted[14]:

> You have so much to be grateful for: your carriage and your fine horses, your home, your gold and silver, your fancy dishes. But look at me. I have a nagging wife, my six children and a skinny goat. And my prayers are very simple: "Wife, children, goat—and I'm done."

As court jester, Hershl played the rebel with a cause. His pranks, though impish, were essentially ventilations against a grinding poverty. Like other fool figures, Hershl Ostropolier unmasked the rich who pretended to be righteous and those who pretended to be learned. Later Yiddish writers created comic characters who snatched ironic victories from the jaws of defeat. Marginalized, the Jews found laughter in the context of tears. Listen to Sholem Aleichem[15]:

> Dear Yankel: You ask me to write you at length and I'd like to oblige, but there's really nothing to write about. The rich are still rich and the poor are dying of hunger, as they always do. What's new about that? And as far as pogroms are concerned, thank God we have nothing more to fear, as we've already had ours—two of them, in fact, and a third wouldn't be worthwhile.... Mendel did a clever thing though; he up and died. Some say of hunger, others of consumption. Personally I think he died of both. I really don't know what else to write about, except the cholera, which is going great guns....

Sholem Aleichem etched memorable portraits of Tevyeh, the dairyman, who argues with God; Motl, the cantor's son, who delights in orphan status because of the attention he receives (*mir iz gut, ich bin a yosum*), Menachem Mendel, *der luftmentsch*, the would-be millionaire, who builds financial castles in the air of stock-speculation. In this literature, humor functions as a cultural line of defense. It mocks the habit of self-absorption and the practice of avoidance.[16]

> My son lost his wife who left him with three children; his house burned down and his business went bankrupt—but he writes a Hebrew that is a pleasure to read.

The great Yiddish writers taught their readers how to extend their arms and box with God. They helped to create a delicate balance between piety and complaint. In the shtetl, "If a poor man eats a chicken, one of them is sick."[17]

Emancipation created another comedic possibility: the wit of retaliation as well as the humor of marginality. To understand this transformation as Jewish humor crossed the Atlantic Ocean, return to a fine model fashioned by Lawrence Mintz, a prolific scholar before retirement at the University of Maryland. Professor Mintz charts four developmental stages. The first features an attack on the out-group by those in power; the second, self-criticism; the third, realism; and the fourth reverses stage one as the oppressed minority gains revenge in assaulting the majority culture.[18]

Stage one can found in 19th century caricature. Leading magazines, *Puck*, *Judge*, *Life*, and *Leslie's Weekly* identified Jews with greed, bargain-hunting, and fraud—principally, arson. In *Puck*, for example, a cartoon depicts two hook-nosed stereotypical Jewish merchants in conversation.

> "Ah, Jacob, I fear I hafe not many tays to live."
> "Nonsense, Fader, you have as much as t'irty years yet before you."
> "No, Jacob, no! The Lord isn't going to take me at 100 when he can get me at 70."[19]

Such stereotypes continue currency in our oral tradition; Jews remain identified with the money obsession[20]:

- How do Israelis take a census?
  Roll a nickel down the street.
- What is their favorite football cheer?
  Get the quarterback!
- Station KVY, Tel Aviv signals: "1400 on your dial, but for you, 1395!"
- Why did Moses accept the Ten Commandments?
  Because they were free.

Status joins money as a favorite pursuit.

What is a CPA? It's a Jewish boy who can't stand the sight of blood and one who stutters.

Sorrow and pleasure fuse when a father discovers that his son is a homosexual but that he's going with a doctor (now a politically incorrect observation). Finally, stage one jokelore retains physical caricature. The Jewish nose is so big because the air is free. When Little Red Riding Hood calls on her bubby, she exclaims: "Bubby, what a big nose you have!" The Wolf replies: "You should talk!"[21]

As Jewish humorists became more comfortable with their newly minted status in America, they took off their kid gloves and began an assault on the icons of our culture. They laughed at themselves as well as their neighbors. A number of jokes help us score some salient points.[22]

- A rabbi, a priest, and minister converse. They are all suffering from a loss of congregants. So they devise a scheme to attract new members: through music. The priest secures the services of Perry Como to sing "*Ave Maria*." The minister hires Andy Williams to sing "Rock of Ages." And the Rabbi solicits Robert Merrill to sing "Gold Mine in the Sky."
- They compare notes. 15,000 join the Catholic Church. 10,000 join the Protestant faith. "How many converts did you make?" asked the minister of the Minister of the Rabbi. "None," replied the Rabbi, "but 50,000 Jews joined the air force."
- A Jewish merchant lay dying. Situated in a room behind the store, eyes closed, he asks for his family: "Sarah, my wife, are you here at my bedside?"
  "Yes, Sam, I'm here as usual."
  "My oldest son, Benjamin, are you here?"
  "Yes, Dad, I'm standing right here."
  "My daughter, Rachel, are you present?"
  "Yes, father, I'm at the head of the bed."
  "And my youngest son, Dovidl, are you here also?"
  "Yes, Dad, I'm right beside you."
  "Then," said the merchant, "who's minding the store?"

In a more aggressive vein, witness this encounter.

A Jewish couple converts. They join a prestigious and restricted country club from which Jews and dogs are banned. She takes a plunge into the chill waters of the restricted pool. Shocked, she yells: "*Oy gevaldt!*" Then, sheepishly, "whatever that means." Later that day, she finds her husband, Mitchell (né Morris), praying to their new God in the old Jewish way with *talith*, *tviln* and yarmulke. "What are you doing praying to Jesus in that garb?" Exposed, he replied: "*Oy, mein goyisher kop!*"

At a subsequent meeting of the male converts, a discussion ensues regarding motivation. Mitchell defends his conversion on spiritual grounds. To which one skeptic retorts: "What do you take us for: a bunch of *goyim*?"

For some, conversion has served as a passport to the "good life." Poised between two—sometimes more—cultures, the assimilated Jew, not unlike a fiddler on a hot tin roof, was sorely tempted to jump. Needless, to say a whole host of jokes surfaced to target would-be jumpers and to maintain some measure of control over a restless flock.[23] Many Jewish wits, from Heinrich Heine to Lenny Bruce, arrived at the realization *as vet gurnisht helfn* (nothing helps). Or as a *yiddishe sphrechvort* (folk saying) puts it, "*A mentsch tracht-un gut lacht*" (A man muses and God disabuses).

In pursuit of *parnoseh* (a living), Jews gravitated to the merchant trades, in which some acquired status and accumulated money. The jokelore that followed the trek from the *shtetl* to suburbia displayed a sharper edge.

> At Eastertime all of the merchants on High Street agree to carry some religious message in their window decorations. George (né *Gedalia*) Horowitz, the only Jewish businessman on the street, agrees to go along. He lined the central window of his store with artificial grass and placed in it several Easter bunnies and a large assortment of decorated Easter eggs. Next to the largest stuffed bunny he placed a sign on which he printed in large bold type: "CHRIST HAS RISEN." And underneath, in smaller letters: "but Horowitz's prices remain the same."[24]

To survive in a hostile world, Jews developed acute antennae and rapier wit: one for defensive purposes, the other for attack. Unable to find a permanent niche in *Gesellschaft*, Jewish wags created a pastiche of group experience. They blended poverty, pain, and "put-downs" with anger, intellect, and "send-ups" which enabled them to enter mainstream America, laughing. Writing with savage mockery or pulsing with coarse vitality, they sought money (*geldt* by association, as George S. Kauffman scoffed) and recognition. Not "high-brow" intellectuals but Jewish vaudevillians, Alfred Kazin correctly observes, introduced America to their culture on favorable terms.[25] However, as in the Horowitz-Easter joke cited above, they proceeded with caution. Initially, they impersonated other ethnic groups. Witness Weber and Fields, Gallagher and Shean, Smith and Dale. Some even hid behind black masks as well as Irish names. Eddie Cantor, Sophie Tucker, George Jessel and especially, Al Jolson waxed hot under burnt cork. Jolson had inherited a Jewish blue note. Fusing this somber, cantorial strain with vibrant, sometimes demonic energy, Jolson touched a vital cord when he conjured up a magnolia-scented South teeming with togetherness or *gemeinschaft*. Oozing *schmaltz* (high cholesterol chicken fat), Jolson pandered to America's darkest stereotypes. His success paved the way for ethnic *landsleit* (fellow travelers) to mix saccharine sentiment and aggressive humor effectively.[26]

Rarely reflective, Jewish entertainers used Yiddish accents, dialect stories, unabashed sentiment, gritty jokes, frantic energy—all, Irving Howe charges, "spin-offs from immigrant experience."[27] The Marx Brothers carried on the vaudeville tradition minus the minstrel masks. Groucho and his brothers debunked all American institutions, slaughtered all our sacred cows. In response to his father's failures in business, Groucho quips: "When I came to this country, I didn't have a nickel in my pocket. Now, I have a nickel in my pocket."[28]

Recently, while watching television, this writer observed the insidious stereotype equating Jews and money purveyed with the seemingly incongruous juxtaposition of Jews and communism. The Jews in the anti–Semitic folk culture get it from both ends. Daniel Bell and Richard Hofstadter have traced the roots of this nativist bilge to the sour dregs of Populism.[29] In the canards of Tom Watson's cracker-barrel bigotry, Jews owned Wall Street. Hence, his hate-laden pontifications promoted the lynching of Leo Frank. Later, during the Great Depression, other "white knights" such as Father Coughlin and Gerald L.K. Smith took up the Populist cudgels to continue their assault on the Jew as banker. Roget's *Thesaurus* identified the word Jew as synonymous with usurer, cheat, extortioner, and schemer.[30] I vividly recall my mother trying vainly to dispel this equation among our less than philo–Semitic neighbors in Brooklyn. "Is Rockefeller Jewish?" she asked. "Or Henry Ford? J.P. Morgan? Marshall Field?"

Even my radical mother of blessed memory, however, could not deny Jewish success in the American marketplace. As Professor Robert Cherry has observed, Jews appear to enjoy a median income 30 percent above the national average.[31] Thomas Sowell even puts it higher: 73 percent above the national average. This is a product of many variables and the subject of lively discussion, indeed debate, among scholars. Some, like David Riesman, stress education. Nathan Glazer points to religious values while Thomas Sowell focuses on cultural values, especially professional education.[32] Whatever the root cause, Jews remain the target of "underachievers" below and the "power elite" above. Pilloried at both poles, Jews continue to laugh, at themselves as well as at their enemies. Once upon a time, religion reconciled us to death, pain, evil, bankruptcy. Now, humor performs this vital function.

Manoff and Siskind met one day for lunch in the garment district. It was hard to tell which of them was more depressed. Manoff began: "Siskind, my friend, life is treating me badly. June was a disaster. Never in my entire career have I seen a June like the one I had. I felt miserable—until July. July made June look good. I didn't make a single sale all month! You had to see it to believe it. In fact—"

"Just a minute," said Siskind. "You think *you've* got problems? Listen to this. My wife has cancer. My brother is getting divorced. And my son, my only son, came to tell me yesterday that he was getting married: to somebody named Harold. Now I ask you, what can be worse than that?" (another anachronism; this observation no longer plays even in Peoria). "I'll tell you," said Manoff. "August."[33]

After the Biblical Jacob wrestled with God, many Jewish humorists like Sholem Aleichem, Woody Allen, Mel Brooks, and his friend Joseph Heller jousted with and jested about *Der Aybishter* (Supreme Deity). In combing through Milton Berle's bountiful joke file, one finds a few gems, if not golden nuggets[34]:

- Most people pray collect.
- God isn't dead. He's just getting a second opinion.
- "He's changing his religion."
      "You mean he no longer believes he's God?"
- God took six days to complete the world. But that was in the days before building permits.
- I don't like to be interrupted while I'm saying a prayer. There's something about putting God on hold.
- What if God takes the Earth back to the shop?
- I think that one of these days God will ask to have his name removed from our money. He doesn't want to go into Chapter Eleven.

The cosmic *kvetch* can be found in one of novelist Joseph Heller's last literary efforts, *God Knows*. King David, the giant killer, is also at twilight time. He frets over his succession, his enlarged prostate, his resettlement to Ocean Parkway, Brooklyn, guilt with regard to his patron, King Saul, whom he dethroned, and his rebellious son Absalom, whose death he caused; above all, God, "the great underachiever," according to the gospel of Woody Allen. Listen to his angry *shpritz*:

> Some Promised Land. The honey was there, but the milk we brought in with our goats. To people in California, God gives a magnificent coastline, a movie industry and Beverly Hills. To us He gives sand. To Cannes he gives a

plush film festival. We get the PLO. Our winters are rainy, our summers are hot. To people who don't know how to wind a wrist watch He gives underground oceans of oil. To us He gives hernia, piles, and anti–Semitism.

Comedy, it appears, provides armor in the confrontation with the *Malechamoves* (Angel of Death). Ultimately, the Jewish comic sensed that the whole business of money and success was "filthy lucre"—in a word, *dreck*.[35] We prefer to run with Woody Allen rather than walk with King David through the valley of the shadow of death. Material success has not brought the "bluebird of happiness" that Jan Pierce used to sing about. Indeed, one is reminded of the messiah watcher in the mythical town of Chelm. Vastly underpaid, he asked the town elders, all sages, for a pay hike. After days of deliberation, they turn him down. Although they concede that the pay is very meager, the work is very steady.[36]

Since the gap between dream and reality persists, Jewish humor provides a necessary bridge linking God, Jews, jokes and money. This bridge carries the Hebrew children across a grim past, a scary present, and future *schlock*. Girded with the armor of wit, the minions of Jewish humor cross over with a secret weapon: one that Arthur P. Dudden, echoing Mark Twain, has correctly called the "Assault of Laughter."

Two

Jewish Men and Women in Vaudeville

Vaudeville—"The Voice of the City"—was based on a simple idea: stage shows that offered something of value to everyone: rough fun for workers; glamour for middle class women; and old country *tam* (flavor) for immigrants longing for home.

A succession of daredevils, comedians, tearjerkers, and crooners proved highly popular and profitable. This combination captured the fancy of America from 1870 to 1930. Vaudeville represented the voices of modern urban society. Vaudeville challenged old codes of behavior and conferred new meaning to American identity. Sweet music emitted some sour notes[1]: grasping businessmen who put money above everything; frustrated artists who did not reach their lofty goals; and ugly racial stereotypes that distorted blacks as people.

Vaudeville arose in the middle of the transition from the 19th century to the 20th century—and helped it along. Italian-American Tony Pastor, born in New York City in 1834, created modern American vaudeville. Pastor's father, a devout Roman Catholic, ran a fruit stand. His mom was more adventurous; she ran a saloon, in which young Tony sang and composed songs. After 1875, Tony sanitized popular entertainment, rendering it family friendly. He banned vulgarity and cleaned up variety shows derived from the Bowery-based entertainment.[2] He opened the Fourteenth Street Theatre in 1881.[3] And the rest is history.

Pastor was superseded by a New England tandem of B. F. Keith and Edward Albee. They managed to corner the vaudeville market, thereby mirroring what corporate tycoons accomplished during our Gilded Age in establishing monopolies and thwarting unionization of employees. Keith opened a Union Square theatre in 1893. His subsequent success reflected the dominant business culture in which systematic organization eliminated competition. Working-class immigrants and their children flocked to vaudeville, which provided escape, entertainment, and group identification along with self-definition.

Vaudeville had bounce, immediacy, and energy to be sure, but managers adhered to a strict formula for grinding out profits. A "dumb" act—usually acrobats or trained animals—opened the show as customers found their seats. A second act, the "deuce spot," featured juvenile acts: singers or dancers usually in front of a closed curtain (known as working "in one") to allow for a scenery setup behind. Third in the lineup was a "flash" act, either a comedy sketch or a one-act play with a major star from the legitimate theatre, followed in fourth place by an eccentric novelty act such as a magician, an escape artist, or a female impersonator. Part one closed, amid the din of customers seeking relief for empty stomachs and full bladders, with a celebrity, usually a celebrity of modest talent. Concession stands netted huge profits during intermission.[4] Part two introduced returning spectators to a high-quality "dumb" act, such as a skillful juggler or an animal act. The seventh slot was usually a large musical number. The eighth slot, known in the trade as next-to-closing, was reserved for mega-stars. It brought favorite vaudeville teams to center stage. Author Stefan Kanfer cites that dynamic duo Ed Gallagher and Al Shean (Groucho's uncle). Despite their disdain for each other personally, they performed admirably. Witness this typical doggerel[5]:

SHEAN: Oh Mr. Gallagher, oh Mr. Gallagher.
GALLAGHER: Hello, what's on your mind this morning, Mr. Shean?
S: Everybody's making fun of the way the country's run.
 All the papers say we'll soon live European.
G: Why, Mr. Shean. Why Mr. Shean,
 On the day they took away our old canteen,
 Cost of living went so high
 That it's cheaper now to die.
S: Positively, Mr. Gallagher.
G: Absolutely, Mr. Shean.

The last act was known as a "chaser" or "haircut act" because it was so inane it inevitably prompted the audience members to exit en masse, leaving the untalented performer with a view of the back of patrons' heads. For rarely more than a one dollar admission, audiences made up of urbanites and immigrants got their money's worth of entertainment. Performers with high hopes and great expectations received, through trial and error, a priceless education.

On this uneven road to fame and fortune, Jewish comedians played a large role. Most of them hailed from New York City's Lower East Side.[6] Jews replaced Irish performers. They started at candy stores, trying out bits and hits. Among the pioneers, Joseph Weber and Lew Fields were both born in 1867. They met at age eight during a neighborhood scuffle. Starting their vaudeville career one year later, they assumed various personae as blacks, Germans, Irishmen, even Jews. Building in minstrel tradition, they used verbal byplay popularized by Tambo and Bones.[7]

> Who was that lady I saw you with last night?
> That was no lady. That was my wife.

As Mike and Myer, they wore loud checkered suits with large pads under their garb and ill-fitting derby hats. At five feet eleven inches and five feet four inches, respectively, they resembled a highly kinetic Mutt and Jeff. The taller Fields (1867–1941) impersonated the con man; the smaller Weber (1867–1942) the innocent dupe. Like the various immigrants they portrayed, they fractured the English language. Here are examples[8]:

> FIELDS: Vot are you doing?
> WEBER: Voiking in a nutt factory.
> FIELDS: Doing vot?
> WEBER: Nutting.
> FIELDS: Sure. But vot are you doing?
> WEBER: Nutting.
> FIELDS: I know, but vot voik are you doing?
> WEBER: Nutting, I tole you.

A precursor of Abbott and Costello's famous routine "Who's on First?":

> WEBER: So tell me the street you work on. I'll come and pick you up.
> FIELDS: Watt Street.
> WEBER: The street you work on. So I come pick you up, we go to lunch.
> FIELDS: Watt Street.
> WEBER: The street you're working on.
> FIELD: Watt Street.

Their verbal misplay and rough-house comedy provided a channel by which immigrants could release their pent-up anger. While Weber and Fields showed the way for Jews to follow, their violent-prone style coupled with ethnic caricature offended many co-religionists by the 1920s.

Among their many disciples, Joseph Sultzer (1884–1981) and Charlie Marks (1881–1971) surfaced as Smith and Dale. Based upon a Jewish preoccupation with sickness and health, they developed a popular sketch, "Dr. Kronkheit," later immortalized by Neil Simon in *The Sunshine Boys*, a successful play as well as a popular movie. Listen[9]:

SMITH: Are you a doctor?
DALE: I'm a doctor.
S: I'm dubious.
D: I'm glad to know you, Mr. Dubious.
S: I'm still dubious.
D: Mr. Dubious, are you a married man?
S: Yes and no.
D: What do you mean yes and no?
S: I am but I wish I wasn't.

In another routine, a more belligerent note reverberates[10]:

D: You owe me ten dollars.
S: For what?
D: For my advice.
S: Well, doctor, here's two dollars. Take it. That's my advice!
D: You cheapskate! You come in here—you cockamamie—
S: One more word and you only get a dollar.
D: Why—
S: That's a word. Here's the dollar.

Although gentiles B. F. Keith and Edward F. Albee dominated vaudeville management after Tony Pastor's departure, Jewish entrepreneurs began to compete. Working-class Jewish immigrants discovered vaudeville at Loew's on Delancey Street. Oscar Hammerstein I opened his majestic Olympia Theatre on Broadway between 44th and 45th Streets, establishing a foothold in the first tier in 1895. Three years later, Marcus Loew took over. Abetted by New York City's first subway line in 1904, Times Square experienced a boom featuring bright lights and palaces of popular culture, including its apogee: the Palace on 47th Street and Broadway.[11] At the Victoria on 42nd Street and Seventh Avenue, Oscar Hammerstein's son Willie introduced air conditioning, sort of, and a coarser form of vaudeville. Secondary business districts in Brooklyn and the Bronx as well as in Manhattan offered top shows where Jewish performers could gain acceptance and, hopefully, ascendance.

Jewish management and agents helped their *landsmen* (and women) enter vaudeville. A German Jew named Zelman Moses "butterflied" into William Morris. He had clerked for George Liman, a top vaudeville agent. In 1898, Morris started his own business. Soon, he had a galaxy of stars—Al Jolson, Eddie Cantor, Sophie Tucker, and the Marx Brothers—under contract.[12]

One that got away, Natie Birnbaum (1896–1996) found a non–Jewish partner who loved lamb chops. I refer to George Burns and Gracie Allen. He started out dancing for nickels at age five and subsequently singing on street corners as part of the Peewee Quartet. At age ten, he quit school and formed a dance team named after a local coal company: the Burns Brothers. He changed names and partners frequently. After several years of trial and error on the small-time circuit—more error than trial—George found a partner in Gracie Allen, eleven years his junior. Introduced to each other by Jack Benny (1894–1974) and his then girlfriend, Mary Kelly, a beautiful damsel damned by excessive drink, George and Gracie (1906–1964) teamed up in Boontown, New Jersey, in 1922 before a fine romance blossomed. Originally, in their comic song-and-dance act, she played it straight to his comic persona. When Gracie garnered most of the laughs, Burns used his *yiddisher kop* (Jewish smarts) and reversed roles. He assumed the straight role; she the laughter generating force that transcended the traditional "Dumb Dora" character.[13] Four years and one marriage later, they made it to the Palace. In a signature bit, they entered the stage. She turned around, beckoned to a man offstage, who came out and kissed her. She returned this amorous gesture. He exited and Gracie returned to a stunned George at stage center.[14]

GRACIE: Who was that?
GEORGE: You don't know?
GA: No. My mother told me never to talk to strangers.
GB: That makes sense.
GA: That always happens to me. On my way in a man stopped me at the stage door and said: "Hiya, cutie, how about a bite tonight after the show?"
GB: And you said?
GA: I said, "I'll be busy after the show, but I'm not doing anything now," so I bit him.
GB: Gracie, let me ask you something. Did the nurse ever happen to drop you on your head when you were a baby?
GA: Oh, no, we couldn't afford a nurse. My mother had to do it herself.
GB: You had a smart mother.
GA: Smartness runs in my family. When I went to school I was so smart my teacher was in my class for five years.
GB: What school did you go to?
GA: I'm not allowed to tell.
GB: Why not?
GA: The school pays me $25 a month not to tell.
GB: Gracie, this family of yours, do you all live together?
GA: Oh, sure. My father, my brother, my uncle, my cousin, and my nephew all sleep in one bed and...
GB: In one bed? I'm surprised your grandfather doesn't sleep with them.
GA: Oh, he did, but he died, so they made him get up.

The career trajectory of George Burns and Gracie Allen illustrates how vaudeville served as an inspiration to immigrant children. They could rise on merit, find "the blue bird of happiness" in the marriage of diverse cultures, and celebrate America's "Melting Pot." Other Jews, seeking sanctuary in *die goldine medine* (the golden land), would follow this trajectory into mainstream culture.

Vicious pogroms and grinding poverty had driven Jews from Russia to the United States. Between 1880 and 1890, three out of four settled in New York City's Lower East Side. In 1900, population density at 700 people per acre exceeded congestion in Calcutta.[15] By 1920, ⅓ of New York City was Jewish. By the same token, Jews constituted a disproportionate number of vaudevillians.

Arguably, the quintessential Jewish entertainer, Eddie Cantor (1892–1964), went from the city streets to vaudeville to stardom on radio and in film. In each medium, Cantor projected the changes that he experienced. Born on Eldridge Street in 1892, as Isidor Itzkowitz, he was raised by his grandmother. He lived a rough and tumble boyhood. In the summer, he entertained fellow campers at Surprise Lake.[16] With pal Dan Lipsky, he played weddings, bar mitzvahs, club socials, and local theatres. After these "gigs," he went solo. Eddie found success in 1908 at the Bowery Theatre: winning an amateur-night contest with a $5 prize. One year later, he worked the summer in Coney Island as a singing waiter. Back on the Lower East Side, Cantor acted as emcee or *badchn* at weddings. Discovered by juggler Roy Arthur, Eddie was invited to serve as his valet at $30 per week. Soon, he elevated on "gigs" in England and California from 1914 to 1915. In 1917, he made it to the *Ziegfeld Follies*, where his boundless energy gained him handsome salaries ranging from $200 to $400 per week. Demonic energy, observed critic Gilbert Seldes, marked Jewish entertainers.[17] No exception to this rule, Cantor shed the skin of assimilation to perform many bits with Jewish *tam* or flavor. In a high-pitched tenor voice, a supple body with effeminate gestures, Eddie danced, pranced, and belted out such signature songs as "If You Knew Susie," "Ma, He's Making Eyes at Me," "Yes, Sir, That's My Baby," and "Yes, We Have No Bananas." Waving a handkerchief, arms akimbo, fingers snapping to a ragtime rhythm, Cantor threw Yiddish words and Russian phrases, along with English punch lines—anything for a laugh—into his frenzied act.[18]

Other Jewish comics entered laughing. Lou Holtz (1894–1980) created Mr. Lapidus, George Jessel (1898–1981) the telephone routine, Joe Sultzer and Charlie Marks their Smith and Dale act, and the irrepressible Marx Brothers' comic chaos. Forced into the business by their dream-driven mother, Minnie, and aided by her brother, Al Shean, the Brothers Marx, after many abortive attempts, stumbled into stardom in 1910 with a skit: "Fun in Hi Skule." Groucho (1890–1977) played the teacher; Harpo (1888–1964) the moronic student. Soon, all five brothers got into the act. When Gummo (1892–1977) went off to war, Zeppo (1901–1979) replaced him. From vaudeville, they moved to Broadway in 1924. The play *I'll Say She Is!* displayed their multiple talents: music, mimicry, comedy, dance, verbal facility, and, above all, anarchy. Groucho played Napoleon in a musical revue that typified their brand of comedy[19]:

> NAPOLEON: Forgive me, my queen. I don't doubt your love. When I look into your big blue eyes, I know that they are true to the army. I only hope it remains a standing army...
> JOSEPHINE: Napoleon, when you go, all France is with you.
> NAPOLEON: Yes, and the last time I came home all France was with *you*. And a slice of Italy, too.

In this sketch, Groucho hears the melody of *La Marseillaise* wafting across the stage, to which he says: "Ah, the Mayonnaise. The army must be dressing." He and his brothers trampled on every ideal or sacred cow such as fair play, romantic love, honesty, business, opera, medicine, law, higher education, lower classes and, as suggested above, the martial spirit. Theirs is preeminently the comedy of deflation, a carryover, no doubt from Central Europe, the origin of their parents. ("When I came to this country, I did not have a nickel in my pocket. Now I have a nickel in my pocket.") So much for the Horatio Alger myth. "Whatever it is, I'm against it" as President Quincy Adams Wagstaff (Groucho) sang in the opening scene of *Horse Feathers* (1932). The song followed a brilliant takedown of academic arrogance in his inaugural address as the new president of Huxley College[20]:

> Members of the faculty, faculty members, students of Huxley and Huxley students—I guess that covers everything. Well, I thought my razor was dull until I heard this speech. And that reminds me of a story that's so dirty I'm ashamed to think of it myself. As I look over your eager faces, I can readily understand why this college is flat on its back. The last college I presided over, things were slightly different. *I* was flat on my back. Things kept going from bad to worse but we all put our shoulders to the wheel and it wasn't long before I was flat on my back again. Any questions? Any answers? Any rags? Any bones? Any bottles today? Any rags? Let's have some action around here. Who'll say 76? Who'll say 1776? That's the spirit! 1776!

An ensuing dialogue pits the retiring president against Wagstaff, his successor:

> RETIRING PRESIDENT: I am sure the students would appreciate a brief outline of your plans for the future.
> WAGSTAFF: What?
> RETIRING PRESIDENT: I said the students would appreciate a brief outline of your plans for the future.
> WAGSTAFF: You just said that! That's the trouble around here: talk, talk, talk!

> Oh, sometimes I think I must go mad. Where will it all end? What is it
> getting you? Why don't you go home to your wife? I'll tell you what, I'll
> go home to your wife and, outside of the improvement, she'll never know
> the difference. Pull over to the side of the road there and let me see your
> marriage license.
> RETIRING PRESIDENT: President Wagstaff, now that you've stepped into my
> shoes…
> WAGSTAFF: Oh, is that what I stepped in? I wondered what it was. If these
> are your shoes, the least you could do was have them cleaned.

At this point, Groucho belts out his signature song: "Whatever it is, I'm against
it." Refusing to join a prestigious country club to which he was invited, years
later, Groucho explained, "I don't care to belong to any club that would accept
people like me as a member." Self-deprecation to be sure; Jewish to boot; but
there were many more kicks in various encounters on stage and in films for
Margaret Dumont, that pillar of piety, WASP stolidity, not to mention stupidity. Karl Marx would have laughed, too.[21]

While the Marx Brothers were growing up in Yorkville, a young Georgie
Jessel was living in Harlem. Jessel started out as a singer, first in his grandfather's tailoring shop, and later at the old man's lodge. Thanks to a job at the
Imperial Theater, he sang in a trio that included Walter Winchell. He was
only nine years old at his show business debut. Prompted by friends—he had
a few—George Jessel later developed a novel telephone routine that offered
a less sentimental view of *die yiddishe mamme*, shades of Sophie Tucker. Having also dealt with tough-minded mothers through humor, many Jewish sons
could appreciate the ambivalence that coursed through Jessel's *beaux* jests.[22]

> Hello Mama. George. George. Your son, from the money every week. How
> are you feeling? You still see spots before your eyes? Have you got your
> glasses on? They're on your forehead? Well, long does it take to get them
> down? You got them down…. You see the spots better now.
> Say, mom. How did you like that bird I sent home for the parlor? You
> cooked it! That was a fine thing to do. That was a South American bird….
> He spoke four languages. He should've said something?

Jessel moved onto the "the Great White Way" as *The Jazz Singer.* A close friend
of Eddie Cantor, he did not copy Cantor's puppet-like movements or his mat-
rimonial style—a long marriage to one woman. Jessel played the field and
became known as Toastmaster General. His "overt Jewishness," Lawrence
Epstein contends, diminished his popularity in middle–America along with
his comedic career.[23]

Arguably, one of vaudeville's most successful alums was Milton Berle,
born Mendel Berlinger on July 12, 1906. Known as "Uncle Miltie" and "Mr.
Television" to millions of fans from 1948 to 1954 at the height of popularity,

he had a long roller-coaster career in show business with spectacular "ups" and precipitous drops. Like "Ol' Man River," he kept on rolling until his death, at the age of 95, on March 27, 2002.[24]

His parents, Moses and Sarah Berlinger (née Glantz) sired five children: Phil, Frank, Jack, Milton, and Rosalind. Milton grew up in Harlem across the street from Georgie Jessel. Prodded by an ambitious stage-struck mother with unconcealed oedipal tentacles, Milton appeared in bit parts in an estimated 50 silent films. Milton shifted to the legitimate stage in a 1920 Schubert production of *Floradora*. As a 12-year-old novice, young Berle received a dual initiation in sex and in Broadway theatre. He teamed up with Elizabeth Kennedy to perform a "kiddie act" which played the Palace on May 2, 1921, and lasted for two years.[25] Since child stars had to avoid the scrutiny of the Gerry Society, a watchdog agency dedicated to prevent the exploitation of child labor, stage-struck mother, Sarah, now Sandra, circumvented the watchdog and secured various jobs for her talented son as an actor/singer.[26]

More derivative than creative, Berle developed a series of imitations of current stars Al Jolson and Eddie Cantor. With high energy, *chutzpa*, and talent, Milton plugged away at the comedy game. Along the "great white way," he encountered many hurdles, including the first of several encounters with anti–Semitism. When famed comic Frank Fay referred to him as "a dirty little Jew" and "kike" in 1925, Milton lashed out at the bigoted star and smashed his face.[27] Working the vaudeville circuit enabled the young entertainer to hone his skills and learn his craft. When Jack Haley, the future "Tin Man" bereft of a heart, canceled a stint at the Palace, Berle filled the vacuum and achieved stardom over a ten-week run. Soon, on the road again as a wandering Jewish entertainer, he appeared in nightclubs, theatres, and eventually on radio. He also performed in an experimental telecast in 1929.[28]

Recurrent visits to Broadway started in 1932 with the *Earl Carroll Vanities* led to a hefty weekly salary of $1,500 and billing with Bing Crosby, Bob Hope, and Eddie Duchin at various benefits and "gigs." Vaudeville, radio, movies, nightclubs, and burlesque (a one-night stand only) beckoned to Berle, who even co-authored a musical parody salted with Jewish humor: "Sam, You Made the Pants Too Long."[29] Berle's identity as a fast-talking ad-libber who would do anything for a laugh developed over many years of trial and error. The comic, however, took union membership seriously: even picketing with striking stagehands at the Roxy Theatre when he was supposed to be on stage early in his career and later, in 1967, as his glory days on TV waned when ABC canceled his show. Defending his stand, he said[30]:

> I belong to every union in the business—actors, writers, directors, even stagehands and cameramen.... That's so I can do anything I want oh a set—

move a table or change a camera setup—things that actors aren't supposed to do under union rules. The other day I was walking to my office when I saw pickets around the Hollywood Palace, where I did my show. NABET (National Association of Broadcast: Employees and Technicians) was protesting the use of new automatic cameras that don't need operators. The boys asked me if I was going to cross the picket line. Cross it? I joined, it!

During the 1930s, he toured in the Harold Arlen–Yip Harburg musical revue, *Life Begins at 8:40*, hosted a radio show sponsored by Gillette, and, accompanied by his predatory mother, he went to Hollywood, where he was a featured actor in *New Faces of 1937*. In the early 1940s, he appeared in several mediocre films, including *Sun Valley Serenade* (1941) and *Margin for Error* (1943).

Trying to look less Jewish, Milton "bleached" his act and bobbed his nose. In his own words "I cut off my nose to spite my race." The new nose morphed into "a thing of beauty and a *goy* forever." But he could never shed his ethnicity. While working a Chicago club, Berle attacked a thick-necked heckler for calling him a "Jew bastard" and "kike." Unable to laugh it off in an improvisatory *shtick*, the comic pummeled the anti–Semite to a bloody pulp.

Eventually, Berle learned to channel his rage into aggressive humor. To a vocal critic: "You've been heckling me for twenty years. I never forget a suit." To a bleached blonde in the audience: "You look like Judy Holliday, and the guy next to you looks like 'Death takes a Holiday!'" When *schlock* journalist Walter Winchell called him "The Thief of Bad Gags," Berle wore this rubric as a badge of honor and often engaged in highly Semitic self-deprecatory wit at his alleged thievery. "I laughed so hard—I almost dropped my pencil." Imitation may suggest the highest form of flattery, but Berle's purloined material sparked anger among his peers. Bert Lahr, a great clown as well as the Cowardly Lion, absolutely loathed him and blocked Berle's entry into the Lambs fraternity.[31]

Superstardom eluded Milton Berle until 1948. For starters on the nascent medium of TV, Berle, given a budget of $10,000 to $15,000 per show, hired Pearl Bailey; Señor Wences, a pseudo–Hispanic comic with Jewish roots; a ventriloquist; and circus performers. Originally, Berle was slated to alternate with Jack Carter and Henny Youngman as hosts of the Texaco-sponsored variety show. NBC executives reversed course and tabbed Berle as the "Top Banana" exclusively. On September 21, 1948, television welcomed ethnic *landsleit* (fellow tribesmen) Smith and Dale and Phil Silvers (who would eventually knock his benefactor Berle out of prime-time TV in 1956) for the premier show. In two months, ratings vaulted skyward. Milton Berle owned Tuesday night for the next five years. Viewers, glued to their sets until 9 P.M., rushed to bathrooms, reducing water levels to a danger point in Detroit. Nightclubs closed on Tuesday nights in deference to the Texaco show.[32]

Berle's success caused a rapid rise in the sale of television sets throughout the nation, from 136,000 in 1947 to 700,000 in 1948. Even the hotly contested presidential election in 1948 could not preempt this ritual of Berle watching. Suddenly a national star with front-page coverage on *Newsweek* (May 16, 1949), Milton crested with rapid-fire gags, a phenomenal memory bag of jokes (10,000, Berle boasted), broad clowning, versatility, and hard work. Shamelessly, he barged into the acts of his guests. Wearing a whistle, he demanded attention while Sarah (née Sadie), the "Whistler's Mother," led the live audience in a chorus of laughter. Berle dressed as Howdy Doody, sang with Elvis Presley in an Elvis wig as he wiggled his pelvis. Berle was dedicated to the premise of "anything for a laugh," a product of the Borscht Belt, coupled with vaudeville. So the call for "makeup" invited a belt from an oversized powder puff in your face. He who got slapped with cream pies or squirted with seltzer elicited peals, if not pearls, of laughter. Guests pulled at his hair as he "mugged" for the camera. Anything could (and did) happen on this often ad-libbed show. Red Buttons lost his clothes, including his undergarments, in a stunt that went awry. So did the "Brazilian bombshell" (and undergarment-free) Carmen Miranda.[33] Significantly, Berle opened doors of opportunity for performers of color and ethnicity.

Despite mainstream popularity, Berle never lost his Yiddish *tam* (Jewish flavor). In one of many cross-dressing capers, this time as a Contessa, unable to fix his hair, he bellowed: "My *shytel* (a wig worn by orthodox or balding Jewish women) is falling!" Another sketch found him encased in a heavy sailor suit to which he *kvetched* (complained): "I'm *shvitzing* (sweating) in here!" Berle favored outlandish costumes to impersonate historical as well as fictitious figures: a caveman with a club and missing teeth, George Washington standing in a bathtub instead of a boat, Cleopatra in drag, Carmen Miranda going bananas, Superman in tights, Sherlock Holmes in robes. To generations bred in the Depression and tempered by war, Berle provided cathartic release through high octane Jewish *shtick* (bits of comic business) as well as traditional American slapstick. He morphed into a *meshugginer* (crazy) uncle who urged the kiddies—his countless nieces and nephews—to be good. While climbing the career ladder to success, Milton Berle never lost his commitment to *tzedakah*. He raised millions of dollars for the Damon Runyan Cancer Fund and other charities at innumerable benefits as featured performer.

Perhaps, as author Lawrence Epstein has argued, "Berle proved too Jewish for America."[34] His early popularity was grounded in an urban Jewish base. As television moved westward, middle Americans preferred a blander kind of humor as practiced by Herb Shriner, George Gobel, Johnny Carson and, more recently, David Letterman. Renowned theatre critic Frank Rich advances several theories to explain Berle's spectacular rise and precipitous fall. When people crowded into an affluent neighbor's home to watch "Uncle Miltie," the contagion of "group hysteria" made Berle seem funnier. That comic effect dissipated as viewers purchased their own sets. Competitive variety shows—Ed Sullivan's and Sid Caesar's—hurt. Sitcoms did not help either. Certainly, Berle's grating in-your-face persona alienated gentile viewers who preferred the benign characters on *Father Knows Best* or the sermons of Bishop Fulton Sheen. Rich concludes that Milton Berle fell victim to a medium that confers instant stardom and rapid oblivion in our throwaway culture. The remarkable thing about Berle is that he kept at it. He could not rest, contented with the lifetime contract (actually 30 years, at $200,000 per annum), which NBC tendered in 1951. After his last show for NBC was canceled in 1959, he attempted a comeback with *Jackpot Bowling* (1961) and another, after renegotiating his NBC contract, on ABC in 1967.[35]

When opportunity knocked, Berle continued to perform: in Las Vegas, on Broadway, in films, and as master of ceremony at celebrity roasts. Interviewed for a documentary on Jewish humor, Berle offered this joke.[36]

> A handsome, elegantly dressed man in his late sixties sits at a dining room table in the Borscht Belt. A woman on the prowl, bejeweled and farputzt (with lots of make-up), approaches. "Hello," she starts. "Have we met before?"
> "Not likely," he replies politely. "I've been away for thirty years."
> "Traveling?"
> "No. I was in the joint, the can."
> "You mean the toilet?"
> "No. That's an expression for prison."
> "Oh. What did you do?"
> "I murdered my wife."
> "Oh," she responds happily. "So, you're single?!"

A sick joke to be sure, but Mendel Berlinger told it with impeccable timing, crystalline diction, and an eye twinkle that framed the punch line perfectly.

Highly libidinous and richly endowed, Berle had many affairs before matrimony claimed him in 1941 with a beautiful if vacuous showgirl, Joyce Matthews, whose passion for shopping unnerved Milton and his oedipally attached mother. Divorce ended the marriage in 1947, but remarriage brought them together again for a year in 1949. When queried on this bizarre behavior, Milton justified the "double jeopardy" because Joyce reminded him of his first wife. After playing the field with Marilyn Monroe and other sirens, he settled into a long third marriage with publicist Ruth Cosgrove until her death in 1989 to cancer. At the age of 82, Berle found another bride in fashion designer Lorna Adams. Almost to the end of his long, active life, Milton Berle craved an audience and welcomed approval of his many gifts, which spanned serious drama as well as low comedy. At the advanced age of 87, he earned an Emmy nomination for his poignant portrayal of an Alzheimer's victim. Frank Rich provides the most fitting summation: "Berle was to television what an electric cord is to a socket, sheer energy the moment someone plugged him in." If heaven exists, no doubt, Milton Berle is *shpritzing* others, stealing jokes from fellow comedians, flicking ashes from Cuban cigars, and upstaging God with a standard Berlesque "saver"—"just kidding."[37]

A large slice of vaudeville featured women, too. Witness Nora Bayes, Belle Baker, Fannie Brice, and Sophie Tucker. Vaudeville paved the way because, fortified with an egalitarian spirit, it was open to all people—women as well as men—of talent. Sophie Tucker (1884–1966) is a case in point. Born in Russia when en route to America, Sophie grew up in Hartford, Connecticut, where her parents ran a delicatessen with a rooming house upstairs. This fat—145 pounds at age 13—coarse-featured girl sang to attract customers while working as a waitress. Married at 16 to Louis Tuck, and mother of an infant son, she ran away in 1906 to New York City.[38] Sophie joined the Von Tilzer songwriting house on Tin Pan Alley. Helped by fellow Jews—Willie Howard and the Von Tilzer brothers—she entered the vaudeville circuit. In addition, she sang in beer halls and cafés. Because of her less-than-elegant appearance, Sophie appeared in blackface until her make-up kit was stolen. Then, she surfaced as a "red hot momma," in whiteface. At the end of her performance, she removed her gloves and black wig to reveal "her natural blond hair and white hands."[39]

Her songs and routines invite scrutiny in the context of vaudeville. This genre had been marketed by founder Tony Pastor as clean entertainment and sharply contrasted with burlesque with its bawdy, vulgar, sex-saturated style. Gradually those boundaries separating vaudeville and burlesque grew blurred. Sophie blended them. She merged "blue" material with paeans to motherhood, black jazz and sentimental song, *shmutz* and nostalgia. Witness her signature song: "Some of These Days." In 1910, she belted out these words and music by black artist Shelton Brooks[40]:

> Some of these days
> Oh, you'll miss me honey.
> Some of these days,
> You're gonna' be so lonely
> You're gonna' miss my hugging.
> You're gonna' miss my kissing,
> You're gonna' miss me when I'm far away...

Contrast this, is if you will, with "My Yiddishe Momme," a popular ballad, written by Jack Yellin and Lou Pollack in 1925.[41]

> *A Yiddishe Momme*
> *Oy vee bitter ven zie feylt.*
> *Vie sheyn und lichtig iz in hois*
> *Ven die mame's doo*
> *Vie troirig finster vert*
> *Ven Gott neymt ihr oyf Oylam HaBo*
> *In vasser und fayer,*
> *Volt sie geloffen far die kind*
> *Nisht haltn ihr tayer*
> *Dos iz geviss der grester zind...*

The English version is less elegant:

> My Yiddish momme
> I need her more than ever now
> My Yiddish momme
> I'd like to kiss her wrinkled brow
> I long to hold her hand once more
> As in the days gone by
> And ask her to forgive me
> For things I did made her cry...

Sophie Tucker abandoned blackface and embraced her Jewish heritage. Her schmaltzy tribute to *momme loshen* and the women who nurtured *die kinder* crossed over to gentiles. Moreover, her corpulent frame rendered her less threatening when she merged the sensual with the maternal.[42]

Author Sarah B. Cohen puts a slightly different spin on the corpulent onetime coon singer. At a hefty 200-plus pounds, Sophie caricatured the torch singer with her gargantuan appetite for fun, food, and sex. Her added meat, she boasted, provided more "schmaltz to sizzle when I pour the heat on."[43] Sophie assaulted all of the taboos of Puritan culture and WASP gentility. This "red-hot mamma" disdained her "ice-cold papa" as she demanded her due[44]:

> Mistah Siegel, you'd better make it legal, Mistah Siegel. *Mazel-tov*:
> Something happened accidentally
> Consequently, we should marry

Is the complainant a duped innocent or a seasoned *nafkele*? Is the man just a gigolo or a Jewish Clyde Griffith who stumbles into parenthood? *Ver Veyst*? Who knows? Not even the Shadow could answer this *farkochte kasha*. In America, women barter sex for marriage, Sophie opines, while men seem to reject commitment. If men welsh on their marital promise, then the sexy lady should barter sex for mink, an animal act for an animal skin, preferably mink from Mr. Fink.[45] For sixty years—1906 to 1966—Sophie continued to sizzle on the griddle of life. As vaudeville lay dying in the 1930s, she took her act on the road all the way to England. During her long career, Sophie appeared in eight movies, on radio, and brought her sizzling (if aging) *schmaltz* to television. Before she expired, however, she gave life to unionization. Adding new meaning to the rubric, red, this "Red-Hot Mamma" like the legendary Joe Hill—in the stirring lyric of Alfred Hayes to the music of Earl Robinson—"went on to organize." She was elected president of the American Federation of Actors in 1938—"the first woman to hold this office," as Sophie proudly asserted in her autobiography. Trouble followed from alleged misuse of funds by an ex-vaudevillian and then executive secretary. Because of this disconcerting development, the AFA eventually merged with Actors Equity, and Sophie wrote her book.[46]

According to author Sam Berk, as quoted by Robert Snyder, Jewish artists had a *dybuk* (demon) for show business. As a child, Belle Baker, née Bella Becker (1895–1957), became enchanted with music hall entertainment on the Lower East Side. She left factory work for the theatre, the Yiddish theatre initially, where she earned $5 per week. When she crossed over to vaudeville her earnings vaulted to $100 per week. Consequently, she moved her parents and six siblings to a new home.[47] It is important to note that both Sophie Tucker and Belle Baker followed a familiar pattern. They began their show-biz careers on the Jewish stage, which they left for the greener (as in money rather than *felder*) pastures in vaudeville, which appealed to audiences across the ethnic as well as geographical spectrum.[48]

Stardom signified affirmation—not denial—of ethnic identity, as the career of Fanny Brice, née Fania Borach, attests. Born in 1891 to a middle-class family with Alsatian and Hungarian roots, Fanny, at age 13, sang for customers in her parents' saloon when she wasn't entertaining with local newsboys in neighborhood poolrooms.[49] A winner of a contest in Brooklyn's famous vaudeville house, Keeney's Theatre, she earned a $10 prize, plus another $3 from coins tossed onto the stage. Subsequently, she joined a chorus line but suffered a setback when George M. Cohan fired her for deficiency in dance. Fanny blamed it on her spindly legs. At 19, Brice belted out a tailor-made Irving Berlin song "Sadie Salome," which she sang with a thick, indeed artificial Yiddish accent. One author described her: "Tall and gangly like Olive Oyl, with two bright crescent shaped eyes on either side of a parrot-like nose, Brice was always using her mug for low-comedy effect."[50]

In 1910, she appeared in the *Ziegfeld Follies*, where she starred for more than ten years. With boundless energy, a broad range of emotions, and mobile face, Fanny blossomed into a first-rate satirist with an extraordinary gift for caricature.[51] Later, in 1923 she submitted to cosmetic surgery, which prompted a brilliant Dorothy Parker quip: "She cut off her nose to spite her race"[52] (a line obviously stolen by Milton Berle). Onstage, Brice, impersonated an elegantly dressed Madame Du Bary, waved her fan and, in a thick Yiddish accent, confessed to the audience: "I'm a bad voman, but I'm demn good company."[53] Once established, Fanny returned to her ethnic roots but refused to employ demeaning stereotypes.[54] She joined a chorus of *landsmen und landsfroyn* (fellow-travelers: Jewish men and women) into the cacophonic orchestra of vaudeville. Consequently, this group introduced Yiddish into mainstream American discourse with their *shtick* as they *schlepped* around the country with a verbal baggage that included *chutspe, schmaltz, nebbish, klutz, schnook, schmo, schmnedrick, schlemiel, schlimazel,* and my personal favorites, to wit, *putz* and *schmuck*. Indeed, as author D. Travis Stewart points out: "Jews had their own segregated vaudeville circuit."[55] On Houston Street, one could see a show with "'the prophet Elijah,' Hilda the Swedish Handcuff Queen, jugglers, one-act plays, songs and dances, klezmer music, all on the same bill." From these minor, marginal leagues sprang great if not-so-fine artists mentioned above and many that would follow.

One of Sophie Tucker's disciples, Belle Barth was born Belle Suzman in East Harlem in 1911. She trekked through vaudeville to the Catskills, Atlantic City, Las Vegas, and Miami Beach. Like Tucker and, later, Lenny Bruce, she talked dirty to influence people but with scripts heavily salted with Yiddish phrases. Calling herself an M.D. or *Maven oif Dreck* (excrement) she peppered her *shtick* with scatological terms. "Show me a home," Belle sang, "where the buffalo roam and I'll show you home full of *pischachs* (urine: *azoi geht die yorn*). She loved to relate jokes about old farts, like the 90-year-old man who had to be fed rectally. Close to the end, he asks the kind nurse to bring two tubes so they could both enjoy his last supper. Another favorite Barthian jest involves a vaudeville act in which the performer claims to sing opera through his rectum. Asked to demonstrate, he sings two arias beautifully, but, on the third try, he befouls the whole floor with fecal matter. Horrified, the agent rants: "What are you, nuts?! This is a $6,000 rug!" The artiste replies: "I had to clear my throat, didn't I?"[56]

Almost invariably, women are the target of the dirty joke. Belle Barth reversed this pattern. For example, in explaining the utility of Yiddish, she advised that only two words sufficed: *geldt* and *schmuck,* "Because if he has no, he is." After a trip to Israel, she *kvelled* about a group she heard there "called the foreskins."[57] Those acidic (as opposed to Hasidic?) one-liners were often followed by a reference to a darling daughter who packs a roasted chicken in a zippered bag for her mother on her way to Florida. On the train (or plane, in an update) she puts the chicken on a seat next to her. When she falls asleep, a man sits down and places the chicken under the seat. Awakened and hungry, eyes closed, she gropes for the chicken in the dark, unzips the man's fly and puts her hands on his penis. "What daughter I have," she beams with pride, "the neck of the chicken is still warm."[58] According to Professor Cohen, this joke signals a comic reversal in which the woman strips away the man's putative penal power. His instrument, after all, is really "as flaccid as a limp-chicken neck."[59] Our sex machine breaks down feeding Belle's comic demolition derby. She satirizes second marriages in which a woman hollers in simulation (not unlike Meg Ryan's fake orgasm in Katz's Delicatessen in the 1989 film *When Harry Met Sally...*) that it hurts, and a man has to tie himself to the bed "so he doesn't fall in and drown."[60]

For subsequent Jewish comediennes, subtlety eclipsed *schmutz* (filth). They matured in a new "playground"—the Borscht Belt. Like Tucker, Brice, and Barth, Totie Fields exploited our twin passions for sex and food. Fields toted 190 pounds on a small frame of four feet, ten inches. Before cancer ravaged her ample body, she engaged in self-mockery. "Do you think it's easy pushing these fat Jewish feet into thin Italian shoes?" Her favorite meal was "breakfast, lunch, dinner, and in-between." She confessed: "I've been on a diet for two weeks and all that I lost was two weeks." Always on the hunt for a bargain, Fields once bought a bra for 49 cents. The bra had three cups; so, one day she hoped, her "cup will runneth over." Totie philosophized: "Happiness is finding a library book that is three weeks overdue but you are not" or going out to dinner with friends and "getting a brown stain on a brown dress." Even after having a leg amputated she continued to jest. At the Concord, *alova shalom* (rest in peace), she quipped: "I never had good legs anyway." She lost her leg and, ultimately, her life, but never her sense of humor. Professor Cohen concludes that Totie Fields, like Tucker and Barth, "relied on girth for her mirth." Apparently, the counter-image to Hollywood's beauty standards permitted them to be funny, to triumph in a world dominated by men.[61]

One former female vaudevillian almost slipped under our radar screen. Born Celine Zeigman in Paris, France, on January 7, 1911, Jean Carroll teamed up with dancer Buddy Howe who shaped her career incrementally as partner, husband, and manager. Like former vaudevillians, Fred Allen and George Burns, they turned to comedy. Realizing that his wife had more talent as well as beauty, Buddy encouraged Jean to stand up alone. She wrote her own material, wore elegant clothes, and as a budding feminist told "husband" jokes. In these comic reversals, one detects a budding feminist humor. Several examples follow:

- My husband. You should see him. I should see him. So quiet, I'm collecting his life insurance.
- My husband is so stupid. Can't dress by himself. Wakes with a headache because he jumps out of bed head first.
- Wouldn't divorce me because the bedroom set is in my name.

Attracted to her husband because of his pride, she joked: "I'll never forget the first time that I saw him, standing up on a hill, his hair blowing in the breeze—and him too proud to run after it."[62]

Carroll also poked fun at suburban living, a Jewish queen as counterpart to Alan's Jewish King. Her repertoire included jokes about family and shopping. She made her "hippie" daughter shave her beard but let her keep her moustache. Perhaps her best joke surfaced at a major United Jewish Appeal in Madison Square Garden in 1948. Following a list of celebrity speakers, a veritable Who's Who of show business, Jean Carroll confessed: "I've always been proud of the Jews, but never so proud as tonight.... Because tonight I wish I had my nose back."[63]

Up from vaudeville, these Jewish female performers paved the way for a new feminine sensibility. Refusing to play "Dumb Doras," they crafted a subversive persona: one armed with a *Yiddishe kop* (Jewish wit) and *chutspe* (nerve, no, balls) to attack conventional pieties and traditional patriarchy. They engaged in what Mark Twain aptly called "the assault of laughter ... against which nothing can stand," not even phallic power.[64] That may prove to be vaudeville's best legacy and the "unkosher" comediennes' finest hour.

THREE

Yiddish

An exhibit "Let There Be Laughter" was held in Chicago several years go. It drew attention to a frequently neglected dimension of Jewish humor in America: the Yiddish language, culture, and the artists who luxuriated in that allegedly dead or dying tradition.[1] The exhibit also resurrected a dichotomy that plagued Jewish theatergoers and pitted intellectuals against *die proste yidn* (common folk). Writing in praise of Yiddish, Maurice Samuel located the primary roots of the language in Germanic dialects with ancient Hebrew components. In one of many examples, he related a simple declarative sentence: "*Es hot ongemacht a kurbn*" in describing a hurricane. Translated literally, the sentence reads: "It made a destruction." Samuel points out that the initial four words are German while the last is Hebraic. *Kurbn* harks back to the destruction of the Temple in Jerusalem. This construction imparts both general and specific meaning. Another example follows: *In shtub iz geven tishebov*, or figuratively: "It was a house of mourning." *Tishebov*, a Hebrew word, designates a holy day commemorating the destruction of the Temple again, while the other words reside in Yiddish.[2] A third example refers to Moses, the lawgiver, upside down, i.e., *Moyshe Kapoyer*. Samuel likens this phrase to the masculine equivalent of "Mary, Mary, quite contrary."[3] Although Hebrew influenced Yiddish, it remained aloof as a sacred tongue for men only. At home, a child learned to speak Yiddish on his mother's lap; hence, the language acquired another name, *mame loshen*, or mother tongue.[4]

Irving Howe and co-editor Eliezer Greenberg added to our understanding of that dynamic tension between Hebrew and Yiddish. In a foretaste (*forshpeiz*) of a world to come, *ganaydn* (heaven) Hebrew represented the sanctified Sabbath, while Yiddish symbolized the other six days, mostly a struggle to earn a living (*parnuseh*).[5] An intellectual wave called the *Haskala* (Enlightenment) swept through Western Europe in the 18th century and Eastern Europe in the 19th century. This heady movement promoted reason, science, and secularism. One side effect fostered the denigration of Yiddish by Jewish intellectuals who preferred to write and to discourse in the language of their host country.[6] Zionism, an offspring of romanticism coupled with nationalism, also led to an avoidance of Yiddish because of its link to *Goles* (Diaspora) and victimization.

In their edition of Yiddish stories, Howe and Greenberg cite a number of bittersweet, often comedic proverbs[7]:

- The tavern can't corrupt a good man, the synagogue can't reform a bad one.
- A wise man hears one word and understands two.
- A fool grows without rain.
- So many Hamans and but one Purim.
- If you dance at every wedding you will weep for every death.
- A Jew's joy is not without fright.
- The rabbi drains the bottle and tells others to be gay.
- If praying did any good, they'd be hiring men to pray.

Teeming with wry wit and folk wisdom, these proverbs served as coping mechanisms that left room for jousting with authority figures, including God. Listen to this chant, a so-called "loving indictment" emanating from a Hasidic rabbi[8]:

> Good morning to You, Lord of the Universe!
> I Levi-Yitschok, son of Sarah of Berditchev,
> Have come with a claim against you
> On behalf of your people Israel.
> What do you have against your people of Israel?
> Why do you afflict your people Israel?
> And I, Levi-Yitzchok of Berditchev, say,
> I shall not stir from here.
> From this spot I shall not stir,
> There must be an end to this,
> The exile must come to an end!
> Magnificent and sanctified be His Name!

Michael Wex's insightful study of Yiddish language and culture proved a delightful surprise. His book begins with an old Jewish joke that, after much kvetching for water to quench a thirst, ends in the punch line: "Oy, was I thirsty!" Wex notes that kvetching harks back to the Bible when Israelites always complained. No longer slaves in Egypt, they kvetched at Moses for wandering in the desert. Even the prophets kvetched—against God, no less. To kvetch, according to the magisterial lexicographer Uriel Weinreich, is to strain, press, pinch or squeeze: a behavior often encountered on the toilet, like many of Philip Roth's older male characters, battling constipation. Complaint comes naturally to a people, allegedly God's chosen; yet beset with so many woes, kvetching reminds us we are. It is our tribal ID card. How should (note the subjunctive) Jews respond? Why not, "Oy, vey iz mir!" coupled with the *farklemte*, blue note of klezmer music?[9]

Not only does Wex, a linguist, a comedian, a translator, a novelist and a professor, offer wonderful examples of the linkage between Yiddish and humor; he also provides a luminous historical narrative on the evolution of this often maligned language. He notes that French and Italian Jews settled in German-speaking areas, where they adopted the local language. Consequently, Romance language residues in Yiddish shrank and a new golden age of German-Jewish thought emerged during the 12th and 13th centuries. To this day, the major source of Yiddish remains German. Wex cites a simple sentence—"*Du bist alt*" as identical in both languages. If you add the word "Today," they differ: *heint* in Yiddish; *heute* in German.[10] Resistant to the lure of Christianity, Jews resorted to subtle jibes like *nisht geshtoygn, nisht gefloygn* (didn't climb; didn't fly). In jest, Jews could deny the divinity of Christ. Yiddish names mock other religions. Jezebel means "the daughter of garbage" or "Baal" (the pagan idol). Beelzebub equates to "Lord of the Flies." The name Nabal refers to a godless non-believer and vile scoundrel.[11] Jews, in the ancient world, drawn to Greek culture, were called *Epicursim*, or follower of Epicurus, who—in simplistic caricature—projected pleasure over pain. Thus, religious Jews viewed gentiles as sensualists bent on immediate gratification. If the mantra *shiker iz a goy* then the "religious other" drinks, fights, and fornicates. Yet a goy, male of the "other" persuasion, is put on a higher perch than the seductive *shikse*.[12]

Arguably, Wex's most compelling analysis covers the trove of Yiddish curses, or *kloles*. A frequent flyer in this verbal assault is "*Gey in dr'erd*." Literally, this translates: "Go into the earth" or figuratively, "Drop dead," or "Go to hell." Occasionally, a phrase is added: "*Lign in dr'erd un bakn baeygl* (lying in hell and baking bagels). This curse adds torment to one's enemies. As Wex explains, it is the Jewish equivalent to the Greek myth of Sisyphus.[13] A *klole* is a *kvetch* with a mission. While *kvetching* is basically passive, cursing employs action in the subjunctive mode with words like "would" as well as "should." A curse, Wex argues persuasively, is a dream deferred.[14] Does it dry up like "a raisin in the sun"? The worst kind of curse is "*yemach shmoy*," derived from *Leviticus* 26 and *Deuteronomy* 26 and 28. Wex offers several examples; one of which is *Ich vel im bagrobn in dr'erd vie an oytser* ("I will bury him like a treasure"). Another is "*Farchapt zolstu vern*" (You should die suddenly).[15] The most virulent curses involve lingering plagues, illnesses, and painful conditions that cause a slow death.

Citing Robert Graves, Maurice Samuel noted "that the more extravagant the curse, the less venom there is in it."[16] In his chapter on "Maledictions and Benefactions," Samuels totals a ratio of three or four to one in favor of curses. Hebrew curses, he argues, are totally humorless but those in Yiddish earn a higher score in comedy. Powerless to oppose an oppressive society, Jews faced two options: to suffer in silence or to rage against a cruel world with verbal agility in *klolehs*. In his repertoire, Samuels seemed to favor health issues.[17] He cites a favorite: *A cholerye oif im* (he should be infected with cholera). Samuel concludes that benedictions such as "Let us meet on happy occasions" may lift one's spirits, but another departing wish at the end of a funeral: "May you know no more sorrow" is, of course, nothing more than a pipedream: highly favored but ultimately fatuous.[18]

Leo Rosten, a humorist and lexicographer, acknowledged the influence of Maurice Samuel on his own writing. Rosten observed that among Jews "swearing is rare, but cursing common."Rosten savored curses because they put trenchant wit over brute force. Physical violence earned rebuke from Talmud scholars because it violated Jewish ethics. Moreover, Rosten pointed to the "special, swift, sweet catharsis" of curses like[19]:

- May all your insides churn like a music box.
- May all his teeth fall out—except for one (so he can have a permanent toothache).
- Like a beet he should grow—with his head in the earth.

A trip from curses to *shmutz* (filth or dirty jokes) does not require a complex suspension bridge. In 1986, a span of some 29 years in time, at an International Conference on Jewish Humor held in New York City's New School for Social Research from June 9–12, attendees, including this writer, enjoyed a presentation by Moshe Waldocks: rabbi, professor, author, producer, and comedian. His paper, "Scatological Yiddish *Shprechverter* and Their Impact on Jewish Humor" required careful listening because Professor Waldoks raced through the delivery to compensate for an occasional stammer. Waldok's thesis is that *sprichverter* or proverbs preceded jokes, and jokes are transmitted as punch lines. In the oral tradition, he argued that the dichotomy of *prosteh* (coarse) vs. sheyneh (refined) Yidn is false. Both groups told and enjoyed "dirty" proverbs, many of which were derived from religious texts. His catalogue of 227 proverbs focused on bodily functions, flatulence, and urination. Here are some choice examples: Yiddish above; English below.

- *A vort und a fortz ken men nisht tzurick nemen.*
  A word and a fart cannot be taken back.
- *An eigeneh fortz shtinkt nit vie a frendn.*
  Your own fart smells better than a stranger's.
- *Ver es pisht vie a hundt is der vos is gezundt.*
  Whoever pees like a dog is one who is healthy
- *A pish und a fortz, is a reign un a duner.*
  A pee and a fart are rain and thunder.
- *A geveer pisht nit boiml und kakt nit gribenhes*
  A rich person does not pee oil or shit congealed chicken fat
- *Vintshn und kocken is die zelbe zach*
  Wishing and defecating are identical
- *Zie hot gut Moishe vie ahrennlach*
  Her Moses (bush) is as good as her little Aarons (breasts)

Proverbs, according to Waldoks, extol the magical powers of urine. "Where Adam did not pee, no great city can be." Many urination proverbs target other religions, particularly Christianity. "A gentile *putz* (penis) is like a dunce cap; a Jewish one, a derby." Some are directed against Jews themselves. "Why can't Jews win a war? They all get up to pee at the same time." Urination evokes merriment of rainfall and relief. Waldoks regards it as "symphonic elimination." One can conjure up a Jewish counterpart to Rabelais's creature Gargantua: pissing on Paris.

Waldoks did not ignore anal matters. *Mit tuchus oifn tish*, or ass on the line, you can hang many proverbs. Witness:

- You can't dance at two weddings with one ass.
- When you sleep with your wife, your ass faces the whole world [a sexist image, clearly].
- Upper class? Kiss my ass!
- Stick your finger up your ass; make your head feel better fast.
- You can't roll strudel out of shit.

One wonders if Rabbi Waldoks's mother ever asked him: "From this, you make a living?"

At a similar conference, an elegantly dressed gentleman who earned a comfortable living in advertising seeking anonymity as Mr. "P," "hawked" his book: a collection of dirty jokes framed by Yiddish punch lines, plus English translations. One gentle joke featured Jake and Becky, who went to the same room in the same hotel to celebrate their 50th wedding anniversary. Aroused,

Jake wakes Becky at two A.M. for sexual activity. "Becky—*darlang mir die tzeyner, ich vill dir a beis gebn.*" ("Hand me my teeth. So I can nibble on you.")[20] In another joke, a *shadchen* (matchmaker) admonishes a prospective bride for her gross behavior. In the middle of his pitch, she arises and says: "Ich dwarf gayn pishn" ("I have to pee.") The shadchen instructs her to say: "*Anshuldig, ich darf benetsen die blumen.*" ("Excuse me, I have to water the flowers.") At the next interview, she mouths the exact words as directed; then adds: "und kocken eichet." ("And shitting too.")[21] A favorite joke relates an encounter between a famous Yiddish actor and an infamous womanizer (possibly a covert reference to Boris Thomashefsky). After a night of passionate love with a pretty woman, the actor gives her two tickets for his show. Disappointed, she protests: "*Billetn darf ich nit. Ich bin a nofke. Ich darf hobn broit.*" ("Tickets, I don't need. I am a prostitute. I need 'bread.'") Haughtily, he replies: "*Broit vilstu; nextn mol zolst du shlofn und trennen mit a becker.*" ("You want bread? Next time sleep with a baker.")[22] Each of these jokes invites a chuckle or two, coupled with deep thought. Drawn from the same book, Mr. "P" offers political commentary. Two candidates vying for nominations commission their campaign managers to sing their praise. Candidate Levy's manager uses the alphabet to extol his virtues[23]:

A he is ambitious
B he is benevolent
C he is clever
D he is damn clever
E he is efficient
F he is friendly
G he is generous
H he is honest
I he is intelligent
J he is judicious

Cohen's manager interrupts with Yiddish descriptives of Levy:

K *Er iz a kocker* (shitter)
L *Er iz a loiz* (a louse)
M *Er iz a momzer* (a bastard)
N *Er iz a* nudnik (a terrible pest)
O *Er iz an oisvorf* (an outcast or prostitute)
P *Er iz a pisher* (a pisser, unseasoned)
Q *Er iz a kvetch* (a complainer)
R *Er iz a ratz* (a rat)
S *Er iz a shtinker* (same thing minus the "h")
T *Er iz a trombenik* (scoundrel)
U *Er is unik* (eunuch)
V *Er iz a vantz* (a bedbug)

From the sublime to slime, an impotent man goes to the rabbi for advice. The rabbi advises him to put his penis in the torah because *"alles shteyt in torah."* That is to say: "Everything stands (is erect) in the torah."[24] As Irving Howe observed in his magisterial study, *proste yidn* (ill-lettered common Jews) broke loose from moral constraints. Vulgarity erupted as a challenge "to rabbinic denial and shtetl smugness."[25]

What standards should dominate: classical ideals or *shund* (trash)? Abraham Goldfaden started this debate when he invented modern Yiddish theater. Born in Volhynia Gubernya (a province on the Russian border in which this writer's mother was also born) in 1840, young Abraham went into his father's trade at a time when Czar Nicholas I began to torment Jews with oppressive legislation. As a student in a rabbinical seminary, he had a female role in a Yiddish play.[26] Thus, a star was born in "drag." To avoid a 25-year term in military service, Goldfaden, at age fourteen, switched to a Russian school. While studying at this government-sanctioned academy designed to train teachers to promote loyalty to "Mother Russia," he teamed up with Abraham Gottlober to foster Yiddishkeit through folk songs and dramatic presentations. Gottlober had written a comedy, *Der Detukh* (*The Canopy*). Also inspired by the Broder Singers, a group of troubadours from the town of Brody, Goldfaden decided to create "a living theater for the masses." This venture entailed a composite of songs, monologues, spectacles that were derived from festivals, *Purimshpiels* (Purm plays), and weddings. In Odessa, Goldfaden founded a periodical devoted to humor, *Der Alter Yisrolik*, or *The Old Israelite*. Banned in Russia by Czarist *ukase* (edict), Goldfaden fled to the town of Jassy, a Romanian town in Northeast Austro-Hungary. There, joined by Berel Brody and talented imitators, Goldfaden inaugurated Yiddish Theater on October 5, 1876.[27]

As author Stefan Kanfer notes, there were four prerequisites for this development, namely, literacy, adaptability, humor, and Yiddish.[28] All of the above ingredients helped Goldfaden to launch his grand experiment in Romania. With financial support from Israel Gradner, Goldfaden created a thriving theatre in Bucharest the next year. Fancying himself more of a writer than a *shoyshpieler* (actor), he also proved an excellent talent scout as well as a fine musician, although his musical knowledge was limited at best. Goldfaden hired an outstanding clown/mimic Sigmund Mogulesko and pilfered melodies from Beethoven and Offenbach, *oich a Yid* (also a fellow Jew) and dipped into folk songs like *"Rozhinkes mit Mandlen"* (*"Raisins and Almonds"*). Most importantly, Goldfaden created two characters from Jewish folklore, Kuni-Lemel and Shmendrik, both derived from the *schlemiel-schlimazel* tradition. Due to their immense popularity onstage, their names became permanently etched into the Yiddish language.[29] Kuni-Lemel (little lamb), a young Chasid, is flawed with blindness in one eye, a speech impediment, a lame foot; in short, he is "a stuttering pedant" and a loser to boot.[30] In the finale, university students—representing the *Haskalah*—chase the Chasidim off the stage, signaling, in the words of Ruth Wisse, the "triumph of modernity over obscurantism."[31]

Author Sol Liptzin notes that Goldfaden's early comedies exposed "the follies of ghetto life and preached enlightenment for the … masses."[32] He singles out several of his best early comedies, including *Schmendrik* and *Die Beyde Kuni-Lemels*. The first mentioned, performed in 1877, became the most popular of his first phase. Liptzin describes Schmendrik as "stupid but not vicious, gullible but not vengeful … easily reconciled to loss and failure." It is a comedy of errors in which Shmendrick marries his cousin Tsierele rather than the beautiful Rosa, whom he covets but loses in a veiled switch at the altar. Goldfaden touts romantic love at the same time he shows *derech eretz* (respect) for the older generation that adhered to customary arranged marriages. In the other comedy, *Die Beyde Kuni-Lemels* (*Both Kuni-Lemels*), audiences were entertained with a bait and switch at the altar, evoking comparison with Shakespeare's *Comedy of Errors* and providing a stronger case for the coupling of love and marriage. In later works—*Bar Kochba* (1882) and *Ben-Ami* (1908)—tragedy transplants comedy as Goldfaden laments the loss of national identity and yearns for a return to Zion. Obsessed with good and evil, he created memorable characters like Hotzmach *der Blinder* (the Blind man) and the witch, BabbeYachne in *Die Kishenmacherin* (*The Witch*). Children exposed to Yiddish, this writer recalls, would chant lyrics stemming from Goldfaden's *cholem* (dream). The witch lured children with promises in a screechy voice:

Kum, kum, kum tzu mir	Come, come, come to me
Vestu zein gut bei mir	Where, you will happy be

The chorus lacks confidence in the anti-hero:

Hotzmach iz a blinder	Hotzmach is a blind man
Shreyen alle kinder	All the children shout

In the end, however, virtue triumphs over evil and the children go free. Though impaired and often bumbling, the always kind peddler Hotzmach defeats the wicked witch. Liptzin concludes his celebration of Goldfaden with a candid catalogue of assets and debits. In the latter category, he states, that Goldfaden, bereft of musical training, could not read a single note. Nevertheless, he used words and music for both entertainment and comfort in Yiddish theater. In this vital medium, he combined the wisdom of *Maskilim*, enlightened teachers and the musical comedy of the *Badchonim* whose songs conveyed satiric bite. Synchronized with the Jewish *Zeitgeist*, not Hegel's, Liptzin writes: "He had faith in the liberating power of laughter, in the fruitful mating of art and morality in the benign union of beauty and goodness ... directing their [audiences'] attention to a better way of life."[33]

Eminent scholar as well as prolific author Salo Baron devoted most of his 94 years on earth to the study of Jewish history: research, writing, and lectures. Fortified with a photographic memory, Baron would sit at his desk and lecture for hours, minus notes, to the amazement of his students, including this writer in the spring of 1959. He repeatedly insisted that the standard interpretation was wrong because it fixed on what he called the "lachrymose"—oppression, poverty, pogroms, and exile. In an article that he wrote in 1928, Baron asserted: "Surely, it is time to break with the lachrymose theory of pre–Revolutionary woe, and to adopt a view more in accord with historic truth."[34] In revisiting this standard approach, Baron opened up new vistas: one that embraced the other side of a tormented past: laughter and mirth. Ironically, Stefan Kanfer notes that "laughter" is embedded in another word "slaughter." Jews invariably found the joke in their yoke. Even in Auschwitz, they told jokes as survivor/psychiatrist Victor Frankl observed and author Steve Lipman demonstrated in his excellent study, *Laughter in Hell*. Ever since the *Bible* exhorted readers to make a "joyful noise," Jews have responded affirmatively. The *Badchen* (designated clown) emerged during the Middle Ages with a mission to entertain his people, especially at weddings.

In the 19th century, a struggle ensued: pitting the ultra-orthodox against members of the *Haskala* (Jewish Enlightenment). The latter group's faith in reason trumped blind obedience to charismatic rabbis and scholarship by rote. The nascent Yiddish theater seemed to favor the Enlightenment folks. Oddly, however, in order to curry favor with a mass audience, dramatists developed a dumbed-down version of drama designated by the term *shund* or scandal. As it traveled from Eastern Europe to America, Yiddish theater filled a void in immigrant life: "a breath of home ... meeting place, an arbiter of fashion, a common passion."[35] It also provided folk heroes who championed a sense of loyalty to traditional and communal ethics. As religion waned in the "New World," Yiddish theater served to affirm cultural identity and to promote core values.[36] Yiddish masses gravitated to the theater that they loved passionately, even if that ardor was not reciprocated by the actors. Above all, *folksmentschen* (ordinary people) preferred *shund* or art for the masses. It fed, Sandrow insists, the "human appetites for amusement, excitement, escape, affirmation," while intellectuals disdained this vulgar art form that favored intensity over subtlety. Comedians milked each *shtick* (comic routine) for laughs. Stereotypical characters: young lovers, shrewish step-mothers, comic fools, *soubrettes*, weak male figures—all appealed to audiences with minimal education. Nachma Sandrow traces these characters to older forms: *commedia dell' arte* roles with roots in ancient Greek theater, featuring masked protagonists. Favorite actors invited fierce loyalty, occasionally punctuated by punches. Since audiences identified with actor and role, they hissed and cheered during plays.[37] In the 1890s, the public favored "high *shund*," i.e., operatic melodramas with exotic locales, twisted plots, vulgar puns, lavish costumes and enlivened by colorful but budget-constrained scenery. That conceit diminished as folks clamored for comic relief in potboiler domestic dramas like *Dos Yiddishe Hartz* (*The Jewish Heart*) in which Lemech, the fool-figure sings Gilbert & Sullivan–type patter songs and, tangential to the plot, engages in "*kuplets*." According to Sandrow, *kuplets* "took the clown out of the play framework, reasserting the relationship between performer and the audience." A common facet of vaudeville, Al Jolson often used this method—"you ain't heard nothin' yet"—to disrupt a narrative and communicate directly with his audience. In many of his movies, Groucho Marx employs this *shtick*, a strategy reprised by Joan Rivers onstage. Yiddish comedian Jacob Jacobs sang about a cuckold, or impotent man; then would ask a man in the front row why his wife is laughing so hard.[38]

One actor who benefitted from the penchant for high as well low *shund* in Yiddish theater was Boris Thomashefsky. His embrace of trashy melodramas won immense popularity. He and his rivals adopted Goldfaden's formula of "a song, a jig, a quarrel, a kiss."[39] Displaying muscular legs to support an expanding upper body, Boris became a heartthrob who self-identified (the original "selfie") as "America's Darling." Craving *shund*, recent immigrants from the Old Country could not get enough. With rising box-office returns, Boris and his second wife, Bessie, spent lavishly, giving Jewish-American credence to Norwegian-American Thorsten Veblen's theories of "Conspicuous Consumption," if not to "Conspicuous Waste." They bought lavish homes in Brooklyn and upstate in the Catskills. Thomashevsky's great rival, Jacob Adler, who favored serious drama with a tragic bent, reluctantly followed the Thomashevsky lead, not the Stanislavsky method.[40]

During hard times, theatergoers wanted a change. They hungered for escape via entertainment as opposed to moral lessons and political harangues. *Shund*, like Gershwins' John P. Wintergreen, was sweeping the country. As a result of this escape mechanism, Kanfer seems to suggest, many escape seekers fell asleep as Hitler was surging to power in Germany.[41] Several counterpoints embracing high and low culture were evident during the Great Depression. On the Yiddish scene, Moishe Oysher, a renowned singer, did double duty as cantor and opera performer. In one film, *Dem Chazn's Zindl* (*The Cantor's Son*), Oysher played a variation of the Al Jolson part-talkie *The Jazz Singer* (1927). Oysher went from shtetl to Manhattan, where he achieved great success as a performer, but little happiness as a man. So, in search of meaning and "the Bluebird of Happiness," he returns to the shtetl, where he finds fulfillment, a bride, his roots, and healthy box-office returns.[42]

Molly Picon had a similar experience, but one with a curious twist. Born on Manhattan's Lower East Side in 1898, Molly's father abandoned the family after her mother gave birth to baby sister Helen. Molly's mother moved her two girls and her own mother to Philadelphia, where she earned a living as a seamstress at Kessler's Yiddish Theater. At age five, Molly won a contest at a local theater. With five dollars prize money plus tips, she launched her career in American vaudeville. While on tour, she was stranded in Boston as a result of the influenza epidemic of 1919. Her savior, Yankel Kalich, manager of the Boston grand Opera House, became her mentor and husband—perhaps even a surrogate father figure. She was 20 when they met; he, 29. Molly's ne'er-do-well father proved to be a bigamist and parasite.[43] Jacob developed a career for the ebullient Molly, not quite five-feet tall but full of energy, as a kind of Jewish Peter Pan. Under her husband's tutelage, she made her first film, *Das Judenmadel* (1921), in Austria. Molly often played dual roles, as male and female. In 1936, Picon and her husband went to Warsaw to film *Yiddle Mit'n Fidl*. During her successful tenure on the Yiddish stage, Yiddish theatres seem to sprout all over. There were four on Manhattan's Second Avenue, and several more in Brooklyn, Queens, the Bronx, and Newark, New Jersey.[44] Like the future Beatles, Molly Picon was "here, there, and everywhere." As the Yiddish theater faded after Maurice Schwartz closed his Second Avenue theater in 1950, Mollie effected a smooth transition to the American stage and film. She appeared in *Milk and Honey* (1961), *Come Blow Your Horn* (1963), *Fiddler on the Roof* (1971) and two *Cannonball Run* comedies (1981, 1984).[45]

Leftist critics like Nathaniel Buchwald loathed *shund*. Yet, even he and his colleague Moishe Nadir could not deny the success of this genre during the 1930s. Audiences flocked to see Molly Picon, Manashe Skulnik, Aaron Lebedev, Leo Fuchs, and Yette Zwerling. Something happened in 1932 to bridge a gap between *kultur* (high-class culture) and *shund* (low-level entertainment) when Getzel became a bridegroom. Thanks to an excellent recent study by Joel Schechter, we now know more about the positive power of *shund* in Yiddish theater. *Shund* (literary trash) featured several salient qualities, namely, a sense of humor, optimism, perseverance, survival—plus a radical sensibility. Audiences could identify with poverty-plagued immigrant outsiders and their dreams. Even leftist writer Moishe Nadir acknowledged its allure while another left-wing critic, Nathaniel Buchwald, decried *shund* in favor of socially engaged theater with a political agenda.[46]

Something happened, however, during the 1932–33 season to bridge that gap: a play, *Getzel Becomes a Bridegroom*, in which comedian Menasha Skulnik (1892–1970) emerges as both a *schlemiel* and union leader. Joel Schechter provides a compelling narrative that illuminates this important Yiddish play. Actors like Skulnik, Schechter explains, had "signature songs, dances, monologues, routines"—or *shtick*. Using broad gestures, wearing *outré* costumes, and engaged in "burlesque brawling," they did anything and everything for a laugh. Schechter traces this style back to *shtetl* weddings where *badchonim* ruled the comic roast.[47] That methodical comic madness found an exemplar in Menashe. He wore a porkpie hat too small for his large head. He walked with hunched shoulders in a stiff gait. His nasal, high-pitched voice sounded like the bray of a wounded animal, in Schechter's apt description. The predictable plot finds Getzel in search of a bride with the aid of a *shadchen*. It is a match made in Coney Island, not in heaven, to a plain woman with two children. There is a Turkish harem dream scene that allows the extremely shy Getzel to express the latent "id" in this timid *Yid* at the same time that it offers audiences, *shund's* multiple titillations as the super-ego slumbers. A Yiddish Walter Mitty, Getzel awakens with a renewed sense of social responsibility. He abandons Oriental fantasies and returns to Selba, a "kosher woman," and her two children. Operating on the false assumption that his future bride is the *shadchen's* beautiful daughter Eva instead of the less attractive Selba, he discovers the truth under the wedding canopy. Accepting his fate as *schlemiel*, not *schlimazel*, the naïve chicken-flicker Getzel joins and eventually leads a chicken-slaughterers' union. Hence, blessed with two unions—marriage as well as labor—Getzel proposes a ten-year strike against *der balebos*, his bother-in-law, the boss. No doubt a parody of Josef Stalin's five-year plans, Getzel wages a successful strike. At the culminating wedding scene, he becomes both *bodchen* and groom.[48] Thus the *schlemiel*, like the sun, also rises.

Troubled times confronted another Yiddish comic performer, Leo Fuchs. Born in Poland on May 15, 1911, he came to America in 1930, when Yiddish theater peaked. Although economic depression hit hard, assimilation had not adversely affected Yiddish as *lingua franca*, and Hitler's destruction of European Jewry was still only a plan. Fuchs entertained Jewish audiences, seeking relief from domestic *tsores* (woes) with his brilliant application of Yiddish vaudeville enriched by *shund*. Success greeted the young actor in 1936 when he appeared in *Papirosn* (*Cigarettes*). Like Woody Allen's Zelig, and Danny Kaye in many roles, Fuchs morphed into many different characters, often in dream sequences. In the Yiddish film *I Want to Be a Boarder*, he portrays a "greenhorn" as well as a popular nightclub entertainer. The film's central theme song, "Trouble" merged social commentary and vaudeville comedy.[49] Leo is in a troubled marriage with Yetta Zwerling. They decide to divorce, but he remains as a boarder. They role play. The back story derives from a frequent practice in tenement life earlier in the 20th century when impoverished immigrant families rented a room to a single, usually male boarder, to meet expenses.

Some instances led to trysts between boarders and married women in violation of a Mosaic commandment and the sources of ribald revelry in literature.[50] In one dream sequence (together again), Leo Fuchs is transformed into Fred Astaire as he dances his troubles away. He also sings. Fuchs personifies the *schlemiel* with grace who does not fall on his face.[51]

In this role, Fuchs bridges two worlds: the greenhorn as outsider and the assimilated Jew as insider. He goes up and down the social ladder as he trysts and shouts. A better world beckons through song, dance, community, and laughter. Awakened from his *cholem* (dream), he chooses to remain a *lebedik un freilach* (lively and happy) boarder than unhappy, henpecked husband. The audiences reveled in Leo's contorted, highly "eccentric dance."[52] This wild dance anticipates Elaine Benes, of *Seinfeld* fame, only with far more agility and grace. An accomplished violinist, Fuchs felt freer onstage than in film to perform *shtick*, like fiddling behind his back, a far, far more difficult task than fiddling on the roof. Throughout his career he performed brilliant *kuplets*—special songs, impersonations, and comic dances, often inviting audiences to sing along.[53] Critic J. Hoberman *kvelled* (rejoiced) over the vaudeville bits in this Yiddish film. He regarded the *Boarder* film as "a kind of missing link between the Marx Brothers and the Yiddish stage." He called Leo Fuchs "a people's clown" akin to Groucho Marx in *Animal Crackers* talking directly to the audience: "Pardon me while I have a strange interlude."[54]

Leo Fuchs had a long career that crossed linguistic and cultural borders. In the 1950s, for example, he played a Yiddish detective in Yiddisher Dragnet, a parody of taciturn Jack Webb's Sgt. Joe Friday as well the central character in *Katz on a Hot Tin Roof*, a sendup in English of Tennessee Williams's famous play. Back to the Yiddish stage in 1962, he portrayed a Jewish cowboy who goes to Israel to raise Goldstein instead of Holstein cows. Along with countless others in the audience, this writer joined in a chorus of laughter (*mir hobn gekeikled fun gelechter*) from the opening line "Shalom Partner" to the final curtain. Schechter, on whose book this take on Leo Fuchs is largely based, indicates that in a stage play, *Here Comes the Groom* (1973), Fuchs amazed theatergoers with uncanny imitations of Maurice Chevalier, Menashe Skulnick, and Jimmy Durante. Switching to Hollywood again, Fuchs played a Polish Rabbi opposite Gene Wilder in *The Frisco Kid* (1979) and Hymie, the brother of Sam (Armin Mueller-Stahl), who cut the turkey prior to his arrival and that of his older brother Gabriel (Lou Jacobi) at their annual Thanksgiving dinner, in Barry Levinson's excellent film, *Avalon* (1990).[55]

Schechter correctly pairs Fuchs with Yetta Swerling, his female counterpart in several Yiddish shows: *Motel the Operator, The Jewish Melody, The Great Advisor*, and the above-mentioned *I Want to Be a Boarder*. Often cast as either a *yenta* (gossip) or *kochlefl* (agitator or troublemaker), Zwerling prefigures the modern woman with her aggressive behavior and comic antics. Her behavior on and off the stage had a cutting-edge quality that invited acceptance because she was so funny. Humor confers immunity on those practitioners who press the envelope with impunity in search of truth. On the impact of Yetta Zwerling, pioneer *Komiker* (comedian) with *chutspe (nerve)* and *zetz* (punch), astute critic Joel Schechter has the final words[56]:

> Zwerling's films and plays portrayed a new world where Yiddish spoken by a comedienne like her could become part of popular culture, a celebration of a country in which women as well as men were advancing socially and culturally, becoming not only seamstresses and shop girls but also stars of stage and screen. When Zwerling performed on stage, the Yiddish language became "good for women" in the best sense of the words. Her lines made the woman speaking them, and her comic art, more popular wherever Yiddish was spoken.

Wanderers throughout their history, Jews had to rely on what was portable: religion, education, values, and humor; all embodied in words. If Hebrew was slated for Saturday prayers, Yiddish—earthy, colloquial, accessible, expressive—was tailor-made for everyday life. Lawrence J. Epstein persuasively argues that it was ideal for humor.[57] Many Yiddish words invaded the English language, sometimes creating a hybrid known as "Yinglish." Epstein also notes the many character types that entered as well: *schlemiel, nebbish, schlimazel, schlump, nudnick, shmegegge, gonif, schadchen, shnorrer, and maven*. To this list, he adds words that have crossed over as well, namely, *bobe-meiseh, fress, kinder, chutspe, shtick, megillah, nosh, kvell, kvetch*, and the ubiquitous *oy*. Many of the Yiddish types that Professor Epstein cites carried the stigmata of losers. Implicit in the naming process is the mode of mockery that has the potential to transform losers into winners. Jews found latent power in words to forge them into weapons for assault as well as defense. Repressed in Eastern Europe but unleashed in the United States, aggressive Jewish humor flowered. Comic observations of everyday life, from the Yiddish-speaking *shtetl* to affluence in suburbia sandwiched around a thick slab of urban life, fed a hungry public a steadily increasing diet of satire (defined by Lenny Bruce as "tragedy plus time") that provided a reassuring sense of community or *élan vital*, a vital force in this era of "troubled times."

FOUR

Funny Jews

Up from the Catskills—
Danny Kaye and Sid Caesar

Jewish comics enjoy a high profile in American culture. Many emerged from poverty and pain.[1] In their pursuit of *parnoseh* (pay-off) and *fargenign* (bliss minus the Volkswagen), they traveled from vaudeville to movies, from burlesque to television or around the world in eighty jokes. In releasing their stored-up aggression, they provided comic relief *shvitzing* (some like it hot) and *shpritzing* (some prefer a cool spray). While diverting mainstream Americans with stereotype, dialect, caricature, satire, and parody, they earned money and *yichus* (status) beyond the wildest dreams of Tevye, the hairy dairyman.

Generating laughter at the expense of one's group—"Take my tribe, please!"—is the process that allegedly defines traditional Jewish humor. Although there is never enough respect, as Rodney Dangerfield lamented, the work is steady. The Messiah watchers of Chelm and Kasrilevke can confirm this proposition. On this side of the Atlantic, Jewish comics plunged into the mainstream culture. Many worshipped *shiksa* goddesses; some even married them. Jack Benny married within the tribe but the object of his affections, Sadie Marks, metamorphosed—new name, new nose—into Mary Livingstone. Milton Berle once quipped, after rhinoplasty, that "he cut off his nose to spite his race ... a thing of beauty and a goy forever."[2] Assimilation won friends and influenced people. Eddie Cantor could not resist currying favor with Christian prelates except for "Radio Priest," Father Charles Coughlin. When American pop culture banished Jews during the Second World War, no protests were evident.

Then something happened in the 1960s. Wallace Markfield called this dramatic reversal "the Yiddishization of American humor."[3] Several important comic geniuses broke the mold and in the process reinvented American comedy. Danny Kaye, Sid Caesar, Lenny Bruce, Woody Allen, Mel Brooks, and Jackie Mason served as catalytic converters. Their comic engines generated heat, light, and laughter.

Before we trace their existential odysseys, we must identify the salient traits of Jewish humor. Like a leitmotif from an opera by Richard Wagner (you should pardon the reference), a pervasive skepticism courses through this genre. The good doctor, Sigmund Freud, also observed strong self-criticism, a democratic deflation of the powerful and the pompous, social principles inherent in Judaism, revolt against religious and economic constraints. Freud's disciples enlarged on these tendencies.

Theodore Reik, for example, noted four singular traits: intimacy, dialectical thought process, unmerry laughter, and explosive truths. Jewish wit— a term that he preferred to humor—shifts from paranoia to masochism. When released, Dr. Reik alleged, aggression targets social institutions. According to Albert Memmi, a brilliant French-writing Algerian Jew in exile (*vu den*?), the Jewish joke is a plea for love. "Rooted in deep feelings of guilt sparked by periodic rebellions against God and his laws, this kind of humor offers a sacrifice in order to survive." In this confession, we confront the fundamental identity conflict which informs Jewish humor.[4] Even at the abyss, gallows humor provided a last line of defense. In happier days, Jewish humor goes on the offensive. A two-sided weapon, it hones a cutting edge for historical change and social commentary.

As the biographical sketches reveal, Jewish comics continually wrestle with knotty contradictions related to their uncertain place in a mercurial world. On the surface, affluence and acceptance beckon. An elderly Jew is hit by a car. Good Samaritans rush to help. They furnish a blanket and offer support. One asks: "Are you comfortable, sir?" He replies: "I make a living." *Parnoseh* (making a living) is not enough. Anxiety gnaws at complacency. Is assimilation viable? Will orthodoxy play in Peoria? Intermarriage continues to climb (Jacob's ladder?). No half-way house can survive the collapse of the Yeatsian center. Slouching to Bethlehem is no solution. Besides, as my mother warned, it's bad posture. Remaining in limbo, on the periphery, a Jew turns to wit as shield, weapon and "dog," i.e., ID tag. After all, Elliot Oring asserts, we are "the people of the joke."[5]

Post-Depression Jewish comedians started in the local candy store, once the hub of urban culture. Nervous, restless, loud; egged on by their upwardly mobile parents and inflated with too many egg-creams (have I got a recipe for you!), they summered in the city; excelled in self-mockery, pricking the pretensions of their parents to high culture. They grappled with *kunst* (culture) in the candy store.[6] Like their parents, they became masters of the needle trade. Capitalization on verbal wit, parody, needling the opposition prepared these immigrant children for public performance. Some achieved professional status either as stand-up comics or sit-down writers of comedy. Others tummeled to the top.

The candy store yielded to the Borscht Belt. At White Roe Lake Hotel, for example, in the Catskills there emerged an enormous talent: David Daniel Kaminsky, later known as Danny Kaye. Born in Brooklyn's East New York section in 1911, he was the youngest of three sons. His mother, Clara, doted on him and smother-loved him with Yiddish phrases. His parents encouraged the young Dovidl to perform. Funny faces in the school yard endeared him to Lou Eisen (later Lou Reed), who was Danny's first partner in comedy. Their antics drove teachers crazy and propelled Danny to an early exit from Thomas Jefferson High School, at age sixteen.[7]

Danny's mother had died shortly after his bar mitzvah. This loss, plus the onset of the Great Depression, pushed the restless youth off the education track. Danny hung out at the local candy store, where he could receive phone calls. One evening as Lou and Danny were singing in front of their favorite store, a Borscht Belt regular heard them and was impressed. He secured their services for White Roe Lake Hotel, near Livingston Manor, New York. A-tummling they would go. A tummler is Yiddish "for fool or noisemaker who does anything and everything to entertain the customers so that they won't squawk about their rooms or food."[8]

To get to White Roe, 112 miles from New York City, Kaye and Eisen had to take a ferry from 42nd Street to Weehawken, New Jersey, from which they took the Ontario and Western Railroad to Livingston Manor, a four-and-a-half hour ride, absent traffic (I made the same journey with my parents in 1946), followed by three miles of bumpy country roads, a far cry from John Denver's, in a wagon.

Lou and Danny tummled at Sunday-night concerts, weeknight masquerades, campfires, games, and plays (usually on Friday nights). They also tummeled during the day, especially when it rained. From this activity, they earned $75 a summer, plus room and board. Inspired by Fishel (Phil) Goldfarb, they combined British diction with Yiddish fiction and intonation— "dot noble beast, dot marwellos stelyin, dot fency stead." From Kaminsky and Eisen they metamorphosed into Kaye and Reed.

In September, back home, Kaye found neither song nor story. Bereft of a permanent vocation, he became depressed—a condition that would plague him the rest of his days. His brothers worked. He idled. Then summertime summoned Danny back to the Catskills, where he turned on the comic juices. He combined "low comedy and high aspirations." At the behest of Nat Lichtman, another mentor at White Roe, Kaye sang a Yiddish lullaby, "*Oifn Pripet-shik.*" He added a comic signature, a recurrent phrase "gagina rechina," which he borrowed from Goldfarb. Gibberish worked wonders, too. Kaye perfected his trademark talents: conducting orchestras, dancing, singing, pratfalling, acting.

Conducting orchestras became a staple. He would arrive onstage, looking disheveled; in one hand, a telephone book; in the other, several batons. He bangs the batons quickly. They break. The orchestra refuses to follow his lead. He drops his arms; the orchestra plays. A saxophone player blows a wrong note. Kaye pounces off the podium to inspect the sheet music. He flicks a dropping from the sheet music and looks skyward with disdain at the offending bird (later reprised as a funny bit in a Mel Brooks movie). Returning to the podium, he trips, scattering the music of a violin player. He adjusts the stand higher and the violinist rises in response. Another sour note brings Kaye to the offender. He grabs the instrument, plays it, badly, and bops the musician over the head. In wiping the perspiration from his forehead, the handkerchief turns into an endless sheet of music. I recall one riff on early television where Danny began to fence with a violinist: baton to bow. Laughter rolled like thunder as the coda featured "Stars and Stripes Forever." As Kaye bowed, the orchestra played. He spun around; they stopped. After many repetitions, Kaye collapsed in exhaustion as the audience roared with delight.[9]

The country's Depression deepened. "Dr. New Deal" entered with promises of "Happy Days." Kaye didn't derive any immediate benefits. Like Snow White, he drifted (to paraphrase a line from Mae West). In 1933, he decided to go on a tour with his girlfriend dancer, Kathleen Young (the first of several gorgeous gentile girls in his love life) and her partner Dave Mack. They called themselves The Three Terpsichoreans. Dividing $60 a week, they headed for the Far East in 1934, as part of a larger review called *La Vie Paree*. One night in Osaka, a tremendous typhoon cut off the electricity while Danny was about to perform. He called for two flashlights, with which he illuminated his face. And he began to sing and talk nonsense. Panic yielded to fascination; fear to laughter. The double-talk communicated universally. Unable to speak Oriental languages, Kaye developed his own language with a

Git-gat giddle,with a geet-ga-zay.

This Yiddish-flavored nonsense evoked laughter everywhere. Verbal slapstick evoked mock Russian, German, Italian, and French. A homeless Jew found comfort in a zone of funny ambiguity.[10] Audiences connected with this new comic language, which was heavily salted with Yiddish inflection. They appreciated this "Desperanto."

When Danny returned in 1935, he joined the vast army of unemployed. His former honey, the dancer, departed for her home base in the Midwest. Danny headed back to Catskills. Impressed with their returned prodigal, White Roe parted with many dimes to sign Danny to a $1,000 contract. Teamed with Phil Goldfarb, he discovered a new comic voice coupled with a unique style, blending old and new. On Kaye's talents, listen to biographer Martin Gottfried[11]:

> [Kaye combined] ... the low clowning of Bert Lahr, Willie Howard, and Ed Wynn; the musical babble of Jewish entertainers; the burlesque flopping of Bobby Clark; the bawdy verbalism of W. C. Fields; the wise guy antics of Groucho Marx; the suave anecdotalism of Jack Benny and Frank Fay. Ahead lay Bob Hope and wise-cracking stand-up comedians, those relentless pacers of nightclub floors.

Kaye and Goldfarb, unaware of their place in history, borrowed from Smith and Dale and their famous Dr. Kronkheit sketch.[12]

> DOCTOR (GOLDFARB): Where were you born?
> RUSTY (KAYE): In the hospital.
> DOC: Why?
> RUSTY: I wanted to be near my mother.

Kaye wanted to be near the money in 1936, so he moved to the President Hotel. There, he teamed up with Lillian Lux and Alex Olshanetsky to sing Yiddish songs, serve as emcee, and promote Yiddish entertainment. He also met Benay Venuta who got him a "gig" as a comic's stooge (assistant) in a Manhattan club, Casa Manana, after Labor Day.

Sandwiched between long periods of unemployment, Kaye went to London, where audiences did not respond well to his novelty songs. Ousted from his booking, he returned, defeated and depressed. Only when performing to live and appreciative audiences did Kaye return to high spirit. Benay Venuta helped him get a club engagement as a stooge for Nick Long. Kaye performed vintage Catskills, material which included "Minnie the Moocher" and a new routine "Dinah" which my Williamsburg buddies loved to emulate. Audiences did not "dig" this repertoire at first. Kaye bombed in New York as he did in London in 1937.

An opportunity in 1939 changed his life. *Sunday Night Varieties*, directed by recent émigré Max Liebman, was in need of talent. Kaye auditioned; so did Sylvia Fine. Though the play closed after opening night, Max moved the fledgling team of Kaye and Fine to Camp Tamiment. There, they merged their talents. Sylvia set her sights on Kaye, spinning a Venus flytrap for her future partner in marriage.

Sylvia Fine was born August 29, 1913. Her parents were middle class;

her father, a dentist for whom Danny briefly worked as a teenager. Sylvia was an intellectual, a musician, a *macher* (a person of influence) in school. Though far from beautiful, she had talent, personality, and wit.[13] Unlike Danny, the dropout, Sylvia graduated from Thomas Jefferson High School with honors and went on to Hunter College, where she also excelled. Socially conscious and politically aware, Sylvia inclined to the left.[14]

Max Liebman, a fine talent scout, hired Sylvia for Camp Tamiment in Bushkill Fall, PA. A haven for Jewish left-wing vacationers, Tamiment offered cottages with kitchens for rent—a higher class of *kochalayn*. A variety show on Friday and a major revue on Saturday served as entertainment magnets. Whereas vaudeville followed a strict formula of eight acts, ritually ordered and working-class oriented, revues labored for and aspired to sophistication in sketch comedy. It appealed to middle-class people.[15] Kaye left tummling behind.

Fine tailored her comedy for Kaye, featuring high androgyny. She spoofed the rage in theatre: Stanislavsky with Russian—as opposed to Yiddish dialect. Fine partnered, accompanied, and encouraged Kaye. At the end of a successful summer, Liebman decided to take the revue to Broadway while demanding 10 percent of his performers' future earnings for the next four years.

The Straw Hat Revue opened on September 29, 1939, with Alfred Drake, Imogene Coca and Danny Kaye in featured roles. Greeted with mixed reviews, the show lasted eleven weeks. After watching a former flame, Rosie Kaye, get married in Florida, the lonely and the restless Danny—without much fanfare—proposed to Sylvia Fine. She accepted. In a civil ceremony, on January 3, 1940, they tied the knot. *Un mariage du raison*, it smacked of a Faustian bargain—mutually convenient and eventually loveless.

Kaye ventured into a nightclub, a dark inferno conjured up by Dante and emerged a bright, shining star. A twelve-minute act, fashioned by Fine and Liebman, featured Tamiment material: "Stanislavsky," "Pavlova," "Otchi Tchnorniya," and "Minnie the Moocher."[16] He reprised the orchestra *shtick* and led a spontaneous eruption of a participatory "Conga." He took the act to Chicago's Gay Paree. With the assistance of Kitty Carlisle, Fine encouraged Kaye to try out "Anatole of Paris"—a send up of a fey designer.

> Voila, a chapeau
> At sixty bucks a throw

Chicago noticed.

So did Moss Hart (Kitty Carlisle's husband) and Max Gordon. They plotted a Kaye debut in their Broadway show, *Lady in the Dark*. Perhaps a projection of Moss Hart's ambiguity, Danny played an effeminate fashion photographer. He stopped the show with a thrust into Russian culture: "Tchaikowsky" singing the names of 50 Russian composers in 38 seconds. This breathless effusion shows Kaye's penchant for pastiche, heavily layered with Russian-Jewish sensibility.[17]

As the swishy photographer, Danny stopped the show and almost stole it from its veteran star, Gertrude Lawrence. This sensational debut led to an offer Kaye could not refuse.

He jumped ships, rather shows—Cole Porter's *Let's Face It*, which opened on October 29, 1941. Now, in a starring role at double his previous salary, he gained national recognition. Kaye put scat into skit, fusing black and Jewish experiences: "Git gat gittle, giddle-de tommy, riddle de biddle de roop, da-reep, fa-san, skeedle de woo-da, fiddle de wada, reep?" Thus, Danny mimicked a would-be soldier who pleads bad ears, flat feet, ulcers, and decayed teeth in pursuit of deferment. "Shad-ap!" the sergeant bellows; case closed.[18] Rosamond Gilder penned an ecstatic review, describing Danny as "a khaki playboy with an immortal comic mask, infinitely malleable, wide-mouthed, large-eyed, broad in the ear, with hands as eloquent and precise as his torrential speech." After dismissing the plot as old hat, Gilder went on to elevate Kaye to stardom, bestowing critical benediction[19]:

> Now he holds center stage with an opportunity to show his versatility in song and in performance, as well as in his own style of dexterous and lightning-swift patter. His numbers ... are written for him by Sylvia Fine ... and Liebman, and they prove a roaring delight not only to those who like to laugh but also to everyone who finds a special pleasure in skillful and polished workmanship. His "Melody in Four F" is particularly effective since its crack-brained double-talk calls for all-out cooperation from Danny's mobile face, quick-silver hands and plastic body. His comic attack is in the old tradition of clowns and mountebanks of all times. He reaches out to each incredulous delight in the absurdity and joy of living.

Such positive reaction led to a movie contract. Mogul Sam Goldwyn, master of the malaprop, earned Neal Gabler's praise as one of the principal Jews "who invented Hollywood."[20] He also invented the movie persona of Danny Kaye. Initially, he tried to Anglicize Kaye. Signing Kaye to a contract—not an oral agreement which he "insisted is not worth the paper it is printed on"—Goldwyn wanted Kaye to bob his nose. Danny refused. They compromised. Kaye dyed his rusty hair blond.

Before heading for Hollywood, Kaye performed live at the Paramount Theatre off Times Square. With 4,000 seats, it was Danny's largest venue. He faced the future with comedy, music, and dance. His face appeared on magazine covers. Heeding the advice of Horace Greeley, Kaye went west on February 27, 1943, to co-star in the tailor-made movie, *Up in Arms*.

Recycled from a Broadway comedy, *The Nervous Wreck*, later an Eddie Cantor movie, *Whoopie!*, *Up in Arms* conveys Kaye as a hypochondriacal hero in spite of himself. Was this a veiled attempt to depict the Jewish character as fearful of military combat? There is a long tradition in Jewish folklore of anti-militarism harking back to the European experience. The schlemiel-schlimazel duality has been amply documented. Invariably the schlimazel drops the buttered bread. So does the schlemiel with a difference: the buttered side down.

Whatever the motivation, Kaye plays Danny Weems (a play on George Washington's hagiographical chronicler?), nebbish, a close cousin of the schlemiel. The complicated love plot—a quadrilateral affair—features Dinah Shore (also in her film debut), Dana Andrews and Constance Dowling. An aggressive nebbish, Danny opens the film with "The Lobby Number" with "Hello, Fresno, Hello." He previews the film for those waiting in line for tickets, informing them that the movie was "produced by manic and directed by depressive." He manically dashes up the lobby stairs burlesquing movie credits with increasing tempo.[21]

I saw the film with my parents in 1944 when it opened at Radio City Music Hall. Along with other enthusiasts, we contributed to the box-office gross of $3.34 million. We chortled at his "Melody in Four F," reprised from *Let's Face It*, and the concluding "Jive Number." Taking pride in the success of our ethnic landsman (fellow Jew) we eagerly awaited his future films.

We did not have to wait too long, for *Wonder Man* was released in 1945, as World War II was ending on a happy note. The United States had emerged as the premier world power. We had fused the moral vision of Woodrow Wilson and the Realpolitik of Theodore Roosevelt. Despite our imminent victory, Americans faced an uncertain future, one fraught with anxiety. Even before the hot war ended, the cold war had begun. In this context of almost schizoid dimensions, manic energy coupled with Hamletic indecision, *Wonder Man* appeared. Written by Don Hartman and Mel Shavelson, the script called for Danny to play twin brothers: one an arrogant entertainer with ties to the mob; the other, a nerdy scholar. The entertainer is murdered early in the film by Ten Grand Jackson (Steve Cochran), the chief mobster who will suffer if the performer testifies. The bookworm takes over with frequent visits from his brother's ghost. The nerd thwarts his brother's murderer and gets the home-town beauty, Ellen Shanley (Virginia Mayo). Kaye spoofs exotic dancing in "Bali Boogie," concert music in "Otchi Tchorniya," and opera in the "Opera Number." Unlike the Marx Brothers' destructive assault on high culture, Kaye showed great musical gifts. He wanted to belong to the cultural elite. *Time* marched onto the Kaye bandwagon. Profiling the prolific Danny, a writer for the magazine enthused over his "high baritone, with a two octave range. He can impersonate an Irish tenor, mimic a coloratura soprano ... or plead like a Slavic gypsy singer with a basso profundo and schmaltz."[22]

In between films, at least one a year, Kaye tried radio. Here, lacking the spontaneity of a live audience, he proved less than sensational. Writers Goodman Ace and Mel Tolkin found Sylvia Fine more than they could handle. On the first broadcast in 1945, Ace penned this exchange[23]:

> "My sister married an Irishman."
> "Oh, really?"
> "No, O'Reilly."

This was followed by similar pun the next week:

> "The audience gave my stuff a great reception."
> "Oh, really?"
> "No, ovation."

After such jokes, what forgiveness? No wonder the program faded into oblivion.

On the silver screen, Kaye starred in *The Kid from Brooklyn* (1946), *The Secret Life of Walter Mitty* (1947), and a classical musician who converts to jazz in *A Song Is Born* (1948). A child was born to Sylvia and Danny Kaye in 1946. Instead of bringing the family closer as in the lyric "and baby makes three," Danny grew distant. He went off to tour minus the two other Kayes; hardly a blue heaven above. Eve Arden, a lover of five years, trailed along. Without Sylvia, Kaye failed in *A Song Is Born*. No one could write for him like Sylvia. A free fall at the box office ended the Goldwyn relationship. The master of malaprop dropped him like a hot tomato. (Although Kaye later starred in *Hans Christian Andersen*, a Goldwyn/RKO production.)

In search of a new self, Kaye headed for London's Palladium. Starting on February 2, 1948, he took England by storm, something even Hitler could not do. After a period of initial silence, he strode onto the stage and sang "Anatole," "Minnie," and, in Cockney, "I've Got a Loverly Bunch of Coconuts." Then he did the orchestra bit followed by a dance to "Ballin' the Jack." He then pulled an Al Jolson—descending into the audience to bum a cigarette and to engage in chit-chat with the audience. He related the Osaka incident. After a five-minute hiatus, he gathered steam for a triumphant conclusion of the fifty-five-minute act culminating in the ritualistic invocation: "God save the King!" The cool Kaye had connected with his hot audience. One psychiatrist likened the process to a transformation into hysterical children. Elizabeth and Philip, once and future monarchs, became part of Kaye's retinue. They were joined by Britain's royalty of theatre: Laurence Olivier and Vivien

Leigh. Later, King George and Queen Mary visited the theatre and sat with the commoners. Their younger daughter, Margaret, was quite taken with the American entertainer. They became fast friends, perhaps even lovers. Kaye had come a long way from Brooklyn. He had crested.[24] He could now prove Thomas Wolfe wrong. He went home, again. To Sylvia and Deena. Could anything be feener?

Danny returned to a new movie venture and trouble in paradise. The House Un-American Committee tried to ferret out communists long before a junior senator from Wisconsin added his name to an old, infamous witch hunt and a new "Red Scare." Starting under Martin Dies and continuing under J. Parnell Thomas, the committee cast a wide net for Hollywood "pinkos." In 1947, one of the "Jews who invented Hollywood," Jack Warner volunteered as the committee's first "friendly" witness. Ultimately, 24 "friendly" witnesses were summoned, including Robert Taylor, Robert Montgomery, Adolphe Menjou, Gary Cooper, Walt Disney and Ronald Reagan, all goyim except for Jack Warner. Eleven "unfriendlies" prepared to testify. The first, Bertolt Brecht, denied Communist affiliation under oath. He fled the country shortly thereafter. Then there were ten: Alvah Bessie, Herbert Bieberman, Lester Cole, Edward Dmytryk, Ring Lardner, Jr., Albert Maltz, Sam Ornitz, Adrian Scott, Dalton Trumbo, and their leader, John Howard Lawson.[25]

Waiting in the wings, a support group calling themselves the "Committee for the First Amendment" wanted to testify. They included Edward G. Robinson, Humphrey Bogart, Lauren Bacall, John Garfield, Gregory Peck, John Huston, and Danny Kaye. They inclined toward the left but wanted to stay on the high, middle ground. Also waiting in the wings, ready to fly into action, were "tail gunner" Senator Joe McCarthy and his minions. The always-liberal Sylvia Fine and her husband had signed a petition in 1947 denouncing HUAC. Subsequently, they were linked with Fredric March, Olivia de Havilland, and Edward G. Robinson as "swimming pool pinks."[26]

Kaye was slated to film the life of Sir Harry Lauder, a legendary Scotch entertainer, for Warner Bros. However, Jack Warner, eager to please the less than grand inquisitors, scotched the project.

Kaye withdrew from the anti–HUAC movement. He wasn't really "yellow." He just preferred the color of money. Mollified, Warner signed Kaye to do *The Inspector General* (1949), loosely modeled after the Gogol masterpiece. Kaye turned it into a tour de farce. He played Farfel, an illiterate vagabond who is mistaken for the Inspector General. If Danny harbored ill will toward the grand inquisitors who questioned his patriotism, he could channel the fury into this movie. Corruption runs riot in society which the innocent Farfel (Yiddish for a tiny noodle) exposes and exploits simultaneously. In the movie's most ambitious song, "Soliloquy for Three Heads," Kaye sings four-part harmony in four different dialects: Russian, German, English and his own with touch of the "Ink Spots" thrown in for good measure. When my students viewed this film in a class that I teach on humor, they sat on their hands, so to speak. As Fibber's Molly used to say: "T'aint funny, McGee." My students' reaction reflected the poor box office that the movie generated. Yet, when Kaye and Fine went to London, they were greeted like royalty.[27]

After a two-year respite from the movies, Kaye made *On the Riviera* (1951) for 20th Century–Fox. Again, he played a double role: a French ace aviator and an American impressionist. This film reprised two earlier films: *Folies-Bergère* (1935) with Maurice Chevalier and *That Night in Rio* (1941) with Don Ameche.[28] While filming, he acquired a new romantic interest, Gwen Verdon, who appeared in the film as a chorus girl, and a rumored tendency toward homosexuality, with Laurence Olivier as Kaye's leading man. Biographer Martin Gottfried confirms the former allegation concerning the brilliant dancer Verdon and disputes the latter, taking strong issue with Olivier biographer Donald Spoto.[29] Obviously, such a liaison could generate many ribald one-liners such as "comedy screws tragedy" or versa vice. However, Gottfried demolishes Spoto's argument by innuendo. Call Kaye androgynous, asexual, amoral—Gottfried seems to suggest—but not a *faigele*.

Danny Kaye was a frequent flyer. For instance, he flew to Korea with Frank Sinatra to entertain the troops. Psychologically, he descended into periodic depressions and ascended to new heights of creativity. His colleagues noticed "something strange" about him.[30] He portrayed a moody, if brilliant, Dane in *Hans Christian Andersen* (1952). A weak story line was elevated by the magnificent music and lyrics of Frank Loesser and the abundantly talented Danny Kaye. "Thumbelina," "The Ugly Duckling," "Wonderful Copenhagen," and "Anywhere I Wander" resonated throughout the country, perhaps the world. Only the dour Danes were not amused with the fictional treatment of their culture hero, a spinner of fairy tales who may have been a "fairy" himself. To placate the people of Denmark, Kaye flew to the country that spawned Anderson. He won friends, influenced people, quieted critics and mesmerized children. And the picture grossed $6 million. Kaye had everything: fame, fortune, adulation. But he could neither rest nor gain nourishment from his own cultural roots.

Kaye rejected his Jewish past. One observes this thrust toward assimilation in words, music, and movies. He warned a young Alan King, eager for encouragement, that his act was too Jewish.[31] The kid from Brooklyn became a citizen of the world. He parlayed his love for children, desire for service, and enormous talent into a parallel career as spokesman for Unicef. The UN, headed at that time by Dag Hammarskjold, sent Kaye all over the world. He publicized the plight of poor children through film. He raised enormous sums of money, thereby fulfilling ancient Jewish imperatives of *tzedakah* (charity).

Kaye's film career also flourished, no doubt fueled by favorable publicity attendant on his benevolence. Luckily, he decided to form his own production company, with Norman Panama and Melvin Frank. Their first vehicle, *Knock on Wood* (1954), mounted in conjunction with Paramount Pictures, produced a critical success and a large capital gain for Kaye. He plays Jerry Morgan, a "double" who, as a ventriloquist, dabbles in psychotherapy, love (with his "shrink," Mai Zetterling), spying, mistaken identity, and a murder mystery. Sucked into espionage, Morgan cannot convince the authorities that an English gentleman is the true spy. He flees danger, utilizing various disguises. Thrust into a ballet, by turns, Morgan is klutzy and elegant, manic and depressive, like his two dummies and not unlike Kaye himself. In this film, he performed some classic *shtick*: as an Irish roust-about in a pub and as a nebbishy hide-about under the table.

In that same year, 1954, Kaye teamed up with Bing Crosby, Rosemary Clooney, and former co-star Vera-Ellen for an ultra-*goyish* movie, *White Christmas*, with uninspired songs (except for the title song) by Irving Berlin, another Jewish genius who had bleached his material (if not his hair) in pursuit of profit and prestige. Despite an inane plot and patriotic pabulum involving a retired general (Dean Jagger), the movie ranked #1 at the box office that year, with a gross of $12 million. But minus Fred Astaire for whom the original film, *Holiday Inn* (1942) was written, this pallid semi-remake lacked movie magic.[32]

The Court Jester (1956) was a winner on all fronts, except at the box office: a cause for that distinctively Jewish combination of laughter and tears. The picture, shot at Paramount Studios, featured a stellar cast headed by Danny Kaye and supported by Basil Rathbone, Angela Lansbury, Mildred Natwick, Glynis Johns, and Cecil Parker. A satiric send-up of misty medievalism, the movie parodies the romanticized English past. In glittering Technicolor, the picture purveys castle and court, jester and joust. We witness a wicked king; a sinister minister; and a long litany of names with "G" strings: Giacomo, "king of jesters and jester to kings"; Griselda, the witch; Gwendolyn, the princess; and "the grimly, grizzly, gruesome Griswold," the satanic suitor.

A carnival jester of considerable talent (suggesting the future Art Carney), Giacomo (Kaye) becomes embroiled in a plot to restore the good king while playing the bad king's fool. Empowered by the good witch Griselda with a hypnotic trance, Giacomo is transformed into an instant hero by a finger snap. That same gesture, the snap, causes him to revert to cowardice. The film's most dramatic moment is also the funniest.[33] It is a tongue-twisting scene performed with precision by Kaye and Mildred Natwick:

> GIACOMO: Does the chalice with the palace have the pellet with the poison?
> GRISELDA: No. The pellet with the poison is in the vessel with the pestle.
> GIACOMO: The pestle with the vessel?
> GIRLFRIEND: The vessel with the pestle....
> GRISELDA: The chalice with the palace has the brew that is true.... There's been a change. They have broken the chalice with the palace.
> GIACOMO: They have broken the chalice with the palace?
> GRISELDA: And replaced it with a flagon.
> GIACOMO: A flagon?
> GRISELDA: With a figure of a dragon.
> GIACOMO: A flagon with a dragon.
> GRISELDA: Right.
> GIACOMO: And they put the pellet with the poison in the vessel with the pestle.
> GRISELDA: No. No. The pellet with the poison is in the flagon with the dragon. The chalice with the palace has the brew that is true....

True comedy evoked gales of laughter. At a cost of $4 million and a gross of $2.2 million, however, it proved that unlike modern crime, comedy did not pay. Although Kaye continued to make movies in the 1950s: *Merry Andrew* for MGM in 1958, *Me and the Colonel* for Columbia in 1958 and *The Five Pennies* for Paramount in 1959, the winds of change propelled him into a different medium in the 1960s, namely, television.[34]

Despite a few dazzling bits, reminiscent of vintage Kaye, Danny's venture into television 1963–1967 was a disaster. He had aged prematurely. His persona seemed invested in sentimental goo, cutesy poo and Peter Panish infantilism. He gave freer vent to snobbery and arrogance at the same time that he yearned for love. A clue to Kaye's divided soul can be found in an Ed Murrow–Fred Friendly special, *The Secret Life of Danny Kaye*, which aired on CBS in late 1956. The program showed a glittering surface, perhaps façade: Kaye as comic, humanitarian, bon-vivant, children's advocate, family man. It was this latter pose that elicited a skeptical response from critic Marie Torre.[35] She zeroed in on Kaye's mood swings, his distance from his wife, Sylvia, monumental ego bordering on hubris, the tragic flaw that precipitates a fall from high places.

In the twilight of their careers, comedians sometime venture into serious drama. Ed Wynn, Bert Lahr, and Milton Berle spring to mind. Danny Kaye made a fugitive attempt in *Me and the Colonel* (1958), based on a Broadway play by Franz Werfel and S. N. Behrman. Perhaps trying to reconnect with his Jewish roots and aspiring to high culture, Kaye essayed the role of S.L. Jacobowsky, a Jewish businessman in flight from the Nazis as they prepare to capture Paris in 1940. Often cast as the "good" German in Cold-War Hollywood, Curt Jurgens plays the anti–Semitic Polish colonel hired to help Jacobowsky, the Jewish refugee, escape. In this film, Kaye sought to escape comedy, assimilation, alienation. It was the first of several attempts to reconnect with the Jewish experience, which ultimately found fruition late in Kaye's career when he played a Holocaust survivor. *Skokie*, a docu-drama based on an actual confrontation between Jewish survivors and neo–Nazi demonstrators, aired on CBS, on November 17, 1981. Confronting the constitutional parameters of free speech, the drama raised compelling issues and provided a forum for Danny Kaye's reconciliation with Judaism.[36]

Why did Danny Kaye with all his *meilehs* (virtues)—talent, charm, energy, charisma, ambition, genius—fall short of greatness? For British critic, Raymond Durgnat, Kaye represents the chronic underachiever[37]:

> Danny Kaye, like Cantor and Hope, made many comedies for Goldwyn; he had the widest range of the three, and his career is all the more disappointing. His face is at once handsome, sensitive, and infinitely transformable, and he combines a straight romantic appeal with wild plunges into frenetic parody.... But his fancy was rarely free, and outside his git-gat-gabble musical numbers, he was hampered by a milky goodwill which ... smothered his comic attack.... Kaye deteriorated into a charmer whose screen heart is as wide as Cinemascope and as sickly sweet as candy floss.

This became painfully evident in the television years, 1963–1967. Invariably, with a child perched on his knee, like Kolya the little gypsy, he would bill and coo regressing into syrupy childhood. The plea for love remains a constant among Jewish comic entertainers. So does the quest for something more. Kaye became a gourmet Chinese cook, a licensed airplane pilot, a baseball franchise owner, a symphony orchestra conductor, a goodwill ambassador to the world: many characters in search of identity. Larger than life, sports broadcaster Vin Scully observed, Kaye was "a lot of person ... a group photo."

A group of all-stars gathered at the Kennedy Center in Washington to receive honors from President Reagan in 1984. Danny Kaye joined Lena Horne, Isaac Stern, Arthur Miller, and Gian Carlo Menotti for this happy event. Film clips of *Hans Christian Andersen* and *The Secret Life of Walter Mitty* highlighted Kaye's creativity. Students from the United Nations School in New York serenaded Danny as he writhed in pain from arthritis.[38]

Kaye was honored as "King of Brooklyn." Though close to death, he continued to jest, perhaps realizing the wisdom of his wife's one-liner: "A jester unemployed is nobody's fool."[39] Joking, unfortunately, could not defer the

Malachhamoves (the Angel of Death) indefinitely. Drained by an incurable case of hepatitis, not AIDS as malicious rumor had it, Kaye succumbed to heart failure on March 3, 1987. One year later, the United Nations paid tribute to the kid from Brooklyn. UN Secretary General Perez de Cuellar cited Kaye as the man who "heightened global awareness of the plight of unfortunate children throughout the world." Douglas Fairbanks, Jr., conveyed Kaye's secret with children: he "made them feel they were real people." Liv Ullmann, Peter Ustinov, and Harry Belafonte sang his praises. Roberta Peters sang. A choir of 80 children, representing 22 nations at the United Nations School, also sang[40]:

> Danny Kaye, you gave us laughter.
> We'll remember you ever after....
> Thank you! *Merci! Danke!*
> Danny Kaye.

A second pioneer on the frontier of comedy, Sid Caesar was born on September 8, 1922, at the height of Harding prosperity and political corruption to a lower-middle class *mishpoche* (family), whose income derived from a luncheonette. Like Danny Kaye, who would inspire much of his comic attack, Sid was the youngest of three sons. His father was 50; his oldest brother, 18, when young Caesar entered crying: a Yankee from Yonkers. At P.S. 10 and at his father's St. Clair Buffet Lunch, he entertained. Absorbing the sounds of immigrants, Sidney learned to mimic the ethnic *pastiche*. In order to gain attention from busy parents and earn love from angry siblings, he had to be funny.[41]

At age seven, he began taking saxophone lessons. Later, in 1935, when his father went bankrupt, and his brother Dave became a bookie, Sid formed a band. At age 16 he headed downtown where he worked at odd jobs as usher, doorman, saxophonist and comic stooge. In the summers, Caesar attempted to conquer the Catskills, beginning in 1936. Booked as a musician in Monticello's Anderson Hotel, Sid volunteered for sketch comedy. When comic Jackie Michaels flung tomatoes at Caesar, drenching his new white suit, Sid went ballistic; he chased the offender into the audience, where gleeful onlookers thought it was part of the act. Michaels paid for the cleanup and awarded the irate Caesar a raise in pay to ten dollars a week, plus perks.[42] In 1939, after graduating from high school, he formed a band in a place called Vacationland, in Swan Lake, where he doubled as musician and comic foil. Social director Don Appel put on serious plays as well as comic sketches. In one sketch, young Caesar attempted to buy a challah in a bakery; mixing English and Yiddish, he mistook a baked apple for a bekked *teppel*.[43] It was in the Catskills that Sid learned to act and to improvise. He reprised his dual role as comic and musician for three summers, the last in 1941 at Kutcher's Hotel. At this juncture, Caesar moved away from music in favor of comedy. Almost fired, he won a reprieve with a skit called "Crazy House." An inmate on the run, Sid is pursued by two asylum guards. He escapes by throwing toilet paper at them. The audience roared; Caesar kept his job.[44] In 1942, he landed at the Avon Lodge, where he met his future bride and wife of 60-plus years, Florence Levy. In between dances with *meiskeits* (ugly girls), he romanced Florence. They talked endlessly about politics, psychology, philosophy—love.[45]

Caesar entered the Coast Guard on November 9, 1942. He was ordered to enemy territory: Brooklyn's Manhattan Beach. Unable to eat the awful food, he dropped 50 pounds. After basic training, he went on another "dangerous" assignment: Gowanus Canal, also in Brooklyn, and a far cry from Guadalcanal. Caesar covered the waterfront, i.e., he patrolled part of a pier. To kill time, he formed a band with fellow serviceman, Vernon Duke (né Dukelsky). Soon, Friday nights started to jump with dance fever. Caesar also wrote special material for a revue: *Six On, Twelve Off.* One featured a conversation between Donald Duck and Adolf Hitler. He also created a bit in which he compared planes in peacetime with those in wartime. On his weekends off, Caesar continued to court Florence Levy. They married on July 17, 1943; both were 20 at the time. Not only did Caesar find his muse in the mountains, he also learned the craft of comedy. As he candidly put it[46]:

> In the late 1930s and 1940s, the Catskill Mountains were a college for entertainers, myself included. In the hundreds of resorts, hotels, and bungalow colonies, the audiences were rough and demanded quality. The Catskills created a Jewish Brigadoon and provided a training ground for young comedians and musicians.

A talented musician, Vernon Duke received a commission to write a show for the Coast Guard, featuring Victor Mature, Gower Champion, Max Liebman and Sid Caesar. Liebman, a refugee from Vienna who had launched Danny Kaye's career, recognized Caesar's potential. He coaxed young Sid to write a sketch for the revue *Tars and Spars.* They took the show on the road from Palm Beach through Jacksonville, Atlanta, and Baltimore, with performances six times each day on one-week stands. Columbia Pictures sponsored this tour with an option to buy it for a movie version.[47]

After a shuffle off to Buffalo, Sid was ordered by Lieutenant Cook to repeat his number in the show at nine A.M. Enraged, Sid threw a 50-pound sand-filled brick at his commanding officer. The next day, offended by an anti–Semitic slur, Caesar attacked a marine with a jagged glass edge. A benevolent commander, Reed Hill, came to his assistance. He ordered the release of Caesar from the hospital and the return to *Tars and Spars*, accompanied by Mrs. Caesar "for the good of the service."[48]

Florence had a calming effect on the volatile comic. Columbia Pictures optioned the show and replaced Victor Mature with Alfred Drake, who starred in the original Broadway production of *Oklahoma!* Drake had graduated from Brooklyn College and had worked with Max Liebman at Camp Tamiment in the Pennsylvania Poconos. Drake's leading lady in the film was the luscious Janet Blair; Caesar served as comic relief. *Tars and Spars* (1946) bombed at the box office. Fortunately for Caesar, he was paid $1,000 to do another picture, *The Guilt of Janet Ames* (1947), in which he played a stand-up comic who satirized psychiatry, a growing phenomenon in postwar, middle-class America. This film proved a commercial failure, too.[49] Nevertheless, Caesar acknowledged that "if the Catskills were college, Hollywood was graduate school for me as an entertainer."[50]

A return to civilian life proved difficult. Caesar's father died of cancer. Like his older brothers, Sid lived at home with his mother and was expected to contribute to the household funds. All but broke, Caesar left Hollywood for New York, where Max Liebman wrote a nightclub act for him that consisted of 25 minutes' worth of Copacabana material. When Sid took the act on the road, Liebman expanded the set to 45 minutes. Despite periodic temper tantrums, Caesar improved. Offered a part in another revue, *Make Mine Manhattan*, Caesar accepted a two-week contract at $250 per week. In one sketch, he portrayed a "veddy, veddy British" character who, looking back in anger, reverts to Yiddish-accented punch lines honoring the Harry Golden maxim: "Dress British; think Yiddish." He jabbed: "When it comes to a garment, I already forgot what you ever knew." Another bit illustrated inflation: a social date in 1948 compared to one in 1938. Five dollars got plenty of nothing in '48 and almost everything in '38. As a result of Caesar's comic triumph, he demanded—and got—$1,500 per week, plus 5 percent of the box office. At this takeoff stage in his career, Caesar also developed a destructive dependency on alcohol. Scotch on the rocks eased the tension, reduced the pain, and assuaged the guilt of sudden success.

In 1949, Caesar and Liebman lunched with NBC Vice President Pat Weaver to plan a 90-minute weekly TV show for which Sid demanded $1,000 per week. Worth every penny, he did everything: sketches, specialty numbers, production numbers, and monologues. As Hamlet, he dug down to his psychic roots, a tragic-comic everyman. He did a bit as an ardent suitor with a heavily Jewish, self-mocking pitch.[51]

> I've got to make her feel that she's somebody, that I respect her, that I look up to her.... I'll say to her, "Doris, you are a queen, and I am a tiny twinkling star. You are the soft breeze floating over the vast ocean and I am but a pebble on the beach.... You are everything ... life itself, and I am nothing. [Pause]. So you better get somebody else because I'm no good for you."

Then comes the Oedipal assault.

> Mom, what do you mean you don't know her? Don't you remember I intro-
> duced you to her? ... And you said: "You're stealing my boy. I brought him
> up. I washed him. I cleaned him. I fed him. I held him in my arms, and now
> that he he's starting to look like something, you're stealing him from me! I
> hate you! I hate you!" Now it's because of little things like that, she doesn't
> like to come over here so often.

In this mini-family vignette, drama and trauma cross lines. Here, Caesar tapped
the well-springs of American Jewish culture and imparted them with a uni-
versality that transformed American comedy. Always intimidated by European culture, especially of the Teutonic variety, national audiences were delighted
by the comedic assaults and witty reversals generated by this new kind of
humor. High culture was fair game for Caesar's satire. Low culture, too. The
cast started straight, i.e., they sang arias as they died either by suicide or
assassination. Arias faded into "Makin' Whoopie" and "Just One of Those
Things." As "Gallipacci," a clown, Caesar drew a mark on his cheek while
putting on make-up. Without skipping a beat, critic Karin Adir reports, "He
continued singing and extended the mark into a tic-tac-toe game on his
face."[52] Then-current movies and plays provided raw material for the company's blast furnaces. They introduced national audiences to "From Here to
Obscurity," "A Trolleycar Named Desire," and "On the Docks." In the latter
two, Sid did a marvelous Marlon Brando, replete with mumble, slouch, gum,
nasal voice and loutish behavior.[53] If Caesar played Brando to perfection, he
impersonated his Germanic professor character with mastery that invites
critical scrutiny. No expert to my knowledge has ever plumbed Sid's motivation. Even his autobiography does not offer any profundities regarding this
funny figure. In explaining his comic persona, Sid offered several observations. He and Imogene played off clichés. Thus, bringing up babies led to
this exchange authored by Lucille Kallen[54]:

> IMOGENE: I think the old method of spanking a child is passé.
> SID: I say don't just spank a child, reason with him, find out what's on his
> mind. And when you find out the reason, the real cause—then belt him.

Caesar realized that "a guy who is in trouble is a very funny guy." Willingly,
he played the goat. Lovingly, he evoked *shleppers*, sad little guys confronting
the real world. But why the German professor? This character developed
slowly. An expert on all subjects, he emerged from an airplane in tattered
garments and thick with German accent.[55]

> INTERVIEWER: Doctor, would you explain to the audience in simple lan-
> guage the basis of your theory of sleep?

PROFESSOR VON SEDATIVE: Yah. Schleep is vunderbar. Schleep is beautiful. But schleep is no good to you if you is vide awake … I haff a friend vunce, he could schleep anywheres. In der boiler factory, in der foundry, in a stockyard. He could go on a train and right away he fall aschleep. Pass all the stations.

INTERVIEWER: That's wonderful.

PROFESSOR VON SEDATIVE: It was lousy. He was the engineer. He wrecked more trains, dot friend of mine.

In one sketch, Professor Sigmund von Fraidy Katz came on as an authority on mountain climbing. What happens if the rope breaks?[56]

CAESAR: Well, as soon as you see the rope breaking … scream and keep screaming all the way down … this way they'll know where to find you.

REINER: But, Professor, isn't there anything else you can do?

CAESAR: Well, there's the other method. As soon as the rope breaks, you spread your arms and begin to fly.

REINER: But humans can't fly.

CAESAR: How do you know? You might be the first one. Anyway, you can always go back to screaming. That's always working for you.

REINER: Was Hans [a fellow climber] a flyer or screamer?

CAESAR: He was a flying screamer and a crasher, too.

Caesar impersonated many other Germanic scholars: Rudolf von Rudder, an authority on flying; Heinrich von Heartburn on love; Ludwig von Pabulum on children; Filthy von Lucre on money; Ludwig von Fossil on archaeology; Hugo von Gezuntheit on medicine; Ludwig von Complex on animal behavior; von Muscle on sports; Lapse von Memory, an expert on memory, who wrote *I Remember Mama—But I Forget Papa*. These characters are, to quote Cole royalty, Nat and daughter Natalie, "unforgettable." Author Ted Sennett discerns a method in this madness: laughter at erudition gone berserk. Humor maven Steve Allen chortles at these routines but does not even venture an explanation.[57]

I contend that Caesar was acting out a deep-seated anger harbored by a vast majority of Jews against Germany. Their well-springs are easy to locate. World War II ended without full retribution for Nazi barbarism and Hitler's "War Against the Jews." Evil Germans, abetted by anti–Communist clerics, escaped punishment as many found refuge in South America. Most Germans professed ignorance of the Holocaust. Others claimed—re: the Nuremburg Trials—that "they were only carrying out orders." Hence, American Jewish comedians launched assaults of laughter on the enemy. The Jewish response is understandable, but why did non–Jews find the nutty German professor equally funny? German culture or *Kultur* evoked feelings of superiority across the ocean and *unter das linden* while here in America a mirror-image reflected inferiority. Germany represented Bach, Beethoven, Brahms as well as Berlin, Bremerhaven, and *Broiges* (anger). To deflate the pedantic professor was to prick the pretensions inherent in mythic German superiority. During the war, Spike Jones sang "Der Fuehrer's Face," a funny anti–Valentine to Hitler. Sid Caesar carried this assault further and more effectively across the air waves of national television. He deftly coupled Jewish anger and American pride. He targeted the vaunted German efficiency and alleged superiority. Thus, by a powerful comic reversal, German high culture is defeated again. Terror, cruelty, arrogance, racism, genocide all dissolve in the corrosive acids and cathartic bases of laughter.

Caesar surrounded himself with a battery of enormous talent. Max Liebman charged writers Mel Tolkin, Lucille Kallen, Danny and Neil Simon, Mel Brooks and Woody Allen to come up with weekly scripts tailored to the top banana's comedic gifts. Co-stars Imogene Coca, Carl Reiner, and Howard Morris all contributed to the show's amazing success. This stable of talented writers and performers embodied a salient trait of Jewish humor, namely, a gift for parody. Sid Caesar, built like a horse, powered parody and heavily salted satire to success on Saturday night. Described as "the boldest, most compulsive user and misuser of Yiddish," Caesar lampooned foreign films, to wit: a Nipponese romance featuring *gantse mishpoche, gehakte leyber*, and *shmate* or a Gallic farce situated in a dive called *La Fligl*.[58] Taking aim at the cinema, TV's principal media rival, Caesar and Co. scored many direct satirical hits. They spoofed the Westerns. Shane became Strange. A mysterious stranger, Caesar appears greeted by Howard Morris, the farmer and Imogene Coca, his son. The stranger gulps down a gallon of well water leading to this exchange[59]:

MORRIS: You seem mighty thirsty, stranger, Have a long dry ride?
CAESAR: No. Had a herring for breakfast.
MORRIS: What's your name?
CAESAR: Folks call me ... Strange.
MORRIS: What's your first name?
CAESAR: Very. But you can call me Strange.
COCA: Gee, that's a nice gun, Strange. That's a nice holster, Strange. Nice gun-belt, Strange. I like you, Strange. You got nice boots, Strange. You're nice, Strange.
CAESAR: Get away, kid, or I'll blast you.

In a climactic gunfight with the villain, Carl Reiner, Strange forgets to bring a gun. Coca tosses a gun to his idol, who shoots six evil henchmen. The villain cackles triumphantly:

REINER: Six shots. Six bullets. You're empty.
(Caesar shoots a disbelieving Reiner.)
CAESAR: The only seven-shooter in the West. Made it myself.

Coca: Come back, Strange. Strange, come back. Strange (echo) ... Strange (echo) ... Strange (echo).

Caesar (from a distance): Shut up, you rotten kid (echo) ... rotten kid (echo) ... rotten kid (echo)...

Every major movie—foreign as well as domestic—served as grist for Caesar's comic mill. Ted Sennett's marvelous book, *Your Show of Shows* (which I acquired for only one dollar, an *emeser* [true] bargain), describes them in detail.[60] More than 60 years later, they continue to tickle our funny bones. And they issue from a comic perspective: indelibly Jewish.

Stefen Kanfer offers a cogent explanation of Caesar's (and Kaye's) gift for *pastiche* and parody.[61] Imitation is more than a higher form of flattery. It is a mechanism for survival. Forced to cross barriers and boundaries, Jews had to learn their new neighbors' language, manners and morals. With extraordinarily fine-tuned antennae, they picked up the cues and played their parts, brilliantly. Ronald Sanders called attention to a similar trait in music.[62] An example of Caesar's multi-cultural *mishegas* (craziness) follows[63]:

Italian: *Buon giorno, signore e signore. Il fate luo lomani la menta cucelli tuo la lamana de la larote, mangiare! Mangiare supilla a de tuo pillente de las cosa cinque lara senta Madison Avenue. La rotara e la robanda esso lo vehiculo messo de lo typico de Bonnie's. Rutti de la gettina. Bonnie's e rolla in. Notta Bonnie's fia nu, Bonnie's fus mi. Ahma know Bonnie. Che lo mimaldo do lo trico e mimaldo della mangiare* alatta, size of one to two!

French: *Bonjour, messieurs et mesdames, Eh! Contrer d'Isabelle deja vue ballpenne repris a l'on tres bien. Fetes toujees marjoulles de lousondres, toute de suite cabibier that perdit la grande armee. Et elle pour le soldat avec le bayonet. Le bayonet, n'oublie pas, c'est sur son quelque on d'end of de rifle. Le bayonet rabit de facon* very sharp. D'on use fir ni de nails, or cut your hair. Strictly keep it en de case, unless I tell you to change. Then I will not be with you. Non?

German: *Achtung! Was ist mit in die Harnuche eben wahler das garza Romantic Hour. Das heer oder Hermann schlechte Romanz Das Durrementldorf das Lesson von kissen. Das lips von der ahnimal bereben aht dat Pucker und weier denn mi von dan Puck, next to the von dot you luff. Wenn der Puck kommt to der oder Puck, smack it away. Mit der schleck.*

According to Steve Allen, Sid Caesar deserves a place in the comic pantheon alongside Danny Kaye and Charlie Chaplin.[64] Allen extols Caesar's "expressive hands ... rubbery face" and masterful timing. A true dialectician, Caesar scores with exaggeration and repetition. He also invests physical objects with double meaning. In a skit spoofing prison-escape movies and their attendant clichés, Caesar is caught at the wall with the spotlight fixed on him. Caught—a pregnant pause—he shields his eyes from the merciless light. Then, hand on heart, he breaks into song, a Jewish tear-jerker *alova* George Jessel: "My Mother's Eyes."[65]

Unable to escape from the prison shaped, in part, by mother's love and self-loathing, Caesar plunged into a labyrinth of drink and drugs. Depression soured his family life and aborted his vocation. An ambivalence regarding his Jewish roots, in this writer's judgment, exacerbated his role and identity confusion. Like many of his contemporaries, Caesar pounced on Yiddish phrases like *gatkes* (underclothes). He had sent mixed messages to his audiences. Airing dirty undergarments hidden in the cultural closet, Caesar sent signals to *landsleit* (fellow Jews) with snarling references to overbearing Jewish mothers and confessions of ethnic denials. At the same time, Caesar and his comic legions trumpeted their survival. Emerging from a cave of conformity, they beamed in code language: *mir zeinen doh*! (we are still here!). As Irving Howe illustrates brilliantly, embarrassment alternated with contempt.[66]

In pursuit of the gaudy, glitter of success, filthy lucre or *dreck* if you will, they aimed to please regardless of cost. Caesar cashed in his chips but at a tremendous cost, i.e., self-denial, self-effacement, self-exhaustion."[67] Yiddish-flavored comedy marked a loss of innocence and of culture. Sid embraced the new vulgarity. He abandoned the saxophone, his first love. At the height of his fame, he turned increasingly to alcohol. Unable to accept success and plagued with guilt, he stooped and was conquered by chronic depression, which rolled over him "like a poisoned fog."[68] Compulsive eating did not bring relief. Nor did booze. He ballooned to 240 pounds.

In his autobiography, *Where Have I Been?*, Caesar poignantly charts the sine-curve of a meteoric career. He laments the wasted years. Apparently recovered through a process of Jungian self-therapy, he found inner peace. He performed in summer stock, acted in commercials, made movies. No longer the "King of Comedy," Caesar appeared in cameo roles selling Popsicles and reenacted the King of the Rock People in Mel Brooks's *History of the World—Part 1* (1981), in which legend and disciple joined forces to *shpritz* an often hostile world with Jewish humor. In 2002, Caesar was honored at NBC's 75th anniversary celebration. After a thirty-year hiatus in California, this prodigiously talented comedian enjoyed a triumphant return to "the city that never sleeps." Jerry Seinfeld opened the festivities with a clever dig at network executives whose principal function is to close shows and fire actors. An estimated 98 percent of the honorees that evening were fired. That's why, Seinfeld observed, they look older and harbor angry feelings. Not so, Sid Caesar. He had come to terms with his meteoric rise and fall. Through therapy, Zen meditation, and physical exercise, Caesar had exorcised his demons. Satisfied

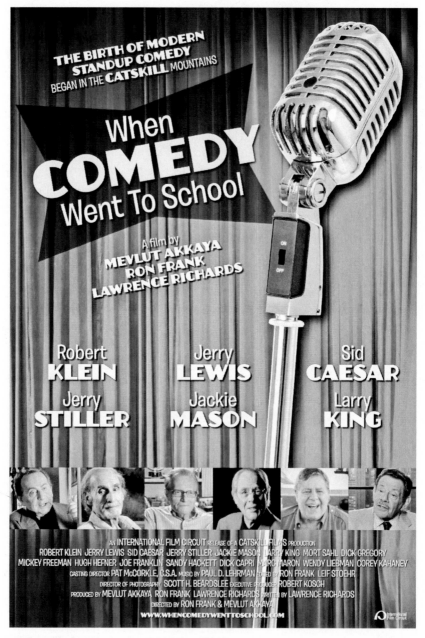

Film poster featuring a galaxy of Jewish stars in comedy and media from left to right: Jackie Mason, Sid Caesar, Larry King, Robert Klein, Jerry Lewis, and Jerry Stiller: all with prominent roles in the documentary *When Comedy Went to School*.

with a third-place finish (behind Lucille Ball and Jackie Gleason) in a poll that ranked television's greatest comedians, Sid beamed with pride. Hailed with a standing ovation, as millions watched, Caesar regarded the event as "one of the highlights of his life."[69] More recently, Caesar participated in a documentary film *When Comedy Went to School* about his Catskill roots. In this film Caesar lauded the various hotels and bungalow colonies in the Borscht Belt or Catskill Mountains for providing a veritable "college for many entertainers." They functioned, he added, as a "Jewish Brigadoon," a kind of "kibbutz with a lot of food" and sex on the side.[70]

After a long illness, Sid Caesar died on February 12, 2014, at the age of 91. The *New York Times* obituary documented the enormous influence that Caesar and his talented writers had on subsequent films and television. It also identified Albert Einstein and Alfred Hitchcock among his many admirers. The latter hailed Caesar as "the funniest performer since Charlie Chaplin."[71] No mention, however, is made of the vital contribution of Jewish humor to his finer hours and the relief it might have rendered during his plunge into drugs, drink, and darkness. That said, let us now praise famous men. Hail, Caesar—and Danny Kaye, too!

FIVE

Catskill Alumni
from Brooklyn

If Danny Kaye evolved into a Renaissance Man, Sid Caesar a comic everyman, Lenny Bruce represented the mad *maggid*; Jerry Lewis, an American clown; Mel Brooks epitomized the *meshuginer* (crazy) who descends from a long line of *naronim* (fools). This coarse type, or *grober yung*, was refined in the Borscht Belt. Born Melvin Kaminsky on June 28, 1926, he was the youngest of four boys. His father, an immigrant from the Danzig corridor, died young, leaving Melvin an orphan at age two. At P.S. 19 in the Williamsburg section of Brooklyn, Mel excelled as class clown. By wit alone he kept the bullies at bay. As he reasoned, "If they're laughing, how can they bludgeon you to death?"[1]

During the summers, young Melvin Kaminsky joined drummer and friend Buddy Rich in the Catskills. There, he honed his comic art. His wildest bit featured a fake suicide. Fully dressed with a heavy satchel, he ascended the high diving board, screamed: "Business is terrible. I can't go on!" Then, he jumped. A non-swimmer, he had to be rescued by the lifeguard on duty. In the Catskills, Mel met a wild saxophone player named Sid Caesar. Inspired by a chambermaid's cry issuing from a moment of panic when she accidentally locked herself in a linen closet, Brooks bellowed: "*Loz mir arois!*" ("Let me out!") If life was indeed a claustrophobic linen closet, Melvin was a Jewish talent yearning to bust loose. His theme "Here I am, I'm Mel Brooks," goes to the heart of *unzer shtick*, or kosher nostra—our tradition.[2]

After a stint in the army, a one-day stay in college, and some experience as a sketch writer, he hit pay dirt with Sid Caesar on television. His first sketch featured a misplaced Tarzan, Jr., roaming the streets of our naked city clad in lion skin. Interviewed by a roving reporter, Tarzan eventually yielded to a pedantic but stupid German professor variously named Kurt von Stuffer,

Siegfried von Sedative, Rudolf von Rudder, Heinrich von Heartburn. Thus, continued Brooks's career-long obsession with Germans as objects of fear and subjects of ridicule. He explained[3]:

> Me? Not like Germans? Why should I not like the Germans? Just because they're arrogant and have fat necks and do anything they're told so long as it's cruel and killed millions of Jews in concentration camps and made soap out of their bodies and lampshades out of their skins? Is that any reason to hate their fucking guts?

Bottled up in a loveless marriage, Brooks turned to psychoanalysis, which elicited funny stuff if not inner peace. After a period of blockage, Mel began to swing with Carl Reiner. In true Catskill tradition, a master of comic deflation, Brooks assaulted the major authority figures—the heroes in history. He even took Freud's measure with this exchange[4]:

> Q: I gather sir, that you are a famous psychiatrist.
> A: That is correct.
> Q: May I ask where you studied psychiatry?
> A: At the Vienna School of Good Luck.
> Q: Who analyzed you?
> A: I was analyzed by No. 1 himself.
> Q: You mean the great Sigmund Freud?
> A: In person. Took me during lunchtime, charged me a nickel.
> Q: What kind of person was he?
> A: Lovely little fellow. I shall never forget the hours we spent together, me lying on the couch, him sitting there beside me, wearing a nice off-the-shoulder dress.

Strangely, Dr. Brooks is a prude who refuses to acknowledge the Oedipus complex ("That's the dirtiest thing I ever heard.") When informed that the ideal of a passionate desire to sleep with one's mother is Greek, not Jewish, he breathes a sigh of relief. "With a Greek, who knows? But with a Jew, you don't do things like that—even to your wife, let alone your mother."[5]

The marriage of Brooks and Reiner sired the bountiful 2,000-year-old man. Fear makes the patriarch's heart pump. In a thick Jewish accent, the old man relates how, before the advent of God, men feared their leader Phil. When a bolt of lightning ended his hegemony, it started the Lord's, also known as Gevalt, Yahweh, Your-Way, His-Way and Goodness. He prays daily so that nothing will fall and his heart will not attack him. He also eats a lot of garlic to ward off the *Malechhamoves* (the Angel of Death). Alternately proud of and disappointed with his progeny he *kvetches*: "I have 42,000 children and not one comes to see me. How dey forget a father?"[6]

Melvin went Hollywood. Mimicking his Uncle Joe, he offered tart commentary on modern art as *ungepatchket* examples of this genre flashed across the screen. For this short film, Brooks won an Oscar. Thus, began Brooks' assault on high culture. His first feature film, *The Producers* (1967), looped back to Sid Caesar's show and the constant battery of Germans as clowns. The centerpiece is a Busby Berkeley send-up: "Springtime for Hitler." Critic Sanford Pinsker argues that Brooks wants to reduce the "grostequerie of the Holocaust world to extremely bad theatre.... His humor is at once a defense mechanism ... and a weapon to beat Nazism senseless."[7] The premise demands that the producers create a box-office flop. Zero Mostel plays Max Bialystock as the Yid with id; Gene Wilder portrays Leopold Bloom, the schlemiel as super-ego. The scheme goes awry: the play is a success and the protagonists wind up in jail, where they start another con game. Justifiably, Brooks claims that he is the only Jew to make a living out of Hitler.

In subsequent films like *Blazing Saddles* and *Young Frankenstein* (both 1974) Brooks offered Catskill comedy in the raw: mixing wild mirth, parody, rage, resentment, dependency, fear, and ethnicity. *Blazing Saddles* is a perfect pastiche: A Jewish Western with a black sheriff. The best parody of the Hollywood Western genre, *Blazing Saddles* violates all of our canons. Mercilessly, as writer, actor, and director, Brooks slaughters all of our sacred cows in this horse opera and parades them before our tear-filled eyes from excessive laughter.

Consider the incongruities. Instead of "sorrow songs," Blacks sing Cole Porter. Following a bean binge, cowboys fart naturally around the campfire. Wizened old women curse and throw haymakers. Mongo (former football star Alex Karras) punches a horse. As Indian chief in bronzed face, Brooks speaks Yiddish when observing African Americans crossing the plains: "*Loz zei geyn; zey zeinen schvartzes. Abee gezundt.*" Many critics, repulsed by the vulgarity, responded negatively. Biographer Maurice Yacower correctly views the Chief impersonated by Brooks as victim and outsider. Far from expressing Jewish ethno-centricity, he represents all humanity; therefore, he speaks Yiddish. Brooks's gift for parody derives from a long tradition of Jewish writers and artists who express their frustration and vent their anger at an unjust dominant society. The film's coda, a film within a film, conveys the multi-dimensionality of Picasso's Cubist period. In response to these critics, Brooks railed against "corruption, racism, and Bible-thumping bigotry. We used dirty language on the screen for the first time, and to me the whole thing was like a big psychoanalytical session. I just got everything out of me—all my furor, my frenzy, my insanity, my love of life and hatred of death."[8] Citing David Roskies's seminal work, film scholars David Desser and Lester Friedman demonstrate how Brooks tapped into this genre to flail away at his enemies, both real and imagined. In this process, he reaffirmed his Jewishness through humor while simultaneously distancing himself from the less desirable traits embedded in the Jewish experience.[9]

Like Mel Brooks, Woody Allen is a short, Brooklyn-born, Jewish humorist, writer, and filmmaker. By looking at life through a prism of irony, insecurity, and ostensible insecurity, according to author Mark Schechner, Woody crafted a comic self-image not always consonant with reality. Basically a *shtick*, the mask he wears is that of a schlemiel.[10] And a schlemiel, psychologists remind us, is easy prey for bullies. An emotional stutterer, he personifies vulnerability. One can argue that the denigration of this type in traditional humor functions as a form of social control. Each joke that targets the schlemiel reminds the listener that this sort of fool projects a "negative identity"—a concept coined by psycho-historian Erik Erikson, who crafted his own positive, albeit fictive, one, with new name and vocation. Jokes that target the *nebbish* or *schlemiel* constitute a warning to avoid such self-destructive behavior, however funny it may be to the observer.[11]

Woody Allen, however, turned this stereotype on its head when he openly proclaimed his Jewish identity, despite his alleged ineptitude. Critic Gerald Mast astutely observes that Allen, looks notwithstanding, acts and thinks Jewishly as a way of life. "Allen, unJewish," Mast wrote, "is as unthinkable as Chaplin without his cane, Groucho without his cigar, or Fields without his nose."[12] Before he experienced a Kafkaesque metamorphosis into the Woody Allen we either love or hate, Alan Stewart Konigsberg was born on September 1, 1935. Eric Lax, among several biographers, brought to light a few facts that belie the so-called *nebbish* persona. We now know, for example that Konigsberg hated school, that he played a lot of "hooky," that he ignored homework in favor of card tricks, and that he frequented magic shops. In addition, he played baseball with skill and the clarinet with fluency. Alan also took a jab at the Golden Gloves boxing tournament until his parents refused consent to continue. Nothing, however, could stifle his love for the great Willie Ways or curb his enthusiasm for Willie's team, the New York Giants, despite his Brooklyn roots. As he evolved into Woody Allen, he ended his formal education at age 18. Instead, he matriculated in joke writing. His gag bag issued from his Brooklyn Jewish roots.[13]

From 1951 to 1962, Woody served his apprenticeship by writing jokes for others. Watching Mort Sahl perform with newspaper in hand and topical joke on tongue inspired Allen to try center stage, too.[14]

Prior to Sahl, comedians were essentially visual clowns, often dressed in tuxedos, who put down their mother-in-law and were surrounded by scantily clad chorus girls in big dance production numbers projecting, in the argot of Lenny Bruce, "tits and ass." Not only was Sahl subversive in content; he also started a new trend in presentation. Informally attired in slacks, sweater, and shirt opened at the collar minus a tie, he affected a casual "Joe College" image. Strictly a verbal comedian, Sahl relied on subtlety, ideas, and wit. Unwilling or unable to wait for a timely explosion of laughter, he peppered his audiences with a constant spray of jokes: cueing approval with his laughing bark. Sahl developed "savers," too. To hecklers, he countered, "This is not the first time that you failed in the dark." Setting up an aggressive joke, Sahl rhetorically asked: "Is there any group I have not offended?"

Woody Allen followed suit. He came on as a sad-faced, twitchy, alienated urban Jew. Covering the metropolitan beat as cultural critic in 1962 for the *New York Times*, Arthur Gelb discovered Allen in a downtown comedy club and wrote: "The most refreshing comic to emerge in many months is a bespectacled, unhappy-looking, former sketch writer of 26 [who] approaches the microphone ... as though he were afraid it would bite him."[15] Inspired by Mort Sahl—and Bob Hope—Woody emerged. One can trace his progress as a comic pilgrim with an array of one liners.[16]

> I was breast fed through falsies. My parents worshipped old world values: God and carpeting. We were too poor to own a dog; so my parents bought me a pet ant. My grandfather was very insignificant man. At his funeral, the hearse followed the other cars. My neighborhood was so tough, the kids stole hubcaps from moving cars. They broke my violin and left it embedded in my body. I went to a school for emotionally disturbed teachers. I stole second when playing softball. Guilty, I returned to first. I went with a girl who had a child by a future marriage. My first wife was so immature; she sank my boats in the bathtub. During sex, I think of playing ball and as she's digging her nails into my neck I pinch-hit for Willie McCovey. My cousin was very successful, a lawyer. He insured his wife with Mutual of Omaha for orgasm insurance. If he failed to deliver, she collected. I spent $1,000 to have my nose fixed. Now, my brain won't work. My apartment was robbed so often, I put up a sign: "We gave already." I moved to a safer apartment, with a doorman. Two weeks later I was mugged—by the doorman. Not only is there no God, try getting a plumber on a weekend. At the horse track, mine was the only one with training wheels.

Laughter creates distance from as well as protection against an oppressive world. In line with Lenny Bruce, Mel Brooks, and Philip Roth, Woody Allen used wit to ward off his demons. When he became a filmmaker, he brought a vast store of Jewish cultural baggage to this art form. In one his first films, *What's Up, Tiger Lily?* (1966), some Japanese characters speak Yiddish. Moreover, the hero is named Phil Moscowitz, who, mortally wounded, calls for a rabbi. And the parody of Samurai films is pure Sid Caesar, for whom he wrote, along with other exemplary Jewish writers like Mel Tolkin, Carl Reiner, Lucille Kallen, Neil and "Doc" Simon, Larry Gelbart, and Mel Brooks.[17] Critics Desser and Friedman argue that Allen's uses of Jewish stereotypes were both few and largely covert. Yet they concede that Jewish themes tend to crop up in the first film that Woody directed, in 1969, *Take the Money and Run*, and resurface in subsequent films. Virgil Starkwell, for example, is inept at his chosen vocation, that of a thief. In jail, he ingests a drug that turns him into a Hassidic rabbi. Wearing Groucho Marx masks, his parents constantly bicker and *kvetch* (complain) about their son, the schlemiel.[18]

In *Bananas* (1971), Woody pokes fun at Jews who send money to Latino dictator Vargas instead of UJA and Christians who "pitch" New Testament Cigarettes. "You switch to ... and all is forgiven." *Play It Again, Sam* (1972) pits the warm, generous Jewish Alan Felix against the cold vacuous Christian Dick Christie with the assistance of Humphrey Bogart as the blithe spirit. *Sleeper* (1973) identifies Jewish union leader Al Shanker as the cause of World War III because he launched a nuclear weapon in a film that propels the Jewish character Miles Monroe, played by Woody Allen (named after his New York Knick basketball idol Earl "the Pearl" Monroe), into the year 2173, where he makes trouble and stirs up rebellion against a robotized Orwellian world. *Annie Hall* (1977) arguably Allen's best film, juxtaposes two worlds: Alvy Singer's vis-à-vis Annie Hall's. The twin focus on both families at the dinner table delineates the vast gulf between two cultures. The Christian family is devoid of warmth but full of manners, while the Singers are loud, emotional, and talk all at once. In bed, moreover, Alvy is supercharged sexually; Annie is not that hot. The climax of this Academy Award–winning film frames two jokes derived from Borscht Belt humor. For openers: "Life is like the awful food in a second-rate hotel—but we want larger portions." In the final analysis, Alvy affirms a life leavened by fantasy in a second joke:

> My brother thinks he's a chicken.
> Why not have him confined to a mental hospital?
> We can't, because we need the eggs.

In *Manhattan* (1979), enriched by a gorgeous Gershwin sound track, Isaac Davis, like his creator Woody Allen, searches for life's meaning. A Jewish television writer, he is dumped by a wife who "comes out" as a lesbian and is spurned by many girlfriends, including a seventeen-year-old named Tracy (Mariel Hemingway), not quite a Litvak Lolita, but under-aged. A schlemiel, he suffers identity confusion. In the final scene, angst yields to the reasons for living: Flaubert's *A Sentimental Education*, Cezanne's paintings, Mozart's

41st Symphony, and Tracy's face.[19] That confusion carried over to *Stardust Memories* (1980). Despite a recurrent morbid fear of dying, Sandy Bates, the Allen character, counts his blessings as he rejects the suicide option because of Satchmo's "Potatohead Blues," and Mozart's Jupiter Symphony. Straying from his Jewish roots, Allen expresses guilt indirectly. *Zelig* (1982) provides a case in point. Here, the principal character appears everywhere but he remains a "nowhere" man despite endless therapy sessions with Dr. Eudora Fletcher (Mia Farrow). Allen's efforts to emulate Ingmar Bergman in a series of serious films prompted Allen to return to what he knew best: the Jewish comedic experience, in *Broadway Danny Rose* (1984) and *Radio Days* (1987). In the former film, Woody draws on Catskill roots. As talent agent Danny Rose, he handles oddball acts with a heavy Brooklyn Jewish intonation. The first scene features a bunch of Catskill comedians—Jackie Mason, Henny Youngman, Morty Gunty, and Sandy Baron—sitting around a table in the Carnegie delicatessen exchanging jokes and sharing funny memories of Danny Rose. As one critic describes the film, it is a kind of marriage between the Mafia and Jewish humor, with Mia Farrow and Woody Allen personifying each group. Mia is marvelous as the Italian "hussy" playing off a nebbishy but good-hearted Woody. Danny Rose often punctuates a sentence with the Yiddish word *emmis* (truth) coupled with "my hand to God."[20] A subsequent film, *The Purple Rose of Cairo* (1985), minus Allen as actor but very much the *auteur* (because critic Gerald Mast persuasively argued that the film is set in a gentile world), shows an abused wife, Cecilia (Mia Farrow), who finds refuge in fantasy as film hero Tom Baxter (Jeff Daniels) pops off the screen to bathe the star-struck Mia in much-needed affection.[21]

In many of Woody Allen's later films, he abandons two earlier stereotypical myths: Jews with money and Jews as intellectuals. In their place, Allen fashioned a more complex narrative, as delineated by Professor Mast, combining Marx's economics, Freud's psychoanalysis, Einstein's physics and Kafka's paranoia. Chief among these influences is clearly Marx—Groucho rather than Karl.[22] Ethnic identity trumps class consciousness in Woody's work. In *Hannah and Her Sisters* (1986), he pits "wasp drama against Jew comedy."[23] Given to hypochondriacal panic and self-doubt, Mickey (Woody) seeks refuge in other religions. In his Catholic phase, he purchases religious artifacts and markers: a picture of Jesus, a crucifix, Wonder Bread, and mayonnaise.[24] When all else fails, including an abortive flirtation with Hare Krishna, Mickey finally finds solace in the comic artistry of the Marx Brothers' 1933 romp, *Duck Soup*.[25]

In *Radio Days* (1987) and *Crimes and Misdemeanors* (1989), Allen grapples with Godlessness. Both films deal with religion and ethnicity more openly than in his prior depiction of Jewish-American life. In *Radio Days*, Little Joey, Woody's prototype as a child, steals money from a *pushke* (money can) designated for a Jewish homeland in Palestine in order to buy a *tschotske*, a magical ring touted on radio. A second *shonda* (scandal) involves a neighboring family with a communist bent, who blast their radio and openly eat non-kosher food on Yom Kippur. Sent to admonish them in an adjacent apartment, Uncle Abe (an obese Josh Mostel) returns, a converted communist mouthing Marxist slogans and eating pork, defiantly. As both God and Marx fade in importance, only art—*auteur* Allen seems to suggest—and entertainment will suffice in a world where the Yeatsian center does not hold.[26]

Crimes and Misdemeanors paints a darker picture of a world—postwar and after the Holocaust—in which God has failed. In tackling a recurring fear in his *oeuvre*, death and an amoral universe minus a just and benevolent deity, Allen lays claim to a plot fashioned by Dostoevsky in *Crime and Punishment*. A happily married, prominent doctor, Judah Rosenthal (Martin Landau) authorizes the murder of his troublesome mistress, Delores (Anjelica Huston). He loses faith, suffers angst, incurs guilt, albeit temporarily, and gets away with murder. If crime goes unpunished, it proves the "silence of God." Life, therefore, has no meaning.[27]

A parallel plot pits the decent but nebbishy documentary filmmaker Cliff (Woody Allen) against the phony Lester (Alan Alda) over the affection of Hallie (Mia Farrow). Both love triangles involve Jewish males and Christian women. A subplot features Holocaust survivor and philosopher Louis Levy, who trumpets love over hate and is the heroic subject of Cliff's documentary film project. Though *auteur* Allen aspires to serious purpose, the film is not devoid of humor. "Trapped in a loveless, sexless marriage," Cliff the *schlimazel* confesses that the only woman he penetrated since the previous year resulted from a visit to the Statue of Liberty.[28]

All things fall apart. Love eludes Cliff. Hallie decides to marry the fatuous Lester. Philosopher Levy commits suicide. In failure, Woody's character concludes that "God is dead" or, at least, blind. Blindness thus becomes the dominant metaphor in this film. Ophthalmologist Rosenthal does not foresee the internal consequences of his mistress's murder; nor does Professor Levy envision the impact of his self-destructive act. In the absence of God, Woody Allen seems to say, there are only movies if you want happy endings. Joy in work, family, and education—the simple pleasures—may offer solace. To survive in this veil of tears, however, one needs blind faith.[29]

Another Catskill alum out of Brooklyn, Alan King, né Irwin Alan Kniberg, was born in Manhattan on December 26, 1927. Before lung cancer ended his life, King enjoyed a successful career as comedian, actor, producer, writer, and philanthropist. Raised as the youngest of eight children in a blended family, a kind of Jewish Brady Bunch, on Manhattan's Lower East Side and Brooklyn's Williamsburg section by immigrant parents, he dropped out of high school to enter show business. His father, Bernie, worked in the garment industry and revered Dubinsky, Roosevelt, and the New Deal, resulting in this observation.[30]

> With the coming of the New Deal my father joined the Democrats. In our house we had two pictures on the kitchen wall. One was a colored print of Moses on the Mount and the other was a rotogravure of Franklin Delano Roosevelt, and until I was fourteen years old I didn't know who came first or who was more important.

Thus, Alan's family revered *die veldt, yener veldt* (this world, the other world) and Roosevelt. Bernie passed on his politics on to his son. Bernie, however, never could earn a steady living or respect from his in-laws. So, he remained an angry *luftmentsh*.

Like his underachieving dad, Alan grew up angry and tough. At age 14, he appeared on *Major Bowes' Amateur Hour*. He sang a Depression favorite, "Brother, Can You Spare a Dime?" in dirty face and torn knickers. Applause and laughter reinforced his determination to become a stand-up comedian. Mother Minnie urged her drop-out son (from Boys High and Eastern District High School in Brooklyn) to learn a trade, quipped King, so that she could tell her friends "what kind of work he's out of."[31]

At age fifteen, King ventured up to the Catskills. There, working his way up from number three comic, porch *tummler*, beauty contest emcee, he crested in the Jewish Alps. The young comic spent summers in the Borscht Belt, and winters in Lakewood. Hired by the Gradus Hotel, he complained: "When you work for Gradus, you work for gratis."[32] King also worked for the Tisch family, who owned Laurel in the Pines, Lakewood's most elegant hotel. He copied every successful comic of the 1940s: Milton Berle, Jackie Miles, Phil Foster, Jan Murray, Danny Kaye, Jerry Lester, Danny Thomas, and Jack E. Leonard. King developed an aggressive style that critic Kenneth Tynan likened to "a [talking] sawed-off shotgun."[33]

King proved adept at memorizing movie dialogue, which he exchanged with another movie fanatic, Sammy Davis, Jr. Both fledgling entertainers experienced the poison of prejudice. King tried to assimilate but could not. Eventually, he learned to wear his Jewishness proudly. At age 16, he went to Canada, where he became a boxer. After 20 wins, he fought a black boxer named King. He lost, badly, but he won a new name—King. He preferred to use his wits instead of his fists.[34] Performing at Georgie Jay's 78th Street Tap Room, he was recognized by Walter Winchell.

Soon, King was seen among the stars. He opened for Frank Sinatra at the Steel Pier in Atlantic City on Memorial Day, 1944. He stretched 12 minutes of comedy into 18, which infuriated the great singer.[35] After a rocky start, their friendship continued despite political differences. King also frequently appeared with Judy Garland during her rueful "days of wine and roses." In 1956, his work with the troubled singer elevated him to stardom.

He developed a persona: a *kvetchy* (cranky), frustrated, angry middle-class denizen bedeviled by the incongruities of modern life. He lashed out at insurance companies, airline food, suburban mores, and "boomer" children. Moving to Long Island may have yoked Alan with heavy debt and some major family problems, but it also gave him fresh material. He had married his childhood sweetheart, Jeannette Sprung, at the East Midwood Jewish Center in 1947. The young couple moved into an apartment in Long Beach. Later, they bought a cul-de-sac house in Rockville center for $22,000. King remembers it as "an upscale Levittown." *Tsores* (trouble) arose, providing grist for his humor mill. A keen observer of suburbanization, he employed trenchant commentary in the role of a funny cultural anthropologist.[36]

As a guest on Ed Sullivan's celebrated CBS show on Sunday nights, Alan King vented his anger in more than 90 appearances (Bruce Weber of the *New York Times* cites only 56 in his obit).[37] He poked fun at zoning laws. A line ran through his home. His kids were zoned for another district. King quipped: "They tried to tell me that if my kids slept in the garage, they could go to schools in Rockville Center."[38] Keeping up with the Joneses and the Cohens was no easy chore. The Kings had to mow their lawns to group specification.

Obsessive cleanliness and finished basements triggered King's comic wrath. Whenever he got up in the middle of the night to use the bathroom, he returned to find that his wife had made the bed. As for finished basements, King observed: "It's so wonderful to walk into a house with an eight-foot ceiling and a basement with a four foot-ceiling and spend an evening like Quasimodo or Toulouse-Lautrec."[39] As many homeowners discovered, you never have enough room. So, adding rooms sparked King's description of how "the open porch became a closed-in-porch. The garage became a study. I had a $22,000 house and lived there for 11 years. We figured out I put $50,000 into that $22,000 house. And you know how much I sold it for? Twenty-two thousand dollars. That's absolutely true."[40]

Equally true and painful were the ground rules for husbands about to host guests handed down by imperious wives.[41]

1. Don't sit on the sofa. I just pulled up the pillows.
2. Stay off the carpets; the pile is up.

3. Don't go into the bedroom. I want to keep it clean.

4. Hurry up and take a shower—but don't use the towels.

So what happens? A man ends up dressing in a dark closet and all night long he walks around with a damp skin, blotting himself with a Kleenex.

The visitors suffered, too. King's narrative resonates with anyone lost in Yonkers or on Long Island.[42]

> Meanwhile … the guests are trying to follow their hostess's directions to the house. Even if you ever received good directions—which is unlikely—it would be virtually impossible to find these places in the suburbs....
>
> Today they stick a street between two trees, and even the people who live on the street are not too sure of its name. Every one of these places is called something like Featherbed Road or Poinsettia Place, and someone I know found his thrill on Blueberry Hill.

Kvetching about suburbia aside, Alan King found a creative outlet in political activity. Because of Harry Belafonte, Alan King marched with Dr. Martin Luther King from Selma to Montgomery, Alabama. Flanked by a host of celebrities and common folk, King experienced fear. Spat upon by National Guardsmen and sheltered in a Catholic monastery, he grew angry. He pushed for civil rights under the aegis of Dr. King and both Kennedys. Their deaths by assassination fueled his fury.[43]

Never content to be just a stand-up comic or a political fellow traveler, Alan King ventured into the movies. Movies meant action. Starting in films in 1955 with *Hit the Deck*, a clichéd remake of three-sailors-on-leave formula, King had a small role.[44] He played a gangster in *The Helen Morgan Story* (1957) opposite Paul Newman. *Bye Bye Braverman* (1968) converted King from *gonif* (thief) to rabbi. In the middle of a funeral sermon, he switches from a traditional Talmudist to a hip, new age Oxford-accented hustler articulating these words: "A man lives. And he dies—is there no time for tears?"[45]

In 1980, King gained star billing as garment center tycoon Max Herschel in *Just Tell Me What You Want*. Like the real King, Max bemoans rural America because basically he's New York City, urban, Jewish. Yet he lives in a palatial estate on Long Island. Married to an alcoholic (Dina Merrill) and involved with a sultry mistress (Ali MacGraw), he suffers. This film, directed by Sidney Lumet, conveys a dark vision of assimilation, social mobility and moral rot.[46] A number of mediocre films followed. Then magic in a bottle of lightning struck in 1988. *Memories of Me* paired Alan King and Billy Crystal, who also wrote the script. Producer and star, Alan King likened it to his King Lear.[47] Ultimately, he acted in 29 films.

Once Danny Kaye critiqued Alan King that he was "too Jewish." Ignoring this assessment, the comedian grounded his humor in the Jewish experience, as this favorite joke attests.

A vile individual died in the *shtetl*. So monumental were his evil deeds that no local rabbi wanted to preside at his funeral. The family finally found a willing rabbi in a distant town. He began[48]:

> Here lies.... He was a liar, a thief, a forger, a brute, a bully, an atheist.... Had he died twenty years before, the world would have been far better off. Sitting in the first row, however, are his three brothers from my town. Compared to these louts, he was an angel!

Tzedakah (charity), an ancient Jewish imperative, informed King's finest hours. Founder of a medical center in Jerusalem and a scholarship for American students at Hebrew University, he also served on the board of trustees at the Long Island Jewish Medical Center and as an advocate for emotionally disturbed youngsters in Nassau County.

As a member of the Friars Club since 1945, King often served as master of ceremonies, succeeding Georgie Jessel as Toastmaster General of the United States. In 1961 he co-hosted the Kennedy inaugural party and hosted the Academy Awards in 1972. Not only did he author five books, King also portrayed that master of malaprop, Samuel Goldwyn, in 2002, in an off–Broadway play. Always eager to do stand-up with cigar in hand, he continued to crack jokes at his own expense. At Kutcher's Country Club in August 2003, he observed: "My prostate is now bigger than my ego."[49]

During a Command Performance for Queen Elizabeth II and Prince Phillip in 1958 in Glasgow, Scotland, he was introduced to the British monarch, who according to protocol, greeted him: "How do you do, Mr. King?" To which he replied with polite but leveling common sense: "How do you do, Mrs. Queen." Prince Philip got the punch line and laughed.[50] This is typical Jewish

Author, raconteur, radio and television host, Joe Franklin, seen in 2013, was another Catskill alumnus.

As was comedian Mickey Freeman, shown here at the Friar's Club.

humor, namely, to bring down the high and mighty to common ground. Clearly, we are all going to die and we might as well laugh until we reach that terminal point.

Excessive indulgence in cigars and cigarettes brought the regal comedian down to eternal rest on May 9, 2004. If there is a heaven, one can imagine the King of Comedy high in the sky blowing smoke-rings at the Big Chief Justice, tough, brazen, and Brooklyn with the usual saver: "God, I was only kidding." As for the other two remaining Brooklyn boys who went to comedy school in the Catskill and Pocono Mountains, heaven can wait.

Six

A Sacred Monster in Lamb's Clothing

Jerry Lewis

If Jesus saves, then Moses invests. And that's a 6 percent difference; advantage to my tribe. Jews are funny people: funnier, in fact, than highly serious followers of Christ. Jerry Lewis, né Joseph Levitch, the principal subject of this chapter, was born into the culture of Moses in 1926. But early in the game of life, he discovered that mainstream America preferred a white Christmas to a happy Chanukah (or "Happy Harmonica" in the self-mockery of Groucho Marx). So he changed his name, his partner, his associates and married a snub-nosed shiksa named Patti. He raised six sons, largely in absentia, as Christians. His behavior often bordered on the hellish. To reach the heights of show biz and achieve celebrity status, he cut a deal with the devil, a kind of Faustian bargain. Enter Applegate, his alter ego in *Damn Yankees*, smirking.

Several summers ago, Professor Larry Mintz asked me to a review a book on Jerry Lewis for *Humor: International Journal of Human Research*. Reluctantly, I took the assignment. My admiration for this "Sacred Monster"—in the appellation of French enthusiasts—was at that time well under control. Physical comedy, particularly when it targets the disabled, is offensive, indeed repugnant. The adulation of Lewis in French literary circles baffles this writer and probably illuminates Gallic sensibility, perhaps pedantry, more than it explains our comic genius. While engaged in addressing "the enigma wrapped in a riddle" that is Jerry Lewis, I became more appreciative of this uniquely American comedic force, though not quite ready to blow him French kisses.

I will try to locate Lewis as a Jewish comic in lamb's clothing. Suffering from a Manichean duality, Lewis did not resolve this dilemma of identity until he abandoned his first wife and suffered a near fatal heart attack. Lionized in France and ignored in America in recent years, he made a dramatic comeback when he returned to his ethnic heritage. Concentrating on the early Lewis, one finds discernible tendencies that recur like a haunting refrain or a daunting Wagnerian leitmotif. Author Shawn Levy correctly places Jerry Lewis in the context of Jewish humor, tracing its roots back to shtetl life. There, the *badchen*, "a cultured clown" entertained at weddings. Coming to America, he adjusted to the new environment as a legitimate entertainer, a master of ceremony.[1] This role sanctioned the Jew as court jester. Later, in the Catskill resorts, this character evolved into a *tummler*, a designated comic fool, also with antecedents in the *shtetl* as *nar, letz, kunilemel,* and *schlemiel.*

Immigrants had to escape from the sweltering city in summer. A few pioneers ventured into the country, in the Catskill region. Hotels, bungalow colonies or *kuchalayns* where *yiddishe mames* did their own cooking (no reservations, please!) sprang up. Fresh air and good food were not enough. Visitors needed—no, demanded—comic relief. In charge of this categorical imperative was the "social director." One of the best descriptions of this role can be found in the autobiography of Moss Hart, who penned a bittersweet evocation of Catskill Culture.[2]

A product of the "Borscht Belt," Jerry Lewis grew up as the only child of a show business couple, Danny and Rae Lewis. Infected by the "show biz" virus, his parents pursued their "golden rainbow" often at the expense of their only, none but the lonely, child. They encouraged his antics and he rewarded their attention with a poignant rendition of "Brother, Can You Spare a Dime?" at a benefit in the Catskills in 1932. He was six years old.[3] Also bitten by the entertainment bug, Lewis was hooked. He left school when he was 16. The young native of Newark developed a bit, part Charlie McCarthy, part Al Jolson. He would mime to music with exaggerated, even spastic, movements. He worked his "dummy act" wherever he could get a gig: from hospitals to military dances.

He watched his father, Danny, do shtick at Brown's Hotel in the Catskills. He observed the manic behavior of the kitchen staff. Then something happened on the Sabbath. While the rabbi offered a blessing, Lewis, still known as Levitch, went through the kitchen door, collided with a waiter and in a familiar scene (it happened to me more than once), dropped a tray, loaded with dishes. Recollecting this incident which launched his comedic career, Lewis confesses[4]:

> I wailed, "Oh God, I didn't mean it!" It was a wipeout. Even the rabbi laughed. At which point it seemed like an ideal way to start clowning my way through every meal. The clown. The one guy who could make people

laugh in spite of themselves, giving pleasure by creating an illusion of wild absurdity. It was all I wanted to do in the first place. So, you can imagine the stunts I pulled during those busboy days at the Ambassador. Suffice to say, the more absurd, the more they like it.

Fate brought Jerry Lewis and Dean Martin together in the summer of 1944. Martin already had star billing while Lewis played second banana as emcee and novelty act. Nine years younger, Lewis adored Martin, who had a fascinating résumé: boxer, bouncer, croupier and lady-killer. At a New York nightclub called the Glass Hat, Lewis and Martin began to "poach" on each other's act. Two years later, they improvised a finale to an act, which blended their respective talents.[5]

An instant hit, the crooner and the comic, Italian and Jew, Mr. Cool and Boy Frantic, handsome man and ugly monkey—in short, polar opposites—followed the Catskill kunst (culture) in "letting go." Biographer Levy comments, in an almost futile effort to decipher their act, that the "Playboy and the Putz" (his designation) played to their opposite's strengths and weakness. More germane to my take is the desperate need for the "Putz" to be accepted, flaws and all. Lewis, heavily freighted with Jewish-American baggage, chose to ignore his ethnic roots until later in his career.

An incident in 1952 invites exegesis. In June, veteran crooner Bing Crosby made his television debut with Bob Hope in order to raise money for the U.S. Olympic Fund. Cool and controlled, this much-traveled duo lost their composure when Dean Martin and Jerry Lewis upset their apple-cart. Slated for a two-minute slot, the Italian and the Jew raised havoc in a "manic half-hour." The more aggressive Lewis jumped Hope and showered him with wet kisses. Disturbed, Hope swatted the upstarts with a clipboard. Lewis bellowed: "It's time for the old-timers to sit down." Eclipsed, Crosby retreated into the wings. After some high-octane dancing, singing and mugging, Lewis repeatedly calls for Bing to return. He mimics a dog trainer's manner. While Crosby stays in his den, a bearded lion in winter, Hope counterpunches. Again, he swats Lewis with his note pad and pulls the microphone from his grasp. Defensively, he quips, "Stop talking about my father that way!" Lewis heightens the tension with a simian stance with an exaggerated claw-hand gesture. Unable to control the manic Lewis, who proceeds to conduct the orchestra and howl a song in a shrill stutter, Hope summons Martin to his aid: "When did they cut the strings off him?" The audience laughed. Undaunted, Lewis loped back onto center stage bellowing like Stanley Kowalski for his Stella for Bing to return. Hope regains an edge with another quip: "He's hiding and I don't blame him."[6]

The zany duo's leap to fame carried them to Hollywood measurably beyond

Judy Garland's rainbow and right into the lap of television, our nation's rising medium. Biographer Nick Tosches provides a compelling explanation for their striking success. Crossing boundaries served as a much-needed escape from Cold War anxieties while sustaining, at the same, male camaraderie forged during World War II. Building on this base, critic Frank Krutnick carries the analysis load into deep, perhaps muddy, waters. He argues, for example, that the Lewis-Martin linkage is at its base a sexual bond nurtured in war. Theirs is a distinctively different pairing. Earlier, Laurel and Hardy, Abbott and Costello, Hope and Crosby were all both often predictable and basically similar. Not so Martin and Lewis. While Hope and Crosby used Dorothy Lamour as a non-threatening female, Martin and Lewis represented two distinctive kinds of masculinity joined in sexual hostility.[7] This same sex version of screwball comedy focused on Jerry's feminine side as "a jester in the court of sexual panic," according to writer Ed Sikov.[8]

Allow me a variation on the above themes. Combining psychology and common sense, one can discern a pattern in the Martin-Lewis (cash) nexus. From Jerry's point of view, Deano represented all that he was not: swinger, athlete, singer, cool and, above all, gentile. A good "goy," Martin fulfilled Jerry's psychic needs as the older brother he never had and a surrogate father to replace the absent one he regarded with painful ambivalence. The insouciant crooner also provided a kind of security blanket. "Every small Jew," Mel Brooks pontificated, "should have a tall goy for a friend, to walk with him and to protect him against assault."[9] Yet, Lewis could never completely sever his Jewish roots. In his lip-sync routine, Lewis invariably closed his shtick with the name Feibush Finkel, a prominent Yiddish actor with current crossover appeal.[10]

Alienated from his ancestral roots, Jerry Lewis hid behind "a tall goy." Escape into fame and fortune constituted a rebellion against his parents. His father, in particular, framed comedy in a Jewish mode. Lewis bolted from the flock. We see elements of assimilation in his early—and ultimately unhappy— marriage to Patti, the shiksa (gentile girl) next door. In rapid succession they had six sons (one was adopted). Patti gave up her career for the role of housewife/mother. Jerry would put up a popular front as good husband and good father. He was neither. Years later he erased his youngest son, Joseph, his namesake, his *ben-yuchedl* (youngest son) who had the chutzpa (temerity) to tell all to the *National Enquirer*.[11] Just as his father had rejected him earlier and Dean Martin later, Jerry would reenact this deadly drama. Again and again, he returned—repeatedly and compulsively—to that primal bond of loyalty. He loved all: father, mother, wife, Deano, children, and, a haunting lyric reminds us: "You always hurt the one you love."

Success, at the outset, linked the "swinger" and the "putz." Their first film, based on a hit radio series, *My Friend Irma* (1949), did not overly impress critics. Nevertheless, the usually acerbic Bosley Crowther praised Lewis. "This freakishly built and acting young man ... has a genuine comic ability." The critic went on to describe "the swift eccentricity of his movements, the harrowing features of his face, the squeak of vocal protestations" and his lunacy, which "constitutes a burlesque of an idiot."[12] Crowther found Lewis "the funniest thing in the film." Martin and Lewis also performed onstage in between film showings.[13] Subsequent films would elicit less favorable reviews. Lewis and Martin cut a wide swath in Hollywood. Low-budget films like *Sailor Beware* (1951), their fourth cinematic duet, cost only $750,000 to produce and grossed $27 million. Hal Wallis had discovered a cash cow, which he milked with a simple formula. Martin played the straight lead singer who gets the girl; Lewis, the urban idiot. One of Crowther's colleagues at the *Times* praised Lewis in 1954 for his "needle-sharp impersonation of three foreign medicos in a hospital sequence" as "a piece of comic artistry." The film, *Living It Up* (1954) is a remake of *Nothing Sacred* (1937). Lewis personified the stationmaster as perfect local martyr even though the film failed to match the vintage model.[14]

Critic Krutnik insists that Jerry provides a regressive fantasy of revolt against adult responsibility. In addition, he secretly harbors a passion for his male buddy. Is this a queer—instead of a fine—romance? No doubt Krutnik is onto something. Prodigious research and friendly persuasion support his arguments. But I believe he does not pay sufficient attention to another, perhaps more important, element: Lewis's ethnicity. Lewis tried to lighten his mother load. For many years, he succeeded in this "great escape from Jewish roots." But he paid a high, perhaps prohibitive price. In a real sense, Lewis cut a Faustian deal to secure fame and fortune. The rakish Martin began to chafe at the bit and bay at the moon.

Hit in the eye with a big pizza pie, Martin bolted from the Paramount stable, leaving Jerry in a cloud of dust. Aptly, his liberation occurred on July 4 after finishing their last film, *Hollywood or Bust*. Initially, as their careers diverged, Dean's personal stock soared in film and later on the "tube of plenty." Indeed, television was ideally suited to the aloof performer, whose mask matched his manner. Life after their divorce in 1956 proved problematic for the younger comic, who had worshipped the gentile singer/actor.

A product of a troubled relationship with his own father, Danny Lewis, Jerry must have sensed another paternal rejection in this breakup. The reinvention of this complex, rootless comic was no easy task. Many critics found Lewis's extreme form of comedy repugnant. Bosley Crowther, a powerful movie critic at the *New York Times,* savaged this would-be king of comedy. Thus demonized, Jerry quickly became the whipping boy of the cognoscenti. Even the castor oil treatment could not purge this creature from American popular culture.

One reason for this resilience was his mass appeal. Let me explain by reference to personal experience. Many years ago while working my way through graduate school, I taught in a junior high school deep in the heart of Harlem. On certain days, when education was put on hold for administrative reasons, we had to cope with hundreds of restless students going through the rite of puberty. What could we do? The favorite respite from uninspiring books and teachers' dirty looks for hundreds of students massed in the auditorium proved to be any film featuring Jerry Lewis! Why? I wondered.

Baffled at first and often repelled by Lewis as a comic, I now know why my students responded so positively. In 1962, the time of my apprenticeship, America was a very different country. Despite laws to the contrary, segregation dominated: overtly in the South, more subtly in our region. The vast majority of my ghettoized students—I learned—had never ventured into Petula Clark territory, namely, downtown. Symbols of white culture saturated the media. Watching a white man, therefore, parading his inadequacies gave the audience a much-needed sense of Hobbesian superiority when black inferiority appeared as the operative mode of our racist culture. Confined to a closed space, these highly kinetic youngsters could roar with impunity. They experienced (shades of Freud) the laughter of release and relief.

Lewis interacted with younger Jewish comedians. For example, he tried to influence Lenny Bruce. Jerry urged Lenny to develop a kinder, gentler act, less larded with political commentary and charged with Jewish idioms.[15] A *nechtikn tog* (a nightly day): no one could change the course of "Dirty Lenny." A link to Woody Allen also merits mention. Woody wanted Jerry to direct *Take the Money and Run* (1969). Since he was unavailable, Lewis urged Allen to direct himself. The film launched Allen's career as an *auteur*. He also asked France's favorite American artiste to direct *Bananas* (1971). Again the veteran comic rebuffed the young filmmaker. Forced to do it again, Allen "remained grateful to Jerry for inspiration and encouragement throughout his career."[16] Allen's alleged rival at this juncture, Mel Brooks, was injecting a Jewish love for humor and a concomitant hatred for Hitler into his first movie, *The Producers* (1967). Brooks also learned from Lewis while working on *The Ladies Man* (1961). Krutnick argues that Lewis created a bridge between old Jewish comic and the younger generation. Their working relationship, however, was less than idyllic. Lewis commissioned Brooks to pen the script for a film. The final draft bore little resemblance to the Brooks original. Contrasting Jack Benny invidiously with Jerry Lewis, Brooks may own the last laugh. To critic Kenneth Tynan, he asserted: "High key comics like that burn themselves out. Lewis could do thirty-one takes, and when you've seen them all that was it. Low-key, laid-back comics like Jack Benny are the ones that last."[17] In his candid assessment, Jerry's biographer acknowledges that his subject repressed overt Jewish tendencies except, of course, putting on the nebbish. Nevertheless, he paved the way for more explicitly Jewish comics to tap into tribal roots and *mama-loshen*.

Exposure to Yiddish culture by parents whose rejection of their only child fueled the young comic's ambition and triggered deep anger. I believe that Jerry subconsciously rejected—point, counterpoint—his Jewish heritage. That is why he gravitated to his polar opposite, Dean Martin. And that is also why the most traumatic event in a life filled with angst was Dean's departure.[18]

In pursuit of self-legitimation, Jerry Lewis, prodded by Judy Garland, added singing to his repertoire. No doubt a daunting challenge, Jerry probably wanted to show his erstwhile partner that he, too, could cross boundaries. In fact, he might even upstage the crooner. Emulating his idol Al Jolson, Lewis, now flying solo, belted out "Rock-a-Bye Your Baby with a Dixie Melody."[19] And a star was reborn.

A pivotal point in Lewis's career as *auteur* occurred in 1963. Released that year, *The Nutty Professor* shows off Lewis's immense talent as performer/writer/director—in short, Renaissance man. Derived from the bi-polar matrix, Jekyll and Hyde, the film projects two sides of Jerry's persona: introverted (Jewish?) intellectual Julius Kelp and chemically charged (Goyish?) ebullient Buddy Love. To woo Stella Purdy (Stella Stevens), the nerdy professor tries a Charles Atlas program of transformation. He fails dismally, if comically. Arguably, a satiric thrust at former partner Deano, Buddy packs a charismatic punch as crooner, boozer and womanizer. Biographer Shawn Levy insists that Buddy is Jerry, not Dean. He is "loud, arrogant, abusive, abrasive, and conceited"—a mirror image of the comic's dark side—first articulated in *The Bellboy* (1960) and reprised in *The King of Comedy* (1983).[20]

Lewis provided a clue to the real persona in his own words. In one account, he claims that Kelp was modeled after a fellow traveler on a train from Los Angeles to New York. A *nebachl*, a small Pittsburgh salesman named Hartman, with glasses perched on his nose, fascinated Lewis, who plied him with drink. At the end of this possibly disingenuous story, the entertainer confesses: "Many people can identify with him because somewhere, sometime, they may have met the likes of him. He may even be a member of the family."[21]

Whose family? Skeletons (white as opposed to red) rattled in his own closet. In a profoundly revealing statement, rich in psychological content, Lewis writes[22]:

> He's Buddy Love, infinitely for himself and disliking all other humans. I made him a glaringly destructive force, despicable to the core, as a balance against the loving professor. Creating the role had me in a sweat, especially when I saw images of Buddy Love creeping out from inside me onto the page. A crying horror! It got even worse during the actual filming. I kept pushing the Buddy Love sequences to the end, procrastinating my ass off, dreading to see him come alive on the screen.

Thus, Lewis's comic bifurcation is tap-rooted in family and culture. Using many Yiddish phrases in his informative book on filmmaking, the *auteur* identifies Chaplin with the schlemiel ("the guy who spilled drinks") and schlimazel ("the guy who had the drinks spilled on him"). Lewis admits, "My idiot character plays both schlemiel and schlimazel, and at times the inter-mix."[23] It is precisely the oscillation between the quest for intellectual attainment, "highbrow" culture and the attainment of filthy lucre, geldt by association, "lowbrow" and "middlebrow" culture. This dichotomy provides the enduring dilemma confronting Jewish-Americans as noted in the work, among others, of Mark Shechner, Albert Goldman, Stephen Whitfield, Joseph Boskin, and this writer.

Diminished popularity and personal problems led to Lewis's virtual absence from the screen from 1970 until 1983. Lionized in France, he was bearded in America and forced to put his pet project, *The Day the Clown Cried*—a film about a German circus clown who winds up in Auschwitz—on permanent hold. Never released, mired in litigation, the film represents a grandiose attempt at self-promotion and Chaplinesque bathos. More significantly, it served to reconnect Jerry with his Jewish roots. This aborted film invites a post mortem. Why did the aging star invest so much time, energy and money into the project?

As originally written, the plot takes a selfish German clown, 78 years of crusty old age, into Auschwitz. His assignment is to entertain the Jewish children prior to their deaths. Indeed, he functions as a Pied Piper, leading his charges into the gas chambers. Hired by producer Nate Wachsberger to both direct and play the lead role based on a Joan O'Brien book, Lewis deliberately revised the story; in his version the clown is transformed into a Jew who reconnects, through the children, with community and self. The final scene of this incomplete and unreleased film fixes on Lewis as he marches with the children into the jaws of death.[24]

Subsequently, Lewis shed his old skin and marched into semi-retirement.

He left his wife for a younger, Jewish woman, SanDee Pitnick, in 1983. Unable to bear children, Mrs. Lewis and her husband adopted a daughter. Strangely, Lewis lavished more love and attention on his adopted daughter than his five biological sons. His official biography, on the Internet, describes daughter Danielle Sara as the "light of their lives and the air in their lungs."[25] After such knowledge, what forgiveness from ex-wife and sons?

Even in the lean years and the in-between years, Lewis remained in the public eye with his annual Labor Day Muscular Dystrophy Association Telethons. In lampooning the host, Lenny Bruce claimed that muscular dystrophy was a disease invented by Jerry Lewis and offered to host a "Clapathon" for victims of venereal disease. Lewis's assessment of his critic is worth quoting[26]:

> Lenny Bruce was the most infuriating man I ever met in my life because he preferred to make his way with four-letter words. He was brilliant but couldn't make it as a straight comic, so he steered that brilliant mind into a joint with fifty-eight people. He could have swung with the best if he'd gone straight. I am not the enemy of Lenny Bruce, rest his soul.

Lewis also attacked Mort Sahl and Andy Warhol for "wasting talent on so few, rather than working for the masses."[27]

Fund-raising also links Lewis with traditional Jewish imperatives. To be sure, the motives embrace both *tzeddakah* and *koved* (philanthropy and respect). Krutnick adds a psychological dimension in his analysis of Lewis's role as MDA spokesman. He is the mediating father figure who, empowered and impassioned with the rhetoric of love—largely absent from his own nuclear family—"rages, cries, pleads and cajoles on behalf of ... the victim-child against the villain of disease."[28] He thus translates guilt and fear into love, a precious kind of love measured in money.

Lewis's regeneration began in 1983 with the release of Martin Scorcese's *The King of Comedy*. Jerry plays Jerry in a strikingly—for him—understated performance. The 1990s witnessed a resurgence of interest in and admiration for Jerry Lewis. *Washington Post* media critic Tom Shales led the chorus of cheers.[29]

> What do you know? The French were right—Jerry Lewis is a genius after all. At least, a genius of sorts. He wants to be thought of as a great film director, but it's as a performer that he's earned his honors. He is a comic genius. He also has a genius for surviving and is, inevitably, a symbol of hope. Who better to host the biggest telethon of the year?

The hyperbole came from a critic not known for hyperbole, and this view was shared by younger comedians like David Letterman, Steve Martin, Robin Williams and Martin Short, all of whom have acknowledged their debt to Lewis.[30] Clearly, Eddie Murphy's 1996 remake of *The Nutty Professor* pays homage to Lewis "as symbolic godfather" to contemporary screen comedians.

Seeking love—a staple of Jewish comedians from the shtetl to suburbia—and fulfilling his dad's dream to "make it" on Broadway, Jerry Lewis achieved apotheosis in 1995. He had traveled a long way from the Jewish Alps. From there to fame, from here to obscurity, he resurfaced as Applegate: the Devil in the revival of *Damn Yankees*. His Faustian bargain had at long last paid off. Thus, the sacred monster of medieval carnival culture that opposed the social order and generated visceral laughter among the masses returned to national favor. Were the French indeed right all along or was Leo Tolstoy's observation that "God sees the truth but waits" the appropriate measure of Jerry Lewis? American academics—this writer included—had underestimated him. My students, vintage early 1960s, deserve the last words: "He funny." The absent predicate represents the laughter that crosses class (lost?) boundaries and reinforces the bonds of our common humanity. In the final analysis, the healing power of the laughter may save more souls than the zealous minions of either Jesus or Moses.

Since I wrote this coda, Jerry Lewis was relieved of his role as chief fundraiser of the MDA telethon. Ever resilient, he resumed his career as entertainer. More significantly, he contributed his immense talents to a film, *When Comedy Went to School*, which opened on July 31, 2013, at theatres across America.[31]

Evidently, the "Sacred Monster" and Jewish Genius lives!

SEVEN

Comedy's Changing Landscape

Two Jews and a Black Crossover Artist

"America was born in the country," historian Richard Hofstadter astutely observed, "and grew up in the city." Applying this pithy observation, author Joseph Boskin linked that transformation to our national humor. Thus, 19th century vintage country humor featured long narratives with homespun wit issuing from Mark Twain. Twentieth century demographics, however, converted us into an urban nation with little time and less patience for extended deliveries, however humorous. Consequently, one-liners eclipsed old forms. Blarney was out; Henny Youngman was in.[1]

- I take my wife everywhere, but she keeps finding her way back.
- My wife will buy anything marked down. Last year, she bought an escalator.
- My wife is on a new diet. Coconuts and bananas.
  She hasn't lost weight, but can she climb a tree.

When the old-time religion waned, humor became a substitute for faith as urban folks ran around in secular circles. Protest, resistance, and heightened ethnic identification fueled the new comedy. By 1970 only 3 percent of the national populace, Jewish practitioners represented 80 percent of the top comedians in America. Blacks, led by Dick Gregory, joined the assault of laughter. Starting out in the 1950s and gaining momentum in the 1960s, comedians vaulted toward the cutting edge of cultural criticism.[2]

One of the most able chroniclers of the 1950s, David Halberstam is silent on the role of comedy during that placid decade. Perhaps he found nothing worth reporting on our protean subject. During the early 1950s, mainstream

American humor was "good natured, trivial, kindly," author Mel Watkins observed.[3] Beneath that bland "I like Ike" exterior, however, lurked darker impulses, indeed cultural demons rife for exorcism. Out of this cauldron of boiling ingredients emerged several comedians who not only challenged tradition but changed American culture with their caustic wit and "in-your-face" style. Most were Jewish.

Mort Sahl and Lenny Bruce dramatically departed from their peers, whose constricting formulae of "pee pee, doo-doo" dirt by innuendo jokes that had dominated the comedy scene. As children of Depression, war, Hollywood fantasies, comic books, muckraking newspapers, these innovative non-conformists mined a vast store of funny stuff. Psychologically, they used humor as a coping mechanism in confronting a hostile world.

Born in Montreal on May 11, 1927, raised in New York and Los Angeles, Mort Sahl was a precocious only child of progressive parents. He grew up addicted to women, sports cars, jazz, and fancy watches. Influenced by radio and films, he loved to talk. After graduation from Compton Junior College, he became a Trojan, i.e., a USC student. He worked at various jobs and tried comedy in small clubs. Sahl gained recognition at San Francisco's Hungry I. Sporting a casual outfit of sweater and slacks rather than tux, cummerbund, and tie, he scouted the daily newspapers for topical humor. Author Gerald Nachman describes him as intense, cerebral, aloof, icy, and flashy. He used Latin phrases and big words punctuated by a nervous cackle. His one deficit was a lack of warmth.[4] Sahl changed comedy's look, sound, and delivery. A jazz aficionado, he incorporated riffs as well as rhythms of this authentic American music. He spun out ideas that he improvised; then punched quickly with a barking laugh, and darted to another subject. Uneven in delivery, he forced audiences to listen intently as he tripped over his own codas. Eschewing *shmutz* (smut), he worked clean, thereby elevating comedy's style and substance. Sahl loved to shock as well as to inform his audiences.[5]

Sahl's first big joke targeted Washington's junior senator. Joe McCarthy, he quipped, fashioned a new jacket. It's really the old Eisenhower jacket with an extra flap to fit over his mouth. Mort took the high ground vacated by Will Rogers minus the rope tricks and the bumpkin mask. This casually attired graduate school dropout peppered the Republican establishment.[6]

- Ike's first election: We needed a man on a white horse. Well, we got the horse, but there's nobody on him.
- Ike: He kept us out of Mars.
- Nixon: He's been on the cover of every magazine except *True*.

- Answer to Senator McCarthy: Sir, I didn't mean to be subversive but I was new in the community and I wanted to meet the girls.

Sahl branched out to other subjects.

- Folk-singers. They wear velvet shirts open to the navel. But they have no navels. This is the ultimate rejection of mother.
- Scientific experiments on the adverse influence of tobacco that use laboratory animals prompted a moral question: Should mice be allowed to smoke?

Politics, however, fired his verbal guns and remained his bread and butter. On the 1960 election, Sahl observed that Nixon is trying to sell the country while Kennedy is trying to buy it. "Their chances look good. How about ours?" After the Kennedys, both our ship of state and Sahl's comedic sail lost wind. Thereafter, he seemed to emit more gas than gags. Following JFK's tragic assassination, Sahl's incipient paranoia, a recurrent theme in Jewish humor, hardened into the real thing. He grew callous to his own ethnicity. Queried by the *Realist*: "Do you consider yourself Jewish?" Sahl replied: "No, I belong to me. I don't consider myself anything to me. I don't consider myself anything."[7] To spite his race, Sahl sported a new nose and new jokes that failed to fly.

A true innovative force in American comedy, Sahl grew more bilious with age. He sneered at feminism. "A woman's place is in the stove." To hecklers, he used this saver: "I guess that's not the first time that you've failed in the dark."[8] As he grew more cynical and conservative, Sahl failed in the dark, too. He was galled by the success of younger comics like Woody Allen and David Steinberg. He once confessed that he smoked Cuban cigars with General Haig because they reasoned (or rationalized) that "they were burning Comrade Castro's Cuba down to the ground."

Several failed marriages, including one to China Lee, a former *Playboy* model, produced his only son, Mort Sahl, Jr., who ended his troubled life, a suicide. Now happily married to a much younger woman, Mort Sahl can take pride in his salutary influence on other comics, Woody Allen, whom he maligned, and Lenny Bruce, who took his newspaper gambit and ran with it to new comic territory.[9]

Leonard Alfred Shneider was born on October 12, 1925, the only child of an odd couple. Biographer Albert Goldman contended that Lenny's father was a Jewish mother in disguise while his mother, Sadie Kitchenberg, abandoned husband and son for a career in show biz. Only five when his parents separated, Lenny shifted from one family to another. Denied either a bar-mitzvah or a secular Jewish education, Bruce became an *amhoretz* (ignoramus). Possessing neither ethnic pride nor cultural anchor, Lenny went to sea in 1942. Later, he secured a discharge by posing as a homosexual.

Upon liberation, he intermittently worked odd jobs, returned to the sea as a merchant seaman, and studied drama. Under his mother's tutelage, he became a comedian. Starting in Brooklyn, he introduced striptease acts and performed tasteless *shtick*. His break occurred in 1949 on the *Arthur Godfrey Talent Scouts* program. Introduced by his mother, posing as Sally Marr, talent scout, he impersonated Edward G. Robinson, James Cagney, and Humphrey Bogart in a bizarre German accent. He tied for first place.

This led to better bookings. While on the road, he met stripper Honey Marlowe. After another stint at sea, he married her. Playing Pygmalion to her Galatea, he tried to convert her into a successful *chanteuse*. A near-fatal car wreck aborted that experiment. Fascinated by Honey's Roman Catholic religion and propelled by a need for "bread," Lenny impersonated a priest, Father Mathias, who raised money for a leper colony in Africa. Exposed, Bruce received a judicial rebuke but no jail time. He returned to the legitimate theater.[10]

Lenny Bruce stumbled into stardom around 1958. While Sahl hacked at politicians, Bruce blitzed all hustlers, especially men of the cloth. The only Jewish kid in a predominantly German-American Long Island community, Lenny had grown up thoroughly assimilated. This may have stimulated his almost stridently compulsive use and misuse of Yiddish phrases and overwrought mannerisms, which reminded author Nat Hentoff of the Yiddish Art Theater. Consummately nasty, Bruce relished put-downs pickled in Jewish brine.[11]

- Shelly Berman is the *goyishe* Sam Levenson.
- Sophie Tucker was a nymphomaniac *heis* (hot) for
  Puerto Rican busboys.

He gained a large cadre of fans at Enrico Banducci's Hungry I club in San Francisco, where Mort Sahl also started on the road to stardom. In 1960, Bruce earned $3,000 per week and sold 190,000 LP records. Uneasy with success and drawn to drugs, Lenny oscillated between a wish for sainthood and an inescapable sense of his own corruption. He confessed: "I can't get worked up about politics. I grew up in New York and I was hip as a kid that I was corrupt and the mayor was corrupt. I have no illusions."[12]

In his earlier bits, Lenny projected the hustler as the ultimate villain who sparks derisive laughter. He aimed his outrage at religious hustlers and business hucksters. Ad-men, he advised tongue-in-cheek, should make it "cool" as well as "hip" to contract cancer in order to sell more cigarettes. His best bromides were thrust at organized religion. No one escaped—not the Pope, not Billy Graham, not Oral Roberts, not even Rabbi Stephen Wise.

For Lenny, all residents of New York and other big cities were Jewish. "If you live in Butte, Montana, you're going to be goyish even if you are Jewish." Bruce welcomed Italians, Count Basie, Dylan Thomas, Eugene O'Neill, mouths, bosoms, rye bread, chocolate, children tushy kissers as Jewish. Among the *goyim*, he counted evaporated milk, Spam, George Jessel, Danny Thomas, baton-twirling, fudge, gold-star mothers and trailer-park residents.[13] Hip, hyper, urban, and glib, Lenny embodied Norman Mailer's "White Negro." He hung out with hustlers, strippers, and jazz musicians. With life on the edge and work on the cutting edge, he extended the limits. His frenetic delivery resembled bebop jazz, observed author Mel Watkins.[14] He incorporated black speech, jazz jargon, Yiddish phrases couched in the facile delivery of a New York Jew. Obsessively and shockingly, he talked about Jews. As a hustling salesman, he touted a German car: "Here's a Volkswagen pickup truck that was just slightly used during the war carrying people back and forth to the furnaces." Author Lawrence J. Epstein cites another Holocaust joke in which Bruce held up a newspaper with a headline proclaiming, "Six million Jews Found Alive in Argentina."[15]

Lenny served as stand-up therapist. He peeled away society's surface pieties. Epstein incisively argues that the striptease provided the operative metaphor for Lenny Bruce, who also assumed the role of judge and prosecutor.[16] A successful comedian is like a guerrilla fighter. He attacks and leaves quickly to fight again. Lenny stayed in the trenches too long. And he paid a high price: often busted for obscenity; once for using the word *shmuck* in San Francisco.

Bruce claimed that he was victimized by the Roman Catholic Church. He targeted religion in his act. In one bit, he traced the return of Jesus and Moses on a visit to St. Patrick's Cathedral, which took them through Spanish Harlem, where 40 Puerto Ricans were residing in one room while one stained glass window in the church cost $10,000 and the cardinal wore a ring that was worth eight Gs. Bruce pontificated: "More and more, people are drifting away from the Church and going back to God every day."[17]

Like other Jewish comics, Bruce harbored higher aspirations. Unlike them, however, Lenny regarded his role as that of a moralist. Dubbed the leader of America's counter culture, he used dirty words and provocative phrases to shock white Christians and fellow Jews into self-awareness. A latter-day would-be saint, cut from the cloth of Jonathan Edwards, he located our demons and urged us to exorcize them. Unfortunately, Lenny could not purge his own *dybbuk*. Earlier, Lenny had maintained a delicate balance; he could express contempt, yet escape punishment. Haunted by his own corruption—drugs, deceit, vocation, *shund* (vulgarity)—Lenny found himself in a "glass enclosure: from which there was no escape."[18] A chronic optimist, say, in the mold of Menachem Mendel, Bruce tried to break loose and lead his followers to some mythical promised land free of societal constraints and cultural no-nos. "A disease of America," in critic Kenneth Tynan's apt rubric, Lenny Bruce—marginal man, double alien—plunged the ultimate needle inward and self-destructed on a toilet in 1966. "From the 1950s to his death, Lenny Bruce posed a threat to white America. "Heroes," observed comedian Redd Foxx, "ain't made; they're cornered."[19]

Mort Sahl and Lenny Bruce paved the way for future comedians. One of their cultural heirs, Dick Gregory, was born in St. Louis, Missouri, on October 12, 1932. A pioneer, he rose to fame in Chicago at the Playboy Club, in January 1961. Since Professor Irwin Corey could not perform, Dick Gregory answered the call. The club hosted a large contingent of Southern businessmen who attended Gregory's debut. Somewhat hostile, they uttered racially tinged barbs. The young black comedian met the challenge, masterfully.[20]

> Good evening, ladies and gentlemen. I understand there are a good many Southerners in the room tonight. I know the South quite well. I spent twenty years there one night. Last time I went down South I walked into this restaurant. The waitress came up to me and said: "We don't serve colored people here." I said: "That's all right. I don't eat colored people. Bring me a whole fried chicken."
>
> About this time these three cousins came in, you know the ones I mean, Klu, Kluck, and Klan, and they say: "Boy, we're givin' you fair warnin'. Anything you do to that chicken, we're gonna' do to you." About then the waitress brought me the chicken. "Remember, boy, anything you do to that chicken we're gonna' do to you." So, I put down my knife and fork, and I picked up that chicken and I kissed it.

Prior to this sensational debut, Gregory endured years of abject poverty and no-future jobs. Raised in a slum, he learned to survive on verbal wit. Doing the "dozens" and "counter dozens," young Richard learned the ritual of insult.[21] The beneficiary of a track scholarship, Gregory attended Southern Illinois University for three years. After a series of menial jobs, he decided to try comedy.

Drafted into the army in 1954, he endured humiliation and burned with rage. Insubordinate, he chose the role of barracks comedian over that of court "martialee" by winning a contest with jokes like: "When I lost my rifle, the

Army charged me eighty-five dollars. That's why in the Navy, the captain goes down with the ship."[22] Return to civilian life proved difficult. In a brief stint as a postal clerk, Gregory claimed that "he was fired for routinely sorting mail for Mississippi into the 'foreign' bin."[23]

Starting in a several small black clubs, he honed his skills as a comic. Gregory realized that he had to be "a colored funny man, not a funny colored man" and that he had to engage in self-deprecating humor "before I can make jokes about them and their society."[24] Gregory employed guerrilla tactics. He hit hard and retreated[25]:

- Just my luck. Bought a suit with two pair of pants today. Burnt a hole in the jacket.
- Refusing to buy a lifetime membership in the NAACP, he joshed. "Told them, I'd pay one week at a time" just in case integration arrived one night.
- Wouldn't it be a hell of thing if all his was burnt cork and you were being tolerant for nothing?

Gregory artfully positioned himself to be the Jackie Robinson of comedy. He avoided the ghetto style of Redd Foxx and other members of the "chitlin' circuit." Influenced by white comedians on the radio, especially Bob Hope

The great Dick Gregory, the first black cross-over comedian, who, appealing to white as well as African American audiences, spoke out against racism. He used his microphone as a "bully pulpit."

and Red Skelton, Gregory lauded Lenny Bruce as the greatest, indeed as the Einstein of show business. Among the black comedians he drew on were Jackie "Moms" Mabley, "Slappy" White, "Nipsey" Russell, and Redd Foxx.[26] He recycled old jokes from Bert Williams and commissioned new ones from Bob Orben.

During his meteoric, if brief, career as a comedian, Gregory stayed current with biting commentary appropriate to the changing tides.

- I wouldn't mind paying taxes if I knew they were going to a friendly country.
- They say Governor Pat Brown's pink and Nixon's yellow. Does my heart good to see two colored fellows doing so well.

I recall a concert performance at LIU Brooklyn, where Gregory spent over two hours rapping and joking with our students. It seemed that he was reluctant to leave. He never uttered a four-letter word in a set that mixed politics, economics, history, and humor. Clearly, Gregory was moving away from comedy as his primary vocation. His co-author, Bob Lipsyte, contended that Gregory was bound for glory; first as an athlete, later as a comedian, then as a civil rights activist, diet specialist, and a prophet crying out in the urban wilderness against drug abuse, overpopulation, and a host of other causes.

"An artist must take sides" counseled his hero, Paul Robeson, and Dick Gregory embraced this role. Call him flaky, zany, and even borderline; nevertheless, he created a salutary stir in his wake along with Lenny Bruce and Mort Sahl. Thanks to this creative trinity and their many acolytes, "the Lion Act" ended and the Sambo stereotype was at long last laid to rest.[27] In this era of Bush League politics, it is imperative to remember this triad of comedic pioneers. Arriving in the gray 1950s, they turned on a generation of young Americans with their minds fixed on freedom. Today, we honor their vital contributions.

EIGHT

Jewish Humor in Literature

A vital stream of Jewish humor courses through the modern literature penned by Jewish authors. Harvard scholar Ruth Wisse cogently argues that it begins with Heinrich Heine, although Columbia historian Simon Schama and author Hillel Halkin detect significant traces in earlier writers. Certainly, the German-born, French exile tapped into his Jewish heritage for witty observations often etched in acid. As an assimilated Jew whose conversion to Christianity served as a potential passport to a good life, first in Germany, later in France, Heine expected other members of his tribe to surrender their distinctive garb along with their way of including the "bastard" Yiddish language in favor of full participation in German life. For him, Hamburg, with its large Jewish population, many involved in business, represented "Huckstertown."[1]

An elitist, like fellow apostate Karl Marx, Heine was embarrassed by the Jewish link to commerce or *geldt* (money) by association. He took the plunge into mainstream German currents with a secret baptismal on June 28, 1825, as Christian Johann Heinrich Heine.[2] He ultimately recognized this as a Faustian bargain that proved too expensive an "entry ticket" into European culture. Prof. Wisse cites Heine's self-characterization as "renegade Jew and phony Christian."[3] Ever ambivalent, he regarded Polish Jewish brethren with revulsion. He loathed their appearance, odor, and lifestyle, but expressed compassion for the many engulfed in poverty.[4]

Yiddish, of course, is a funny language. When I. B. Singer was awarded the Nobel Prize for Literature in 1978, he addressed a party hosted by the Swedish King, he explained why he continued to write in Yiddish[5]:

> First, I like to write ghost stories and nothing fits a ghost better than a dying language. The deader the language, the more alive the ghost. Ghosts loved Yiddish; they all speak it. Secondly I believe in resurrection. I am sure the Messiah will come, and millions of Yiddish-speaking corpses will rise

from their graves one day [and ask]. "Is there any new Yiddish book to read?" Thirdly, for two thousand years, Hebrew was considered a dead language. Suddenly it became strangely alive. What happened to Hebrew may also happen to Yiddish one day.

During the festivities in Oslo, Singer gave many interviews flavored with Jewish wit. In one such encounter with the press, he asserted: "We must believe in free will. We have no choice." After this "rim shot," Singer remarked: "The language is ailing. But in Jewish history the distance between sickness and death can be a long, long time." He lived into his 89th year.

Jewish humor is embedded in the Yiddish literature that Singer wrote and was propagated in the Yiddish theater. The latter form found modern expression on October 5, 1876, when Abraham Goldfaden sired Yiddish musical theater. Out this new genre of popular entertainment there emerged a clown figure called Kuni Leml, who embodied a familiar duality of weakness and strength. Conditions in Russia worsened after the assassination of Tsar Alexander II in 1881. Pogroms terrorized the shtetl residents who were consigned to so-called Pale, confined to these segregated hamlets far from the major cities. A mass migration ensued. Modern Yiddish literature featured the social satire of Mendele Mocher Sform, born Sholem Yankev Abramowitz; Sholem Aleichem was born Solomon Naumovich Rabinowitz and I. L. Peretz retained his original name, Isaac Leib Peretz. Each of these authors created sharply etched comedic characters that influenced the exiles: actors, writers, and musicians who came to America, where they continued to entertain the masses. These characters embodied two generic types: the *schlemiel* and the *schlimazel*; the spiller and spilled-on. The former slouched into modern European literature in 1814, the result of Adelbert von Chamisso's story, *Peter Schlemiel*, a man who sold his shadow to the Devil for a bag of gold. The analogue can be found in the Chelm stories of Jewish folklore.[6]

Mendele Moicher Sphorim, or Sholom Jacob Abramovitz (1836–1917), can be considered the grandfather of this literary movement. His portraits of *schlemiels* and *schlimazels* were designed to advance the cause of *Haskala* (Enlightenment) reform. His first major work in Yiddish, *Dos Kleine Mentshele* (*The Little Man*), satirized "corrupt politicians and hypocritical bigwigs … fattening on the spoils derived from taxes and religious imposts which these public benefactors were called upon to supervise," wrote Yiddish scholar Sol Liptzin.[7] Thus, the grandfather of Yiddish literature also sired the satire later employed by Mort Sahl and Lenny Bruce. One of Mendele's most memorable characters, Benjamin III, is not unlike Don Quixote; he even goes on a journey with a Sancho Panza type in Sanderl, his loyal squire. They experience a series of misadventures in pursuit of *die royte yiddelach* (little Red Jews), the remnants of Israel's ten lost tribes across the mythological Sabatyon River. Despondent over the deteriorating condition of Jews in Eastern Europe, he abandoned his poison pen for a kinder and gentler humor.

Sholem Aleichem (1859–1916), né Solomon Rabinowitz, followed. In a signature story, "On Account of a Hat," the principal character, Sholem Schachna, is treated like royalty because while he was suddenly awakened from a nap in a railroad station he inadvertently donned the wrong hat, one belonging to a Czarist official in Russia. Plagued by both guilt and fear, however, he returns the hat and resumes his negative identity. Author Ruth Adler provides psychological insight into this exchange. By giving the main character his own first name, Sholem Aleichem projected an autobiographical element. As Adler points out, he, too, had a shrewish mother-in-law, a carping stepmother, precarious finances, a penchant for gambling, and identity confusion with 23 pseudonyms. Subconsciously, this acclaimed Yiddish writer did not want to leave his old hat, i.e., traditional culture, in the station but he also wanted the personal freedom that the officer's cap symbolized. In short, the "Hat" story reflects Sholem Aleichem's ambivalence. Clearly, during the Haskala (Enlightenment) movement, Jews were unable to embrace core values in gentile society. Nor were Jews, on the other hand, warmly welcomed into mainstream culture. As traditional norms weakened, Jews faced a difficult period of adjustment.[8]

Aleichem's stories weaved similar themes into the fabric of his literature. As a child, I read *Motl: The Cantor's Son*, or *Motl, Peyse dem Chazens* in the original while attending *Shule*, a secular school for the study of Jewish culture.[9] In the chapter that describes the attention lavished upon this young boy after his father's death, he declares: *Mir is gut, Ich bin a yosem!* That affirmation—"It's great to be an orphan!"—reverberates to this day. In a nutshell, pain and joy mix as tears are salted with laughter, conveying the great irony embedded in Jewish humor. The novel traces the trek of Motl's family to America in search of a better life, battles with older brother Eli, the brother's wife, and their friend Pinye. Motl represents the happy childhood that few in the Russian Pale, including his creator, experienced. In America with his extended family, Motl marvels at his new environment[10]:

> The ride into the city of New York is dreadful. The ride itself isn't so bad, but transferring from one trolley to another is difficult. As soon as you sit down—aha! You're flying like eagles through the air over a long, narrow bridge, afraid for your life. They call it the elevated here. Do you think that's it? Just wait a bit. You get yourself out of the elevated, and you have to switch over to another car. You reach it by going down steps, as if into a cellar, where you ride under the ground so fast that your eyes pop out of your head. They call this the subway. Why is one car called elevated and the other subway?

He is innocent, curious, joyful, even mischievous, but never malevolent. Indeed, Yiddish critic Sol Liptzin likened him to Huckleberry Finn.[11]

Indubitably, Aleichem's greatest literary achievement is Tevye, *Der Milchiker* (the Milkman). At this novel's heart, Tevye engages in five monologues featuring five of his daughters: Tzeitel, Hodel, Chava, Shprintze, and Byelke. Their individual stories describe their lovers and husbands paired by a matchmaker. Each mate, A.E. Rivlin observes, represents a certain cultural or ideological type.[12] She views the Tevye stories as semi-allegorical in that they mirror the changes that beset Jews on the edge. Tevye suffers the death of his wife, Golde, the conversion of his daughter Chava and the expulsion from home and village. Despite all the *tsores* of Job, the Milkman retains a survival mechanism: a sense of humor. He talks and talks: functioning as narrator, witness, judge, and observer, a kind of precursor to Jerry Seinfeld. Tevye assumes these multiple roles as he copes with contradictions and complexities "by his faith and his jest."[13]

The great Irish poet William Butler Yeats asserted that from the arguments with others we devise rhetoric; from the arguments with ourselves, we create poetry. Thus, Tevye joins the celebrated few who, through self-reference, versify. In his humanistic monologues, he self-identifies as good-for-nothing, brute, old woman, fool, burden-bearer, and animal. Yet he also rebels—in words, not deeds—against those who exert more power than he does: God, government, gentiles, women, and the younger generation. Ingeniously, Rivlin notes that Tevye's complex relationship with God derives from a common name, Tuv-Ya, because Ya is an abbreviation of Yehovah or Jehovah. To a deity who is called "merciful" how does one continue to endure a life without mercy? And in the absence of a higher authority to whom does one appeal? The only option for Tevye is the cosmic *kvetch*. His language teems with words, proverbs, commentaries and inside-jokes. Creatively, he throws new light on old adages. The Milkman never turns sour. On the one hand, he declares: "all is vanity" yet on the other "everything will be all right."[14] His speech flows like a river, Rivlin insists, gushing and idling in alternating currents. Though the river often overflows into tragedy, Tevye presses onward minus self-pity, syrupy sentimentality, and *mazel* (luck). He must speak out in simple, fluid, vivid style. This speech— laced with puns, gossip, misquotes from Biblical sources, and lost battles— provides mental balance through catharsis, if not therapy. Although a chronic loser, he gains self-esteem with humor, the "weapon of the weak." Like his American counterpart, Mark Twain, Sholem Aleichem intuited a profound truth, namely, "The hidden source of humor is not gaiety but grief."[15]

Sholem Aleichem died before finishing this last novel. Approximately 100,000 gathered to mourn his passing. The Educational Alliance held a memorial service at 197 East Broadway that attracted an overflow crowd of bereaved admirers. His legacy is affirmed in no small measure due to *Fiddler on the Roof*, a brilliant transformation of the Tevye stories to the Broadway stage in 1964 and, in 1971, to the silver screen. Not always faithful to the original text, the updated version, elevated by a wonderful score (by Sheldon Harnick and Jerry Bock) and Hollywood *glitz* (as opposed to *galitzianer*), brought the tragi-comic Jewish experience to millions of viewers around the world. His final wishes for burial demonstrated his true identification as *folksmentsch*: a man of the people."[16]

> Wherever I die, I wish to be buried not among aristocrats, big shots, or wealthy people, but precisely among ordinary folk, workers, the real Jewish people, so that the gravestone which will be placed on my grave will beautify the simple graves around me, and the simple graves will beautify my grave, just as the simple, honest folk during my life beautified their folkwriter.

Apparently, for this extraordinary writer/humorist Sholem Aleichem, death as well as life was with ordinary people.

Aleichem's contemporary, I. L. Peretz (1852–1915), preferred a more serious approach, culminating in Bontsche Shveig or Bontsche "The Silent." After a life of dire deprivation and benevolent deeds, Bontsche receives a warm welcome in heaven. The angels offer to reward his most virtuous life by granting him a reward of his own choice. All he asks for is a hot roll with fresh butter each morning. And the angels sighed in disbelief while the prosecutor, Bontsche's adversary smirks. This self-mocking irony courses through all Jewish literature from the Middle Ages to the present. In the 12th century, poet Solomon Ibn Ezra wrote[17]:

> If I sold shrouds, no one would die
> If I sold lamps, then in the sky
> The sun, for spite, would shine by night.

American Jewish writers borrowed from their European predecessors. Among the many who tapped into this vital tradition, a remarkable trio invites attention in our study. In chronological order, Saul Bellow, Bernard Malamud, and Philip Roth enter kvetching as well as laughing. Trailblazer Saul Bellow, Canadian born, Chicago raised and grazed, represents a new kind of author along with his colleagues whom he dubbed in a literary "selfie" the "Hart, Schafner, and Marx" of American-Jewish writers.[18] Why not? After all, for many years, Jews have mastered the needle trades. This triad of immensely talented writers provoked envy and evoked mockery in the works of Gore Vidal, Truman Capote, Edward Hoagland, Katherine Anne Porter, and John Updike (more gently). Easy targets, this gifted trio refused to be packaged or identified as Jewish writers, per se. Bernard Malamud conceded that he wrote about Jews because they fired his imagination. In his literary *oeuvre*, Jews became prototypes of universal suffering, in fiction as well as in life. Bellow insisted, via Augie March, that he hailed from native soil, in these words[19]: "I am an American, Chicago born—Chicago that somber city—and go at things as I have taught myself, free style, and will make the record in my own way; first to knock, first admitted; sometimes an innocent knock, sometimes a not so innocent." Among the three, only Saul Bellow won the coveted Nobel Prize for literature. A deserving Philip Roth speculated how he could have gained this elusive prize: "I wonder if I had called *Portnoy's Complaint... The Orgasm under Rapacious Capitalism* if I would have earned the favor of the Swedish Academy."[20] Both Roth and Malamud had to settle for many other (but lesser) prizes.

One neglected facet of Bellow's work is his attempt at playwriting "mental comedies." He deserves credit, critic Keith Opdahl argues, for expanding his range. Theater allowed Bellow to indulge in farce: coupling high and low, "earthy and sublime, the passionate and sentimental" after the fashion of Yiddish theater and vaudeville.[21] Bellow's principal characters seek freedom from WASP hegemony. Like his two partners in fiction, Malamud and Roth, he resisted the rubric of Jewish writer. Most pointedly, Opdahl demonstrates how deeply Yiddish influenced Bellow's writing style with repetition, question, inversion, allusion, and inflection."[22]

Critics seem to agree that Bellow's first two novels did not evoke either a strong Jewish identity or his best work, though principal characters in each—Tamkin personifies a shtetl *shnorrer*, and Wilhelm, a klutz. In subsequent novels, Henderson and Humboldt are portrayed as *meshugoyim*, or crazies.[23] Clearly, Bellow furnishes his novels with Jewish types who wrestle with polar pulls towards the secular and the sacred.[24] Before he became famous, Bellow and his friend Isaac Rosenfeld enjoyed crafting parodies of poetry in Yiddish. Here is one particularly hilarious spoof of T.S. Eliot's "The Love Song of J. Alfred Prufrock."[25]

Nu-zhe, kum-zhe, ich un du
Ven der ovnt shteyt unter dem himl

Vi a leymener goylem af tishebov
Lomir geyn gichm durch geselech
vos dreyn zich
Vi di boar bay dem rov...
In tsimer vu die wayber zenen
Redt me fun Marx un Lenin
Ikh ver alt, Ich ver alt
Un mayn pupik vert mir kalt.

Nu, let us go, you and I,
When the evening stands beneath the sky
Like a clay golem on Tisha B'av
Let us go through streets, that twist themselves
Like the rabbi's beard
In the room where the women are
They speak of Karl Marx and Lenin
I grow old, I grow old
And my navel grows cold.

Augie March introduces us to the first genuine Jewish-American novel, *sans souci* (without regrets or apologies) to a broad spectrum of readers. Jewish derivatives of Spain's Don Quixote and the picaresque adventures of Augie are laced with Yiddish words as well as ghetto rhythms. Loose, colloquial speech, according to critic Allan Guttmann, defines this comic anti-hero. With a profoundly Jewish self-critical laughter, Augie made a "joyful noise."[26] Not until we encounter Herzog do we see the wise fool in action. Practically a schlemiel, Herzog projects Bellow's own messy private life, with intellectual animosity, petty jealousy, and obsessive womanizing. Bellow switches from the colloquial to the rhetorical style and back.[27] Professor Sarah B. Cohen added that this so-called wise fool is a deviant, a masochistic, narcissistic, anachronistic bungler. He goes from the kitchen to metaphysics. In the process, he forms a bridge between the world of Sholem Aleichem and urban America's "abrasive idiom." The comic mind, Cohen concludes, leavens intellectual flaws because it is self-critical, while satire fixes on the failings of others.[28]

Herzog, essentially a self-caricature, according to critic Stanley Edgar Hyman (no mean womanizer himself at Bennington College), was on the best-seller list for 42 weeks and sold 142,000 hard copies. James Atlas argues that the novel provides an anthropological record of Jewish life in Chicago through a glass brightly. Bellow, like Herzog, disdained Ivy League intellectuals, including Jewish scholars like the esteemed critic whom he contemptuously called a "Harvard kike."[29]

Critic Leslie Fiedler, with whom this writer tangled briefly at a 1974 Popular Culture Conference, argued that Saul Bellow and Norman Mailer, both alienated intellectuals, tried to imagine themselves as mythical Gentiles by aping Hemingway.[30] Perhaps, they tried too hard to play the *macho* card. Politically, Bellow started out as a liberal (like the vast majority of American Jews) with support of SANE, CORE, civil rights, and teach-ins, but, as biographer James Atlas insists, Bellow always resisted "the party line."[31] Ultimately, as evinced in *Mr. Sammler's Planet*, Bellow balanced German pessimism with Jewish optimism. And the latter won.

If Bellow ranked number one with a Noble Prize, Bernard Malamud trailed at number two. Like Nathaniel Hawthorne and other members of what critic Richard Chase called "The American Prose Romance," Malamud embraced religion, myth, folklore, and ritual in his literary creation. This is clearly the case in his artful short stories collected in *The Magic Barrel*.[32] *A New Life* conjured up a strangely familiar world for this writer and is possibly Malamud's most Jewish in tone. Reading this novel en route to California in the summer of 1964, after a brutal break-up of a two-year romance and just before starting a full-time tenure-track position as a junior professor at Newark State College (now Kean University) in New Jersey, I discovered a striking parallel to Levin. He was a depressed drunk, an anti-heroic schlemiel who belatedly heeded the advice of Horace Greeley to "go west and grow up with the country" at Cascadia College, a mediocre institution, as a low-ranking professor in the English Department. In stark contrast to his new milieu, Levin, a liberal humanist with a dark past, hides behind a thick beard (as did I) to conceal a clownish schlimazel persona in search of a democratic future. Levin's quest, salted with Jewish humor, courses through the novel like salmon returning to their spawning grounds. His new vocation is situated in the English Department, which teems with conformity, Babbitry, and boosterism.

Nature, however, lures Levin to a new sensibility. Although Levin finds the academy drab, even stultifying, the surrounding country exudes a pristine, primeval beauty. Sexual urges invite *tsores* (trouble). Thrust into nature, Levin sleeps with an undergrad female student, evoking guilt. Later, he finds a more appropriate mate in Pauline, the estranged wife of his departmental chair, in the woods, where he fondles her flat chest in pursuit of pleasure. Eventually, Levin learns to drive a second-hand car with a second-hand wife (shades of Fanny Brice's lamentation of "Second-hand Rose"), who is pregnant with her third (his first) child. Unable to change Cascadian culture, he lights out for the far country in emulation of Huck Finn, only this time with wife and stepchildren in tow. Although Levin no longer loves Pauline in a carnal sense, he sacrifices sex for love, the Platonic idea of love, ironically.[33] In this pica-resque novel, Malamud explores a variety of subjects, including the Korean War, McCarthyism, Cold war animosity, loyalty oaths, and politics. Almost Rousseauan in style, Levin's substantive return to nature enables him to embrace moral responsibility and social leadership.[34] Author Cynthia Ozick concludes that *A New Life* lines up favorably with Fitzgerald's *The Great Gatsby* "as exquisite in its evocation of American transformation." She adds that it is more than "another academic novel." And indeed, Ms. Ozick is on to something here. In conjuring up Nick Caraway's last lines in Fitzgerald's novel, Levin moves, finally, "against the current," unable to shed his old life: burdened by self-doubt, loss of idealism and love—the quintessential Jewish anti-hero or the salmon waiting to be smoked. Thus we are left with "ironic affirmation" in this undervalued novel and in the one that followed, *The Assistant*: regarded by some authorities, including Philip Roth, to be his best novel. In modern life, literature, and secular culture, a state of grace does not guarantee a return ticket to paradise.

My introduction to a deeper reading of Malamud resulted from a previously mentioned 1974 conference on Popular Culture, where I met author Sheldon Hershinow, who then was completing a book based on his dissertation. In that work, he formulated a thesis that illuminated Malamud's "double edged comic irony." Derived from the Yiddish folk tradition and issuing from the somber situation of East European Jewry, Jewish humor infused Malamud's prose in his attempt to reconcile spiritual aspirations with actual conditions. According to critic Robert Alter, Bernard Malamud employed *Yiddishkeit*, or Jewishness, as both ethical symbol and moral stance in that verbal portrait of the schlemiel-schlimazel duality. Malamud deftly delineated the conflict between old (as in orthodoxy) and new values in modern America as *shadchen* Pinye Salzman, reeking of white fish, encounters Les Finkle in *The Magic Barrel*.[35]

The most fascinating, if not the best, writer in our secular trinity is Philip Roth. I have no complaint with his Portnoy. Indeed, in concurrence with acclaimed critic, Harold Bloom, Roth garners rave reviews in this corner. Many less able writers have won the Nobel Prize, including one who wrote only one novel and a lot of short stories. One can easily imagine many of Roth's admirers emulating Howard Beale in Paddy Chayefsky's last film, *Network* (1976), opening their windows and screaming: "I'm mad as hell. And I am not gonna' take it anymore!" Enough bile; let us now praise a famous man. Roth's debut with *Goodbye, Columbus* hooked many young readers in 1959, including this writer who read Roth with great gusto. Larry Peerce's brilliant 1969 film adaptation captured the essence of Neil Klugman's angry young man as he bade farewell to Jewish American Princess Brenda Patimkin, her bratty sister, and her athletic but brain-challenged brother who had graduated from Ohio State. The wedding scene is hilarious, a true *tour de farce*. Every story in that collection from "Defender of the Faith" to "The Conversion of the Jews" generated many shocks of recognition and induced peals of laughter as we read them aloud. At Columbia University, my home away from home, Roth enjoyed iconic favor.

When Roth began writing novels, we avidly followed his ascent. In *Letting Go*, for example, there is a scene where Gabe Wallach visits his friend Paul's parents and his former girlfriend Doris and her husband, Maury, in Brooklyn. Gabe—probably Roth's alter ego—describes both their furniture and attire. Maury "so young, so fat ... hogged a Swedish chair that cradled his behind no more than three inches off the carpet." Doree—Maury's affectionate moniker for his pretty but paunchy wife with sagging shoulders, is bedecked in a white blouse and black toreador slacks. Left alone, Doree talks non-stop and Gabe listens, patiently, to her babble about her former boyfriend Paul who left her to marry a shiksa because she refused "to put out" for Paul and then married Maury. Gabe ends this brief encounter with a kiss aggressively planted on Doree's lips, after which she files her fingernails. This scene,

so artfully sketched, reads like a story arc that would find fruition in Jerry
Seinfeld's apartment.

What is this thing, to borrow a lyric from Cole Porter, called Jewish
writing? Is it like a Porter tune composed in a minor key? Philip Roth furnished an answer in *The Paris Review*, edited and published by his good
friend George Plimpton. In this article, cited by biographer Claudia Roth
Pierpont (no relation), Roth points to salient traits: "nervousness, excitability,
arguing, dramatizing, indigestion, obsessiveness, play-acting—above all, the
talking." For Saul Bellow, another close friend, it was the mix of "laughter
and trembling."[36]

Since it is impossible to take full measure of the genius that is Philip Roth
in one chapter, let us focus on several seminal works to probe the connection
between humor and identity in the Jewish groove. After two so-called academic
novels, *When She Was Good* and *Letting Go*, Roth published his comic masterpiece *Portnoy's Complaint* to the pleasure of many, including gentiles, and
to the consternation of those Jews who bemoaned another *shanda far die goyim*
(shame before the non–Jews). Portnoy, like his creator, transgresses. He goes
overboard in acting out sexual as well as psychological fantasies. According to
author Robert Greenberg, Roth's parents oppressed him: demanding perfection
and generating guilt. Consequently, this fictional son [or self] tastes forbidden
food: a *traife* lobster or masturbation on a bus sitting next to a sensual *shiksa*.
In sync with Lenny Bruce, Roth's comic persona is "brutally honest and ingeniously comic." He draws on a rich trove of stand-up comedians, sit-down
authors (Kafka is one), radio, films, ads, jargon and Yiddish dialect.

Earlier at Yeshiva University, in 1962, at a conference on "The Crisis of
Minority Writers of Fiction" featuring Ralph Ellison and Pietro de Donato,
Philip Roth incurred the audience's wrath. During the usually innocuous Q
& A, hatred inflamed the crowd, with Roth the principal target. He felt
branded.[37] This traumatic event also proved liberating in the long run. Five
years later, during that long, hot summer of 1967, with a new lover—May
Aldrich—Roth stayed on Martha's Vineyard, where he made friends with
Robert and Norma Brustein. To entertain them, he created Portnoy at the
dinner table.[38]

Leaving his estranged wife behind in New York, where she later died in
a car accident, thus liberating him anew, Roth moved to Princeton. Intensive
psychoanalysis and a little help from his Jewish friends enabled him to finish
Portnoy, the novel.[39] Regarded as one of three great novels in post–World
War II America (along with Malamud's *The Assistant* and Bellow's *Augie
March*) and a comic masterpiece, it generated sufficient controversy to propel
Portnoy to the top of best-seller lists. Jewish ire fed anti–Roth fire while the

author cried all the way to the bank, as a newly minted millionaire. To explain his sudden success, Roth cited Franz Kafka as his inspiration. He also ably fended off attacks launched by members of the Jewish establishment.[40]

So, why do we laugh *at*, not *with* Portnoy? Because, posits Roth expert Jay Halio, of his manner of speech, his penchant for over-the-top melodrama, and his agonized soul. Unlike his idol Kafka, Roth found a way to strike a balance between moral impulse framed by Jewish suffering and his ability to create his [or her] comic mode.[41] Finally, a good *shpritz* refreshes as it liberates. Roth accurately assessed the assimilated Jew. Oedipal guilt—*Es epes Oedipus*—produces a sense of Jewish righteousness, intellectual superiority, and ethnic sensitivity.[42] Though some Jews despise gentiles, critic Sheldon Grebstein argues, they pursue them and curry their favor. Portnoy must have his "monkey" on her back. This marginal man, anti-heroic schlemiel, archetypal Jew, is basically a loser, but one who does not quit. Professor Grebstein attempts to "decode" Roth's style. He detects an element borrowed from Mark Twain's synthesis of American folk humor, namely, the written word coupled with live performance as in vaudeville comedy. Grebstein notes an improvisational harvest, not at all random, of three bits or skits: bedroom, i.e., sex, bathroom, and kitchen.[43]

Author Jay Halio notes many parallels between Saul Bellow and Philip Roth. Both wrote about Chicago: Bellow in *The Dean's December*; Roth in *Letting Go*. Both attended Chicago University, a decade apart, and both taught there. Both used humor to cope with predicaments, often sexual in nature, in search of solutions. Halio further writes: "Portnoy's inner conflict rages between his moral self and his powerful hedonistic urges."[44] Portnoy's excesses entertain Roth's readers. As the many French who love Jerry Lewis attest, we too love freaks because we admire their courage, coupled with their human frailty. Halio insists that such freaks nurture compassion in us. Another critic, Hermione Lee, detects a clue to Portnoy's problem in an essay by Sigmund Freud in which the good doctor linked masturbation and constipation. *Merde!?*[45]

Psychobabble aside, Roth never strayed far from issues of Jewish identity. In one of the several Nathan Zuckerman novels, *The Counterlife* (1987), Nathan's younger brother Henry gives up a successful dental practice to become a right-wing, gun-toting Zionist émigré, who moves from New Jersey (Red Bank?) to Israel's contested territory, the West Bank, to shore up his Jewish identity. This was Roth's first attempt since Portnoy to grapple with *goles* (diaspora) and the role of Israel from the vantage point of an American. Themes of sexual failure surface anew. What also appears new, however, is the dialogue between brothers Henry and Nathan. While Roth clearly identifies with Nathan, the writer, he fortifies him with powerful words in defense of *Aliya*.[46]

> Everybody escapes.... They [grandparents] were escaping history! Here
> they're making history! There's a world outside, the Oedipal swamp,
> Nathan, where what matters ... is what you do—not what decadent Jews
> like you think but what committed Jews like the people here do! Jews who
> aren't in it for laughs.... Here they have an outer landscape, a nation, a
> world! This isn't a hollow intellectual game! This isn't some exercise for the
> brain divorced from reality! This isn't writing a novel, Nathan! Here people
> don't jerk around like your fucking heroes worrying twenty-four hours a
> day about what's going on in their heads and whether they should see their
> psychiatrists.

Living the "counterlife," brother Henry packs a powerful counterpunch.

While researching Roth, this writer experienced an epiphany of sorts. I learned to appreciate Professor Elaine Safer. My brief encounters with this scholar at various humor conferences were less than pleasant. At one particular conference, she refused to stop reading her paper on the premise, presumably, that what she wished to impart was too precious to withhold or to encapsulate despite the repeated and defeated urgent pleas of her panel chairperson to curb her endless chatter in defiance of time limits. In 1995, at another conference in Birmingham, UK, she entered a room in which I was discoursing on "Funny Jews"—now a chapter in this book—to ask for a glass of water. Rudely interrupted, I said: "No," politely. Recollecting this incident in tranquility almost twenty years later, I should have answered with a quote from W. C. Fields: "Water!? You mean what children drink and fish fuck in?"

I realize now that professor Safer has much to say and says it expertly in "Tragedy and Farce" on Philip Roth's novel *The Human Stain*. The novel fascinates for several reasons. A black man, Coleman Silk, passes as a Jewish intellectual who teaches at a rural New England college. He invites comparison with Anatole Broyard, former editor of the Book Review section of the *New York Times*. He incurs the wrath of a female colleague who openly hates but secretly loves him. A kind of schlemiel, Professor Silk makes an innocuous, ironic remark that a black student misinterprets as a racial slur that leads to Coleman's forced retirement. A passionate affair with a college employee who is physically abused by Lester Farley, her estranged Vietnam War veteran hate-filled husband, leads to a double murder. Finally, identity reversals conjure up minstrel and vaudeville shows wherein Jewish entertainers put on blackface to perform their soulful songs and crack their hurtful, stereotypical jokes.

So, Professor Safer aptly asks, should we laugh or cry? This predicament prompts a link to President Clinton's ordeal by impeachment in 1998. In both critical cases, moral vigilantes sought to destroy a powerful but vulnerable figure. Safer does not evoke Hawthorne's "Scarlet Letter" or Monica Lewinsky's stained dress. Rather she shows how author Philip Roth shifts from black humor to farce by calling attention to Roth's reminder "that we live in a bizarre cartoon world, where the ludicrous and the calamitous coalesce."[47] Safer zeroes in on Silk's archenemy Delphine Roux, who personifies "political correctness." Doctor Roux reeks with moral outrage, yet is attracted to Coleman, fatally. She provides grist for Philip Roth's humor mill and grinding wrath at modern society and the academy. Another farcical figure, crazed Lester Farley, epitomizes philosopher Henri Bergson's theory of humor, to wit "the mechanical incrusted upon the living." With machine-like precision, he kills his wife and kills Coleman Silk for being a Jew as well as his estranged wife's lover.[48] And Farley gets away with it.

In 1987 Philip Roth suffered a major mental breakdown. His mother's death, his father's decline, his failed marriage with actress Claire Bloom, poor reviews, loss of friends, and writer's block; all may have contributed to a lingering and debilitating depression.[49] Ever resilient, however, Roth returned to his rigorous writing regimen. In *Operation Shylock: A Confession* (1993), for example, put to rest the canard that he was immersed in Jewish self-hatred. Writing about Israel, Roth spiced his narrative with Jewish jokes and cartoonish names. Contrary to the uncritical celebration of Israel, à la Leon Uris, Roth unbound dealt with moral complexities facing Jews. In this controversial narrative, Roth satirizes Columbia Professor Edward Said—Ziad in the novel—as an outraged American Palestinian whose wife urges a return to comparative literature, coupled with anger management. Said, who spent most of his youth in Egypt, not Palestine, was photographed with his son hurling rocks at Israeli military police. Upon his return to Morningside Heights, Said managed to infuriate students and colleagues alike with his verbal missiles and false narratives. Several years later in a *New York Times* interview, Roth might have imagined Said in his crosshairs when he derided ideologues, critical theorists, and humorlessness.[50] In addition, Roth threw a counter punch against the holiday season punctuated and dominated by Christmas songs, the best of which—if not the most—were written by Jews like Mel Torme, Jerry Adler, and Irving Berlin. The alleged self-hating Jewish writer that the Semitic establishment loved to target counterintuitively found a viral strain of tribal affirmation, which he revealed in *Operation Shylock*[51]:

> The radio was playing "Easter Parade" and I thought, But this is Jewish genius on a par with the Ten Commandments. God gave Moses the Ten Commandments and then He gave to Irving Berlin "Easter Parade" and "White Christmas." The two holidays that celebrate the divinity of Christ—

the divinity that's the very heart of the Jewish rejection of Christianity—and what does Irving Berlin brilliantly do? He de-Christs them both! Easter he turns into a fashion show and Christmas into a holiday about snow. Gone is the gore and the murder of Christ—down with the crucifix and up with the bonnet! *He turns their religion into schlock.* But nicely! Nicely! So nicely the goyim don't even know what hit 'em. They love it. *Everybody* loves it. The Jews especially. Jews loathe Jesus. People always tell me Jesus is Jewish. I never believe them. It's like when people used to tell me Cary Grant was Jewish. Bull*shit*. Jews don't want to *hear* about Jesus. And can you blame them? So—Bing Crosby replaces Jesus as the beloved Son of God, and the Jews, the *Jews*, go around whistling about Easter! And is that so disgraceful a means of defusing the enmity of centuries? Is anyone really dishonored by this? If schlockified Christianity is Christianity cleansed of Jew hatred, then three cheers for schlock. If supplanting Jesus Christ with snow can enable my people to cozy up to Christmas, then let it snow, let it snow, let it snow!

Critics were less than kind. *New York Times* reviewer Michiko Kachitani carped on repetition, self-indulgence, and too much talk. The acerbic Ms. K missed the point. Jews talk and talk. That's our *métier*. A more hurtful review issued from a friend, John Updike, in *The New Yorker*. Saul Bellow's fifth wife, Janis, entered the fray with a spirited defense of her husband's acolyte and dear friend, Philip Roth.[52] Thanks to Janis Bellow, the friendship between Roth and her husband deepened. Indeed, Roth was blown away, as it were, by Bellow's "uncanny powers of observation, the naturalness, the seeing into human faces." Compared to this Nobel Laureate, Roth confessed that he felt like an amateur.[53] They stayed close during Bellow's fading years. While waiting for the end, they made each other laugh; about which Roth commented in despair: "He was saved by death."[54] In fact, Roth luxuriated in Augie March's opening lines exalting the process of being/becoming American.[55] In 2003, esteemed critic Harold Bloom wrote: "Roth has earned a place in American literature by a comic genius that can never be doubted again, wherever it chooses to take him next."[56]

Everyman (2006) visited the subject of mortality with these words: "Oh death, thou comest when I had thee least in mind." Touched by these words from an anonymous writer in 1485, Roth crafted a novel that is part autobiographical and which grapples with life's finality. There is no escape from a diagnosis of a terminal illness unless one takes refuge in a classical Jewish joke's punch line: "I'll see another doctor for a second opinion." In *Exit Ghost* (2007) Roth came to terms with life's vicissitudes. He dealt with that widening gap between old and young, the "no longers" and the "not yets." Still the contrarian, as Roth crossed over to his eighth decade, he mourned the loss of dear friends, and eulogized George Plimpton: a life force no longer. Despite the turmoil and because of the drama, Roth decided to remain in the New

York Metropolitan area, close to his abode in Connecticut. A Jewish atheist, the author of *Everyman* offers little or no solace for everyone.[57] Paradise regained for Roth, I imagine, is not fixed on some future mythical real estate in heaven; rather, it is situated in childhood innocence before the glands and the complaints of Portnoy kicked in. Much of Roth's fiction evokes the last lines of *The Great Gatsby*: "So we beat on, boats against the current borne back ceaselessly into past."[58] He adds a Jewish twist, of course, combining laughter and tears.

NINE

Dialectical Jewish Humor

Mickey Katz, Sam Levenson and Jackie Mason

Jewish comedians did not follow a linear path or fixed compass on their road to success. Some gained fame in situation comedies on radio; others on television; while quite a few never went far beyond their Catskill roots and Florida finishes. Over the years, they grappled with identity issues. Even the most famous tried to play down their tribal ties while engaging in the amusement business. To illustrate this almost toxic atmosphere, we will examine several salient performers and their diverse identities.

Author Henry Popkin, writing in *Commentary* when it still had a liberal political orientation, lamented the vanishing Jew in American popular culture. Popkin saw this as a defensive measure against the rise of fascism coupled with the resurgence of anti–Semitism on "native grounds." Another possible explanation stems from the frequent use (as well as abuse) of stereotypes originating in vaudeville and perpetuated in comedic arenas during the 1930s and 1940s. Popkin was correct in calling our attention to this disturbing pattern but the remedy that he proposed, like his analysis, was flawed. The debate started with an article by Irving Kristol, not yet the super neocon, who intimated that Jewish humor teetered on the brink of extinction, also in a *Commentary* article. Sam Levenson joined the argument, in the same journal, urging that "the dialect comedian"—not Jewish humor—"should vanish." Teacher turned comedian, Levenson felt that crude caricatures coupled with "mockey" accented English demeaned the Jewish people. Hence, he urged Myron Cohen, among other fellow comedians, to abandon this method to secure cheap laughs. Eventually, Cohen followed Levenson's lead and discovered that he could generate positive laughter with impeccable diction and excellent timing.

Sam Levenson had painfully absorbed a bellyful of grotesque Jewish characters on radio. The most successful purveyor of ethic stereotypes on radio was Jack Benny. While affecting a middle–American persona, acquired from his home base in Waukegan, Illinois, Benny's popular radio program featured two Jewish characters: Mr. Kitsel and Mr. Shlepperman, both of whom fractured the English language in order to titillate gentile listeners. Eddie Cantor did likewise with appearances from obvious Russian-accented Jewish characters like Rubinoff. That mode of teasing laughter from mass audiences stems from the vaudeville era when Negroes, Irishmen, Germans, and Jews emerged as standing targets for mass entertainment.

One exemplar who did not heed Sam Levenson's corrective advice was Mickey Katz, the father of Joel Grey and the grandfather of Jennifer Grey (who danced with the stars and won). Born Myron Meyer "Mickey" Katz on June 15, 1909, to Latvian-Lithuanian immigrants, he lived in Cleveland, Ohio. Before becoming a Mickey, he grew up in a warm atmosphere steeped in *Yiddishkeit*. Author Josh Kun, who wrote the introduction to the 2002 version of Katz's autobiography, makes a forceful but not fully persuasive argument for his subject's significance. Kun asserts that Mickey Katz is the missing link between early 20th century comedians like Menashe Skulnick and "Yinglish" pioneers like Leo Fuchs, as well as the all–English wags exemplified by Allan Sherman.[1]

Kun points out that Mickey was a fringe player. Minus Catskill roots, he never made it on radio, television or film although he created a Borscht Belt lyric—"I'll Be Coming Round the Catskills When She Comes" to amuse us. In the twilight of his career, despite Kun's assertion to the contrary, Katz did perform in the Catskills. As a Jew, Mickey rejected total and rapid assimilation. He wore his tribal identity on his sleeve. Unlike singer Tony Bennett, Katz never went "from rags to riches." No linear narrative led the diminutive Mickey to Hollywood.[2] Mixing and running freely from English to Yiddish and back, Katz satirized iconic figures like Davey Crockett. In 1950, a little-known actor named Fess Parker impersonated Davey Crockett on the silver screen, bringing instant fame and subsequent fortune while we Brooklyn-bred youngsters preferred Mickey's parody, "Duvid Crockett."[3]

Mickey learned to mix and match Yiddish and English from his father. In his comic routines, he parodied names of prominent Jews as a form of ironic return. For example, Katz recalled that his father, an avid radio listener, referred to Clifton Fadiman as Clifton Fetterman and Lauren Bacall as Lauren Bagel. Names of actors that his father could not remember were replaced by descriptives like *"der shayner"* (the handsome one) for Robert Taylor, "the tough guy" for James Cagney, and for Humphrey Bogart "the Queen of Africa."[4] It is author Kun's contention that Katz must be understood as well as appreciated in historical context. Anti-Semitism was rife in the U.S. during

Mickey's formative years, in the so-called "Roaring Twenties." Racially biased and pseudo-scientific theories fueled immigration-restriction legislation that barred Hitler's future victims from entry. Revived after World War I, Ku Klux Klansmen gained inroads in Northern states where they targeted Jews and Catholics in addition to Negroes. Henry Ford infamously circulated conspiracy theories and thundered against Tin Pan Alley for converting American music into "moronic Jewish music."[5]

It was against this threat that Mickey Katz, fortified by his father's malaprops, launched his counter-attack with parodies of children's literature that he labeled "literary matzopieces" or "not-very Grimm-fairy tales."[6] This catalogue included "Little Red Rosenberg," "Hansel & Ganzl," "Yoshke and the Beanstalk." Later, Katz took on the *cognoscenti* with "The Barber of Schlemiel."

After an IRS audit left him broke, he joined the ranks of what proletarian writer Michael Gold called "Jews without Money."[7] Looking backward rather than forward, Katz created a musical melting pot in which nothing melted, And nothing was sacred, not even a kosher cow. Consider Katz's "Kiss of Meyer" in lieu of a Georgia Gibbs torch-song hit: "Kiss of Fire."

An entire inventory of clever parodied songs caught fire in Katz's cauldron of favorites. Here are some titles:

"Shleppin' My Baby Back Home"
"Geshrai of the de Vilde Kotschke"
"Borshct Riders in the Sky"
"Herring Boats Are Coming"
"Dot's Morris, Not Amore"
"Come ona' My Hois"
"The Little White Knish That Cried"

Like so many other Jewish comedians, Mickey Katz had a musical start. He played the clarinet in a variety of bands. Following the precedent established by other musicians-cum-comedians, he plunged into parody. That venture elicited joy from his fans, including this author, and fear among the assimilationists. One of the patter routines that remain fixed in the "mystic chords of memory" is a riff on a wedding *simcha* (party):

> What's de matter, Mr. Fox? You can't do the one-two-three box?
> You're graceful like a piece lox.
> Mr. Meltzer, grab a seltzer!
> *De bubbe gecholished* (grandma fainted)!

Katz tried to capture a cross-over audience with a Broadway show, *Borscht Belt Capades*. A comparable variety show opened at the same time. Arguably it was too Jewish for the 1950s. What worked well in a niche audience or on 78 RPM records lacked staying power on the stage. Investors lost interest as well as principal. A despondent Mickey took to the road again, a choice that actually carried him to the Catskills for a career extension.

One of the saddest moments for this fan of Mickey Katz was his subsequent trip to South Africa, where he was greeted by enthusiastic audiences. To be sure, that warm reception was good for Katz and netted him some much-needed cash. Nowhere, however, in his autobiography is there any mention of apartheid. How could a Jew who faced anti–Semitism and witnessed the corrosive effects of racism remain silent? The sweltering heat of oppression eluded the ebullient dialectician. Feted by state officials and fellow Jews, he luxuriated in self-absorption but remained silent. The obligatory commitment of prophetic wisdom to social justice eluded the little man from Ohio.

Despite this serious flaw, Mickey Katz worked "clean" in stark contrast to contemporary comedians who sling four-letter words like short-order cooks used to do with hash, the kind you ate, not smoked. They hyphenate mother with a sexual act and offer little or nothing about social concerns. Don Imus, a "shock jock" attempting to emulate Lenny Bruce, resorted to racist and sexist stereotypes and almost aborted a lucrative career. The less we say about Howard Stern, another would-be Bruce, the better. Thus, a view from the bridge at another Jewish humorist with a social conscience provides welcome relief. What a pleasure, therefore, for this writer to discover a mother-lode of wisdom and wit in the Sam Levenson archives housed in the library of his alma mater, CUNY's Brooklyn College. What follows is drawn primarily from this treasure trove.

After graduation from Brooklyn College, Sam became a teacher. For several years, he taught Spanish at Samuel J. Tilden and Abraham Lincoln high schools. During the summers, the young pedagogue ventured up to the Catskills, where he discovered another vocation: "comedy tonight." Among the hotels that Levenson listed in his résumé were the Arrowhead Lodge, The Copake Country Club, Maud's Summer Ray (where this writer worked in the summer of 1955), The Fallsview, Kutcher's, The Flagler, Paul's, The Pines, Raleigh, Windsor, Tamarack, and Klein's Hillside. One Borscht Belt night of entertainment featured a spoof on the "Ballad for Americans," which Levenson called the "Ballad for Galitzianer" or "The Salad for Americans."[8]

At Arrowhead Lodge, Chester's, and the Nevele Hotel, Levenson crafted skits and polished parodies. One routine featured Sam, along with Moe and Henry Foner, that went:

HENRY: In your Easter bonnet/ With matzoh farfel on it
    You'll be the cutest lady at the Easter Parade.
SAM: Our sponsor Gloria's Castoria.
HENRY: Switch to Gloria's Castoria
    You can go twice a day, *kinnahorya*
    It will change your complexion
    And speed up your action
    The Scott's tissue boys will adore ya.
HENRY: Don't fake it—make it…. Listen to Dr. Kronkheit.
SAM: A man came in "Save me Dr.," I've been saving it for three weeks
HENRY: What did you do for him?
SAM: I prescribed a double dose of Gloria's Castoria.
HENRY: Did he move?
SAM: He moved once before he died and twice after.

In another skit, they spoof a popular film, *King's Row* (1942), involving a future president. The Ronald Reagan character bellows: "Cut off my legs and call me shorty." Often a "class" collaborator with the four Foner Brothers, Levenson refers to them as the "Four Flying Foners."

1. Prof. Jack, BA, MA, PhD, authority on Neanderthal man, his cousin Benny and uncle, the Fuller Brush Man
2. Prof. Phil, 23 degrees Fahrenheit, authority on the Punic war, Peloponnesian War, 30 years War, and winner of the European Peace Prize.
3. Prof. Morris Foner, author of that stirring novel, *Transfer—Out of Night, Into the Day Session* and *Life with Foner*, which brought plenty of Jack and "Four Sons," who brought plenty of trouble.
4. Prof. Henry, BBA 1939, *magna cum difficulate* at present indoctrinating stenography in the New York City high schools.

A better meatball, he added, can found in Foner's Fricassee Institute. Henry retaliated with this bit of doggerel in 1939.[9]

> Sammy tells us funny jokes
> Some are nice and some are naughty
> He is only 28 years old
> The jokes are over forty!

Author/comedian Joey Adams paid homage to "Uncle Sam" Levenson in his book *The Borscht Belt*.[10] Without bobbing his name, nose, or his identity, Levenson worked the mountains, which had everything: "girls, handball, bedbugs, chicken … and nature." Sam remembers funny lines.[11]

- Bellhop: "You won't forget me, Mr. Harris?"
  Mr. Harris: "No, I'll write you regularly."
- Proud Mother: "My daughter won a cha-cha scholarship at the Nevele."
  "The place is just what I expected: soft breezes, beautiful evenings, soft music—and no men."
- Sign in the bathroom: "Watch your children. Don't throw anything in the bowl."

Author Stefan Kanfer observes that "in Sam Levenson's comedy, the words were in English but the melody was Yiddish, a gentle ironic strain based on exchanges he had overheard in hotel lobbies"[12]:

> "I don't do exercises. Too old."
> "Just for the manager, make a little exercise. How can you go home and tell your friends you didn't make any exercise?"
> "All right, one exercise I'll do."
> "Good. You see your valises down on the floor? Lean over and touch them without bending your knees. That's the way. Now, while you're down there would you mind opening the valises and giving back the towels."

Levenson loved the Catskills because it conveyed a sense of immortality. While guests came and went, the teacher/comic seemed to stay forever. The Jewish Alps provided Sam with fresh air, college tuition, and excellent subject matter for a future career in comedy.

In his *New York Post* column "the Lyons Den," Leonard Lyons noted, on July 25, 1941, that three CCNY instructors (the Foners) who were suspended "now are working in the Catskills Mountains resort. They call themselves 'Suspended Swing.'" They worked at the Arrowhead.[13] The levity turned sour when the Red Scare experienced a revival after World War II. Eleven years after the Foners were ousted from City College, Sam Levenson was summoned to testify before the McCarran Senate Sub-Committee on Internal Security.[14] The red-hunting senators questioned Levenson, then at the height of his career in television. They cited a story in the *Daily Worker* on September 22, 1946. The American Labor Party (ALP) had sponsored a rally at Brooklyn's Parkway Theater. Committee members wanted to know Levenson's association, if any, with actor Sam Wanamaker, an alleged communist, who left for London in order to escape the Blacklist in America. Sam Levenson denied knowing the actor. He also denied membership in the ALP. "I am apolitical," he asserted, and provided his registration record as proof that he voted Democrat. No doubt assisted by an able counsel, Levenson pointed out that a "friendly witness," Harvey Matusow, had retracted his accusations.

Levenson conceded that he worked with Josh White but he insisted that his work was "purely commercial." Hence, his relationship with the crimson-tainted People's Artists had a simple rationale, namely, "I was eager to get ahead in my career." On other occasions, Levenson was not aware of "subversive" sponsorship." The entertainer did his "bit" to combat anti–Semitism at a Brownsville rally, collected his fee and left. Other agencies—William Morris and MCA—hired Levenson as well. To project a patriotic, rather than popular, front, Levenson cited his presence at functions at VA hospitals, Holy Name Society, Red Cross and other mainstream venues.[15]

Then, in a masterful move, Levenson cited an attack on him launched in the communist press. A hard-line *apparatchik*, brilliant but pedantic, Louis Harap maligned Levenson, as the humorist claimed with some hyperbole, as a fascist, warmonger, a preacher of anti–Semitism, and a reactionary. Wrested from context, Harap's quote assails Levenson for being "like a Nazi storm-trooper..." "I am called vulgar, uncouth, and generally anti–Semitic," clearly "not a favorite of the Communist Party." Finally, Levenson pulled out another chestnut from the political fire, a letter from his former principal, Abraham Lefkowitz, an ardent anti-communist, who touted Sam's patriotism, professionalism, and loyalty.

Fascinated by this turn of events, I decided to probe Louis Harap's diatribe. The document issued from the Levenson Archive, Box 353. There, a copy of an article printed in a magazine, *Jewish Life* (precursor of *Jewish Currents*) in January 1949, offers an insight into Harap's idiocy and Levenson's escape. The pedantic scholar begins with a sneering commentary which castigates Jewish intellectuals for "separating" from their people. Erroneously, he excoriates the use and abuse of humor that leads to "the clubbing of a Jew" and "the lynching of the Negro." He accused Sam Levenson, shades of Emile Zola, of supporting corporal punishment for children, the use of Yiddish curses, ridicule of immigrant parents' aspiration to high culture (as opposed to sports and low popular culture). Citing the humorist's alleged advocacy of "Anglo-Saxonism," male superiority, and the vulgarization of Jewish folk tradition, Harap compared Levenson invidiously with Sholem Aleichem. He took strong exception to the humorist's equation of a *mikvah* to a kosher aquacade. Harap posed the question, "Is Sam Levenson funny?" Yes, we affirmatively answer. And clearly, Louis Harap, the not-so-grand inquisitor, is patently *unfunny*.

In one brochure, there is a funny takeoff of Yiddish phrases.[16]

> *Kreplach*—The eternal triangle
> *Chrane*—A Jewish eye opener
> *Tsibeles*—All this and herring too

Mishpoche—Foreign relations committee
M'choten—Leader of the opposition
Naches—Something you get only from grandchildren
Shochet—Cutthroat
A Minyan—An orthodox stag
A Groyser Knocker—A man who does crosswords with a pen
A Fargenign—Front row seat at a burlesque show
A schnapps—Jewish antifreeze

Absolved, Levenson's career continued in high gear. Senator McCarran, somewhat different from his Republican colleague from Wisconsin, tried a more moderate route: eschewing a blanket indictment based on guilt by association. He gave several artists a slap on their wrists and a sermon on proper conduct. Several artists had to eat humble pie. Judy Holliday, née Tuvim, for example, played the dumb blonde despite her genius. Blessed with an IQ circling 170, she *mea culpaed ad nauseam*. Holliday attributed her subversive activities dating from 1941 to sheer stupidity. Defended by former Judge Simon Rifkind and heckled repeatedly by Utah Republican Senator Watkins, she cut a pathetic figure in an era charged with absurdity.[17] Also summoned, Burl Ives and Phillip Loeb swore that they were never communists or knowingly connected. *New York Daily News* columnist Ed Sullivan exhorted TV executives to ferret out communists while an editorial from the same paper claimed that McCarran's committee was too kind to Ives, Loeb, Levenson, and Holliday. Influential columnist and radio broadcaster Walter Winchell defended Sam Levenson in his syndicated column in the *Daily Mirror* on September 22, 1952. As a rabid "Cold Warrior" and fierce anti–Communist, his support carried considerable clout. *New York Times* writer C. P. Russell reported on the hearing more objectively, but his coverage could not save Loeb's job as Molly's husband, Jacob, on *The Goldbergs*. Philip Loeb committed suicide on September 1, 1955.[18]

As a former teacher, Levenson made many pithy observations on pedagogy. Confronting overzealous parents, Sam offered a few examples[19]:

- I'm giving Arthur a zero. He doesn't deserve a zero but that's the lowest mark I'm allowed to give.
- Time will pass, but not Richard.
- Not only is your Donald the worst-behaved kid in the class, he has a perfect attendance record.

Students had "savers," too.

- That's no zero, Pop. Teach ran out of stars; so she gave me a moon.
- F for spelling equals phenomenal!

- I don't wanna' make trouble for you, Teach, but my mom says if I don't get a better report card next time somebody's gonna' get killed!

Then there are euphemisms.

- Richard is very relaxed. He sleeps all day.
- In music, [your son] contributes nicely to group sing—by helpful listening.
- George is trying—very trying.
- David will graduate with the lowest possible honors.

Levenson's capacity for combing the past for words of wisdom coupled with wit endeared him to many admirers. Frugality dominated his early years. Asking Poppa for one penny generated a third degree: "You want *what*? Who gave *me* pennies? You're a good asker. Maybe you should work for the UJA [an anachronism]. You mean I have to pay you for living with us? You mean you want your *yerushe* (legacy) while I'm still alive? Just because you're asking, you're not gonna' get."[20]

Momma used a more subtle technique: "Sure, find my pocketbook." Not even the FBI could find her pocketbook. Even if found, there was never any money in it. "That's life," she philosophized, "an empty pocketbook, a cup of tea, a pebble in your shoe, or like an onion. You peel away layers and layers and come to—nothing." Sam concluded that his parents were permissive, especially his father, because he permitted the children to work. When his older brother Joe indicated that he wanted to go to college, Poppa replied: "So, who's stopping you?" Brother Jack said that he wanted to be a dentist. "Good!" Poppa interjected. "I need one."

The Levenson Archives contain a partial transcript of a television program hosted by Bob Lape on February 6, 1977, on which Levenson appeared along with fellow guests Bel Kaufman and Joseph Landis. The subject, "Jewish Humor," elicited pithy commentary. A Jewish joke, Sam asserted, contains certain salient features: consciousness, pride, linkage to the outer world, and an honest picture. Taking the long view, he cited incongruity as the motor force behind humor. Poverty, not wealth, powers the Jewish joke. He cited Bel Kaufman's *zeyde* (grandpa) as the exemplar. Through his creation, Tevye, he took God to task. Even during the Holocaust, Jews resorted to humor, as Auschwitz survivor Viktor Frankl revealed. Troubled by Yiddish crossover words to English that were primarily pejoratives, Levenson cited as examples: *sheister, mezzuma, geldt, gonef, nudnik, chutspa, shtik, and tuchus*. For Sam, a joke like "I owe God for my soul and a butcher for my meat" elicits either a "bitter laugh" or a "beautiful laugh."[21]

In this discourse, Levenson repeated his distaste for dialect jokes and humor that demeans. When moderator Lape asked why so many comedians were Jewish, Levenson responded that this apparent paradox is explained by "democracy in action." In a war of wit, Jews outsmarted their opposition. Swapping jokes, Lape's guests wrestled with the import of Jewish humor. The last joke belonged to Levenson. A dying rabbi calls for the town atheist. "Why?" his devoted congregants want to know. "Because," the rabbi pontificated, no, reasoned, "all the others I am going to see again; so I want to say goodbye."[22]

Near the end of his life, perhaps as a goodbye gift, Sam sent copies of his last book, *You Don't Have to Be in Who's Who to Know What's What,* to associates in the world of humor. One respondent, author Harvey Mindess, commented: I am devouring it with relish (we ran out of mustard)."[23] Nominated for 1980 Literary Father of the Year, Levenson received a letter from a teacher, Nettie Silver at Richmond Hill High School. She thanked Sam for "capturing everyone you met and [leaving] us with heart filled with laughter and love." That big heart bursting with love and laughter gave out on August 27, 1980. Before his untimely death at age 69, when he crossed over the River Jordan, Sam Levenson bequeathed to his grandchildren "a prayer for peace." It reads[24]:

> All the "aint's will become "ises" and all the "ises" shall be for all, even for those you don't like.
>
> I leave you unpaid debt, greatest assets. Everything I own, I owe.
>
> 1. To America I owe a debt for the opportunity it gave me to be free and to be me.
>
> 2. To my parents I owe America. They gave it to me and I leave it to you. Take good care of it.
>
> 3. To the Biblical tradition, I owe the belief that man does not live by bread alone, nor does he live alone. This is also the Democratic Tradition. Preserve it.
>
> 4. To the six million of my people and to the 30 million other humans who died because of man's inhumanity to man, I owe a vow that it must never happen again.
>
> 5. I leave not everything I never had, but everything I had in my life time: a good family, respect for learning, compassion for my fellow man, and some four-letter words for all occasions, words like help, give, care, feel, and love.
>
> Love, my dear grandchildren, is easier to recommend than to define.

With these powerful and poignant words, Sam Levenson, champion of the "VUPs" (very unimportant people) left all of us a legacy of love, leavened with laughter.

Arguably, the most successful contemporary Catskill alumnus is Jackie Mason. A Talmudic scholar with a cantorial voice from the Lower East Side by the way of Wisconsin, where he was born in 1930, Jackie graduated from City College—CCNY, or Circumcised Citizens of New York—with a B.A. while he studied for the rabbinate. He went to a North Carolina congregation, where he sensed *tsores* ahead when, discoursing on the danger of earthly pleasures, he fixed on a "fan-tastic girl" in the third row. He lost his place and space. So, he surrendered the religious vocation, which he had shared with his father and brothers. Putting his faith in gags and girls in one basket and liberated by the death of his father in 1957, he headed straight for the Catskills. There, he did jokes with a Yiddish beat. When he reached out to a larger audience, he was rejected as "too Jewish"—Mason contended—by Jews. As a waiter in Brickman's in 1958, I remember my colleagues warning me that Mason was always asking: "Where are the girls? Do you know any girls?"

Riding the *shlock* circuit, he paid his dues and tasted defeat. Mason, however, persevered with his signature sing-song style[25]:

> I'm still recovering from a shock. I was nearly drafted. It's not that I mind fighting for my country, but they called me at a ridiculous time: in the middle of a war! Now, I'm not a conscientious objector or anything like that, it's just that I'm afraid. Not of guns: guns don't bother me at all—but bullets!
>
> You may notice that I don't do much on the stage. Did you ever see Sammy Davis, Jr.? He comes on, tells a joke or two, dances, sings, does a tap routine…. It's because he doesn't know what to do. If one thing doesn't work, he'll figure he'll try another. Not me. I've got too much class. I don't have to do that. I just stand there.

Gaining confidence in his craft, he turned to self-analysis. He was so self-conscious that at a football game when the teams huddled, he thought that they were talking about him.

> I went to a psychiatrist. I said: "How much do you charge?" He said: "Fifty dollars." I told him: "For fifty dollars, I don't visit. I move in."

He developed "savers," such as: "You understand what I'm saying?" If no response followed, he would quip: "It's the foist time I ever saw dead people smoke." He went from $300 per week to $8,500. His fellow comics began to badmouth him. Then, that slip of the finger on *The Ed Sullivan Show* sent him into limbo. (Whereas Sullivan insisted that Jackie had "given him the finger," Jackie claimed that he was merely imitating the host's hand gestures.) With the help of his "yente" manager, Jyll Rosenfeld, a perky blonde with a slight lisp who became his girl Friday in 1975, Jackie Mason made it big on Broadway. *The World According to Me!* proved to be as successful as it was unexpected. Audiences—this observer included—roared with laughter to the point of tears and throbbing headaches.[26]

Everyone is amazed at the unbelievable might of the Israeli army. It's a direct contradiction to the image of the Jew. It's an historical fact that Jews were never fighters. Jews were always pacifists. Why do you think you never saw a tough Jew in this country? You never do. I never saw four people walking down the street saying, "Watch out, there's a Jew there!" Let's be honest about it: Did you ever see anybody afraid to walk into a Jewish neighborhood because he might get killed by an accountant? In this country Jews don't fight.... Every Jew almost killed somebody, They'll tell you: "If he said one more word.... What's the word? Nobody knows what that word is. Italians are just the opposite. *Bang!*

Reprised several times with updated jokes but with the same format, Mason scored successive triumphs. He had come a long way from rabbinical roots and mountain gigs. The critic Jon Garelick in the *Boston Phoenix* called his latest hit, *Much Ado About Everything* in 1998, a "Borscht Belt minstrel show." He vents on fellow Jews. Mason mimics *landsleit* at a cocktail party: eschewing the drinks in favor of the hors d'oeuvres. "You ever see how much food a Jew can hold on a cardboard plate?" He satirizes the grabby, pushy, hungry Jew who can find a cure for polio but cannot change a light bulb. Mason tartly observed a transformation. As Jews assimilate, they will avoid the Catskills "because there is nothing to do" and will go to Martha's Vineyard instead, where their activity consists of *shvitzing* and strolling with an ice-cream cone. Since Miami Beach is too Jewish, they go to Mexico: "the shithouse of the world."

In the second act, this increasingly conservative Mason mocked then–President Clinton as an amoral nebbish whose poll ratings go up with each crisis. "If he gets caught one more time, he'll be emperor of Japan." His imitations of Nixon and Kissinger—one, an unindicted felon; the other a notorious war criminal—are hilarious, if familiar. Updating a Zero Mostel quip, Mason claims that sushi is killing more Jews than Hitler. Both President Clinton and his *nafkele* are chided for their dalliance. "A Jewish girl is not interested in oral sex—in an oral surgeon, maybe." Mason needles Americans who buy imported water—"imported from a sink in Pittsburgh."[27] And despite his hostile attitude toward women, gays, blacks, Hispanics and liberals, he continues to engender laughter among gentiles as well as Jews.

As Mason zeroes in on our foibles, he reminds us that once upon a time in America, there was a special place: east of Eden, west of the moon and north of New York City, where the hills were alive with the sound of laughter, music, and tumult. Indeed, our entire cast of Catskill comedians contributed immeasurably to American culture because they put the Id back into Yid and the Oy into Goy (re: Philip Roth's Portnoy).

TEN

Up from the Bronx

Red Buttons, Billy Crystal and Robert Klein

Versatile actor, comedian, toastmaster and "roast master general, the "first Jewish leprechaun," Aaron Chwatt was born to immigrant parents on February 15, 1919, and raised on the Manhattan's Lower East Side. An indifferent student, young Aaron was questioned by a teacher: "Who killed Lincoln?"

"I didn't do it!" he shot back.

His parents, Michael and Sophie, were summoned to P.S. 105 on East 4th Street so often that, he observed, "They should have graduated with me."[1] Upwardly mobile, the family, including brother Joe and sister Ida, moved to the Bronx. Dressed in a sailor suit, aged 12, Aaron won an amateur contest at the Fox Crotona Theatre, with a high-pitched rendition of "Sweet Jenny Lee." A star was born.

Four years later, while attending Evander Childs High School, Aaron worked as a singer-bellhop at Ryan's Tavern, where he wore a uniform bedecked with multiple buttons. Coupled with his mop of red hair, he earned a permanent moniker, Red Buttons, from orchestra leader Charles "Dinty" Moore. After high school, encouraged by his father, Red scored a job in the Catskill Mountains as a singing bellhop at the Beerkill Lodge in Greenfield Park, New York, for which he was paid $1.50 per week, plus room and board. Since his voice was changing, Red switched from music to comedy, and from baggage to dishes. As a rebel with a cause (greed and gratuities) busboy, he filled fountain pens with cream for beverages during meat meals in defiance of kosher laws: charging up to a quarter per squirt.[2] In the so-called Borscht Belt, Buttons also mastered the art of stealing and relating jokes. He teamed up with a tall gentile, Robert Alda, who played his straight man. Short, impish, blessed with an infectious grin, Red entered show business, laughing. His new career continued in Lakewood, New Jersey, under the aegis of Danny Lewis, social director and Jerry's father.

Back in the city, he became a "club comic"—playing weddings, bar mitzvahs, conventions, and picnics. Once he played four in one night, earning $60. An experienced performer, he gravitated to Minsky's Burlesque, where he was spotted by Jose Ferrer. Since burlesque was banned in New York, courtesy of Mayor LaGuardia's fiat in 1942, Buttons found a new home, thanks to Ferrer, in the legitimate theatre as a supporting actor to the stars, Ferrer and his then wife, Uta Hagen, in *Vickie*. One year later, Buttons joined the Army Air Corps and the cast of *Winged Victory*, first a play, then a movie, featuring many stars promoting the war effort.

After the war, Buttons resumed his career on and off Broadway. A mediocre musical of 1948, *Hold It*, caught the attention of TV moguls and led to appearances on the new medium as a guest of megastar, Milton Berle. In one sketch, preparing to examine Red, Berle inadvertently ripped off his clothes along with funny undergarments to the surprise and delight of all but the victim of this prank gone wrong.[3] Buttons also showed a dramatic flair in his portrayal of ill-fated comic Joe E. Lewis. In 1953, CBS gave him a show. In a sensational start, Red impersonated several stock characters: Rocky, the punch-drunk fighter; Mugsy, the juvenile delinquent; the Kupke Kid, a dumb nebbish; and Keeglefarven, a Teutonic lout. Between acts, he would cup his ears, evoking the Catskill years minus the Yiddish phrases, and sing: "Hey-hey, ho-ho, strange things are happening." That refrain caught on. Youngsters, vintage 1950s, loved this comic everyman. A three-year run on two networks, CBS, later NBC, resulted in failure, especially among older viewers. Lacking depth, author-comedian Steve Allen argued, Red's characters ran out of gas. He fired writers left and right, sparking a self-destructive flame that served as an inspiration for Billy Crystal's movie, *Mr. Saturday Night* (1992). Superficial charm proved insufficient. "Dying," as thespian Edwin Booth (or Donald Wolfit, allegedly) lamented, is easy. Comedy is hard." (This famous quote has also been attributed to veteran character actor Edmund Gwenn.)

Resilient, Buttons turned to drama. Director Josh Logan reluctantly cast him as Sgt. Joe Kelly in a film adaptation of James Michener's novel *Sayonara*. In the story, Kelly defied army regulations as well as racist policies to marry a Japanese woman (Miyoshi Umeki) during the Korean War. Unable to sustain married life together, they commit suicide. For this updated and democratized version of *Madame Butterfly*, Buttons and Umeki won Academy Awards for Best Supporting Actor and Actress of 1957. This award-winning performance led to important roles in many films, including *Imitation General* (1958); *The Big Circus* (1959); *Five Weeks in a Balloon* (1962); *One, Two, Three* (1961); *Hatari!*

(1962, the last movie shown at the Brooklyn Paramount); *The Longest Day* (1962); *A Ticklish Affair* (1963); *Your Cheatin' Heart* (1964); *Harlow* (1965); *They Shoot Horses, Don't They?* (1969); *The Poseidon Adventure* (1972); *Gable and Lombard* (1976); *Movie Movie* (1978); *When Time Ran Out...* (1980); *Alice in Wonderland* (TV movie, 1985); *18 Again!* (1988); *The Ambulance* (1990); *It Could Happen to You* (1994); and *The Story of Us* (1999). Buttons climaxed his film career with two documentaries: *Goodnight, We Love You* (2004) and *Sid Bernstein Presents* (2005).

Red Buttons returned to television in *Knotts Landing, ER, Roseanne* and *The Love Boat*, and as a pitchman for Century Village condos. A ubiquitous presence at celebrity roasts, he delivered some very funny lines.[4]

- Sophia Loren just had a baby. His first words were: "Is all that for me?"
- Most singers are Italian, and most comedians are Jewish. And yet there's not much difference between them—one year of high school.
- Do you know why Joe Torre gave up catching for managing? Because he was too chicken to play catcher. He was afraid they would call him "Chicken catcher Torre."
- Elizabeth Taylor is building a half-way house for young women who don't want to go all the way.

On the road again, Buttons performed in Atlantic City, Las Vegas, and back to his roots in the Borscht Belt. In 1995, salted with Catskill *shtick*, he did an autobiographical show, *Buttons on Broadway*. He brought the house down with a rousing rendition of "Sam, You Made the Pants Too Long!" (which I witnessed from the balcony). His most memorable routines, however, stemmed from the televised *Dean Martin Roasts*, especially "Never Got a Dinner." Among the many major figures denied dinners were[5]:

Ghandi's mother, who urged her son: "Eat a cookie. Who's gonna' know?"
Henry VIII, who said to his lawyer: "Forget the alimony. I've got a better idea."
Moses, who said: "Stop calling me Charlton!"
Abraham Lincoln, who said: "A House Divided is a condominium."
Amelia Earhart, who said: "Forget about me; look for my luggage."
Moshe Dayan, who donated his eye to CBS.
George Washington's dentist, who said: "Knock on wood."

General Custer, the first man to get an Arrow shirt.

Sunny von Bülow, who said to Claus on their honeymoon: "Stop needling me!"

In his dramatic roles, Buttons demonstrated versatility, pathos, and impeccable timing, no doubt derived from his comedic experience. Whether a desperate marathon dancer who succumbs to a heart attack; a prissy bachelor who survives disaster at sea and the clutches of *yenta*-matchmaker Shelley Winters; a paratrooper trapped in his parachute on a church rooftop in Ste. Mere-Eglise, France; Red Buttons was there. Buttons tied the knot three times: two (with Roxanne Arlen and Helayne McNorton) ended in divorce; a third produced two children, Amy and Adam, and heartache when his wife, Alicia Prats, died of a drug overdose 2001.[6]

Red Buttons finally got a dinner in 1982, when the Friars Club honored him with an award, coupled with a roast. Although there is no record of his last laugh or last supper, he earned an Emmy nomination for his last appearance in a recurring guest role as Jules "Ruby" Rubadoux in the hospital drama *ER*, in 2005. He died of vascular disease at his home in Los Angeles, on July 13, 2006. The ultimate tribute came from *Washington Post* writer Tom Shales[7]:

> Part of an audience's fascination with Buttons was his apparent, astonishing agelessness. His red hair stayed red ... and his boy's face retained its confounding boyishness.... Endearingly fearless, ... Red Buttons rarely met an audience he couldn't conquer. Sides were split, guts busted and that quintessential merry little man invariably left crowds happier than he'd found them.

Robert Klein also ascended from the Bronx. Born on February 8, 1942, he was raised in an apartment house, a vertical existence, as he described it in a documentary film *When Comedy Went to School* (1913). "We never went out; we went down. We never went in; we went up." He fondly recalled the scents of that experience: "The hall smelled of pies baking in the afternoon, and boiled chickens and broiling lamb chops in the evening."[8] His father, a textile salesman, did impressions and "hung out" with Myron Cohen while his mother played the piano by ear. At DeWitt Clinton High School, as a teenager in love with music, he formed a doo-wop group, "The Teen Tones." The group competed and lost to a one-armed piano player on *The Ted Mack Amateur Hour*. Undeterred by defeat, Klein headed up to the Catskills, where during the summer he worked as a lifeguard, "bussed" dishes in hotel dining rooms, and entertained guests; all in an effort to increase gratuities as well as to finance higher education at Alfred University in upstate New York. Once enrolled, he imitated snooty professors to the delight of his fellow students.

Moving up the Borscht Belt ladder, he became an M.C. or *tummler*. Like his talented father, Robert did impressions, including a popular impersonation of Jimmy Durante, and delivered jokes with punch lines in Yiddish.[9]

Back in school, he played Shylock in Shakespeare's *Merchant of Venice*, which later became a subject for a cerebral but funny discourse on anti–Semitism. After graduation from Alfred, he went to Yale Drama School, where he studied movement, acting, elocution, and telling jokes. Antsy (a better phrase would be the Yiddish word, *shpilkes*), Klein left New Haven for New York City. In between auditions for Broadway shows, he worked as a *per diem* substitute teacher in junior and senior high schools. Sy Rose, a dear friend who coached basketball and taught physical education, remembers Robert Klein as a colleague with colorful attire and a funny persona to match. On several occasions, the school principal had to tone down Klein's exuberance and call his attention to punctuality. Perhaps lateness was the inevitable result of Robert's appearances at Greenwich Village folk clubs with frequent comic observations of a substitute teacher.[10]

After trial by ordeal at the Bitter End Club, the young and restless Klein lit out for the far country: Chicago, Illinois, and its famous school, the Second City. According to a fellow student, Fred Willard, Klein appeared "very political, very opinionated." He continued his gifted impressions of James Dean, Lyndon Baines Johnson and "gung ho" military men whose macho chatter lacked synchronicity with their action under fire. Richard Zoglin, whose excellent book provided most of this biographical data, believes that Klein benefitted from Second City's innovative methods, especially its forte in improvisation. On the road again, after a one-year apprenticeship with Second City, Klein returned to New York City and a part in a play, *Apple Tree*, with a high-powered cast: Barbara Harris, a Second City alum; Alan Alda; and Larry Blyden. He also returned to stand-up comedy.[11]

Tutored by Rodney Dangerfield (aka Jacob Cohen and alias Jack Roy), Klein found his comic voice in 1966 at the Improv. With improved delivery, Klein refined old bits (teacher as sub) and added new material to his repertoire. He dwelt on traumas caused by the "Cold War" and tapped into baby boomer nostalgia. One of his "hot" riffs, hiding under school desks to ward off a nuclear attack, evoked shocks of recognition along with ripples of laughter. He lampooned authority figures, including obscure presidents like James Garfield, whose only claim to fame was "assassination by a disgruntled office seeker."[12]

Inspired by Lenny Bruce and Jonathan Winters, Robert Klein sought relevance and spontaneity. Second City schooling provided the latter; keen observation and rigorous practice the former. Taping each performance for critical scrutiny enabled the young and restless comedian to find his groove.

Cigar-chomping agent Jack Rollins agreed to represent him. The big move upward occurred in January 1968 on *The Tonight Show Starring Johnny Carson*. First, he sat with Carson for a convivial chat; then he stood up, performed, and scored.[13] As a television performer, Klein inspired a young Jerry Seinfeld to follow suit. Seinfeld loved Woody Allen, too, but preferred Klein, who was warmer, more accessible, and less psychoanalytical.[14] In the early 1970s, Robert was really hot. Mocking commercials, he scoffed at the logic of hair-replacement pitches by an owner who was also a client. Klein also took exception to a condescending Geritol add: "My wife—I think I'll keep her." He challenged the fascist agenda of insecticides that kill "cute bugs." Author Zoglin cites Klein's application of incongruity based on the comedian's experience as a lifeguard at a Catskill hotel. A pesky child named Oscar defied warnings and ventured into the deep end of a pool and began to drown. Klein jumped in to save the obnoxious child, whose parents then tipped the heroic Robert five dollars. By what calculus, Klein wondered, does the rescue of a child rate that amount of money? Uncertain of the answer, he mined that experience in a comedy routine for future delivery.[15]

The young comic experienced rocky encounters on the road. Too cerebral for Las Vegas, not hip enough for college crowds, he had to recalibrate. A record, *Child of the 50s*, released in 1973, gave his career a big boost. A sellout crowd at Carnegie Hall did not hurt either. Two additional albums helped Robert Klein get a bid from HBO to launch a comedy series, *On Location at Haverford College*, in 1975. With the New Year's Eve airing, Klein scored a triumph that inspired younger comedians, including Steve Martin.[16]

Why, Zoglin asks, given his looks, talent, range, vocabulary, and timing, did Robert Klein fail to reach the top of our entertainment pyramid? A good question deserves a substantive answer. Perhaps, one clue is *mazel* or luck, which Klein lacked in critical moments. Another problem might have been a lack of judgment, illustrated by his turning down a co-starring role on *M*A*S*H*. Politics may have contributed to his less than stellar career. During the Watergate scandal, he peppered the Nixon administration with sardonic jokes. Klein caricatured Nixon's loyal if not always truthful secretary Rosemary Woods, whose "shuffle" caused an 18-minute gap in a crucial, incriminating tape. Klein accurately aimed his verbal barbs at disgraced Vice President Spiro "the Zero" Agnew, and Nixon, the "Crook-in-Chief," who tried to appoint a doddering senior senator from the South, John Stennis, to review the tapes that would eventually force the president from the office he had so palpably disgraced. Was Klein too risky or too safe? Zoglin asks. Neither, this writer contends. He was simply too smart for an American public that was in the process of "dumbing down."

As an actor, Klein exhibited far more range than any contemporary comedian, including the manic, self-destructive Robin Williams. Opposite Lucy Arnaz in the Marvin Hamlisch–Neil Simon musical, *They're Playing Our Song*, he was sensational. Though he performed superbly as guest host on *Saturday Night Live*, producer Lorne Michaels, harboring hostility towards Klein's agents, Rollins and Joffee, offered no opportunities for Klein to return. Nevertheless, at age 73, he still sparkles with timely wit. In a documentary *Robert Klein: Unfair and Unbalanced*, a satirical thrust at the alleged integrity of Fox News, Klein chanted:

> Barack Obama
> Don't *shtup* Madonna
> You're not the President of France
> Try to keep your pecker in your pants
> Go chase Osama
> Barack Obama
> Use your head, not your penis
> And for God's sake, keep it in your pants!

Klein serenaded disgraced South Carolina governor Mark Sanford with a refrain from *Evita*, the musical. "Don't *shtup* for me, Argentina!" He chided Senator Larry Craig for homosexual dalliance in a Minnesota airport after voting against gay marriage legislation. That airport, with good churches and schools nearby, Klein joshed, is now a major tourist attraction. He also *shpritzed* former New York governor Elliot Spitzer for his high-priced *nofke* (prostitute), thereby disproving the stereotype that Jews always get bargains. On the subject of fellatio, Klein created a soliloquy worthy of Shakespeare.

> Oh sweet Fellatio is dead.
> Blow thy winds, howl
> Come … come

Klein performed a brilliant riff on this subject at the premiere of *When Comedy Went to School*, in which he served as the narrator. During the Q-and-A after the film was shown at the JCC of Manhattan, Klein delighted attendees with a spew of Shakespearian words, à la King Lear, inspired by fellatio. Moreover, in his musical riffs on the aging process, with odes to Viagra and colonoscopies, Robert Klein justifies his position among the best and brightest on comedy's cutting edge. It's easy to see why Jerry Seinfeld regards him as a mentor: "Klein was a hipper guy [than Woody Allen], but he was talking to unhip people and getting them to laugh."[17]

Every comedian needs a mentor, plus a role model. Like his Catskills-trained mentor, Billy Crystal has been happily married to the same wife for

44 years. Unlike Alan King, however, Crystal was born in the Bronx on March 14, 1947, and grew up in a middle-class home in Long Beach, Long Island. His father managed the music shop in the Commodore Hotel. His uncle, Milt Gabler, a famous record producer, founded Commodore Records, which featured many great black jazz artists, including Billie Holiday. An avid Yankee fan, Billy's dad took his youngest son to Yankee Stadium for the first time on May 30, 1956. There, Billy found a hero: Mickey Mantle. When he played baseball in high school, Crystal affected a limp just like Mantle's. At his bar mitzvah, he inflected his Hebrew portion with an Oklahoman drawl. The idyll ended when his dad died suddenly in 1963.[18]

Comedian, actor, singer, harmonica-player, and narrator of *When Comedy Went to School*, Robert Klein, a "child of the seventies," lifted the legacy of Lenny Bruce to a more cerebral perch and influenced many comedians in subsequent generations.

According to *Slate* author Bryan Curtis, Crystal launched his career in comedy by watching a *meshuginer* (crazy) Catskill comedian "prowling the stage like a panther." Bitten by the comic bug, he borrowed the routine, replete with dirty jokes, which he hurled at members of his family.[19] After high school, Billy attended Marshall University. During a summer vacation in 1966, he succumbed to Goldfinger—Janice. Their first date was a night game at Shea Stadium on July 30, 1966. He transferred to Nassau Community College, where he majored in theater. He directed and starred in a production of *The Fantastics*. He moved on to NYU, where he studied film under Martin Scorsese. After college, he married Janice in 1970 and moved back to Long Beach, where he earned his daily bread as a substitute teacher. His wife gave birth to a daughter, Jennifer. Mrs. Crystal became the breadwinner while Billy played Mr. Mom. At night, he ventured into New York to perform at comedy clubs, such as The Bitter End, in Greenwich Village. In an interview with James Lipton, Crystal confided: "I had to rehearse material for a fraternity party on my eighteen-month-old daughter. Aside from a little dribbling, her feedback wasn't that positive."[20]

In his autobiography, written with Dick Schaap, Crystal traces his start in show business. He got a few laughs on the way to the hospital, prenatally. "It was the best womb I ever played."[21] At age six, he imitated his relatives while hanging up their coats. Influenced by television, Billy and his two older brothers, Joel and Richard, honed their own comedy routines based on what they saw. For example, they converted Mel Brooks's 2,000-year-old man into the 2,000-year-old teenager. Later, he drew inspiration from the insipid but campy *Joe Franklin Show*. Teaming up with two students, Dave Hawthorne and Al Finelli, whom he befriended at Nassau Community College, Billy began to write and act in comic sketches. The trio worked the college circuit for $150 per night. Billy's first solo gig was a fraternity party for $25. Twenty minutes built around a Howard Cosell–Muhammad Ali routine became one hour of solid material. Crystal would thereafter work alone.[22]

During a stand-up performance, Crystal caught the eye and ear of Norman Lear, who gave the young comedian several spots on *All in the Family*. Billy also appeared on the ill-fated Howard Cosell variety show. Dick Schaap needed a comic to grace a *Sport* magazine banquet, honoring Muhammad Ali, in 1975. Since Robert Klein could not make it, Schaap, close to panic, took Billy on the rebound. So this timid occasional substitute teacher on Long Island sat on a dais with Neil Simon, George Plimpton, Melba Moore, and Ali. Crystal strode to the microphone to perform[23]: He was fully prepared to take on the roles of Cosell and Ali.

> "Muhammad—may I call you 'Mo'?"
> "Sure, Howard, but don't call me Larry or Curly."
> "How fast are you, Mo?"
> "I'm so fast, Howard, I can turn off the light and jump in the bed and be under the covers before the room gets dark."

It was a sensational debut.

Billy schlepped his family to the West Coast to launch a film career. Stand-up led to the role of Jody, a homosexual, on *Soap*, an evening soap opera satire. Crystal invested the gay character with wit, coupled with dignity and compassion: arguably, a first in television history. Catskill alumna Joan Rivers employed Crystal for the starring role in her film, *Rabbit Test* (1978). In this farce, he played a man who is pregnant. In 1984, he joined the cast of *Saturday Night Live*. As a writer/performer/host, he created an amazing array of characters: Sammy Davis, Jr.; Rooster, an aging black baseball player; an old Jewish weatherman; Buddy Young, a stereotypical nightclub comic; Penny Lane, a transvestite piano player; gullible Ricky; self-abusive Willie; and Fernando in his Hideaway, a hilarious synthesis of Fernando Lamas and Joe Franklin.[24]

Billy hooked up with Alan King in a poignant film, which Crystal wrote: *Memories of Me* (1988). King plays a Jewish Lear who is alienated from his family until an unwanted reunion with his son, played by Crystal, reestablishes his humanity. Some viewers found the film a bit maudlin, a danger whenever comedians veer toward tragedy. This cinematic venture brought the two Jewish comics, one from Brooklyn who lived on Long Island; the other from Long Island who lived in L.A., together. A close friendship issued from this not-so-brief encounter. Crystal pumped King for information about the history of entertainment and the latter dropped names and topped the younger comic in their verbal *mano a manos.*[25]

In *Mr. Saturday Night* (1992), a vastly underrated film, Crystal deftly synthesized comedy and tragedy. He mined his Long Island past, his association with Borscht Belt comics, and the Hollywood experience to craft a self-destructive yet highly creative figure. Buddy Young, Jr., is a cruel narcissist who, author Lawrence J. Epstein observes, abuses his wife, daughter, and brother. His career draws on other Catskill comics. He begins as a lip-syncher, shades of Jerry Lewis. Like Sid Caesar, he stars in a variety show. Following The Beatles on *The Ed Sullivan Show*, he yields to baser impulses, punctuated with the use of his middle finger, not unlike Jackie Mason.[26] Buddy finally finds fulfillment in Florida, working the senior circuit. Perhaps the film failed to gain box-office success because it depicted the downside of Jewish comedians in pursuit of the American Dream. At one critical juncture, when all seems irretrievably lost, the aging comic visits his comatose mother in the hospital. As she lay dying, Buddy whimpers in Yiddish: "*Es geyt nisht git, mame*" (It goes badly, momma). At the funeral, he delivers the eulogy. "She died at age 91, much too young.... She enveloped us with those big, flabby arms and all was well." Then, humor leavens the pain. "Stan," he asks his loyal brother, "did you get mom's recipe for kugel before she died?" Clearly, food and laughter provide the recipes for survival.

Author Bryan Curtis finds a clue to the genius of Billy Crystal. He personified the "comedian as grief counselor." In his sensational one-man show, *700 Sundays* (2005), Crystal pulls comedic nuggets from grief, as Billy details what it was like to be 15 when his beloved father died. Crystal intuited that, contrary to Hollywood happy endings, life was freighted with sadness; often punctuated with a *yiddisher krechtz* (Jewish groan). Thus, a slightly depressed middle-aged person can identify with the films of Billy Crystal. Just as Harry Burns invites comparison with our lives of "quiet desperation, in *When Harry Met Sally* (1989)," so does the fake orgasm of Sally in Katz's Delicatessen, where the corned beef and pastrami coming through the rye evoke real orgasms. To this point, Alan King once observed: "As life's pleasures go, food is second only to sex. Except for salami and eggs. Now that's better than sex, but only if the salami is thickly sliced."[27] *Memories of Me* (1988), *City Slickers* (1991), and *Forget Paris* (1995) all speak to contemporary *malaise*: aging, alienation, marriage and its discontents, and the generational divide. Crystal combines a tragic sensibility with a comedic perspective. Never taking the big risk of another Catskill alum, Lenny Bruce, he needles Christ, gently. "Oh, I didn't recognize you with your hands down." Bryan Curtis concludes his assessment with a brilliant insight.[28]

> It is often said that Crystal is a peaceful man in a world of wild eyed schizophrenic comedians. In *700 Sundays*, he makes a single gesture of insecurity, a nervous, toothy smile in which the corners of his mouth curl toward his ears. It's his trademark face—what rolled eyes were to Rodney Dangerfield—and it almost always follows a moment when he has gone a shade too dark. It's the smile of the Catskills comedian Crystal so richly admired—a worried grin that communicates angst. But Crystal's smile is so mechanical that it glows with assurance—that no matter how tragic his material, his audience will give in. He unleashes it, and the laughs wash over him.

As healer, Crystal assumed the role of Dr. Ben Sobel, the "shrink" in *Analyze This* (1999) *un noch amol* (once more, with feeling) in *Analyze That* (2002). In both films, he exorcizes the *dybbuk* (demon) from a gangster personified by Robert De Niro. Becoming a doctor, albeit in a Hollywood-crafted fantasy, propels the comic to the pinnacle of parental wishes. An equally compelling symbol of his success is his role as host of the Academy Awards ceremonies in 1991, 1992, 1997, 1998, and 2004. A welcome relief from the ultra-*goyisish* Bob Hope as well as the woefully overmatched Chris Rock, Crystal's clever commentary scored with millions of viewers. His hilarious wordplay with Robin Williams and Whoopi Goldberg produced iconic moments happily "fixed," as another humorist, Abraham Lincoln, felicitously put it, "in the mystic chords of memory."

More recently, Crystal the healer has delivered poignant as well as funny tributes to fallen comrades in comedy. After Sid Caesar's death on February 12, 2014, Crystal recalled a show in which Caesar, covered with a bald cap, parodied Yul Brynner in *The King and I*. Hands on hips in that famous kingly pose, he grabbed his bare foot and bellowed: "Who's smoking in the palace?" Crystal laughed and repeated that line continually at various locales—the beach or the bathtub to induce ripples of laughter in others. Another sketch, a takeoff on *This Is Your Life*, hosted by Ralph Edwards proved inspirational. A shy Sid is feted by friends and relatives. Howard Morris as Uncle Goopy embraces the surprised Caesar, clinging to him like a monkey, as the much larger honoree carries the diminutive Morris across the set: first on his back, then on his legs, evoking hysterical laughter from viewers. Unable to separate, they continue to hug, kiss, and cry. Many years later, Crystal invited Caesar, in declining health and forced to navigate in a wheel chair, to his Broadway show, *700 Sundays*. Awed by what he witnessed, Caesar heaped high praise on the acolyte with a single word: "Wow." They had, as Crystal observed, changed places.[29]

Crystal's role as grief counselor was especially evident in his brilliant tribute to his dear friend Robin Williams at the Emmy Awards ceremony on August 26, 2014. He recalled the late comedian's antics at a ballgame, impersonating a baseball player in Russia who plays for its only team—"the Reds." When he catches a foul ball in the television booth, he shows the baseball to cheering fans and says: "I love America and I want to defect." Sitting with Crystal's older immigrant relatives, who talked about their difficult journey to America, Williams also claimed that he had migrated to America but only after he could fly in a 747 and eat a kosher meal. Tearful but restrained, Billy Crystal enumerated his friend's many virtues and refused to refer to Williams in the past tense because he is "so present in our lives." To mournful and worshipful fans, Crystal healed their spirits as he called Robin "the brightest star in our galaxy" and added "beautiful stars will shine on us forever. Robin Williams: 'what a concept!'"[30] Thus, Billy crystallized the essence of Jewish humor from Sholem Aleichem to the present: a synthesis of laughter and tears.

If we search for an appropriate historical narrative of contemporary American life coupled with comedic commentary, we can find no better example than in the memories of Bronx expatriates as well as in the antics of the Long Island son.[31] "City Slicker" Billy Crystal found Sally and national recognition at another time, in another place: east of Eden, west of the moon, north of New York City, and not very far from the Catskill Mountains.

ELEVEN

Sitcoms from
Benny to Seinfeld

Two forms of comedy have dominated American popular culture since 1945, writes critic David Marc. In his pioneering study, Marc distinguishes between stand-up comedy, the principal theme of this book so far, and its antithesis, situation comedy. Though he evidently favors the stand-up for heroic defiance of the machine-made modern world, his book is devoted to the less heroic form. Both occupy, he argues persuasively, a Janus-faced American portal into American culture because they are oppositional.[1]

Stand-up constitutes an act of bravado against a mechanical, indeed hostile, world. The solo performer either wins the face-to-face audience over or he loses everything, including control. It is like playing chess with a computer. The human player is vulnerable to hecklers, the mood of his or her audience, and the temperature of the room while the sitcom actors play to canned laughter and submit to a multitude of writers, producers, directors, and machines: an assembly line of insiders putting out a finished product. To illustrate his principal point, Marc directs our attention to Richard Nixon: toppled from office because of his Watergate Scandal. In a series of televised interviews with David Frost in 1977 and in staged performances elsewhere—Yankee Stadium springs to mind—in his post presidential and pardon years, Nixon tried to divert blame from himself to his advisors. This self-pitying, unindicted co-conspirator played the martyr disingenuously, if adroitly. Tearfully, he made the extreme sacrifice of resignation to serve his country. As comedian/mimic David Frye captured that hypocritical moment when he bellowed as he aped the president: "I love America! And you always hurt the one you love!" A more accurate reading of that singular moment would have fixed on Nixon, the narcissist with confessions of self-love coupled with self-destruction as the former president almost confessed to Mr. Frost.[2]

Stand-ups also self-destruct. Witness Jackie Mason on *The Ed Sullivan Show*, Mort Sahl with the Kennedy assassination conspiracy theory, and Lenny Bruce on a toilet. Situation comedy is safer, more stable, and less heroic. Whatever the preference, it is safe to say that without situation comedies, from radio to television, there would be little or no Jewish humor for mass consumption. Most of the early family sagas featured Jewish figures in various creative capacities: writing, acting, producing and directing. Too numerous to analyze in detail, we will focus on several signature programs that reflect their time frame and its principal concerns. Ultimately, each show evolved until we arrive at the door of Jerry Seinfeld's apartment. Two years shy of his actual 39th birthday Jack Benny, né Benny Kubelsky, made his radio debut in 1932 as a guest on Ed Sullivan's WHN show in New York City. With typical self-deprecating Jewish humor, he said[3]:

> This is Jack Benny talking. There will be a slight pause while you say, "Who cares?" I am going back to motion pictures in a few weeks. I'm going to be in a new picture with Greta Garbo. When the picture opens I'm found dead in the bathtub. It's a mystery picture.... She and I were great friends in Hollywood. She used to let me drive her car all over town ... of course she paid me for it.

A funny Valentine, Jack Benny was born Benny Kubelski on February 14, 1894, in Chicago. He grew up in Waukegan, Illinois, where his father owned a haberdashery. Hoping that we would become a virtuoso, his parents forced him to take piano and violin lessons. His hatred for this involuntary servitude to music would be vented in his future career through humor. Author Jim Cox notes that Benny also detested school, an attitude reciprocated by the schools from which he was expelled: Central High School and Waukegan Business College. Neither could he obtain steady work with his father, who fired him for "several screw-ups."[4] Despite parental opposition, Benny "hit the road, Jack" for several stints in vaudeville as part of a dual musical act, first with Cora Salisbury, later with Lyman Woods. During World War I, Benny joined the U. S. Navy. During one show, he had a speaking part with flashes of humor. From this transformative experience, Benny emerged as a solo artist with the violin as a prop and his mouth as principal organ. He also acquired a new moniker: "Jack Benny—Aristocrat of Humor."[5] On tour he met George Burns, Gracie Allen, and Sadie Marks, his best friends and future wife, respectively. After the pivotal interview with Ed Sullivan, Benny launched his own radio program on NBC, May 2, 1932.

In 1932, FDR was elected to the first of four unprecedented presidential terms. That year marked the debut of the Jay Gorney–Yip Harburg song classic, "Brother, Can You Spare a Dime?" and witnessed the beginning of Jack

Benny's long career in situation comedy. Like other major figures in this genre, Benny, a Jew, submerged his ethnic identity. On these programs, Benny and friends celebrated Christmas and played golf in high-end country clubs. Only Gertrude Berg as Molly Goldberg—who did not play golf or gather around a Christmas tree—openly identified as a Jew with working-class ties and middle-class aspirations. After 20 years of residence in a Tremont Avenue, Bronx apartment house, Molly and her family, husband Jake, children Sammy and Rosalie, moved to the suburbs, aptly named Haveville. Radio sitcoms also migrated—to television, which encouraged blandness (as in the Blandings' dream house), cuteness, emptiness, and boredom.[6]

Never boring, *The Jack Benny Program* had staying power. Combining some stand-up and lots of vaudeville initially, it quickly embraced a formulaic sitcom style with many writers who ground out weekly scripts that were carefully edited and commercially controlled. Benny emerged from vaudeville, armed with a violin. His successful run in media from 1932 to 1965 was cleverly crafted on continuity of characters. It was simple, familiar, and funny. Recurring themes—stinginess, age (39 perpetually), Maxwell Auto, fake violin virtuosity, vanity, and argumentative interaction with other cast members—offered audiences clean, Sunday night fun—for free. One admirer put it succinctly: "America had an itch and Jack Benny knew where to scratch."[7]

What made this experiment tick was Benny's modest demeanor as well as his close relationship with his writers. The target of most jokes, Benny conditioned radio listeners to laugh.[8] His cast of characters had clearly defined traits: the corpulent announcer Don Wilson laughed heartily and became the target of many "fat" jokes. Tenor singers Kenny Baker and Dennis Day provided loyalty and naiveté with an Irish twist. Aggressive bandleader Phil Harris played himself and spouted slightly Southern-accented jive talk when he addressed Benny as "Jackson." Flippant girlfriend Mary Livingstone (Benny's retiring wife off-mic) and combative valet, raspy-voiced Rochester (a.k.a. Eddie Anderson) rounded out the permanent cast.[9]

As a vaudeville alumnus, Benny incorporated many of its traditional *shtick*, including ethnic stereotypes, in presentation. Offensive at first, they morphed into more acceptable depictions with the passage of time and change in national temperament. Sam Hearn as Shlepperman became Jack's first ethnic foil, a Jewish type whose name in Yiddish means "one who carries heavy burdens," in short, a drag. His comic persona ended in the late 1930s, probably as a result of Hitler's war on the Jews. After World War II, Hearn resurfaced as a country yokel or "rube"—a caricature of a rustic type, comparable to Titus Moody (Parker Fennelly) on Fred Allen's show. In one sequence, he parades his voluptuous wife before the incredulous cast, all of whom are stunned by her beauty. He punctuates this surprise on a note of last-laugh triumph: "I guess I'm not such a rube after all."[10]

The Jewish type also returned after the war. A former photographer for the *New York Daily Mirror*, Artie Auerbach impersonated Mr. Kitzle (Yiddish for tickle; rhymes with pickle) in 1946. Hawking hot dogs at the Rose Bowl (my "gig" at Yankee Stadium and Baker Field in the mid–1950s), Kitzle sings aloud in thick, "mockey" accent: "Peekle in da middle mit dee mustard on top." On another program, he Judaizes certain names like Nat "King" Cohen, a favorite singer.[11] Arguably, the most intriguing relationship paired Benny with Rochester. In 1937, when he first speared as a spot performer, Eddie "Rochester" Anderson typified the black stereotype. He drank, gambled, schemed, dissembled, lied, and womanized. Because his popularity shot up faster than Jackie Robinson on the base-paths, Rochester van Jones (his underutilized moniker) became a regular. The traits that he brought to the microphone, vestigial minstrel traditions by way of vaudeville, gradually eroded if not completely abandoned. Humor expert Joseph Boskin, in charting that progressive trajectory, duly credits Benny for fashioning the "oddest racial couple in American culture. Not unlike the relationship of Huck Finn and Jim, the slave, the bonding brought enlightenment to the white person. Frequently, Rochester assumed the role of critical commentator evolving from cruel caricature to friendly assistant and moral guide as well. In fact, at times he served as super-ego correction officer to Benny's id-iotic behavior."[12]

To his credit—and ultimate profit—Jack Benny made himself the target of "cheap" jokes. During the Great Depression, being frugal was a necessity, not a sin. Therefore, listeners could identify with Jack, who gave them emotional permission to "economize." Also, humor scholar Lawrence Epstein observes that Benny's effeminate behavior (his mincing walk, for example) and his pseudo-talent as a violinist evoked empathetic laughter. Although Benny concealed his religious moorings throughout most of his radio and TV career, his ethnic humor synchronized with his times.[13] In fact, Epstein demonstrates that Benny saved Eddie Cantor's job in 1939 when the banjo-eyed comic attacked Father Charles Coughlin and was threatened with reprisals from radio sponsors. Later, in 1948, Benny emerged from the closet of political and ethnic neutrality and staunchly supported Israel, raising millions of dollars for the fledgling Jewish state.[14] He also encouraged celebrity guests like Ronald Colman to use Yiddish phrases for comic effect. Thus, the articulate British actor referenced "shnook," "schlemiel" and "schlimazel" with impeccable diction. And Jack Benny, true to Jewish comedic tradition, played the triple "S" fool deftly, if not defiantly.[15]

Biographer Milt Josefsberg regarded his "boss" as a kind of Jekyll and Hyde personality, although in a benign way. Onstage, he played the vain, unfair cheapskate for laughs. Offstage, he was kindly, benevolent and sweet.[16] Benny saw himself as a friendly, eccentric uncle. Steve Allen put it more bluntly: "Benny's personal character ... is as warm and generous as his make-believe character is despicable," which may account, Allen argued, for "his limitless success."[17] Although at his best on radio, Benny also had a long film career that spanned 37 years, from 1930 to 1967, including several clunkers like *The Horn Blows at Midnight* (1945), which became fodder for funny self-criticism on radio.[18] Jack Benny's enormous success, however, came with a price. By distancing himself from ethnic as well as religious roots, he established a precedent that many subsequent Jews, like *Mad About You* star Paul Reiser, in prime-time entertainment, felt obliged to follow. The "sha sha" syndrome merged with the "ha ha" laugh track all the way to the bank.[19]

Gertrude Berg's great achievement, author Donald Weber insists, was longevity on radio and success on television. Writer, producer, actor, and pitchwoman, Berg (1899–1966) created Molly Goldberg, a Jewish woman for all seasons and guide to the perplexed of all ethnicities. How she accomplished her goals can be traced to a mother lode of papers situated in the Syracuse University Library, where Weber found this treasure that unlocked the secrets of her 35 years of highly successful mediation.[20] Prior to her debut on NBC's Blue Radio Network on November 20, 1929, Berg had to convince skeptical moguls that a program about a Jewish family in New York City facing and overcoming a series of crises would attract listeners across the United States. From her first program in 1929 to her last, a series of commercials in the 1960s, Berg garnered enormous kudos from listeners who wrote to their favorite Molly.[21]

Unlike Molly, however, that character that she created and impersonated so deftly, Gertrude Berg came from a middle-class family. Her father operated a small hotel in Fleischmanns, New York, in the Borscht Belt. Educated and articulate (with some college credits), Gertrude affected a Yiddish accent to touch ordinary people. She loathed the label of "soap opera" that was often appended to her show. In a magazine article that Donald Weber invokes as well as quotes, Berg explained her vision. Instead of "escapist material," she attempted to show how "other people live ... as a powerful channel for the dissemination of progressive ideas, tolerance, and understanding."[22]

Berg's great achievement—until the "Red Scare" altered her agenda—was to counter residual stereotypes from vaudeville. She used the program to depict an immigrant family striving to gain a slice of the American pie. The Goldbergs imparted a positive image of a Jewish family, coping with acculturation. A Passover program on April 3, 1939, punctuated by a rock thrown into a window that interrupted their Seder, evoked the "night of broken glass" or *Kristallnacht*. On a more positive note, another program conveyed the significance of Yom Kippur to both gentile as well as Jewish audiences. Weber notes that after its initial airing in October 1934, it was reprised on radio in 1943 and for TV in 1949.[23]

A 1948 version of the Goldbergs' happy family reached Broadway. *Me and Molly* entertained theatergoers for 156 performances. One year later, Molly brought her folk humor and wit to television for a seven-year-run. In that span, Berg also brought highly talented Yiddish actors like David Opatoshu, and Joseph Buloff, and a young Italian actress, Anna Napolitano, later Anne Bancroft, onto the show. Social issues surfaced in 1949, including a rent strike when Molly's husband, Jake (Philip Loeb) refused to accept an increase. In line with the rise of consensus politics and the decline of class consciousness, Molly resolved the crisis by baking a cake for the landlord's birthday and brought *sholem bias* (peace), not only with a home-made confection but with a conciliatory assertion: "A landlord is also a person."[24]

Two characters on the show offer insights into how stereotypes influenced Gertrude Berg's craft. Uncle David, played by Menashe Skulnik on radio and Eli Mintz on television, projected a traditional image, favored and reinforced through media, of a whiny, feminized Jewish male. That character—critic David Zurawik maintains—continued to titillate viewers of subsequent television programs, like Stuart Markowitz in *L.A. Law*, and Miles Silverberg in *Murphy Brown*.[25] Uncle David cooks, wears an apron, and cries at the drop of a hat—perhaps Skulnik's porkpie *chapeau*. Zurowick asserts that the unmanly, powerless Jew is "an insidious stereotype"—one of the worst.[26] Molly's daughter Rosalie provides the second stereotype that evoked angry criticism. Serving perhaps as a precursor of the prototypical JAP (Jewish American Princess), in one episode she states her desire to have a "nose job." Her brother Sammy, based on Gertrude Berg's son Cherney, tells his parents that Rosalie is working to save enough money for rhinoplasty. This endeavor poses a challenge to mother Molly who "mixes in" to do some fixin'. Eventually, Rosalie changes her mind (and not her nose) when she meets a pregnant woman in the doctor's office who awaits a baby with a new nose, fearful that her husband will discover the truth when the baby matures. Molly convinces her daughter that she is pretty enough. The nose doctor ends this dilemma with a joke about his wife, a former actress, and her nose.[27]

What could not be dismissed with a joke, until Woody Allen's testimony in the 1975 film *The Front*, was the Red Scare. A scurrilous book, *Red Channels*, listed actor Philip Loeb of being friendly to communist causes. It appears, according to Victor Navasky, that Lee J. Cobb avoided interrogation by HUAC for two years. Fingered by Larry Parks in 1951, Cobb yielded to the less than grand inquisitors in 1953 and "ratted out" fellow actors Sam Jaffe, J. L. Bromberg, and Philip Loeb. Under oath, Cobb said that Jaffe and Loeb "controlled" the left-wing caucus of Actor Equity.[28] So Jaffe and Loeb were designated for termination. Pressure mounted to fire Loeb, Molly's television husband, even though he was voted "Television's Father of the Year" in 1950 by the Boys Club of America. Gertrude Berg campaigned for Loeb's retention but CBS, responding to General Foods' threat to remove advertisements, canceled the show despite its rating as the seventh-best show on TV. Transferred to NBC, the show survived on borrowed time as Philip Loeb was fired and the sponsor dropped its support in 1954. Gertrude Berg did agree to a settlement of $85,000 of severance pay for Loeb or "*geldt*" (money), coupled with guilt by association. Unable to find work and depressed over his son's health, Loeb took an overdose of sleeping pills in the Taft Hotel on September 1, 1955. He died, as one lamentation in the *New York Times* put it, of "a sickness commonly called 'The Black List.'"[29]

Whatever the underlying cause of Loeb's death, it must have generated much pain for his television family, if not for the Jewish titans of their industry, William Paley and David Sarnoff. Succumbing to the witchcraft brewed by that infamous senator from Wisconsin and his zealous minions, their honor stained, no longer "defenders of the faith," they caved in to the troglodytes. In Joyce Antler's excellent study, however, there is a silver lining—the important legacy of Gertrude Berg. She became the prototypical Jewish immigrant as well as American mother. Molly Goldberg served, Antler persuasively argues, as "a consistent force for righteous behavior."[30] Berg crafted a working-class Jewish family that changed with the times in pursuit of social mobility, but remained grounded in traditional values. As the matriarch, she proved that mother knows best and her husband, Jake, all the rest, while the WASPy sit-coms that would follow postwar suburbanization would reverse that trend. Lawrence J. Epstein correctly characterizes "The Rise of the Goldbergs" as a "cross between a situation comedy and a soap opera"— Gertrude Berg's protest against the latter rubric notwithstanding. In her view, each show evoked, shades of Sholem Aleichem, laughter, tears, and a moral lesson. Berg personified an ideal: *die yiddishe mame*. When popular song decried the cold outside, she projected warmth inside the Bronx apartment, where the patriarch Jake pursued "beezness" even on *shabbos* (Saturday), but, thanks to "Blue Laws" at that time, never on Sunday.[31]

To get on television, Berg suffered repeated rejections until she arranged a face-to-face with CBS boss William Paley to pitch her program. Paley surrendered to Berg's charm and intensity. On January 10, 1949, she made her TV debut. After two years, the itinerant Goldbergs, seeking better accommodations, moved to NBC. As "Cold War" tensions heated up with an attendant witch-hunt for the so-called "reds" in media, cowardly potentates surrendered to the red-herring mongers. Caught in the crossfire, Berg opted for a safe, non-political agenda, stressing family values and ignoring other troublesome issues. Despite her valiant defense of Philip Loeb, as mentioned above, she ultimately submitted to their demands: putting her own survival over moral principle that she so ardently promoted throughout her career. Significantly, David Marc's definitive study, *Comic Visions*, makes no mention of the Goldbergs and the equally important Jim Cox study, grants only scant references to this once highly heralded program featuring Mother Molly and her brood. Perhaps, in the long run, it was too Jewish and too tame for an America that was—in the memorable words of Bob Dylan—"a changing!"[32] An activist youth culture must have regarded this family saga as antediluvian.

In drawing further parallels in situation comedy, we need look no further than the Molly Goldberg archetype. Starting in 1988 in a situation comedy that basked in popularity until 1997, Roseanne crafted her own version of a blue-collar, working-class family, minus the Jewish trappings, but invested with dignity.[33] Roseanne Barr's sitcom success also invites comparison, however remotely, with that of Gertrude Berg and Jack Benny. Humor expert Lawrence Epstein incisively explains the appeal of this "outsider's outsider" (his words).[34] Growing up in an ultra-*goyishe* Salt Lake City, she suffered a mysterious illness which left her paralyzed for a period. Later, at age 16, she was hit by an auto, an accident that impacted her physically as well as psychologically. The cure required a long rehabilitation process: eight months in Utah State Hospital. She married young, bore three children, lived in a trashy trailer, and worked as a cocktail waitress. On the job, she coaxed tips from patrons by telling jokes, usually on them. Trying stand-up, Roseanne scored as a female counterpart to Jack E. Leonard (also fat) and Don Rickles. Gaining confidence, she gradually mastered the role that both Leonard and Rickles made famous, namely, "The Merchant of Venom." She also drew on the one-liners of Henny Youngman with a reverse twist: she put down her *husband*. In that vein, she followed Phyllis Diller and Jean Carroll as well. Other female entertainment figures suggest parallels. Because of her large girth and coarse features, Sophie Tucker posed no threat to her female fans. Neither did Roseanne. Like Sophie, however, she demanded satisfaction.

A clue to her rebelliousness can be found in her dysfunctional family. Roseanne's grandparents were immigrants. Her Boobe (grandmother) Mary may have lost her entire family in the Holocaust but not her Jewish sensibility and survival skills. Roseanne's mother lacked both as she emulated Heinrich Heine in a sense by becoming a Mormon and a missionary in search of a better life. When Roseanne's father cuffed her small brother, Boobe Mary, a 300-pound avenger, rose, slapped her father across the face, and warned him that he must never do that again. Grandmother Mary encouraged Roseanne's theatrics at an early age and fostered a tie to Judaism on weekends, at least. Her stage persona was crafted, Antler insists, with Boobe Mary in mind. On the sitcom, the overtly Jewish actress, Shelley Winters played a character named Nana Mary. Although self-advertised as "Domestic Goddess" in a white trash milieu (she lived in a trailer with husband number one), she was really a Jewish mother minus the *mezuzah*. Pushing the envelope, Roseanne Barr brought to this anti–Molly Goldberg her whole baggage of feminism, marriage, weight issues, nonconformity, identity confusion, rage, and return, albeit subtle, to Jewish roots.[35]

Unlike Molly Goldberg's personification of the perfect *yiddisher mame* "the self-sacrificing mother and tireless *ballasbuste*" that Sophie Tucker extolled in sentimental song, Roseanne exuded malice and sloth; she was also, clearly, a ball-buster. She told her television children that they were adopted, urged them to play in traffic, and fed them *ersatz* frankfurters and real Doritos. In order to remain on television, Roseanne had to sand her hard edges and moderate her malice.[36] Concession to necessity granted; during her seven-year tenure on the tube, Roseanne symbolized a new kind of feminism. Not by coincidence were second-wave feminism's founding mothers of Jewish or half–Jewish descent as manifested by Betty Friedan and Gloria Steinem, respectively. Despite her many personal difficulties offstage—broken marriages, off-key renditions of our national anthem (with hand on crotch), fights with producers, admissions of plastic surgery, accusations of child abuse—Roseanne Barr retained her Jewish identity as outsider. Like the character Howard Beale in Paddy Chayefsky's *Network*, she seemed to shout: "I am mad as hell and I won't take it anymore!" In that message, Lawrence Epstein asserts, Roseanne Barr spoke for the "new Jews and American women."[37]

Second viewings sometimes lead to accurate reassessments. That applies to the Seinfeld phenomenon. When a dear friend, Stan Kanter, first urged me to watch a new sitcom, *Seinfeld*, my reaction was underwhelming. During that record-shattering nine-year-run, I tuned out, turned off, and ignored Seinfeld and his stable of schlemiel and schlimazel friends. It seemed like a flock of horse feathers and a lot less funny than the Marx Brothers. When a *Wall Street Journal* reporter, Cynthia Crossen, asked me to comment on the state of American humor, I replied with *Seinfeld* in mind[38]:

The humor I see on television and in the clubs today is the humor of the narcissist ... of trivia, of people engaged in lives of little substance and less social significance.

Now, 14 years later, this author wishes to recant that sad attempt at cynical sophistication of a *fineshmecker*. As advertised "a sitcom about nothing" proved quite the contrary. Besides becoming the most successful experiment in this genre in network history (it earned NBC $200 million per or 40 percent of its profit in a single year), *Seinfeld* carried far more social significance than I had imagined.[39] I experienced a shock of recognition on a visit to Florida.

At the dinner table, my elderly in-laws urged my wife and me to finish quickly so that we could all watch *Seinfeld* re-runs promptly at 7:30 P.M. Incapacitated by a major stroke, my father-in-law wheeled himself into the living room as both eagerly watched their favorite programs and chortled with health-restoring laughter. Soon, I too watched, listened, learned, and laughed. Far more satisfying than the rush through dinner, the program that evening provided ample food for thought, conversation, and laughter. After all, it was a Jewish-centered program primarily written, produced, directed by Jews. And to our great relief, they did not have to "blacken up" like Al Jolson, blend like Jack Benny, and hide like George Burns.

Seinfeld's initial proposal to NBC encountered opposition from NBC President Brandon Tartikoff who regarded it as "too New York" and "too Jewish."[40] Earlier, especially in the 1940s and 1950s, ethnic diversity found expression on media via the Jewish Goldberg family, 1948–1954, the Norwegians in *Life with Mama*, 1949–1956, and the Italian *Life with Luigi*, 1952. Interfaith marriages harked back to the late 1920s, with *Abie's Irish Rose*. That trend resurfaced in the 1990s with Jewish male liaisons with gentile women.[41] Jewish characters entered American popular culture with a bang, not a whimper, during the 1960s, with what author Wallace Markfield aptly analyzed as the "Yiddishization of American Humor."[42] That transformation paved the way for the rise of Jerry Seinfeld. Born in Brooklyn on April 20, 1954, Jerry and his family moved to Massapequa on the trail blazed by our modern Moses— Robert—to suburbia. Young Jerry intently watched Ed Sullivan's show on Sundays and cottoned to Bill Cosby, along with Rowan & Martin on other nights. By age seven, Seinfeld had already chosen his future career in comedy. Educated in public schools, Jerry started college at SUNY Oswego but homesickness brought him back to Queens College, where he matriculated for two years and graduated. In the summertime, Jerry confessed to Mark Kutcher that he had sneaked into Kutcher's Hotel to see the shows. Bored by acting, he opted for stand-up comedy fortified by health foods, yoga, and Zen meditation.[43] In an early performance at Catch a Rising Star, he froze, blaming the flop on excessive booze. Carefully scrutinizing his bits on tape, he realized that he had not memorized the routines. Jerry developed one too many observational bits with a discourse on "left-hand negatives." His renewed efforts earned praise from Jackie Mason and mentoring from Robert Klein. His comeback, greeted warmly, dissipated the "flop sweat." While improving his craft, Jerry worked at odd jobs.[44]

Seinfeld sensed that sitcoms from 1960 to the 1970s were dominated by Anglo-Saxon types. One striking example was *The Dick Van Dyke Show*. Originally slated for its author, Carl Reiner, about his life in show business, the show featured Mary Tyler Moore along with the ultra goyish Van Dyke. Carl Reiner and Morey Amsterdam, two Jewish types, were consigned to supporting roles. As countervailing forces from outside, Lenny Bruce and Woody Allen put their stamp on contemporary comedy with Jewish sensibility, if not subversion, as they critiqued American cultural mores. Unlike these two transformative humorists, Seinfeld stood up on less controversial ground.

He honed his craft relentlessly. A frequent performer at open mike opportunities in local clubs, he rose through the Improv in New York City. Following the mantra of Horace Greely, Seinfeld ventured westward to Los Angeles. After much trial and a few errors, he established a comic identity as, Richard Zoglin notes, a "truth telling everyman, exposing our secret thoughts and airing our dirty laundry—even when it was just laundry." One example springs to mind: his sock appeal anecdote about losing one wayward stocking in the washing machine or dryer. Author Zoglin identifies Jerry Seinfeld as a representative of a "little guy's battle for sanity in a crazy world."[45] Subject to panic, Seinfeld's voice often ratchets up a notch with a tremor.

Like Philip Roth, Jerry Seinfeld does not wear his tribal identity on his sleeve. In fact, he often exuded semi-detachment from Judaic roots. Critic David Marc defines him as a single straight white guy living in New York City with more success than his dysfunctional friends "full of wise cracks utterly bereft of political or social idealism."[46] In concert with other famous Jewish comedians, Seinfeld used his real name. *Er Shuckelt*, he shuffled along on the sitcom while indulging a *shtick* called *kuplets*—a staple in Yiddish theater—of departing from the script's narrative and speaking directly to the audience while living a fictional life. Ambivalence marks his persona, but David Marc contends he is Jewish and "he enjoys the money and the small nosed glamour girls."[47] Thus, openly Jewish and New Yorkerish, Jerry struts as a "sarcastic, wisecracking cynic with an overbite" leading a life without purpose, surrounded by friends. In his book, *Sein Language*, friends are extolled as "the DNA of society. They are the building blocks of life. If you

have good ones treasure them like gold."[48] Really? On the show that made
him rich as well as famous, who are his friends?

His best friend, George Costanza (Jason Alexander), is a loser: lacking
Jerry's skills as both lover and entertainer. He is short, fat, bald, and neurotic.
A fool, George emerges from I. B. Singer's menagerie alongside of Gimpel:
schlemiel and *nebbish* rolled into a single lump. George also invites comparison with Phil Silvers's Sergeant Bilko, whom John Stratton describes as "a
manipulative and self-serving liar." In this role, on CBS from 1955 to 1959,
Silvers impersonated a schlemiel, covertly Jewish, whose schemes always
ended in failure (shades of Sholem Aleichem's Menachem Mendel).[49] In real
life, Silvers was a compulsive gambler who lost almost everything, including
a wife, to this endemic (if not ethnic) vice. Totally inept, in one episode, George
Costanza blows a sure sexual score when an attractive date invites him up to
her apartment for coffee and post-coffee coitus, presumably. He refuses her
offer on the grounds that coffee keeps him awake at night. In another bit,
unable to conceal his urgent need to pleasure himself in "master of domain"
privacy, he is caught in the act of masturbation by his irate mother.[50] Author
Bill Wyman argues that George Costanza is a stand-in for Larry David, also
an infantile, enraged white male, who is selfish, cheap, untruthful: full of self-
pity and "flattened ambition."[51]

**Jerry Stiller, who plays Frank Costanza, George's hot-tempered father on *Sein-
feld*, and daughter Amy combine as well as continue the ethnic strain of humor,
tapping both Jewish and Irish roots (via Anne Meara). They also personify the
generational bridge over "troubled waters" with comedy as creative coping
mechanism in *When Comedy Went to School*.**

Juxtaposed to him, Jerry is heroic. Jerry's former girlfriend turned bosom buddy, Elaine Benes (Julia Louis-Dreyfus) is obviously Jewish and so deeply neurotic that it is accentuated negatively in her spastic, indeed frenzied, dancing. Like Jerry, she is bent on sexual fulfillment but broken on the wheels of fortune by frequent flyer failures in the dating game. In one episode, Elaine and George spar over a descriptive: "handsome man." Revealing his sexual anxiety, George refuses to utter this perfectly—to Elaine—innocuous phrase. Writing about the sitcom's subtext, Joanna L. Di Mattia concludes that both George and Jerry remain ineffectual and childish in their relations with women because in their world, companionship, as Seinfeld confided in his book, trumps marriage.[52]

Cosmo Kramer (Michael Richards), based on a real person of the Jewish persuasion, is a manic chameleon who invites comparison with Ed Norton, Ralph Kramden's dopey neighbor and best friend. An uninvited consummate shnorrer, Kramer raids Jerry's refrigerator, co-opts his property, girlfriends, and other valuable commodities. Author Bill Wyman claims that all of these characters are flawed. Although he paints a dark picture of this confused, hostile, isolated quartet, Wyman identifies Jerry as part of a "bad boy" tradition in America that embraces Huck Finn and Holden Caulfield, the latter, a J.D. Salinger construct of a Jewish lad masquerading as a Christian everyman-child. Since Seinfeld embodies the American male who refuses to grow up, the kind who finds Howard Stern funny and Imus wise, he fits his time frame or *zeitgeist*, deftly.[53]

Author Carla Johnson views Jerry Seinfeld's claustrophobic urban milieu of small rooms and crowded restaurants, and citing critic Leslie Fiedler, as the "gradual breaking up the Anglo-Saxon domination of our imagination." Our rural myths have gone, she seems to argue, with Margaret Mitchell's wind, propelled by Seinfeld's wit.[54] Johnson further argues that while Costanza is a *schlemiel*, Seinfeld is a *schlimazel* because Jerry is both more rational and more passive.[55] His dark humor, however, reveals our worst traits: immaturity, narcissism, and venality. Irwin and Carl Hirsch maintain that audiences were induced [or seduced?] to accept shared sensibilities of these unpleasant, if entertaining, characters. On a positive note, for the first time, a clearly defined Jewish character rose to first place repeatedly in the Nielsen ratings.[56] As a camera eye, Jerry comments but cannot act. Gargling six times a day, he is extremely anal and is unable to find the perfect woman, like Leonard Cohen's Suzanne, to match his imperfect body. That body is always in danger of erupting at both ends. Masturbation raises its ugly head in a novel way for television while the four feckless and needy New Yorkers engage in "homosociality."[57]

The last episode in this phenomenally successful series merits close reading. Thanks to Joanne Morreale's excellent interpretation, we can now clear away the cobwebs that might have obscured our earlier vision. The four principal characters wind up in jail as befits four shallow, self-absorbed neurotics who embodied the fantasies of their avid viewers. What constitutes a proper atonement for these four remorseless characters bereft of "future ... fulfillment and ... redemption?"[58] Critic Roy Rosenbaum acerbically expressed agony over the ecstasy that Seinfeld and friends evoked for nine years. While this gang of four sits in jail, viewers continue to chortle at their antics in reruns.[59] No need to send in the clowns; they never left. They remain in the corners of our minds representing the lesser angels of our nature. One poet wrote: "After such knowledge, what forgiveness?" David Zurowik forgives. His coda, despite all of Seinfeld's flaws tripled with those of those of his friends, is that the show is both Jewish and American. It also merged two genres, standup and sit-com, successfully—indeed far above Yip Harburg's rainbow. Thus, the answer to an old question is a resounding—as broadcaster Marv Albert used to herald a winning shot: "*Yes!* It was good for the Jews."[60]

TWELVE

Shpritzing and Jiving

Jews and Blacks

A young black man sits on a New York City subway train and appears to be reading a Yiddish newspaper. An old Jewish man approaches him and asks: "*Du bist a Yid*?" To which the Black man replies: "Man, I have enough trouble (*tsores*) being black (*shvartz*)!"

Trouble indeed links the two marginalized groups, a formidable "odd couple" in American culture. Both groups faced prejudice and suffered discrimination. Jews are demeaned in the Oxford Dictionary, and the Bible seems to sanction racial prejudice. "Black boy," or its "N" word equivalent, vies with "Jew-boy" as the number-one target of bigotry's "hit parade" in my troubled youth. As a child, I recall hearing such epithets. A familiar chant mixed racial and political pejoratives:

> Roses are red, violets are blue
> You court the niggers, I'll court the Jews.
> And we'll stay in the White House
> As long as we choose.

An unflattering descriptive of FDR's New Deal coalition, this doggerel echoed in another:

> Sheeny, sheeny, alley picker
> Your father was a Jew
> And your mother was a nigger.

Jews and blacks have been baited, mated, and equated:

> What do you get when you cross a black and a Jew?
> You get a janitor, but he owns the building.

In his cogent analysis on which this chapter builds, folklorist Nathan Hurwitz persuasively argues that blacks and Jews are rebuked and scorned in

170

sacred writings, folklore, and in the humor of dominant Christian society. A notorious scholar of smut, Gershon Legman insisted that behind every joke lies infinite aggression. In our collective unconscious, blacks represent *id* while Jews reflect *superego* imperatives. Both are perceived as sexual threats to the dominant white Christian "male animal." Put in economic terms, blacks constitute a working—Jews, a trading—minority.[1] Both function in American joke lore as objects of derision or, as in Emma Lazarus's unfortunate phrase, "wretched refuse." Examples follow.

When a Negro courier tried to deliver a message directly to J.P. Morgan, the banker's secretary declared: "You can't go in there, that is J.P. Morgan of J.P. Morgan and Co."

"Dat's all right," replied the messenger as he whizzed past her, "I'm the coon of Kuhn, Loeb & Co."[2] The latter, one must hasten to add, was a Jewish firm. Our subject is invested with rich ambiguities and poor delineation. Too often the masks adopted by each group were taken at face value. Clearly, both Jews and blacks as pariahs were compelled to develop certain strategies of survival. Among them, humor proved most effective. When all else failed in the eye of adversity, humor functioned as a line of defense. Indeed, for the Jews, Irving Howe and Eliezer Greenberg insist, it was the *only* line of defense.[3]

Following the rationale of Heinrich Heine's conversion discussed earlier in this study, a Jewish couple converts to Christianity to join an exclusive country club where no dogs or Jews are allowed. One morning, the female convert plunges into the pool's chilly waters. She shrieks: "*Oy vey is mir!*" Exposed, she looks around sheepishly and declares, "Whatever that means." A black variant of this revelation pits a beautiful black woman, Cindy Ella against the magic mirror. "Who is the fairest one of all?" she asks the mirror.

The mirror replies: "Snow White, you black b___h, and don't you forget it!"

White bigots are also unmasked in the joke lore genre. When a Southern senator told many reporters that he had many friends who were Negroes, that he was completely devoid of prejudice, and that he was writing a book about his famous Negro friends: athletes, singers, and statesmen, the reporters asked: Senator, what is the title of your book?"

He replied: "Niggers I have known."[4]

The late South Carolina senator Strom Thurmond might have appropriated this title as a subtext to "knowledge" in the Biblical sense.

Gallows humor appeals to both blacks and Jews. In the pre–Civil Rights era, a Northern black tourist asks a Southern sheriff: "What time is it, officer?"

Because the query was not punctuated by the word, "sir" a reference to deference, the sheriff barks: "Three o' clock!" and, with his club, cracks the black man three times.

The victim offers a strange response: he laughs.

"Why are you laughing, boy?" the angry sheriff demands.

"Because, sir, I'm sure glad that it ain't twelve."

Jews have also indulged in this kind of humor. Before he reinvented himself as the leading neo-conservative intellectual, Irving Kristol dabbled in Jewish humor. In a stimulating article in *Commentary*, he prematurely interred our subject as an alleged consequence of the Holocaust. Ironically, gallows humor experienced resurgence during and after Hitler's apocalyptic rule.[5]

Much of Jewish humor is preoccupied with death. Author Stephen Whit-field has argued that it is a way of keeping the *Malachhamoves* (Angel of Death) at bay.[6] Witness the Hitler jokes as illustrative examples:

- After coming to power, Hitler insisted on positive propaganda for his Third Reich. Thus, a German teacher describes the great benefits that *Der Fuhrer* has bestowed on a grateful people. "He is like a father to us. Is there anything you would ask 'father' to do for you?"

   "Yes," replied a little Jewish boy, "to make me an orphan."
- In Hitler's early days as dictator, his finance minister approached the financier Rothschild for a large loan.

   "What are your assets?" Rothschild asks.

   "Coal underground and Hitler above ground."

   The famous banker responded: "I would gladly help you if you could reverse the situation."
- Extremely superstitious, Hitler went to the best fortune teller in Germany, who happened to be Jewish. Looking into her crystal ball, she informed the "great dictator" that he was going to die on the eve of a Jewish holiday. "Which holiday? Hitler asked anxiously. "Anytime you die," she answered, "the next day will be a Jewish holiday."
- During the mid–1930s, a German Jew indicated that he preferred to read the vicious Nazi newspaper *Der Sturmer*. Why? his friends wanted to know. Because, he explained, the honest press reports on tragedies, pogroms, round-ups, and humiliations, while *Der Sturmer* articles relate how Jews own the banks and wield world power.
- During the war, Jewish residents in Warsaw compared their ghetto

to Hollywood because of all the stars (yellow armbands) seen on the streets.

Mordant and macabre to be sure; but levity in the face of annihilation speaks volumes, which invites further study. Author Steve Lipman has answered that call with an illuminating book, *Laughter from Hell*.[7]

It is not clear whether all of the jokes cited above sprang spontaneously from horrific events at that time or were the distillation of "emotion recollected in tranquility," to borrow Wordsworth's definition of poetry. What is certain, however, are the beneficent effects of humor in extremis, as stated in these trenchant words of Holocaust survivor Dr. Viktor Frankl[8]:

> It is well known that humor, more than anything else in the human make up, can afford an aloofness and an ability to rise above any situation, even if only for a few seconds. The attempt to develop a sense of humor and to see things in a humorous light is kind of a trick learned while mastering the art of living. Yet it is possible to practice the art of living even in a concentration camp, although the suffering is omnipresent.

According to William Novak and Moshe Waldoks, Jewish humor is substantive. It usually salts something of moral fiber with didactic flavor. As Dr. Freud observed, essentially democratic, Jewish humor targets authority and punctures pomposity. Baring a critical cutting edge, it disturbs as it amuses. In the contest of wits, little people often win. *Shpritzing* or attacking dogmas, institutions, celebrities, and enemies, Jewish humor does not even spare God.[9] When bloated with *tsores* (trouble), the Jewish joke purges one with suddenness and effectiveness of seltzer. It spells relief.

On the flip side of the comic coin, African American humor is equally functional. The litany of black jokes serves survival, escape, and self-criticism, while contributing to conflict and control. Arising from an African base, slave humor turned abominable situations, at least psychologically, around. Trickster humor, wherein cunning trumps strength, especially appealed to Negro slaves. Consider the following example: When an enraged master caught trickster-slave John stealing food, he bellowed: "You scoundrel, you ate my turkey!"

"Yassuh, massah," the slave countered, "you got less turkey but you sho' got more nigger." The master was mollified and jollified.

Historian Gil Osofsky cited a battle of wits in slave narratives.[10]

> Pompey, how do I look?
> O' massa, mighty.
> What do you mean "mighty," Pompey?
> Why massa, you look noble.

What do you mean by "noble?"
Why, sar, you look just like one lion.
Why, Pompey, where have you seen a lion?
I see one down in yonder field the other day, massa.
Pompey, you foolish fellow, that was a jackass!
Was it massa? Well you look just like him.

Who was *really* foolish? Osofsky refers to other examples of funny irreverence. Surrounded by slaves and family at his deathbed as he commanded, a plantation owner groaned in both pain and in fear. Consoling him, a "faithful servant" said: "Farewell, massa! Pleasant journey: you soon be dere—all de way down hill!" In a third tale, one slave boasts to another that he can cuss out his master whenever he desires. Evidently, venting anger makes him feel good. His friend tries it and his master punishes him.

"Where was he standin'?" The first slave asks.

"Right there in front of me."

"That's the *wrong* way," the wise slave advises. "When I cuss my massa out, he's up at the big house and I'm in the field, near the creek."[11]

The comedy of avoidance—or evasion—worked effectively. African American humor, until the civil rights movement, resided underground. The messages were dressed in animal tales. A kind of in-group joke lore incorporated double meanings, word-play, self-deprecation, play-element, and aggression against the Man. Some coded messages found their way into music as in the song, "Raise a Rukus Tonight." In the Alan Lomax version, the principal theme states[12]:

> My ol' mistress promise me, Raise a rukus tonight
> When she died, she'd set me free, Raise a rukus tonight
> Live so long twell her haid got bal', Raise a rukus tonight
> Give up the notion of dyin' at all, Raise a rukus tonight...

Coded humor also featured the "Dozens"—often dirty and involving family members. Clean "Dozens" also entered the arena of in-group contests; for example[13]:

- Your father's drawers have so many holes in them that when he walks, they whistle.
- Your house is so small that roaches walk in single file.
- Your family is so poor the rats and roaches eat lunch out.

Clean or dirty, these verbal jousts have sparked scholarly controversy. Anthropologist Radcliffe-Brown was the first to explore "the joking relationship as an institution by which a person is expected, sometimes required, to make fun of another who, in turn, is required to take no offense." These relations were prevalent among tribal societies in Asia, Oceania, North America, and in Africa as well; arising when people experience ambiguous relationships with one another.[14]

A scholarly pioneer on the frontier of racial relations, Yale professor John Dollard viewed the "Dozens" as a "valve for aggression in a depressed group." He argued that they provide a safe substitute for physical violence, a theory that evoked a rebuttal from a fellow anthropologist, Roger Abrahams. Studying black youths in Philadelphia, Abrahams concluded that the "Dozens" provided a ritual to liberate black adolescents from their overprotective and fearful mommas as a way of resolving acute Oedipal and identity problems. Historian Robert Levine found fault with all single-cause interpretations. Conversely, he noted two principal functions in the ritual of insult: training in verbal skill along with training in self-discipline.[15]

Do we slip the yoke, as Ralph Ellison contended, when we change the joke? By playing the American buffoon, the Negro gained certain benefits in slavery. After abolition, however, choices were available. Despite societal constraints, or because of them, many Negro (the preferred rubric then) entertainers continued to play a stereotyped role. They struck a Faustian bargain. Whites, at one end, figured that as long as the Negro seemed funny he was not dangerous. Thus, the Negro's laughter, author Margaret Butcher observed, was "often contrived and artificial" rather than natural and spontaneous. Either as unthreatening clown or brute beast, the Negro was locked into white fantasies, though poet/critic Sterling Brown detected five additional stereotyped roles in American literature. These roles probably assuaged white guilt rendering the appearance—as tranquilizing as it was false—that blacks were happy.[16]

Industrialization coupled with urbanization sent shock waves through 19th century America. First the minstrel and, later, the vaudeville shows, helped mass audiences to cope. This "brave new world" rested on an ideological base, namely, the Protestant Ethic. Success depended on order, industry, cleanliness, punctuality, frugality. One had to delay instinctual gratification. Sublimation, however, was no guarantor of success. Fear of failure was a nagging concern. Projecting their fear and fantasy onto blacks, white folks fashioned an anti-self. Epitomizing passion, lust, and license, blacks objectified the distance between societal norms and man's natural self. (Women were not yet part of the social equation.) Therefore, the principal comic mode, to wit, travesty, turned on the disparities between actor and costume, position and name, life and language. Slaves, for example, had high and mighty names: Brutus, Pompey, Caesar; freedmen emerged as Washington, Jefferson, Jackson, et al. Stage Negroes used ornate language peppered with malapropisms. They engaged in social pretense. In the highly popular minstrel shows, the Jim Crow persona caricatured the rural black while Jim Dandy burlesqued the urban Negro. Later, intellectuals may have regarded Marcus Garvey as a parody of Jim Crow while the "Black Moses"—argued historian Nathan Huggins—viewed the supremely gifted W.E.B. DuBois as a Jim Dandy. To Americans, who were everybody and nobody, a jumble of masks, a kaleidoscope of costumes, a bundle of uncertainties, life mirrored art.[17] The man who helped to make the mold of the minstrel mask was a mass of contradictions. Joel Chandler Harris was born in 1848, a bastard. His mother worked as a servant. At age 13, he became an apprenticed printer. Lonely, shy, insecure, he turned for solace to Negroes. The Uncle Remus stories which Harris pilfered were published in 1880. Fortune followed; fame, too. Strangely, Harris did not sense the schizoid in the Negro psyche. B'rer Rabbit celebrates the code of survival. Profoundly anti–Christian, the code stresses slickness, deceit, evasiveness, and ruthless self-interest. If one wants to know what thoughts lurk behind the black mask, the animal tales, properly interpreted, provide a better clue than the spiritual or sorrow songs. According to Bernard Wolfe, in Harris's first book, Rabbit, who symbolizes the Negro, appears 26 times. In 20 encounters with Fox, Rabbit whips him 19 times. When pitted against the strong, namely Wolf, Bear, and Fox—all representations of white power—Rabbit invariably wins. In addition, other weaklings—Buzzard, Bullfrog, and Terrapin—consistently beat the Fox. Harris was neither the first nor the last white poacher who ventured into black territory for psychological comfort and material gain.[18] Cultural theft has reaped huge profits.

For the black performer, on the other face, blacking up with burnt cork provided a rite of exorcism. If blacks on stage represented the anti-self and its spectrum of values, whites also assumed the mask in a quest of catharsis. Audiences howled as they perceived the incongruity between affectation and reality. The laughter of derision managed to put the pretender in his place. Black artists wanting a piece of the entertainment pie insisted, despite Ernest Hogan's best-selling song "All Coons Look Alike to Me," that real "coons," as Bert Williams and George Walker billed themselves, could do it better. Not only did commercial considerations encourage blacks to parody whites who were aping blacks in the minstrel mode, but, as Robert Bone contended, the mask served as a way of distancing the superego's middle class values from the dark recesses of the id. As recently as 1950, many—if not most—black comics on the TOBA or chittlin' circuit still blacked up. Even after the NAACP applied pressure, John Hudgins resisted the new look. He confessed: "I feel so naked out there." Harlem audiences at the Apollo

Theatre found the burnt-cork comics appealing, which Malcolm X found appalling.[19]

Blackface both liberated and chained America's finest black artist, Bert Williams. He was born in Antigua, in the West Indies, in either 1874 or 1875 (depending on what source one cites). Williams grew up in fairly comfortable circumstances. Failing health prompted his father to move to Riverside, California, in 1885. Only a mediocre student despite superior intelligence, Williams pursued a career in show business. Teaming up with George Walker in 1893, Williams soon became one of America's premier entertainers. Not only did the association with Walker prove pivotal, so did the use of burnt cork. Williams explained, "Then I began to find myself. It was not until I was able to see myself as another person that my sense of humor developed." Like clown white, the black mask permitted an entertainer to achieve artistic distinction. Stifled as a man, he crested as a comedian. Williams poked fun at societal institutions: churches, marriages, and funerals. As a wise fool, he uttered common sense. As a Jonah man, Bert portrayed the black *schlimazel*. He famously sang.[20]

> My luck started when I was born
> Leas' so the old folks say
> Dat same hard luck's been my bes' frien'
> To dis vary day
> When I was young, Mama's friends—
> To find a name they tried
> They named me after Papa—and de same day Papa died, fo'
>
> I'm a Jonah, I'm a Jonah Man
> My family for many years would look at me
> And den shed tears
> Why I am dis Jonah
> I sho' can't understand,
> But I'm a good substantial, full[fledged]
> Real, first-class Jonah Man

Originally the straight man to Walker's comic, Williams, as Jim Crow, the slow rural black, stole the show from his partner, the urban Jim Dandy. Steeped in the Protestant Ethic gospel, according to Booker T. Washington, Williams thought his stage persona was helping to "elevate the black man. Shuffling along, battered by a heartless world, he never succumbed to self-pity. But his humor, on and off stage, turned to melancholy. "It's no disgrace to be a Negro," Williams confessed, "but it is very inconvenient." Although he earned much money (especially when he was featured in *The Ziegfeld Follies*, which he was almost continuously from 1910 to 1919), he had to sleep in segregated hotels, ride freight elevators, and work as a solo after his partner succumbed in 1911, to paresis, an advanced stage of syphilis.[21]

One of his best bits involved a black fish peddler who climbs a mountain to sell fish to white folks. "No, we don't want no fresh fish today," he is told. He descends to the bottom, greeted by a snow slide that almost buries him. He looks up and the little white man on top of the mountain beckons to him. "So I sez to myself 'Praise God, that w'ite man is done changed his mind.' So I climbs back again up the mountain, seven thousand feet high, till I comes to the plum top and w'en I gits there the w'ite man is standin' there waitin' for me. He waits till I'm right close to him befo' he speaks. Then he clear his throat and he sez to me, he sez: 'And we don't want none to-morrow either.'"

In another bind because of bad times, he is forced to take a job in the circus. Cornered in a lion's cage, unable to escape, he falls to his knees in prayer. "And this Bengal tagger leaped toward me and jus' as my heart was gettin' ready to stop for good, that tagger took and leaned over and I heard him whisper right in my ear, 'Don't be skeered, pal. I'm colored same as you.'" In fact, there is a comparable Jewish tiger in Hitler's circus. Common to oppressed people, these crossover jokes appeal to Jews as well as blacks.[22]

Pulling laughter from pain animated Williams, who mastered this process. He chanted.[23]

> When life seems full of clouds and rain
> And I am full of nothin' but pain,
> Who soothes my thumpin', bumpin', brain?
> Nobody!
>
> When winter comes with snow and sleet,
> And me with hunger and cold feet,
> Who says "Here's twenty-five cents, go ahead
> And get something to eat?"
> Nobody! …
>
> I ain't done nothin' to nobody
> I ain't got nothin' from nobody, no time
> Until I get somethin' from somebody, some time
> I'll never do nothin' for nobody, no time.

After Walker's death in 1910, Williams began to drink more heavily and plunged into chronic depression. W.C. Fields, no mean drinker himself, remembered Williams as "the funniest man I ever saw and the saddest man I ever knew."[24] Well read, highly articulate, and painfully funny, Bert Williams had to score points in this kind of dialogue[25]:

A man is brought before the judge for chicken stealing, and sentenced. The white Judge is curious: how could he steal chickens with dogs in the yard? "Hit wouldn't be of no use, judge, to try to explain things to you all, if you was to try it you would be like as not get your hide full of shot an' get no chickens either. If you want to engage in rascality, judge, you betah stick to de bench whar you am familiar."

About marriage, a favorite target: "If you have two wives, that's bigamy, if you have many wives, that's polygamy; if you have one, that's monotony." Actors' Equity refused to accept dues from Williams, despite his success in mainstream entertainment. He remained in a constant state of exile "from the white culture," Ann Charters wrote, "from which he was barred because he was a Negro; and from his Harlem neighbors and theatrical acquaintances because he remained at heart a West Indian."[26] Poor health and excessive drinking took their toll on Williams; his heart gave out on March 4, 1922, when he was only forty-seven years old. As he shuffled along to that great fish-fry in the sky, many mourned. Poet Paul Lawrence Dunbar may have contributed an unintended but most appropriate epitaph for Bert Williams when he wrote[27]:

> We wear the mask that grins and lies
> It hides our cheek and shades our eyes—
> The debt we pay to human guile:
> With torn and bleeding hearts we smile.

Mr. Dunbar knew whereof he sang. He, too, put on the minstrel mask when he composed lyrics, such as "Who Dat Say Chicken in Dis Crowd" and "Hottest Coon in Dixie" for blackface vaudeville. Like a haunting refrain, that tradition lingered. In the ensuing years on stage, radio and film, blacks appeared to be locked into stereotypical performance as coons, Uncle Toms, fools, and tragic mulattoes. Mantan Moreland, Stepin Fetchit, Eddie "Rochester" Anderson, Bill Robinson, Hattie McDaniel, Butterfly McQueen, and even Dooley Wilson personified these types. Fortunately, the Civil Rights movement generated a dramatic reversal of this deplorable long-term trend. Comedian Dick Gregory helped launch what scholars Arnez and Anthony aptly called "third stage image creating public humor."[28]

In the 1917 *Ziegfeld Follies*, Bert Williams starred in a skit with Eddie Cantor as his effeminate, blackfaced son Eddie (of the goggled eyes and the frantic whoopee) called Williams "Papsy" (the Jewish comic Cantor also hid behind the minstrel mask). Thus, black father and Jewish son made the comedic scene together: the objects of common linkage in dark laughter. Other Jewish entertainers followed suit. The most famous blackface performer, of course, was Al Jolson. Born in St. Petersburg, Russia, in 1886, Jolson and his family settled in Washington, D.C., where his father worked as a cantor. Adjustment to American life proved difficult. Jolson wound up in a Catholic home for troubled youth in Baltimore, which also housed future baseball immortal Babe Ruth. After release, Jolson tried odd jobs, one as a singing waiter. He was a mediocre performer until 1904 when a valet suggested that he use blackface. The rest is both a fable as well as history with a pendulum swing. As Bert Williams's popularity went down, Al Jolson's went up.[29]

Behind the mask, many forces—aggression, nostalgia, guilt, loneliness, anxiety—coalesced. As Stanley White demonstrated in his provocative article, Americans wanted, indeed requested, an emotional release from the daily assaults unleashed by urban society on the old order. Entertainers like Cantor and Jolson pandered to wish fulfillment, which conjured up a mythical South where whites ruled, black mammies took care of things, and Negro children frolicked from sunup to sundown. Jolson had inherited a Jewish blue note. Fusing this somber, cantorial strain with vibrant, sometimes demonic energy, Jolson captivated audiences all over America. Whether he sang of the Old South in "Swanee," or unrequited love in "After You've Gone," or parental grief in losing one's "Sonny Boy," Jolson struck a responsive chord in his listeners. *Yiddishe schmaltz* (Jewish chicken fat), larded with blackface sentiment, proved a formidable recipe. This recipe worked for Sophie Tucker, Eddie Cantor, George Jessel, and especially Al Jolson. Stanley White's summation is worth quoting[30]:

> All that mattered was to evoke the image of the once servile black for an emotional outlet in a dehumanizing, disjointed age—the mammy for security and comfort, and the Negro male for ridicule and jest. Whereas the Negro's body had once been in bondage, now it was his personality that was enslaved to satisfy the white man's immediate psychic needs.

Pulsing with coarse vitality, Jewish comedians had sharpened their skills in the streets. They mimicked hoity-toity teachers, snarling rabbis, fat cops. Since *landsleit*, or fellow Jews, owned and operated many theatres, careers in comedy were open to talent. Initially, many worked as teams of two. Weber and Fields, Gallagher and Shean (the latter, Jewish), and Smith and Dale spring immediately to mind. Soon they acquired confidence, developed *chutspe*, and started to stand or sit alone by the telephone like George Jessel, the original Jazz Singer on the Broadway stage. Listen.[31]

> Hello Momma, this is Georgie, who sends you the check each month. I'm sitting with Wendell Wilkie, no Momma, not Mendel. He talked about the Four Freedoms. What did he say about our neighbors—the four Friedmans? I am going to browse in an art gallery. Yes, it's respectable. I'll bring Whistler's Mother home for the living room. No room? She'll have to sleep with sister Anna? I also a picked up a Rubens. A sandwich? No, a painter. You want him to paint the kitchen?

Aggression alternates with embarrassment in this routine. The Americanized son plays of the immigrant mother. Momma's mistakes evoke exasperation as well as recognition.

Critic Alfred Kazin, observed that great writers, did not establish "the Jew in the national consciousness as a distinctly American figure"; rather, this contribution came from a collective effort embracing the Marx Brothers, Eddie Cantor, Al Jolson, Fannie Brice, and George Gershwin. Two traditions attracted the Jewish artist: the blackface strain and European operetta. Blackface had a brassy, lowdown, earthy quality, as opposed to a bourgeois mentality. In the other ear, European operetta sounded mellow, genteel. Most gravitated to black culture because it granted freedom from conventional restraints and served as American libido. This attraction occurred when cultural pundits like Oswald Spengler were lamenting the alleged "decline of the West and poets like T. S. Eliot were raining metaphors of sterility on their respective 'wastelands.'" Thus, a coarse, vibrant ethnic humor and music—*pastiche*, in Ronald Sanders's arresting formulation—appealed to vast American audiences.[32]

Impulsively, Jewish entertainers used Yiddish accents, dialect stories, unabashed sentimentality, gritty jokes, frantic energy—all, Irving Howe charged, were "spin-offs from the immigrant experience."[33] The Marx Brothers, for example, plunged into "gleeful nihilism." They assaulted all–American Institutions with "ruthless deflation"—a staple of Jewish humor. No one—profession or person—remained safe from their demolition derby. As Hitler mounted his diabolical crusade for world hegemony, *sha-sha!* ("Be quiet! Don't make waves!") passivity led to the disappearance of the Jew from American popular culture. Jews, like blacks, became almost invisible. Radio had celebrated, Philip Roth noted, Jack Armstrong, the "All-American Goy." Roth added that our dream girl, fabricated in Hollywood was a blonde *shikse* "nestling under your arm whispering love, love, love, love!"[34]

When the Jews as entertainers resurfaced after World War II, they fused several baser metals: *shnorrer* and *schlemiel* types from the *shtetl* and the Catskill *meshuginer* (crazy), that "wild irresponsible disconnected buffoon who oscillates between the frantic edges of obscenity and tearful sentimentality." Jewish vulgarity "busted loose" from genteel constraints. Stand-up comics, from 1950 to 1970, emitted snarling references to Jewish parents. Shame still made their comic engines pump. Only this time, the needle-trades assumed a more malevolent, indeed savage, style. Not only their dirty underwear in the closet proved embarrassing but their identifying evasions, as Lenny Bruce pontificated ("'I'm proud to be Jewish' means only that I made the adjustment"), also triggered self-contempt. They suffered, Irving Howe persuasively argued, from a moral duality. The gaudy glitter—gold dust if you will—of making it was, at bottom, *drek*, or shit. Always "overwhelmingly social," Jewish humor had an obligation to foster spiritual values and group cohesion in the face of materialistic temptation.[35] In the 1960s and 1970s, authors Leslie Fiedler, Earl Rovit, Irving Howe, and Sig Altman conferred low grades in their evaluation of Jewish entertainers. Rovit complained that Jews had failed to produce a Charlie Chaplin, a Mark Twain, a Sinclair Lewis. He attributed this failure to facile adaptation. He added that, on major controversial issues, Jewish humor, in contrast to its black counterpart, had accepted, without struggle, the middle-class belief system. Even the cerebral Woody Allen trumpeted the uselessness of intellectual activity. He quipped about the courses he took in college prior to dropping out, namely, Truth, Beauty, Advanced Beauty, and Intermediate Truth. In this vein, Allen seemed to say that all academic activity is futile.[36]

Arguably, the most important comic in postwar America, Lenny Bruce, proved transformational. Before his untimely death of a drug overdose, he developed a unique, cogent kind of humor that shocked as it amused. Drawing on folk sources, black as well as Jewish, Lenny questioned conventional wisdom as he undressed our would-be emperors. He wielded strong and salutary influence on contemporary comedians, especially blacks. Redd Foxx adored him.[37] As he said:

> Lenny Bruce was the greatest human being I ever met. He was honest. He said things that were not conventional to say. But they need being said and Lenny was the first to say them. He was crucified for telling the truth. He was a great influence on me.

Foxx's "Fuck Kate Smith" routine many have been inspired by a bit wherein Lenny Bruce offered audiences a chance to test the imperatives of race and sex. How would a white man choose between, say, Lena Horne and Kate Smith? Or which one would a white woman choose—Charles Laughton or Harry Belafonte? Most passionate people, Lenny asserted, would pick handsome Harry and lovely Lena.[38] Lenny Bruce also inspired Richard Pryor, George Carlin, Robert Klein and Norman Lear. From his years as a hack comic in his early career, Bruce became a "speechifying comic Jeremiah." Frenzied resentments bubbled up in his elaborate, spontaneous *shpriizes*. Instead of currying favor with powerful people by projecting a hearty, honest, and lovable image, Bruce's sweeping gestures, Yiddish phrases, and fierce sense of moral outrage linked him to a radical component of Jewish tradition. Beyond the pale, his flights of fantasy took off from supposition of what if…[39]

The Lone Ranger was making it with Tonto and Silver?
Christ and Moses returned to earth and walked through Harlem?

Hitler was made Chancellor of Germany by central casting?

Madison Avenue sold "Religions Incorporated" through an ad campaign?

We used ethnic and racial slurs openly until they lost their power to inflict pain?

Lenny Bruce tested the limits in stand-up comedy, salted with a unique sensibility, which author Maurice Yakower aptly defines as[40]

> essentially Jewish. The performer stands alone and without a prop before a crowd of strangers. By his wit he attempts to forge a sense of community with them. By his brain and humor he tries to gain their acceptance, the laughter that denotes approval.... Despite his strangeness and alienation, he must persuade them that he is one of them.... So he stands alone in front of a silent and alien audience, spinning out his line self-deprecating patter or charming cheek (*chutspe*). The stand-up comedian is the eternal outsider, the Wandering Jew.

Before self-destructing with a little help from the law, Lenny Bruce provided ample food for comic thought, which subsequent humorists, black as well as Jewish, digested. Most Jewish comedians, until recently, sought status, success, and *shikses*. They also crave love, and fear death. All of the above apply to Woody Allen and Mel Brooks. Woody Allen does not exactly fear death, he confessed: "I just don't want to be there when it happens." Death inspired some of his best one-liners, to wit.[41]

- Death is an acquired trait.
- Death is one of the worst things that can happen to a Cosa Nostra member, and many prefer simply to pay a fine.
- I do not believe in an afterlife, although I am bringing a change of underwear.
- Yea, I shall run through the valley of the shadow of death.
- Dying doesn't make you thirsty. Unless you get stabbed after eating herring.
- Also there is the fear that there is an afterlife but no one will know where it is being held.

Woody's obsession with death is shared by another leading American Jewish comic artist. Mel Brooks wants to live forever. His 2,000-year-old man is Jewish and therefore vulnerable to "hostile man, nature and God." Brooks prefers to "swing, shout, and make noise!" Humor is "another defense against the universe." He affirms life: "Let's not mimic death before our time comes! Let's be wet and noisy!" In *The Producers*, Melvin Kaminsky (his real, as opposed to reel, name) reduces the horror that was Hitler to an extended joke. In *Blazing Saddles*, a super-macho black sheriff (originally designed for Richard Pryor) restores law, order, sex, and laughter to a frontier town. This new genre, the Jewish Western, is replete with vulgarity, effusiveness, and in-jokes. Witness the reference to the confluence of black and Native Americans as the Indian chief allows a caravan of African Americans to cross into his tribal territory with these words: *Zei zeinen shvartzehs—loz zei geyn*! (They are blacks—let them go). Thus, use of Yiddish is a means to revive a dying voice in a fading culture.[42]

One African American who did not reach the far country of nirvana was a comedic genius, a legatee of Bert Williams, named Richard Pryor. Although his early life remains somewhat mysterious, thanks to contradictory sources, we now know some salient, if troubling, facts: that he was born in 1940 in Peoria, Illinois, that his grandmother ran a string of whorehouses; that his mother worked as a prostitute—her clients, local "johns," including white men—and that she turned the money from "tricks" over to Richard's father; that he slugged a local teacher and engaged in other acts of violence; that he tried various jobs—shining shoes, serving as a janitor (who did not own the building), playing a piano in a nightclub, serving in the army—before embracing comedy. Despite what appears to be a traumatic early life as an only child, Pryor insisted that his parents were honest: "They had great dignity. My mother taught me about being decent."[43]

Pryor was 12 when he appeared onstage for the first time, in *Rumpelstiltskin*. Through aggressive humor, he earned respect from classmates and peers. After he assaulted a teacher with fists, not wit, he was expelled from school. Subsequently, army life offered additional opportunities for comic exploration as well as violent outbursts. Stationed in Germany, he got into a fight with a white soldier, whom he stabbed in the back. That ended his army career. After his discharge, Pryor entered show business with "gigs" in bars and clubs on the "chitlin' circuit." Encouraged by the success of black pioneer comedians with crossover appeal, like Dick Gregory, Nipsey Russell, Godfrey Cambridge, Redd Foxx, and especially Bill Cosby, he came to New York's Greenwich Village in 1963. Discovered by talent scouts, he guested on television shows, branched out to the largely Jewish Catskill hotels and top nightclubs, winging his way to top-banana status in 1967 by emulating Bill Cosby's "mellow Jello" style. Suddenly, he fell apart on a Las Vegas stage: one of several mental breakdowns. Leaving the Las Vegas Aladdin Hotel stage, he bellowed: "What am I doing here? I'm not going to do this anymore!"[44]

Egged on by his second wife, a white Jewish woman from Brooklyn named

Shelley Bonus, Richard began to find his truth. Nurtured in a show-business family—her father was Danny Kaye's business manager—and finding fulfillment in the civil rights movement, under the aegis of Dr. King, Ms. Bonus urged her husband to add radical ideas to his repertoire, as their daughter, Rain, recalled.[45] While chilling out, as it were, in Berkeley, California, Pryor read *Malcolm X Speaks*. In what might be construed as an epiphany, he realized[46]:

> I wasn't crazy. Someone else thought what I thought; And it freed me. I wasn't gonna' stand up there and wear a tuxedo anymore. There was something better to do. I got my head out of the white man's dream.

As the mute piano player in the film *Lady Sings the Blues* (1972), Pryor started a brilliant comeback. Both as writer and as actor, he continued to shine in a succession of money-making movies. Having found his authentic voice, his stand-up comedy performances propelled him to the artistic summit. He played variations, like Redd Foxx, on the theme of "nigger." In a variety of personae—pool room shark, "Super Nigger," hustler, wino, wise old man, prostitute Big Bertha, or precocious child—he got down to the core of African American culture.[47] In his Grammy-winning record, *That Nigger's Crazy* (1974), Pryor developed a bit in which he pitted the vicious Count Blacula against a wise wino, who questions his foe: "*Count Blacula*? What kinda' name is that for a nigger? You dig blood, huh? Why don't you go to a blood bank? It's just down the street. I hope your ass gets sickle cell."[48]

Artist as Everyman, Richard Pryor got on everybody's case. With extraordinary gifts for mimicry, he could morph into a white hayseed in one presentation and impersonate Mudbone, the black equivalent of Mel Brooks's 2000-year-old man, spinning yarns drawn from a vast treasury of folklore. Pryor's preacher man also invites comparison with Flip Wilson's the Reverend Leroy. Both were crafted as charismatic characters, with a touch of guile. For members of the growing black middle class, they may have engendered embarrassment, but satire, especially in the biting words of a once-poor Richard, defied groups, let alone self-censorship.[49] Success did not spoil his N—r image. *Newsweek* chronicled a long litany of Pryor's bizarre behavior. He set fire to a girlfriend's mink coat; he exchanged blows with co-stars in the film *Blue Collar*; he riddled an ex-wife's car, a Buick, with bullets; he did time for income-tax evasion; and he almost burned himself into oblivion while freebasing cocaine on June 9, 1980. According to critic Richard Zoglin, Pryor actually tried to commit suicide by pouring a bottle of cognac over himself and setting off a fire with a Bic lighter. Coached back to life by football immortal and "Superspade" cinematic hero Jim Brown, along with an excellent staff at the Sherman Oaks Community Hospital Burn Center, Pryor made a stunning comeback, culminating in a film, *Richard Pryor: Live at the Sunset Strip* (1982), only 18 months after his brush with death.[50]

Dressed in a bright red suit (suggesting, perhaps, a return from hell), Pryor gave a masterful performance, partly powered by drug use. He let it all hang out. Peppered with four- and ten-letter words, his routine featured fewer "N" words. No group was spared in his comedic assault, not even his agent. "I trusted him because he was a brother. Well, the brother took me hook, line, and sinker. And on dry land!" Dramatic tension animated his body movements. His nimble fingers punctuated the narrative: highlighting every punch line. Relating an experience while filming *Stir Crazy* (1980), with Gene Wilder, he observed[51]:

> Eighty percent of the prison population at New Mexico State Penitentiary is black. There are no blacks in the state. I think they bus 'em in. I asked the inmates: "Why did you kill everyone in the house?" The reply: "Well, they were home." Thank God for penitentiaries! These motherfucking murderers are doing triple life. When they are reincarnated, the teachers say to them: "Get your little asses out of kindergarten. Back to the penitentiary! You have to watch out for the Double Muslims because they can't get into heaven 'less they take twelve motherfuckers with them.

Pryor recounted an experience prompted by his white girlfriend and future wife, Jennifer Lee Pryor, whom he married twice (after and between divorces). She had urged him to go to Africa. He went. There, he experienced one of several epiphanies. He saw colored people of different hues, shapes, and cultures, but "no niggers!" When he realized that all human life started in Africa, he cried at the shock of recognition. Unable or unwilling to refrain from stereotype, however, after this startling realization, Pryor revealed that riding in car next to a sweaty African, he had to cover his nose because of the awful stench.

The film's climax is pure psychodrama as Richard re-enacted his death wish. The devil's voice issues from the cocaine pipe. Id attempts to seduce ego in a soft, mellow, seductive voice.[52]

> ID: Time to get up, time for some smoke, Rich. Come on now, we're not gonna do anything today. Fuck your appointments—me and you are just gonna' hang out in this room today.
> EGO: When that fire hits your ass, that will sober you up quickly. One thing I found out: When you're on fire and runnin' down the street people get out of your way.

Not unlike the resilient anti-heroes of Sholem Aleichem, Richard Pryor, that red-suited Lazarus emerged from *Gehenna* (hell), drawing on the humor of survival from his ordeal by fire. Pryor's genius must be assessed in the historical context of African American humor. Scholar Arnez and Anthony proposed a three-stage paradigm. The first stage carries us back to "Ol' Virginny," and beyond. In response to a concerted effort by the white ruling class to obliterate African culture, slaves developed a covert comic stance, laced with coded language. Whites heard only accommodated humor as black wit turned inward because aggression would have invited instant retaliation. Therefore, blacks learned to laugh in a box. They also put on masks. Behind this Sambo exterior, however, lurked a future Nat Turner, harboring murderous rage that was just waiting to explode. Like his predecessor Lenny Bruce, Richard Pryor attacked corruption symbolically. After his breakdown in Las Vegas, however, he took on the role of shaman who purges our "private fears and submerged fantasies," in scholar Geza Roheim's formulation.[53] In this role, Pryor plumbed our deep-seated anxieties and assaulted the phantom of death. As the preacher man, he proclaimed[54]:

> We are gathered here today, on this sorrowful occasion, to say goodbye to the dearly departed. He was dearly, now he has departed. Thus, we have the dearly departed. In other words, the nigger dead.

His commitment to truth put Pryor on a collision course with our personal evasions as well as our societal euphemisms. Nervously, we sit in the arena. Will we accept the truth as purveyed by comedians like Richard Pryor and Lenny Bruce? Comparable to the effects of Malcolm X's pilgrimage to Mecca, Pryor's trip to Africa, apart from noxious body odors, brought a pivotal awareness that man is doomed if he doesn't make a multiracial society. On the journey to self-awareness, he discovered that he wasn't inferior.[55] The rich language of African Americans spiced with slang, jive, biblical language, cliché, obscenity, and double-meanings served the dual purposes of control and conflict. Pryor embraced this language and covered all three stages of avoidance, acceptance, and aggression.

Humor pressed from the comic vineyards of Woody Allen or Mel Brooks, as well as Bert Williams and Richard Pryor, is never sour grapes. Rather, their labor invites comparison with Paul Tillich's Protestant theology; both are existential philosophies of ultimate concern. Preoccupation with death as one *leitmotif* alternates with joyful, one is tempted to say Dionysian, transcendence. Though rooted in *tsores* (trouble) that appears to be timeless, our subject is a comedy of affirmation and continuity with a "fluid connection to history."[56] As a cultural force, blacks and Jews have imparted renewed vitality to a slumping America. Through their humor, lubricating as well as abrasive, they have recharged our nation's post-industrial machinery. Tuned in, we hear the electric hum of their talent, which reciprocally turns us on. Put less elegantly, the ethnic comedian provides a much-needed tonic—or enema?—for our ailing White Anglo Saxon Protestant *corpus*. Peter Schrag's epitaph—the Decline of the WASP—appears a bit premature since humor has buttressed conservative as well as radical structures. Little change, Christopher Wilson observed, can ever result for a process that, contrary to popular belief, is rarely anarchic and subversive. Often, jokes are potent instruments in protecting the status quo. The efficacy of protest humor remains a moot, if not mute, subject. According to various studies, ridicule is often "directed downwards and laterally through a hierarchy." For every Lenny Bruce, there are a multitude of Andrew Dice Clays and Howard Sterns. In lieu of "the dearly departed" Richard Pryor, there are too many Jimmy Walkers and Martin Lawrences. Since the professional comedian is a social success and potential role model, deviance must be stifled, if not "dynomited." Bill Maher, for example, was ousted from the ABC network after uttering controversial remarks after 9/11, while other mavericks like George Carlin, Jon Stewart, and Sarah Silverman were consigned to cable network outposts (the deceased Carlin on reruns) to where they can still be seen and heard. One example of the above dynamic issued from the Norman Lear TV series *All in the Family* (1971–79). Though Lear clearly intended to make the woefully ignorant and shamelessly bigoted Archie Bunker the butt of his sitcom humor, the opposite reaction occurred. Many viewers, if not the majority, laughed with Archie, not at him. In this recurring process, inequities, along with inequalities, remain. Bigotry's face is masked with a smile. Wilson concluded his analysis on a somber note: "Through its pleasures and personal utility, humor recruits and bribes us to become laughing conservatives."[57]

Clearly, derisive laughter may indeed shore up the social order, however unjust. Humor, in larger measure, is a defense against life's finite limits. We may wax wittily at death's doorstep—not so much in Promethean defiance, but more to dull the edge of fear at twilight time. We can also adopt Mel Brooks's strategy of eating a clove of garlic every evening. When the *malachamoves* knocks, we open the door, exhale, and ask loudly: "Who's there???" In a parallel struggle, Richard Pryor, after surviving a suicide attempt with a cocaine-induced fire, dialogued with the devil, who had attempted to restore his addiction. Laughter could not cure his other ailments, including multiple sclerosis. Thus, in their quest for survival, coupled with a penchant for social justice, unable to reject their destiny, blacks and Jews adjust. When they cannot adjust, they laugh.[58] Since the rupture of the black–Jewish alliance on the civil rights front, and in other vital causes during the 1960s, the humor of exclusion and the wit of aggression have gained primacy. What two authors described as a "bittersweet encounter" had degenerated into a relationship of sour gripes. As racism and anti–Semitism fester, progressive-minded persons fell into despair over the demise of Roosevelt's New Deal reform. The politics of hope renewed common ground during Barack Obama's successful presidential campaigns in 2008 and 2012. Obama's closest advisors, as well as his financial backers, were Jewish. Competing agendas on affirmative action, Israel, immigration, religious identities, however, precluded a full reconciliation.

Despair invites transcendence. Sigmund Freud viewed life as a dialectical battleground between Eros and Thanatos, or love and death. Based on his psychoanalysis of soldiers adversely affected during and after World War I by their traumatic experience, he sensed the prevalence of Thanatos inexorably leading to a tragic view of life. Bruno Bettelhein, a fellow practitioner in the field of Freud, conceded victory to the death drive but, he added, while we live we can struggle on the side of Eros. From his study and treatment of Holocaust survivors as well as his own incarceration in a concentration camp, Bettelheim concluded that we must live and love well.[59] We also need positive laughter, echoing the assertion of humor scholar Joyce O. Hertzler. Indeed, the humor of blacks and Jews serves Eros. Black humor, wrote Saunders Redding, represents "an escape into pride and dignity."[60] Similarly, Jewish humor signifies a transcendence of destiny. Comedians from both cultures have affirmed life in the face of adversity. They have kept the faith of their people aglow like a phoenix rising from the ashes.

THIRTEEN

Yip's Rainbow

Songs of Social Significance

Historically, Broadway Theatre has played an important role in heightening America's awareness of social issues. An effective vehicle in this pursuit is the musical, which has often served as a catalyst for cultural and political reform. Examples abound; a few merit mention. *Of Thee I Sing* (1931) satirized political corruption. *Show Boat* (1927), *Finian's* Rainbow (1947), and *South Pacific* (1949) excoriated racial prejudice. *Bloomer Girl* (1944) put a positive spin on feminism, and *La Cage Aux Folles* (1984) projected a favorable image of gay men. No one creative artist did more to, in the words of Harold Rome in his opening number in *Pins and Needles* (1937), "Sing Me a Song of Social Significance" than Isidore Hochberg.

In this study, I will concentrate on several signature songs and Broadway musicals, especially *Finian's Rainbow,* to explore the masterwork of the lyricist who "morphed" into E. Y. "Yip" Harburg (1896–1981). Though tainted, painted, and red-listed, "Yip" persevered, indeed prospered. Yip's success was a result of the rich vein of Jewish humor that courses through his career. His life and legacy give us much to ponder and to praise. Never a Mr. Blandish or a Mayflower Yankee like Miles Standish, sometimes a bit outlandish with a touch of sugar-candish, always kind of grandish with a social message to brandish, Yip continues to fascinate. As wars heighten our anxiety and raise questions about current policy, more than ever, Harburg has much to tell us, if only we would listen, for example, to "Leave de Atom Alone" or "Napoleon Is Only a Pastry"—and learn from his witty words of wisdom.

A "Red Diaper Baby," I was weaned on the principles of social justice and the lyrics of E. Y. "Yip" Harburg. I remember Father (mine, not Clarence Day's autocrat at the dinner table), a World War I veteran and 1932 Bonus Marcher. He loved songs of social conscience. His favorite had to be "Brother,

Can You Spare a Dime?" for he often conveyed the poignant message in a powerful baritone. My mother, a political activist, also a singer, steered me into "progressive" and secular pursuits. So on a brisk March Saturday in 1947, she invited two of my Jersey City cousins, Judy and Sandra Mandel, to join us for a Saturday matinee. Freshly scrubbed and nattily attired, we posed for a family photograph before we—three "Babes" and I—set off on "the yellow brick road" to Broadway to continue a not-so-sentimental education. Our destination, *Finian's Rainbow*, was a far cry from the local *shul* (synagogue) where my friends mumbled prayers they did not quite understand, seeking, I believed then, future real estate in heaven.

Only the second musical that I had ever attended—*Call Me Mister* had been the first—*Finian's Rainbow* transfixed us. What a show! Ella Logan did not perform that day. In her stead, a beautiful Dorothy Claire played the female lead minus Ella's Scottish burr. Impish David Wayne and handsome Donald Richards headed a stellar cast, which thrilled us with the "Begat" song, the ensemble dances, the magical moment when the bigot Senator Rawkins becomes black, and the rousing chorus numbers. At age ten, the romantic subplots, like Cole Porter's alcohol, did not thrill me at all. However, I did get a kick out of the political message, namely, that poor people—white as well as black—could become "the idle rich." Although I have searched in vain for Harburg's Rainbow, I never forgot that dazzling show. As I grew older and viewed life, as it were, through a glass darkly, the lyrics of *Finian* still resonate. Therefore, when I learned, belatedly, that Hofstra University was putting on another major conference, I hastily submitted a proposal in order to join the bandwagon. Fortunately, for me at least, it won approval. In joy, I shouted: Yip, Yip hooray!

Born Isidore Hochberg on 8 April 1896 (some sources insist on 1898), the youngest of four surviving children to Russian immigrants, Harburg spent his early years in a Lower East Side tenement. The family earned their "daily bread" in sweatshops. Grinding poverty forced young Isidore into odd jobs as messenger, meat packer, and clothes packer. "Yip"—the nickname that he earned for his small body type, scurrying quickly to and fro, allegedly derives from Yiddish, though Uriel Weinrich's impressive *Yiddish-English Dictionary* contains no such word for squirrel. Whatever the source, the name "Yip" became inseparable from the man. In high school he befriended Ira Gershwin, a shy, bespectacled sophisticate, who introduced him to the lyrics of W. A. Gilbert and later to the music of Arthur Sullivan. At Townsend Harris High School on East 23rd Street and later at CCNY on Convent Avenue, they emulated the wit of Gilbert.[2]

Ira dropped out to team up with his younger brother, George, for a spectacular career in musical theatre, while Yip, after earning a degree, took a detour to Uruguay as South America literally "took him away" from possible involvement in World War I and a literary career. Over there, he supervised a meatpacking factory. Returning to New York in 1920, he became a "card carrying" capitalist as an entrepreneur dealing in electric appliances. On "Easy Street" until the '29 Crash, Yip enjoyed affluence. Propelled out of electricity, he suffered what Edmund Wilson aptly called "the shock of recognition," and turned to music. The Great Depression functioned as a bane and a boon, a shock as well as a prod. Encouraged by his old friend Ira Gershwin to place items in Franklin P. Adams's column, "The Conning Tower," he submitted light verse that attracted the attention of composer Jay Gorney.[3] They soon teamed up to write songs for a show called *Americana* (1932). "Brother, Can You Spare a Dime?" (which was almost cut from the show) triggered fears of class warfare and spurred an attempt to censor this "national anthem" of the Great Depression, which failed after the twin towers of American popular song, Bing Crosby and Rudy Vallee, recorded it. This magnificent song invites careful reading and renewed discussion

"Brother" … was masterful: not too maudlin, not over-the-top in aggression; just right. I have heard several renditions, including a haunting interpretation by Fred Hellerman of "The Weavers." However, none ever matched Crosby's. Author William Zinsser astutely points to the song's impact as "the anthem of the Depression and a goad to Roosevelt's New Deal."[4]

Devoid of clichés, the trenchant lament was completed in one take by crooner Crosby, who delivered the message, according to biographer Gary Giddins, in a "perfectly pitched statement of protest and empathy, dignified but not somber, rueful but not bitter, heroic but not overwrought."[5]

Yip's son, Ernie, his co-author, Harold Meyerson, and Lewis A. Erenberg offer the most imaginative interpretation of this lyric and the voice behind it.[6] All dressed up with no place to go, youngsters of the 1930s experienced a power failure. A vanishing species, the male animal, shades of James Thurber and Elliot Nugent, languished. Crosby's lament in "Brother…" expresses an inability to build skyscrapers to the sun or forge high-speed railroads. *Homo Americanus*, as well as Mencken's booboisie, had lost their phallic power. The nation suffered a serious loss of cultural memory in consigning Al, once "Al all the time," to oblivion. Bing offered the right mix of pain and resolve.

In my history classes, I often evoke this song when lecturing on the Great Depression. Huddled in a tattered raincoat and faded hat with hand extended, I emulate the Great Crosby minus the wonderful voice. The notes fly up; the scale changes. Less than artful; however, my plea elicits a positive response. Students toss several coins in my direction. Unruffled, I collect the loose change. Born in 1936, I identify with this fearful generation. With tears coursing down my cheeks, I remember my father's soulful baritone voicing a generation's despair. Later, I realized that he was singing this poignant song Bing's way. My dad shared lyricist Harburg's political bent, which was far to the left of Crosby's.

Writing in 1967, Harold Rome, who coined the concept, recalled that "social significance climbed right to the top of the hit parade with E. Y. Harburg and Jay Gorney's theme song of the depression, 'Brother, Can You Spare a Dime?'"[7] Renowned raconteur and master of oral history Studs Terkel interviewed Yip, who explained the idea behind the song. He wanted to show the agony of the working-class American without sacrificing the "little man's dignity."[8] Anger, protest, doubt, and bafflement derive their power and purpose from concrete imagery and the less tangible *zeitgeist*, the spirit of the age.

Under the aegis of Franklin Delano Roosevelt, America began to recover. New Deal "alphabet agencies" sprouted, offering hope and providing renewal. The "forgotten man" was pulled from obscurity along with other marginals: women, Jews, blacks, artists, and intellectuals. Roosevelt's mastery on the domestic front, however, could not translate to control over international affairs. Goose-stepping robots followed the fascists in Spain, Italy, and Germany. Right-wing reactionaries proved cause for consternation elsewhere: France, England, Norway, Poland, and Hungary. Political disenchantment pervaded America, fueled by a Senate investigation of the underlying motive of America's entry into World War in 1917. Senator Nye, speaking for a majority on his committee, argued that money, J. P. Morgan money, $2.3 billion lent to France and Britain made American intervention on their behalf inexorable. Thus, a revisionist reading of history powered a return to isolationism and led to a new hard-boiled cynicism. Yip did not escape that malaise. Witness *Hooray for What?* (1937).

The plot of *Hooray...* is eerily prescient. Ed Wynn, for whom the play was designed after Victor Moore and Bobby Clark, in sequential order, proved unavailable, invents a deadly gas: so deadly that it can be used to conquer the world. Happily, the mad scientist, a recurrent figure in popular culture, refuses to share his secret. Fortunately, spies—who cannot copy accurately let alone shoot straight—reverse the formula and produce laughing gas, instead of lethal gas. So, everyone winds up kissing rather than killing each other. Yip's son Ernie observed that this play marked an important transition in his father's life. Not only did he establish a bi-coastal life; he also took control over future projects and moved closer to "full blown political book musicals."

The senior Harburg confessed that he left his heart at the stage doors of Broadway, where intellect was valued more than in Hollywood, which catered to viewers sporting a 12-year-old mental age.[9]

Two songs from *Hooray ...* invite scrutiny: the title song and "God's Country." "Hooray for What?," a caustic commentary on global events, the lyric carried a sharp anti-war message, dulled, alas, by the clownish antics of star Ed Wynn, who turned the show into a personal parade of favorite *shtick*. Perhaps to counteract the cynical lyrics, in "God's Country" Yip etched a gentler portrait of America, warts and all.[10]

Sniping at Europe and America, Yip clearly prefers the latter. The "camp" in our popular culture dwarfs the concentration camps abroad. Yip captures the conscience and consensus of America, vintage 1937. While his idol, Franklin Delano Roosevelt, was fiddling around with "Quarantine" strategies, Europe and Asia continued to burn during that grim year. In scanning this lyric, one should note the Semitic overtones. Harburg invidiously contrasts Mussolini and Hitler with Jessel's mother and Jolson's mammy, Benny's Jello and a guy named Fiorello: all Jewish by birth and sensibility. The lyric also contains references, one might term Semitic, to Cohen, Rubinoff's fiddle and Gracie Allen, wife of George Burns, né Nathan Birnbaum.

Again working with Harold Arlen, son of a cantor paved "the yellow brick road" to Hollywood and a date with the *Wizard of Oz*. Since this conference concerns the musicals of Broadway, not "Tinseltown," I will be brief on the Arlen-Harburg 1939 epic. A parable on populism, the script comported well with Yip's politics. Citing an analysis by Henry Littlefield, Myerson and Harburg *fils* profess that Frank L. Baum wrote a veiled lament for the demise of populism. Lacking a heart, Jack Haley's Tin Man represents the industrial working class, while Ray Bolger's brainless Scarecrow symbolizes the farmer. Bereft of courage, Bert Lahr's cowardly Lion is a caricature of the putative populist and inept perennial Democratic presidential candidate, William Jennings Bryan. Frank Morgan's phony wizard is a cruel (though accurate) caricature of our federal government, unable (or unwilling) to effect substantive reform. Although Meyerson and Harburg doubt that Yip grasped the essence of this allegory, they credit him for inserting "Ding, Dong" as a song of liberation and demystification.[11] Yip's lifelong distrust of, even contempt for, organized religion surfaces in *Oz*'s happy ending, coded with his political credo.

The next big thing on film for the dynamic duo of Harburg and Arlen was an all-black musical, *Cabin in the Sky* (1943). Vincente Minelli directed this pioneering effort. Politics evidently played second fiddle to the "bottom-line" in this depiction of the black experience. Author Gene Lees, invariably insightful, called the script "embarrassing." He added: "It is so awful, so drenched in racial stereotypes, that it exerts a certain morbid fascination." The Arlen-Harburg score was one of the few redeeming features that Lees found.[12]

Restless in Hollywood, Yip yearned for New York action. Opportunity knocked in 1944. Film director Frank Capra, in a series of documentaries commissioned by the Office of War Information, tried to explain "Why We Fight." Some of the best films from this era, such as *Casablanca* (1942), provided answers. The wartime musical forced us to define why "we were the good guys," argues critic Ethan Mordden.[13] With *Oklahoma!* as the new model of an integrated musical, Harburg decided to combine history, nostalgia, reform, music, and humor. With Arlen in tow, Yip engaged Fred Saidy and Sig Herzig to frame a new kind of "message" musical. Out of this collaboration came *Bloomer Girl* (1944). To be sure, Yip's radical circle of friends had discussed and debated current events; but it was the socially committed lyricist who transferred cutting-edge commentary on social issues to the Broadway stage. Feminism, abolition, and just war entered front and center. Largely derived from the precedent-shattering *Oklahoma!* integrated musical, Harburg even imported several featured participants in this Rodgers-Hammerstein classic, namely, actors Celeste Holm and Joan McCracken, choreographer Agnes DeMille, not to mention set designers and an orchestrator. *Bloomer Girl*, under Yip's creative aegis, however, aimed to enlighten as well as to entertain.[14]

Set in imaginary Cicero Falls, c. 1861, a stone's throw from Seneca Falls, New York, the birthplace of American feminism in 1848, the script pits "Dolly" Bloomer and her niece Evalina against the establishment personified by Evalina's father, who arbitrarily betroths her to a Southern slaveholder. A runaway slave, Pompey (Dooley Wilson), provides dramatic conflict in a complex plot that ends happily. Like so much of the Harburg *oeuvre*, the serious message was rendered palatable, indeed leavened, by his yeasty sense of humor. One case in point follows[15]:

> EVALINA: Whatever happened to that young man of yours, Aunt Dolly?
> AUNT DOLLY: He came to a bad end—got to be governor.

When the paternalistic slaveholder-suitor expresses a desire to free his slave, Pompey, but wants to know why he ran away, Dooley Wilson, no longer the subservient Sam from *Casablanca*, refuses to play the same old song. Instead he sings about the eagle's need for freedom in "The Eagle and Me."[16]

Feminism was advanced by another song, "It Was Good Enough for

Grandma"; radical politics, by "T'morra, T'morra." The play's 654 perform-ances proved that socially significant, as well as intellectually stimulating, musical theatre could also be profitable.

The year 1944 ushered in a fierce political campaign, during which Yip hitched his wagon to a star, in FDR. Harburg helped to launch the Hollywood Democratic Committee and played a major role in the election-eve broadcast: contributing three songs to this victorious effort. Roused by a Red Cross directive to segregate blood banks, Yip joined Earl Robinson, a young com-munist composer from Seattle, to pen a caustic lyric: "Free and Equal Blues."[17]

When Yip tried to recruit Arlen for another musical, the composer felt that his frequent collaborator was becoming too political, too didactic, and too propagandistic. Earl Robinson lacked the capacity at that time to write a complex score for Broadway. So Yip turned to Burton Lane and created a classic: *Finian's Rainbow*. Meyerson and Harburg contend that *Finian* "allowed Yip the fullest and most successful expression of his talents and politics" and constitutes for the first time, "a work of socialist analysis in the form of an American musical."[18] Spurred by anger, Yip took up the cudgels against racism, class prejudice, capitalism, fetishism, and hypocrisy—with humor to boot.

The plot charts the pilgrims' progress of Finian McLonergan, an Irish dreamer and schemer who steals a pot of gold and tries to grow more in Mis-situcky, a mythical Southern hybrid state deep in the heartland of America. Here, Finian and his daughter, Sharon, encounter the racist Senator Billboard Rawkins, a composite of Congressman John Rankin and Senator Theodore Bilbo, two actual Southern bigots housed in Congress; Woody Mahoney, a charismatic leader cut from the same cloth as troubadour Woody Guthrie; and Oz, the lascivious leprechaun (with a touch of Yip), who is seeking to retrieve his stolen treasure.

There are so many wonderful songs in this brilliant show, but our pri-mary concerns are those which impart a social message. *Necessity* forces men and women to renounce the pleasure principle in favor of work. It speaks to Marxian determinism. Contrapuntally, a cockeyed optimism invests Har-burg's vision. Ultimately, on "That Great Come-and-Get-It Day," the dialectic will end happily.[19]

Religious visions dance alongside of materialistic "goodies." Apocalypse Now arrives with a burst of American affluence, an accurate reflection of post–World War II culture. This leads to a third song of social commentary, "When the Idle Poor Become the Idle Rich."[20]

In "The Begat"[21] not only does Yip poke fun at the world's population explosion along with Bible-belting rhetoric, he also takes on certain sacred elephants: the Daughters of the American Revolution, as well as the Republican Party. According to author Gene Lees, Harburg was inviting trouble and possible retaliation from HUAC, Joe McCarthy, and the G.O.P. By targeting disorganized religion in its pious pursuit of pleasure, Harburg refused to conceal his disdain for "faith-based" charity. Perhaps he intuited what Lenny Bruce would later assert, namely, that "the only anonymous giver is one who knocks up your daughter."[22]

Finian's Rainbow holds up a mirror to America. Harburg found much that was repugnant on native grounds. His anger turned bilious in Act Two. Therefore, composer Burton Lane threw a tantrum, demanding substantive changes in the script that converted rage into realism, bile into humor. He won that round, but relations between the two soured.[23] In a pithy evaluation, Ethan Mordden observes that wry humor tempers Yip's cynicism. True, to succeed in this culture, you are either a crook or a stooge, but everybody lives well. Finian must reassure his daughter who, mimicking Rooseveltian rhetoric, wants to know: "Are there no poor in America, no ill-housed, no ill-clad?" To which her father replies: "Of course, Sharon, but they're the best ill-housed and the best ill-clad in the whole world."[24] Clearly, *Finian's Rainbow* was highly subversive, yet highly successful. While the "Red Scare" began to intensify in lock step with the "Cold War," Yip continued to thrive on Broadway. He was less fortunate in other media: film, radio, and, television. In 1950, for example, the advent of armed conflict in Korea coincided with Yip's exile from Hollywood. He was forced to leave a project with Burton Lane to create an MGM musical version of *Huckleberry Finn*. Yip fought for his professional life. He parried the charges with an affirmation of his credible credo in a letter to a lawyer at MGM.[25]

> I am a Franklin Delano Roosevelt Democrat, believing firmly in everything he stood for. As a firm, almost fanatical believer in democracy, as a proud American, and as the writer of the lyric of the song, "God's Country," I am outraged by the suggestion that somehow I am connected with, believe in, or am sympathetic with Communist or totalitarian philosophy.

Yip waxed proud over his patriotic *oeuvre*. To his credit, he refused to name names incurring the wrath of right-wing reactionaries and, surprisingly, condescending commentary from Victor Navasky for trying to play ball, so to speak, with the enemy.[26] Yip had paid dearly for his lyrics, his linkage to left-wing activities, especially the Henry Wallace campaign for president in 1948, for which he wrote a campaign song and composed a speech for Paul Robeson at a Madison Square Garden rally (which I attended).[27]

Thank God for Broadway! She came through for many red-listed artists during "Scoundrel Time." Indeed, in the very eye of the McCarthy-powered hurricane, Yip constructed his most radical critique of capitalism. No doubt,

Flahooley (1951), co-written with Sammy Fain, composer of "I'll Be Seeing You" did not synchronize with the creeping conservatism and raging paranoia over Reds under our beds. The plot is a less than subtle attack on our system: corporatism, consumerism, and political witch-hunts. Even box-office failures such as *Flahooley*[28] (only 48 performances) have redemptive features. The title song springs to mind, where crass Christmas commercialism gets its comeuppance, shades of George S. Kaufman, in "Sing the Merry."[29]

Strong stuff for 1951, Meyerson and Harburg argue cogently, but a neglected point here is a thick undercurrent of Jewish humor. One of its salient characteristics, as I have indicated in several prior publications, is a democratic tendency to level the playing field, to deflate the pompous, to topple the powerful from their perch, and to criticize religion. Yip paid homage to his mentors, Gilbert & Sullivan. Their gibes at the Establishment, however, are gentle at worst. Harburg, in my judgment, should have looked to the Jewish rainbow or chrysalis. What could be more Jewish than Yip's quips as cited in the *Burlington Free Press*, November 4, 1970? Humor set to music is "the most formidable art form" and "when you attack with humor, you show your enemy you're not afraid."[30] Although he sometimes minimized the influence of Jewish culture on his work, Harburg revealed the roots of his inspiration (and, happily, confirmation of my thesis) to Bernard Rosenberg and Ernest Goldstein in their masterful study, *Creators and Disturbers: Reminiscences by Jewish Intellectuals.*[31]

> The Yiddish theater was my first break into the entertainment world, and it was a powerful influence. Jews are born dramatists, and think[ing] born humorists too. Yiddish has more onomatopoetic, satiric, and metaphoric nuances ready-made for comedy than any other language I know of. Jewish humor was the basis for much great vaudeville, my next passion.

Starting with Boris Tomashevsky, the great *shoishpiler* (actor) in Yiddish theatre, Yip cites a litany of favorite Jewish performers: Al Jolson, Fanny Brice, Willie Howard, Ed Wynn, and Bert Lahr.[32] Bert's son, John, confirms the Yiddish connection. He notes the role that Louis Hochberg played in his son Yip's formative years: reading Sholem Aleichem over a *glezele tay* (a small glass of tea); imparting lessons in survival through humor; prodding his clownish antics; and nurturing his son's socialist sensibilities.[33]

Years later, Harburg delivered a speech attacking "witch-hunts." The opening line, a play on Descartes; a plague on HUAC, was: "I think therefore I am—in jail." In this clever, satirical thrust at the "Red Scare," Harburg jested as he suggested that we make the Smith Act retroactive so that we can posthumously prosecute Walt Whitman, Abraham Lincoln, and Thomas Jefferson. He envisioned a newspaper headline, which read: "Songwriter Gets Five Years for Advocating a Slow Boat to China."[34] Eventually, the red-list abated, but the memory lingered for Yip. In order to do a film with his conservative buddy Harold Arlen on "Nellie Bly," an MGM film project, Harburg had to gain clearance from Roy Brewer, head of IATSE, a super-patriotic organization. Confronting Brewer, who wore a second hat as an American Legion executive, and Cardigan, a paid informer, Yip defended his aid to Chinese relief and to Spanish loyalists fighting against the Franco-led fascists. Finally, his grand inquisitors asked which Joe was the recipient of his "funny Valentine" song "Happiness Is Just a Thing Called Joe." "Joe Stalin?" they insinuated. Yip "blew" the interview but exited, pride intact, laughing at these contemptible, far from grand inquisitors and denigrated the *Legionnaire* as a fourth-rate magazine.[35]

Yip's anger was channeled creatively into vintage Jewish humor. After an involuntary twelve-year absence from "Tinsel Town," Harburg joked: "It's nice to be back in Hollywood—after being kicked out by Joe McCarthy." Citing his "Monkey in the Mango Tree," he questioned Darwin's premise that we represent the "survival of the fittest." Groucho Marx, another Jewish wit, joined in the joyful welcome: singing and *tummling*. Sylvia Drake, *Times* staff writer, provided a quick study of the returning prodigal. "He's a natural storyteller, armed with disarming charm, *Hebraic wit* [emphasis mine], and exuberant politics."[36]

We academics love to talk. Not unlike the Flahooley toy, you wind us up and we go on indefinitely. Like Groucho (for whom Yip wrote "Lydia, the Tatooed Lady" in 1939), I must be going. Before departing, I feel constrained to end this journey somewhat short of the rainbow—in *Jamaica*. Staged in 1956, it brought Harburg and Arlen together again, alas, for the final time. Designed originally for life with Harry Belafonte, the play changed directions, title (initially "Pigeon Island"), and star after the great calypso singer left to undergo throat surgery. Retailored for the sultry Lena Horne, under producer David Merrick's dictatorial aegis, the musical lost its original scope and Harburgian message. Nevertheless, several signature songs, bearing Yip's commitment to social commentary and political reform, resurfaced.

It behooves us today to revisit *Jamaica* for moral instruction. "Push de Button" satirized our gadget-driven society; "Hooray for the Yankee Dollar" lampooned tourist-imperialism; "Monkey in the Mango Tree" questioned the Darwinian paradigm. These Arlen-Harburg gems throw a laser light on what Freud aptly called "civilization and its discontents." Where are the Menckens and the Harburgs of today?

In the final analysis, how do we measure E. Y. Harburg: Jewish leprechaun, word-*mayvn*, and *mentsch* for all seasons? Perry Como knew: "It's impossible!" So did the Beigelman *shvester* (read Barry Sisters). "*S'iz umayglach zein."* John Lahr, Harold Meyerson, and Ernie Harburg did it far better than I can. To avoid an assessment, however, would constitute a "cop-out." Yip hated such evasions. So, for the record, permit me a brief coda as well as a true confession. I love Yip Harburg. He is my Hemingway hero because he confronted adversity with grace under pressure. Yip integrated the Broadway musical, placing black and white dancers in the same ensemble, and raised issues of class, race, and gender, all hitherto taboo subjects. More-over, he was generous to a fault, doling out "dimes" (and more) to friends, fellow victims of McCarthyism, in need. For example, Yip helped Howard Fast, Barrows Dunham, and Jack Gilford, among many others.[37] Exemplifying the Jewish/Muslim/Christian moral imperative of *tzedakah*, Harburg pro-vided funds to fellow victims, even though his own income had markedly diminished. Though red-listed for 12 years, Harburg never lost his moral compass. His active, creative, and socially significant life constituted the best revenge. Over the abyss, he brought rainbows. He spoke truth to power. I sing the praises of Isidore Hochberg, and "If This Isn't Love ... the Whole World Is Crazy!"[38]

Who could say anything more except to follow the fellow who follows the dream? And sing out as did the late Pete Seeger, the Pied Piper of folk music who contributed to a memorable march for peace on February 15, 2003, by singing "Over the Rainbow."[39]

FOURTEEN

Coda

Around the World in Eighty Jokes Plus

Now, dear reader, it is time for a more than brief summation. Why so many Jewish humorists? Why not? A Jew invariably answers a question with another question. One small book, Robert Menchin's *101 Classic Jewish Jokes*, contains a large amount of funny stuff. On the very first page, the author cites cultural equations. Russia is identified with ballet; Italy with opera; France with cuisine; and Jews with humor.[1] Menchin refers to Jews as a people, not Israel as a nation-state, in this coupling. Indeed, one scholar, Salcia Landmann, argued that the creation of a Jewish state in 1948 would signal an end to that mother-lode of wit and wisdom codified as Jewish humor because it issued from powerless people suffering from poverty as well as from pain.[2] Constantly on the move in search of a secure life, Jews developed both a defensive fortress in humor and a retaliatory weapon in *die goldene medina*, America the "Golden Land."

We have touched on many creators of humor in different genres: vaudeville, burlesque, Yiddish theater, musical theater, nightclubs, radio, television, literature, film, and the Catskill Mountains, where comedy went to school. Unable to cover every contributor to this this rich trove of Jewish humor, we were compelled to omit several important figures, to be sure; but we have labored to highlight those transitional figures, including African American humorists, whose work changed the way Americans laugh. Some relevant observations, absent from what preceded this final chapter, invite discussion. Those comedians who never quite made it to the elusive top demand our attention as well. If Lawrence E. Mintz and Stefanie Koziski Olson are correct in regarding stand-up comedians as cultural anthropologists, who register significant changes in society, then Mal Z. Lawrence deserves further study.[3]

Undoubtedly, the funniest Catskill comic who worked the "Borscht Belt" circuit from New York to Florida is Bronx-born Mal Z. Lawrence. He started in the Catskills in 1955 as social director at Ellenville's Sunrise Manor. From 1955 to 1965, dancing was hot and mambo was king in the Catskills. Women dressed to kill and "men wore Machito shirts: big blousy things with white cuffs sticking out of the suit jacket."[4] Mal Z.'s collaboration with Freddy Roman, Dick Capri and Marilyn Michaels as the original cast of *Catskills on Broadway* brought these excellent jokesters a vast new forum for their talents. For decades, hotel goers thrilled to their riffs. Mal Z. played on the Jewish penchant for *fressing* (overeating), gambling, *shtuping* (indulging in carnal knowledge) and other delights. As a cultural anthropologist, Mal Z. zeroed in on tribal behavior. As a modern shaman, he purged our demons and provided an escape through laughter. A *New York Times* reporter quoted this comic observer when the Borscht Belt began a free fall in the mid–1980s.[5]

- The Concord is very big into athletics and entertainment. The bigger the star, the sooner they walk out. Some nights you get a crowd, you say, "Good evening ladies and gentlemen" and they say, "Oh, enough already."
- At the Pines, I tell a little more of a family joke. Brown's is an older crowd. They want to eat and play cards. I do my eating routine there, they die.
- Grossinger's is more religious. They got a lot of young Orthodox singles. They wear windbreakers and crocheted yarmulkes with a bobby pin. During succoth, at Grossinger's, they go out to the succah and smoke a joint. Hasidim are in this year. Everybody wants to look like Boy George.
- What a day here at the Pines: the hustle, the bustle, the yawning, the yawning. Something came back into your lives that you haven't done in years—it's called a walk. Where? We'll walk out. We'll look at the fence. We'll smell the flowers, we'll look at the guard's booth, we'll walk back.
- We need gambling here—not Atlantic City. What symbols on the slot machines! No cherries, no oranges—*prunes*.

    Three prunes and you go to the crap table. Here in the Catskills they will clean you out one way or another.

    At the conservative slot machine, if you get three prunes, you get to kiss the Torah. At the orthodox one, three prunes will allow you to walk around the room and have others kiss the Torah.
- Can you imagine what casinos will be like here? "Excuse me, could you tell me where they're playing Hide the Matzoh?"

During Chanukah, they play the draydl game. "Shake the gimmel and watch that sucker spin!" Food remains an obsession with guests. Harvey & Myrna Frommer, authors *It Happened in the Catskills*, quote Mal Z. Lawrence on this vital topic: "Like everyone else, I started in the Catskills." Fast forward to the dining room[6]:

- You know it's lunch because they see that the other people are beginning to move. In the dining room, people who haven't read a newspaper in years begin to study the menu.
- Apple juice, apple juice. Who wants apple juice. Apple juice, tomato juice, who wants? "What kind of juice do you want? ... Who wants a schav? You want a schav? Wanna schav?"
- "You want a borscht? Potato? No potato? One potato. Two potato. Garni? What is garni? Did you ever eat garni? Jellied yellow pike ... Uhgghhh."
- The more you read, the less you know what you want. People are really confused now. They look at each other in desperation. They say the same thing at every table.
- "What are you going to get? You want to share something?" "Come on, we'll split something. I'll have half of yours. You'll have a half of mine. Because, really I couldn't eat the whole thing."
- "Waiter, you know we normally don't eat like this. I'll just have a little herring on the side, just half a lox, a side dish of herring, a side dish of beef, a side of white fish, a side of—MOBY DICK!"
- And then there's "For later." "These Danish are for later. Not now. Later! We'll have them with coffee—on November 23rd."
- I remember the announcement. "The tea room is open." There were no coffee shops at first. The hotels themselves supplied cake and cookies. Before you knew it, the tea room started to serve pickled herring, lox. It became the eagerly awaited fourth meal. Every mother would say: "Eat! Eat! We're paying for it."[7]

Mal Z. kept working at "gigs," both small as well as big, seeking "The Blue Bird of Happiness" of Catskill graduate Jan Peerce. Yet, he punctuated most of his performances with a *krechtz*, a Jewish blue note. "It's so nice to be here, ladies and gentleman. This is the end of a career. Please, on your way out, leave a stone on the top of my car."[8]

Finally, he charts the sociological change in Catskill culture. "Years ago," he observed sadly, "you used to sit down for dinner, your waiter was named Mendel, Yankel, Yussel, Moishe. Now it's Pablo, Xavier, Chico, Julio. Julio says to you: "Hey man, wanna kipper, man? You want some horseradish, man?" Did this signal a new era—that of the Spanish Alps?[9] Unfortunately, a Yiddish phrase rings true: *Vos is geveyn iz geveyn un iz itz nishtu* (What once was is in the past and is no longer here). This lament applies to Mal Z. Lawrence, due to a lingering illness, and to the Catskill hotels, at one time the largest resort complex in the America.

One neglected element, indeed a missing link in most history books until recently, is gender. Clearly, women have received short shrift. Therefore, in order to right (and write about) this wrong, as Arthur Miller's Linda Loman in *Death of a Salesman* reminded us: "Attention must be paid." Thus, we pay tribute to a pioneer: Joan Rivers. The "mouth that roared" was silenced by death on September 4, 2014. Born in Brooklyn in 1933, to a pretentious mother, Beatrice, and a henpecked father, Dr. Meyer Molinsky—both Russian immigrants—Joan Sandra Molinsky grew up under the shadow of an older, bright as well as beautiful, sister, Barbara. Beset with many complexes, Joan insisted, "I was so fat; I was my own buddy in camp." Despite her carefully crafted comic persona, Joan was a brilliant student, having graduated from Barnard College with high honors, in 1954.

Ignoring her parents' pleas, Joan pursued a career as an actress and singer. But comedy proved a better fit. A long apprenticeship that included performing in the Catskill hotels (because she had a car and agreed to drive her peers there and back), a stint with Chicago's Second City ensemble, many nightclubs, and some "toilets" ultimately led to success capped by a brilliant ten minutes on Johnny Carson's *Tonight Show* in 1965. Inspired by Lenny Bruce, who had encouraged her to expand her vocabulary, Rivers began a barrage of *shmutz* (dirty words) to engage audiences in the pursuit of truth as *Yente*-in-Chief. After watching her perform, Bruce wrote her a note: "You're right and they're wrong."[10] Billed as a writer, Rivers was 32 when she vaulted to stardom. Her early *shtick*, shades of traditional Jewish humor, featured self-deprecating jokes, especially about her allegedly "ugly duckling" appearance. In fact, before multiple cosmetic surgeries, she was actually quite pretty, if not drop-dead gorgeous. Here are examples culled from an excellent essay in which critic Sarah Blacher Cohen placed her in the historical context of "Unkosher Comediennes."[11]

- On our wedding night, my husband said: "Can I help with the buttons?" I was naked at the time.
- You've heard of A Cup, B Cup, and C Cup. Well, you're looking at demitasse.
- They show my body to men on death row to get their minds off women.

- Three stagehands saw me naked. One threw up and the others turned gay.
- My body is so bad; a Peeping Tom looked in my window and pulled down the shade.
- Dress by Oscar de la Rental; body by Oscar Meyer.

Obviously, she posed no threat to the *femmes fatales* or *macho* males in the audience. As a Jewish comedienne, she evaded the lethal blows of anti–Semitism by mocking our tribe and herself[12]:

- I want a Jewish delivery—to be knocked out in the delivery room and wake up two weeks later at the hairdresser's.
- A Jewish porno film is made up of one minute of sex and six minutes of guilt.
- Jews get orgasms in department stores.
- A Jewish computer punches in three times five which equals fifteen but, for you, twelve dollars and ninety-five cents.

Unlike most of her female predecessors, the attractive Rivers wrote her own material and launched an arsenal of verbal missiles. In the late 1970s, she became more aggressive, her jokes a deeper shade of blue. Average folks identified with Rivers when she attacked celebrities, the rich and so-called beautiful people, namely, Elizabeth Taylor, Christina Onassis, Nancy Kissinger, and Bo Derek. Rivers declared that Bo Derek, the putative "Ten," "is so dumb she has to study for her Pap Test" and that she turned down the role of Helen Keller because she couldn't remember the lines.[13] As she rhetorically asked her fans with a pseudo-intimate rallying cry—"Can we talk?—Rivers defended this dramatic departure as a response to "tasteless times." In a real sense, Rivers spoke to the disaffected if not "silent majority"—for outsiders and women who lacked power but possessed other assets. Joan Rivers urged women to "marry rich. Buy him a pacemaker, then stand behind him and say BOO!" This strategy was open to contradictory claims: one as a feminist rebel; the other as a pre-liberation *femme fatale* or *kurve* (a woman of commercial affection) who barters, as Sophie Tucker advised, sex for material rewards.

Growing more conservative in the 1980s, Rivers lampooned the Democratic ticket of Mondale and Ferraro as "Fritz and Tits." If elected in 1984, they would constitute "three boobs in the White House." The strategy of offending feminists and befriending Nancy Reagan was tailored to a new Joan Rivers persona. On the subject of tailors, Elizabeth received no mercy from Rivers.

- Her thighs are going condo. She wears stretch caftans.
- She has more chins than a Chinese phone book.
- She blew up like a balloon on which you could put the stamp of Goodyear and use at the Rose Bowl.
- When mosquitoes see her, they scream: "Buffet!"
- When she put on a yellow dress, thirty kids thought she was a school bus and tried to board her.

Later, Rivers confessed that these remarks were prompted by envy—not malice: both deemed by medieval Christian philosophers as two of the "Seven Deadly Sins." Whatever the rationale, Rivers did not withhold verbal darts from "horsey" Nancy Kissinger whom, she alleged, "wears saddles by Gucci" and rebuffs Henry's sexual advances with "Neigh, neigh, neigh." Of the rich and troubled Christina Onassis, Rivers remarked: "People thought she had a fur coat on, but she was wearing a strapless gown. When she raised her arm, they saw the Greek National Forest." Rivers also created a *shtick*, in which an abrasive Gloria Steinem–type mocks patriarchal society for putting women down, especially the gynecologist.[14]

> I wonder why I'm not relaxed. My feet are in the stirrups, my knees are in my face and the door is open, facing me. And there's always a guy in the waiting room you went to high school with…. My doctor always tells jokes. "Dr. Schwartz, at your cervix." You know what it's like to be in the stirrups and your doctor walks in wearing a snorkel. "I'm dilated to meet you," says he…. "Nurse Kelley, come here. Want to see some cob webs? Bring that Endust." We have spent the whole morning taking a bath, showering, powdering, perfuming, shaving and douching and that son of a bitch has the nerve to wear a rubber glove. Who is *he*?

Crossing boundaries, pushing envelopes, seeking acclaim, Joan Rivers exhibited what the ancient Greeks called *hubris*. When Rivers, in accord with her husband-manager Edgar Rosenberg, decided to compete with Johnny Carson on the Fox network at the same time slot, things fell apart. A furious Carson permanently broke off relations with his former acolyte. The experiment failed after only one year. Fox executives fired Edgar. Depressed and separated from Joan, Edgar committed suicide.

Undaunted, resilient, a "cat" with many lives, she clawed back to fame with "gigs" on the red carpet alongside her daughter, Melissa. There were nightclub performances, guest appearances on television as a shopping network pitchwoman, and at college venues. This author attended one at Brooklyn College. That memorable evening featured RuPaul, a transgendered performer, who was compelled to leave the stage prompted by a chorus of boos. Joan Rivers followed with a masterful comedic act but not before gently chiding the audience for its intolerance and urging all to be more open-minded. In 2010, critic Roger Ebert, not known for easy praise, wrote this[15]:

> I think *Joan Rivers: A Piece of Work* [a documentary] is fascinating and has a lot of laughs in it. It's more than that. It's the portrait of a woman who will not accept defeat, who will not slow down, who must prove herself over and over again. A brave and stubborn woman, smart as a whip, superbly skilled. You want to see what it looks like to rage, rage against the dying of the light? Joan Rivers will not go gently into that good night.

Before that brilliant light dimmed, then died, Joan Rivers's rage, heavily salted with Jewish humor, gave us loads of healing laughter.

Joan Rivers paved the way for a whole host of female comediennes, many of them members of the Jewish tribe, like Elayne Boosler, Emily Levine, Corey Kahane, Carol Leifer, Sandra Bernhard, Rita Rudner, Adrienne Tolsch, Sarah Silverman, and Wendy Liebman. Essentially stand-ups, they had to share the spotlight with Jewish women who flocked into sitcoms, a subject in an earlier chapter, like Roseanne Barr, Fran Drescher, Lisa Kudrow, and those who ventured to films, like Bette Midler, Gilda Radner, Madeline Kahn, Estelle Getty, Sarah Jessica Parker (half Jewish). Though extremely funny, too, they seemed to lack Rivers's strong sense of Jewish identity, no doubt a reflection of assimilation's lure.

When I began the research for this book, the most astonishing discovery issued from a disconnect between the proliferation of Jewish comedy work-

Corey Kahaney: a Jewish comedienne with an Irish name, she continues to evoke laughter on a trail blazed by Joan Rivers and Elayne Boosler.

Award-winning comedienne Wendy Liebman, 2013.

ers—writers, directors, producers, agents, stand-up performers, females as well as males, sitcom creators, and critics—and the small number of Jews among the world's population. "Anywhere I wandered, everywhere I go" (to echo a popular song crafted by composer Frank Loesser, blessed with Jewish wit), in Russia, Germany, Canada, France, Great Britain, Austria, and Australia, one finds Jews among the elite humorists. Evidently, "They got talent." When I consulted Emil Draitser, an eminent expert and exile from the USSR, I asked, "How do you account for this extraordinary phenomenon: is it nature or nurture; genetic or environmental?" He replied: "Genetic! It comes from Genesis!" The pun, as in *punim*, has a Jewish face. Draitser's published works, including a delightful Russian-English book called *Forbidden Laughter*, document the proliferation of Jewish humor in Russia. Even Joseph Stalin, a notorious anti–Semite, loved Jewish jokes. While hunkered down in the Kremlin under relentless Nazi assault in those terrible years, 1941–1942, Stalin commanded his Jewish associates to regale him with humor. Although expressly prohibited by the Soviet Constitution in 1936, anti–Semitism increased markedly after World War II, when Stalin orchestrated another purge that propelled Jewish writers, intellectuals, and political figures into oblivion. Humor went underground, so to speak, except for a favored few.

One comedian who escaped the gallows after performing satiric skits that teemed with gallows humor was Arkady Raikin. In a career that spanned the eras of Stalin, Khrushchev, and Brezhnev, he appeared in October 1984 with a head framed by a large white pompadour and shoulders stooped with the weight of Jewish history. As an audience of 2,500 looked on gleefully, Raikin interrupted his silent entrance with these words[16]:

> Oh, maybe it's not worth it. Maybe we should just keep silent tonight. We're all so good at keeping silent, and they say silence is golden. I could, for instance, keep my mouth shut tonight for three hours plus intermission. That way we won't take any risks. Or maybe we should talk about that ... about, about. No, about that people are keeping silent these days on every street corner.

Fifty years prior, Harpo Marx was sent to Russia in 1934 as a goodwill ambassador and spy after the United States established diplomatic relations with the Soviet Union. Evidently, Harpo enthralled audiences with his silent capers, while offstage he funneled information (strapped to his leg) to his handlers in government.[17]

In Central and Western Europe during the 1920s and 1930s, Jewish humorists were busy challenging authority and mocking conventional pieties. Recently resurrected by novelist Jonathan Franzen (who refused to be marketed by Oprah Winfrey), satirist Karl Kraus, a Viennese Jew, who converted to Catholicism in 1928, but left the church in 1933, lampooned *Kitsch* or middlebrow culture in his magazine *Die Fackel* (*The Torch*). His favorite targets, Edmund Fawcett wrote in the *New York Times*, were "warrior-politicians, profit-driven businessmen, faddish taste and, above all, the 'educated press.'"[18] Fawcett cites a few of Kraus's best *bon mots*:

- Diplomats lie to journalists, then believe the headlines.
- Psychoanalysis is the disease that takes care of the cure.
- Snobs are not reliable. Some things they like are good.
- Dogs are loyal, yes, but to us, not to other dogs.

Another German-Jewish writer with a rapier wit, Kurt Tucholsky invites a second look. A veteran of World War I, he became an ardent pacifist as well as a vocal leftist. Arguably the most mordant wit in Weimar, Germany, Tucholsky was equally adept in poetry and prose. Journalist William Grimes identified the source of Tucholsky's bile as "the reactionary institutions of the old regime, the follies of the Weimar Republic, the pretentions of Berliners and the peculiarities of the German character."[19] Aware of his powerful satire that threatened the myth of Nazi supremacy, Hitler had his books burned and stripped Tucholsky of German citizenship. An exile in Sweden—unable to live in a world of tyranny triumphant—the brilliant satirist committed suicide in 1935. He was only 45 years old.

Unlike their Central European cousins, Jewish humorists in America were more optimistic. They railed against authority figures without incurring the wrath of potentates that led to prison, exile, and/or suicide. One dramatic example can be found during the Watergate crisis of 1973–1974. Although by that time Lenny Bruce was dead, others took up the cudgels of criticism. Author Philip Roth savaged "Tricky Dicky" in his novel *Our Gang*. Comedians David Steinberg, Mort Sahl, David Frye, and Robert Klein used their comedic "bully pulpit" to take down the sitting president. Jackie Mason suggested that Nixon was plagued by syphilis, not phlebitis. "You don't get phlebitis from screwing the country." Cartoonists Herblock, Jules Feiffer, and David Levine punctured the Pinocchio-prone president with brilliant, if vicious, caricatures, featuring a nose that lengthened with each lie. Impressionist Frye captured the flittering eyes, paranoid posture, and disingenuous declarations: "I love America and you always hurt the one you love." Not unlike Captain Queeg in Nixon's favorite novel, Herman Wouk's *The Caine Mutiny Court Martial*, Frye's send-up transforms the president into Humphrey Bogart, clinking steel balls while "blaming Haldeman, Erlichman, and Dean for robbing strawberries on the ship of state."[20] Columnist Art Buchwald called for a new annual holiday on June 17: a celebration of the Watergate break-in by "tapping other people's telephones, spying on their neighbors, wearing red wigs, and making inoperative statements."[21] All of the above escaped punishment, except for possible inclusion on the president's long enemy list, which some (like Groucho Marx) wore as a badge of honor.

For telling a joke in Stalin's Russia, you could get an involuntary trip to a gulag in Siberia. Witness this exchange between two inmates[22]:

> How much did you get?
> Fifteen years.
> What's your crime?
> No crime at all.
> Lie. For no crime you get ten years nowadays.

In Hitler's Germany a comparable joke could lead to death. One woman, Marianne Elise K., told the following joke in 1944: Hitler and Goering are standing on top of Berlin's radio tower. Hitler says he wants to do something to cheer up the people of Berlin. Goering suggests: "Why don't you jump?" Overheard by a fellow worker, Marianne was charged with "undermining the war effort with spiteful remarks," and executed.[23] Arguably, the best joke in the Herzog book provides its title, *Heil Hitler, Das Schvein Ist Tot! Lachen unter Hitler*[24]:

> Hitler and his chauffeur are driving across the countryside when *bang!* there's some kind of impact. So the chauffeur stops the car and takes a look and it turns out they've actually run over a pig.

So Hitler says, "Look, we've got to confess to the farmer that we've run over his pig." The chauffeur walks off and he's away for ten minutes. Then 15 minutes go by, then 30 minutes. Eventually he comes back after an hour, totally drunk, and he's got a basket with sausages and champagne. This is the middle of the war, it's even difficult to buy butter, and he's got all these things and he's completely drunk.

And Hitler says, "My God, what on earth did you tell the farmer? And the chauffeur says, "I just said 'heil Hitler, the pig is dead,' and then they gave me all these presents."

Author Rudolph Herzog concludes with this lament.[25]

I think we Germans suffered a lot from the incredible brain drain that happened during the war. A lot of Jewish comedians were killed and Jewish actors emigrated. Even in the field of humour there was a punishing brain drain from which Germany hasn't really recovered.

In the United States, insult comedy, largely a Jewish innovation linked to "Fat" Jack E. Leonard and perfected by Don Rickles, is highly regarded and its practitioners richly rewarded. When Bill Maher, half Jewish on his mother's side, adds a political dimension to this genre, as Leonard Cohen famously sings: "Democracy is coming to the USA." Long ago and far away, Dr. Sigmund Freud put his definitive stamp on and supplied profound analysis of Jewish humor. Not only does it promote skepticism, democratic thought, social principles, and self-criticism; Jewish jokes also constitute a rebellion against oppressive institutions. Thus, we derive both catharsis and therapy at a very low price. In times of *tsores* (trouble), like ours, who could ask for anything more?

Chapter Notes

Introduction

1. Pew Research Center 2013 Survey of U.S. Jews, February 20–June 13, 2013, as cited in Gary Rosenblatt, "What Pew Does—and Doesn't—Tell Us," *The Jewish Week*, October 11, 2013, 1, 7.

2. Sarah Blacher Cohen, "The Unkosher Comediennes: From Sophie Tucker to Joan Rivers," in *Jewish Wry: Essays on Jewish Humor*, ed. Sarah Blacher Cohen (Bloomington: Indiana University Press, 1987), 115–17. For St. Paul's fulminations against humor, see the quote in D. Travis Stewart, *No Applause—Just Throw Money* (New York: Farrar, Straus and Giroux, Faber & Faber, 2005), 14.

3. The Bible-humor dichotomy is addressed in several sources: Sig Altman, *The Comic Image of the Jew* (Rutherford NJ: Fairleigh Dickinson University Press, 1971), 128–30; Nathan Ausubel, *A Treasury of Jewish Folklore* (New York: Crown, 1948), 265–66; Richard Boston, *An Anatomy of Laughter* (London: William Collins, 1974), 43–47; Israel Knox, "The Traditional Roots of Jewish Humor," *Judaism* (Summer 1963): 12:3, 330–31; Salcia Landmann, "On Jewish Humor," *Jewish Journal of Sociology* 4 (1962): 193.

4. Mark Zborowski and Elizabeth Herzog, *Life is with the People: The Culture of the Shtetl* (New York: Schocken Books, 1978), 279–80; Israel Abrahams, *Jewish Life in the Middle Ages* (New York: Athenaeum, 1969), 133, 198; Ausubel, *Treasury*, 264. On a mordant note, Mark Zborowski turned out to be a Soviet agent who conspired to kill Leon Trotsky's son and perform other heinous deeds, according to the decoded Venona papers.

5. Ausubel, *Treasury*, 15, 286, 304–19; Irving Howe and Eliezer Greenberg, eds., *A Treasury of Yiddish Stories* (New York: Viking Press, 1965), 26, 614–19.

6. Howe and Greenberg, ibid., 620–27; Ausubel, ibid., 326–42; for a variant of clerical jousting, see Lawrence E. Mintz, "'The Rabbi Versus the Priest' and Other Jewish Stories," in *Jewish Humor*, ed. Avner Ziv (New Brunswick, NJ: Transaction Publishers, 1998), 129; and Ed Cray, "The Rabbi Trickster," *The Journal of American Folklore* 77 (1964): 341–42.

7. Abram L. Sachar, *A History of the Jews* (New York: Alfred A. Knopf, 1967), 184; Howe & Greenberg, 26, 28–42, 50–58. The phrase, "wandering between two worlds, one dead/ The other powerless to be born" is derived from Matthew Arnold's poem "Stanza from the Grande Chartreuse," http://www.poetryfoundation.org/poem/172861.

8. Altman, *Comic Image*, 144, 163–67; also see Bernard Rosenberg & Gilbert Shapiro, "Marginality and Jewish Humor," *Midstream* 4 (1958): 70–80.

9. Ruth R. Wisse, *No Jokes: Making Jewish Humor* (Princeton: Princeton University Press, 2013), 37.

10. Stephen J. Whitfield, "Laughter in the Dark: Notes on Jewish Humor," *Midstream*, 24:2 (February 1978): 48; for additional sources of Heine's style of humor, see Louis Untermeyer in *Heinrich Heine: Works of Prose*, ed. Herman Kesten (New York: L. B. Fisher, 1943), 8–11; William Rose, *Heinrich Heine: Two Studies of His Thought and Feeling* (Oxford: Clarendon Press, 1956), 133–34, 154; Sigmund Freud, *The Basic Writings of Sigmund Freud*, translated and edited by A. A. Brill (New York: Random House, 1938), 705, 728–30.

11. The Mintz model is an abstract from a paper at the Second International on Humor Studies on August 24, 1979, which the author graciously sent me. Levinson's humor was deftly captured by Richard F. Shepard, "Dr. Levinson Proves Laughter Is the Best Medi-

cine," *New York Times*, November 22, 1979, B2.

12. Mintz model abstract.

13. Earl Rovit, "Jewish Humor and American Life," *American Scholar* 36 (Spring 1967): 237; the oft-quoted White caveat is quoted in Larry Wilde, *How the Great Comedy Writers Create Laughter* (Chicago: Nelson-Hall, 1976), 51. My colleague Joseph Boskin deplores its use and abuse.

14. Wilde, *How the Great Comedy Writers Create Comedy*, 89.

15. Leslie Fiedler, "The Jews as Mythic Americans," *Ramparts* 2:2 (August 1963): 34–35; Whitfield, "Laughter," p. 48, furnishes many references in this paragraph to *unzer shtick* and *malechamoves*. For a provocative portrait of the Jewish penchant for *pastiche*, see Ronald Sanders, "The American Popular Song," in *Next Year in Jerusalem: Portraits of the Jew in the Twentieth Century*, ed. Douglas Villiers (New York: Viking Press, 1976), 197–219.

16. Nathan Hurvitz, "Blacks and Jews in American Folklore," *Western Folklore*, 33:44 (October 1974): 309. Other themes in the above paragraph were covered in greater detail in Stanley W. White, "The Burnt Cork Illusion of the 1920s in America: A Study in Nostalgia," *The Journal of Popular Culture* 5:3 (Winter 1971): 530–49; Steve Allen, *The Funny Men* (New York: Simon & Schuster, 1956, 65, 66–69, 71; Mary Livingstone Benny, et al. *Jack Benny* (Garden City: Doubleday, 1978), 235, 65–66.

17. Ed Cray, "The Rabbi Trickster," *Journal of American Folklore* 77 (1964): 332–33; Dan Ben Amos, "The 'Myth' of Jewish Humor," *Western Folklore* 32:2 (1973): 118, 129–30; Jeffry H. Goldstein, "Theoretical Notes on Humor," *Journal of Communication*, 26:3 (Summer 1976): 110. The psychoanalysis of Jewish humor can be charted through Sigmund Freud, *The Basic Writings of Sigmund Freud*, translated and edited by A. A. Brill (New York: Random House, 1938), especially 689–91, 705–39, 803; Theodore Reik, *Jewish Wit* (New York: Gamut Press, 1962), 188–240; Edmund Bergler, *Laughter and the Sense of Humor* (New York: Intercontinental Medical Book Corporation, 1956), 46–47, 111–13; Martin Grotjahn, "Jewish Jokes and Their Relation to Masochism," in *A Celebration of Laughter*, ed. Werner M. Mendel (Los Angeles: Mara Books, 1970), 135–42.

18. The "glass enclosure" metaphor comes from the ill-fated jazz great Bud Powell, as quoted in "Talk of the Town," *New Yorker*, August 20, 1966, 25. I canvassed this new trend in comedy earlier; see Joseph Dorinson,

"The Jew as Comic: Lenny Bruce, Mel Brooks, Woody Allen," in *Jewish Humor*, ed. Avner Ziv (Tel Aviv: Papyrus Publishing House, 1986), 29–43. There are many fine recordings of Bruce in action, but the best, in my opinion, is *Lenny Bruce at Carnegie Hall*, United Artists UA 9800.

19. For a painfully detailed death scene and a searing spiritual, see Albert Goldman, *Ladies and Gentleman, Lenny Bruce!!* (New York: Random House, 1974), chapter 13.

20. Richard Schickel, "The Basic Woody Allen Joke…" *New York Times Magazine*, January 7, 1973, 33, 35, 36, 37; Whitfield, *Laughter*, 57; Phil Berger, *The Last Laugh: The World of Stand-up Comics* (New York: Ballantine Books, 1975), 11, 112. Although *dos kleine metschele* was actually sired by Mendele Mocher Sforim, I believe that his spiritual grandchild belongs in the happier family of Sholem Aleichem. See Sol Liptzin, *The Flowering of Yiddish Literature* (New York: Thomas Yoseloff, 1963), especially chapters two and seven.

21. Leonard Probst, *On Camera* (New York: Stein & Day, 1978), 258, 260.

22. Natalie Gitelson, "The Meaning of Woody Allen," *New York Times Magazine*, April 22, 1979, 98.

23. Eric Lax, *On Being Funny: Woody Allen and Comedy* (New York: Charterhouse, 1975), 33.

24. William Wolf, *Landmark Films: The Cinema and Our Century* (London: Paddington Press, 1979), 383.

25. Most of the above insights were gleaned from Albert Goldman's illuminating article "Laughtermakers," in *Jewish Wry: Essays on Jewish Humor*, ed. Sarah B. Cohen (Bloomington: Indiana University Press, 1987), 80–104.

26. Pauline Kael, "The Current Cinema and Our Century," *New Yorker*, September 25, 1978, 151, 152, 154, 157; Charles Michener, "Comedy's King Leer," *Newsweek*, August 29, 1977, 78–79; Richard Schickel, "Woody Allen Comes of Age," *Time*, April 30, 1979, 63–65.

27. Lawrence E. Mintz, "The 'New Wave' of Standup Comedians: An Introduction," *American Humor: An Interdisciplinary Newsletter* 4:2 (Fall 1977): 1.

28. Kenneth Tynan, "Profiles: Frolics of a Short Hebrew Man," *New Yorker* (October 30, 1978): 68–69, 80; *tsores*, as the motor force that powers Jewish humor, is found in several sources: Steve Allen, *The Funny Men*, 212, 213, 215–16, 217, 218; Albert Memmi, *The Liberation of the Jew* (New York: Orion Press, 1966), 43–54; Nat Hentoff, "Yiddish Survivals in the

New Comedy," in *Jewish American Literature*, ed. Abraham Chapman (New York: New American Library, 1974), 691–92; Whitfield, *Laughter*, 53.

29. Berger, *Last Laugh*, 295; Whitfield, *Laughter*, 53; Landmann, "On Jewish Humor," 193–94, 204.

30. Robert Alter, "Jewish Humor and the Domestication of Myth," in *Veins of Humor*, ed. Harry Levin (Cambridge: Harvard University Press, 1972), 256.

31. Howe & Greenberg, *Treasury*, 26.

32. My coda was inspired by a memorable phrase coined by John Dos Passos, which reads: "In times of change and danger when there is a quicksand of fear under men's reasoning, a sense of continuity with generations gone before cam stretch like a lifeline across the scary present." This quote is found in Richard Hofstadter, *The American Political Tradition and the Men Who Made It* (New York: Random House Vintage Books, 1954), v.

Chapter One

1. Sigmund Freud, *The Basic Writings of Sigmund Freud*, translated and edited by A. A. Brill (New York: Random House, 1938), 689–91, 705–30, 803.

2. Leo Rosten, *Hooray for Yiddish!* (New York: Simon & Schuster, 1982), 24.

3. Richard Raskin, "God versus Man in a Classic Jewish Joke," *Judaism* 40:3 (Spring 1991): 39–51.

4. Ibid., 4749.

5. Eliezer Greenberg and Irving Howe, eds., *A Treasury of Yiddish Stories* (New York: Viking Press, 1965), 38–42, 50–55.

6. Rosten, *Hooray*, 25.

7. Maurice Yacower, *Loser Take All: The Comic Art of Woody Allen* (New York: Frederick Ungar, 1979), 162–63.

8. A version of this joke is found in "Exploring the Thesis of the Self-deprecating Jewish Sense of Humor," ed. Christie Davies, *HUMOR* 4:2 (1991): 195. In previous articles and a subsequent book, Davies offers pertinent commentary on the importance of ethnic humor in marking social boundaries.

9. Martin Grotjahn, "Jewish Jokes and Their Relation to Masochism" in *A Celebration of Laughter*, ed. Werner Mendel (Los Angeles: Mara Books, 1970), 139.

10. Lawrence E. Mintz, "'The Rabbi Versus the Priest' and Other Jewish Stories," in *Jewish Humor*, ed. Avner Ziv (Tel-Aviv: Papyrus Press, 1986), 129. Also see Ed Cray, "The Rabbi

Trickster," in *Journal of American Folklore* 77 (1964): 331–45.

11. John Cohen, ed., *The Essential Lenny Bruce* (New York: Ballantine Books, 1967), 44.

12. A variant of this joke can be found in *The Big Book of Jewish Humor*, eds. William Novak and Moshe Waldoks (New York: Harper & Row, 1981), 179.

13. Rosten, *Hooray*, 69.

14. Novak and Waldoks, *The Big Book*, 27.

15. As cited in Maurice Samuel, *The World of Sholem Aleichem* (New York: Alfred Knopf, 1944), 189.

16. Irving Howe and Eliezer Greenberg, eds., *A Treasury of Yiddish Stories* (New York: Viking Press, 1965), 26, 53–55.

17. Ibid., 27.

18. Lawrence E. Mintz, "Jewish Humor: A Continuum of Sources, Motives, and Functions," *American Humor* 4 (Spring 1977): 4.

19. The *Puck* cartoon is cited and reproduced in *The Jew in Early American Wit and Graphic Humor*, ed. Rudolph Glanz (New York: Ktav, 1973), 114–15; John J. Appel, "Jews in American Caricature: 1820–1914," *American Jewish History* 71 (1981): 103–118 adds insightful commentary. Both Glanz and Appel argue that Americans caricatured Jews far less viciously than Europeans did. For a different view, cogently presented, see Michael N. Dobkowski, *The Tarnished Dream: The Basis of American Anti-Semitism*, (Westport, CT: Greenwood Press, 1979), 60–63.

20. Alan Dundes, "A Study of Ethnic Slurs: The Jew and the Polack in the United States," *Journal of American Folklore* 84 (1971): 189, 194–95.

21. Ibid.

22. The three jokes that follow are found with minor variations in Joseph Boskin, "Protest Humor: Fighting Criticism with Laughter," in *Bostonia* (December 1980): 52.

23. Ibid. 49–53. Howard J. Ehrlich, "Observations on Ethnic and Intergroup Humor," *Ethnicity*, 6 (1978): 396; this article offers several excellent humorous morsels on the subject of assimilation.

24. A variant of this joke is found in Ehrlich, 394–95.

25. Alfred Kazin, "The Jew as American Writer," in *Jewish American Literature*, ed. Abraham Chapman (New York: New American Library, 1974), 589–90.

26. Stanley White, "The Burnt Cork Illusion of the 1920s in America: A Study in Nostalgia," *Journal of Popular Culture* 5:3 (Winter 1971): 531–43.

27. Irving Howe, *World of Our Fathers* (New York: Harcourt Brace Jovanovich, 1976), 566.

28. Jesse Bier, *The Rise and Fall of American Humor* (New York: Holt Rinehart & Winston, 1968), 3, 270–71.

29. Richard Hofstadter, *The Age of Reform: From Bryan to F.D.R.* (New York: Alfred A. Knopf, 1956), 77–81; Daniel Bell, "The Grass Roots of Jew Hatred," *Jewish Frontier* 11 (June 1944): 15–20. A later variant on this pernicious theme can be found in the fulminations of Leonard Jeffries, Jr., a clown masquerading as an academic. See the *New York Times*, August 11, 1991, E5, and October 30, 1991, B1, B4.

30. Carey McWilliams, *A Mask for Privilege: Anti-Semitism in America* (Boston: Little, Brown, 1948), 90.

31. Robert Cherry, *Discrimination: Its Economic Impact on Blacks, Women, and Jews* (Lexington, D.C.: Heath Lexington Books, 1989), 182.

32. Thomas Sowell, *Ethnic America* (New York: Basic Books, 1981), 98; Cherry, 182–84.

33. Novak and Waldoks, 188.

34. Milton Berle, *Milton Berle's Private Joke File*, ed. Milt Rosen (New York: Crown, 1989), 292–93; also see Howe, 570–71 for the comic assault on authority.

35. For an imaginative application of trickster mythology and psychoanalytic theory to money, see Norman O. Brown, *Life Against Death: The Psychoanalytical Meaning of History* (New York: Random House Vintage, 1959), 234–304; King David's angry *shpritz* is quoted in a harsh critique of Heller's novel, *God Knows*, by Leon Wieseltier, "Shlock of Recognition," *The New Republic*, October 29, 1984, 33.

36. Allen Guttmann, "Jewish Humor," in *The Comic Imagination in American Literature*, ed. Louis D. Rubin, Jr. (New Brunswick: Rutgers University Press, 1973), 331.

Chapter Two

1. Robert W. Snyder, *The Voice of the City: Vaudeville and Popular Culture in New York* (New York: Oxford University Press, 1989), xiv.

2. Ibid., 12–22.

3. Lawrence J. Epstein, *Mixed Nuts: America's Love Affair with Comedy Teams* (New York: Public Affairs, 2004), 18.

4. Ibid., 20.

5. Stefan Kanfer, "Vaudeville's Brief, Shining Moment," *City Journal* (Spring 2005): see http://www.city-journal.org/html/15_2_urbanites-vaudeville.html.

6. Snyder, xiv.

7. D. Travis Stewart, *No Applause: Just Throw Money* (New York: Farrar, Straus, and Giroux, Faber and Faber, 2003), 51–52.

8. Epstein, *Mixed Nuts*, 36.

9. Ibid., 40.

10. Lawrence J. Epstein, *The Haunted Smile: The Story of Jewish Comedians in America* (New York: Public Affairs, 2001), 34.

11. Snyder, 86–87.

12. Stewart, 120.

13. Epstein, *Mixed Nuts*, 5–8.

14. Ibid., 8.

15. Joseph Dorinson, "The Educational Alliance: An Institutional Study in Americanization and Acculturation," in *Immigration and Ethnicity*, eds. Michael D'Innocenzo and Joseph P. Sirefman (Westport Ct: Greenwood Press, 1992), 93.

16. Snyder, 48–50.

17. Irving Howe, with Kenneth Libo. *The World of Our Fathers* (New York: Harcourt, Brace, Jovanovich, 1976), 566.

18. J. Hoberman, "Eddie Cantor," in *Entertaining America: Jews, Movies, and Broadcasting*, eds. J. Hoberman and Jeffrey Shandler (Princeton: Princeton University Press, 2003), 156–157; Epstein, *Haunted Smile*, 11–14, 40–41.

19. Epstein, *Haunted Smile*, 45.

20. As cited in *Film Site* Movie Review (*Horse Feathers* 1932), http://www.filmsite.org/hors.html; and Richard J. Anobile, ed., *Why a Duck? Visual and Verbal Gems from the Marx Brothers Movies* (New York: Crown Publishers Darien House, 1972), 96–98.

21. Larry Wilde, *How the Great Comedy Writers Create Laughter* (Chicago: Nelson-Hall, 1976, 17–18; Pauline Kael, "The Current Cinema and Our Century," *The New Yorker*, September 25, 1978, 151, 152, 154, 157; Charles Michener, "Comedy's King Lear," *Newsweek*, August 29, 1977, 78–79; Richard Schickel, "Woody Allen Comes of Age," *Time*, April 30, 1979, 63–65; James K. Feibelman, *In Praise of Comedy: A Study in Its Theory and Practice* (New York: Horizon Press, 1970), 223–25.

22. Epstein, *Haunted Smile*, 15–17, 35–36.

23. Ibid., 67–68.

24. Lawrence Van Gelder, "Milton Berle, 93, Comic Who Became TV's First Star as 'Uncle Miltie,' Dies," *New York Times*, March 28, 2002, A1, A29; also see Frank Rich, "The Lives They Lived; TV Guy" *New York Times Magazine*, December 29, 2002; Steve Allen, *The Funny Men* (New York: Simon & Schuster, 1956), 85–90. http://www.timesonline.co.uk/article/060-250872,00.html, 1–5.

25. Ibid.

26. Ibid. Also see Milton Berle, with Haskel Frankel, *Milton Berle: An Autobiography* (New York: Applause Theater Cinema Books, 1974), 85.

27. Ibid., 101.

28. Ibid., 121–22, 134–35; Van Gelder, *New York Times* obituary, A29.

29. Milton, Berle, *B.S. I Love You* (New York: McGraw-Hill, 1988), 144; Van Gelder, A29.

30. As quoted by Bob Thomas in a syndicated column that appeared in *The Cumberland News,* Maryland, January 28, 1967.

31. *Milton Berle: An Autobiography,* 180–82.

32. Ibid., 271.

33. Ibid., 279–80.

34. As cited in Robert Gluck, "Very Jewish Milton Berle Inspired Modern Comics," *The Jewish Star,* September 2014, 7; also see Berle's *Autobiography,* 293–94.

35. Epstein, *Haunted Smile,* 133–34.

36. Van Gelder, A29.

37. Berle related this joke in a television documentary film on Jewish humor.

38. For additional information and referenced observations, see: Steve Allen, *The Funny Men* (1956); Milton Berle, with Haskel Frankel, *Milton Berle: An Autobiography* (1974); Milton Berle, *Milton Berle's Private Joke File* (1989); Lawrence J. Epstein, *The Haunted Smile: The Story of Jewish Comedians in America* (2001); Frank Rich, "TV Guy," *The New York Times Magazine,* December 29, 2002; and Lawrence Van Gelder, "Milton Berle, TV's First Star as 'Uncle Miltie,' Dies at 93," *New York Times,* March 28, 2002.

39. Sarah B. Cohen, "The Unkosher Comediennes: From Sophie Tucker to Joan Rivers," in *Jewish Wry: Essays on Jewish Humor,* ed. Sarah B. Cohen (Bloomington: Indiana University Press, 1987), 106–07.

40. As cited by Jody Rosen, "A Century Later, She's Still Red Hot," *New York Times,* August 30, 2009, AR, 13.

41. Snyder, *Voice,* 131, 148.

42. D. Travis Stewart, *No Applause,* as cited in http://www.youtube.com/watch?v=BEzsT6W3Y4E.

43. Ibid., 148; June Sochen, "Fannie Brice and Sophie Tucker, 'Blending the Particular with the Universal,'" in *From Hester Street to Hollywood: The Jewish-American Stage and Screen,* ed. Sarah Blacher Cohen (Bloomington: Indiana University Press, 1983), 53–54.

44. Cohen, *Jewish Wry,* 107.

45. Ibid.

46. Ibid., 109.

47. http://womenshistory.about.com/library/bio/blbio_tucker_sophie.htm, 2). This source provides salient biographical information about Sophie Tucker. She was truly a "Union Maid." For details of Sophie's triumph and unwavering support of unions, despite Ralph Whitehead's misadventures, see *Some of These Days: The Autobiography of Sophie Tucker* (Garden City, NY: Doubleday, Doran, 1945), 301–07.

48. Snyder, 45, 46.

49. Ibid., 62.

50. Epstein, *Haunted Smile,* 48.

51. http://travsd.wordpress.com/2013/10/29/stars-of-vaudeville-71-fanny-brice-2/.

52. Epstein, *Haunted Smile,* 48.

53. http://jwa.org/discover/infocus/comedy/brice.html), 4.

54. The quote is from http://thinkexist.com/quotation/i-m-a-bad-woman-but-i-m-damn-good/347347.html; also for context, see Howe, *World of Our Fathers,* 563.

55. Epstein, *Haunted Smile,* 32.

56. Stewart, *No Applause,* 177.

57. Cohen, *Jewish Wry,* 111, 112. The author offers a slightly different version of the excremental joke.

58. Ibid.

59. Ibid.

60. Ibid., 113.

61. Ibid.

62. Ibid., 113–15.

63. http://www.quotedb.com/quotes/1066.

64. Mark Twain and William M. Gibson, "The Chronicle of Young Satan," in *Mysterious Stranger Manuscripts* (Berkeley: University of California Press, 1969).

Chapter Three

1. http://www.news.wisc.edu/4742.

2. Maurice Samuel, *In Praise of Yiddish* (New York: Cowles Book, 1971), 4.

3. Ibid., 5.

4. Ibid., 9–10.

5. Irving Howe and Eliezer Greenberg, eds., *A Treasury of Yiddish Stories* (New York: Viking Press, 1965), 3.

6. Ibid., 12–21.

7. Ibid., 611–12.

8. Ibid., 8–9.

9. Michael Wex, *Born to Kvetch: Yiddish Language and Culture in All of Its Moods* (New York: St. Martin's Press, 2005), 1–6.

10. Ibid., 15–16.

11. Ibid., 20–25.

12. Ibid., 66–67.

13. Ibid., 40–41.

14. Ibid., 117–18.

15. Ibid., 124–25.

16. Samuel, *In Praise,* 223.

17. Ibid., 226–28.

18. Ibid., 233–34.

19. Leo Rosten, *Hooray for Yiddish! A Book about English* (New York: Simon & Schuster, 1982), 92–93.

20. Mr. "P.," *The World's Best Yiddish Dirty Jokes* (Secaucus, NJ: Citadel Press, 1984), 3.

21. Ibid., 6.

22. Ibid., 74.

23. Ibid., 91–92. Uriel Weinreich's *Modern English-Yiddish, Yiddish-English Dictionary* (New York: YIVO Institute for Jewish Research. McGraw-Hill, 1968), 109 equates eunuch with *aynuk*, a slightly different version than that of Mr. "P."

24. Ibid., 49.

25. Irving Howe, with the assistance of Kenneth Libo, *World of Our Fathers* (New York: Harcourt Brace Jovanovich, 1976), 558.

26. Ruth Wisse, *No Joke: Making Jewish Humor* (Princeton, NJ: Princeton University Press, 2013), 73.

27. The information regarding the founding of Yiddish Theater in the above paragraph was largely culled from Sol Liptzin, *The Flowering of Yiddish Literature* (New York: Thomas Yoseloff, 1963), 33–38, and Wisse, Op. Cit.

28. Stefan Kanfer, *Stardust Lost: The Triumph, Tragedy, and Meshugas of the Yiddish Theater in America* (New York: Alfred A. Knopf, 2006), 8–14.

29. Ibid., 20–22.

30. Ibid., 22.

31. Wisse, *No Joke*, 74.

32. Liptzin, *Flowering*, 38.

33. Ibid., 50–51.

34. As cited by Michael Stanislawski in the *Columbia Alumni Magazine* (Winter 2005) http://www.columbia.edu/cu/alumni/Magazine/Winter2005/llbaron.html.

The original quote is from Salo Baron, "Ghetto and Emancipation: Shall We Revise the Traditional Review?" *The Menorah Journal* 14 (1928): 515–26.

35. Nahma Sandrow, *Vagabond Stars: A World of Yiddish Theater* (New York: Harper Row, 1977), 77.

36. Ibid.

37. Ibid., 99–102.

38. Ibid., 123, 127.

39. Kanfer, *Stardust Lost*, 67–68.

40. Ibid., 108–10.

41. Ibid., 159–60.

42. Ibid., 217.

43. Molly Picon, with Jean Bergantini Grillo, *Molly! An Autobiography* (New York: Simon & Schuster, 1980), 9–11.

44. Ibid., 46.

45. For additional biographical information, consult http://www.haaretz.com/news/features/this-day-in-jewish-history/.premium-1.596379. This Day in Jewish History / Birthday of legendary Yiddish performer Molly Picon; also see Molly Picon, *All American Maydl* http://www.ajhs.org/publications/chapter.cfm?documentID=291.

46. Joel Schechter, *Messiahs of 1933: How American Yiddish Theater Survived Adversity through Satire* (Philadelphia: Temple University Press, 2008), 26–27, 101, 141–44.

47. Ibid., 144, 146.

48. Ibid., 152–56.

49. Ibid., 177–78, 183. For additional biographical information about Leo Fuchs, see Bernard Mendelovitch, "Leo Fuchs Obituary" in http://www.independent.co.uk/news/people/obituaries-leo-fuchs-1568528.html.

50. Richard F. Shepard and Vicki Gold Levi, *Live & Be Well: A Celebration of Yiddish Culture in America, From the First Immigrants to the Second World War* (Worthington, MA: Hilltown Press, 1982), 25–26.

51. Schechter, 185–86.

52. Ibid., 187–88.

53. Ibid., 180, 182, 269 (notes 8 and 9).

54. J. Hoberman, *Bridge of Light: Yiddish Film between Two Worlds* (New York: The Museum of Modern Art/Schocken Books, 1992), 219, as cited in Schechter, 188.

55. Schechter, 190; Mendelovitch, "Leo Fuchs Obituary," Op. Cit.

56. Ibid., 201.

57. Lawrence J. Epstein, *The Haunted Smile: The Story of Jewish Comedians in America* (New York: Public Affairs, 2001), 297–99.

Chapter Four

1. Samuel Janus, "The Great Comedian: Personality and Other Factors," *The American Journal of Psychoanalysis* 35:2 (1975): 169–74; also see "Analyzing Jewish Comics," *Time*, October 2, 1978, 76.

2. Anthony Lewis, "The Jew in Stand-up Comedy," in *From Hester Street to Hollywood: The Jewish-American Stage and Screen*, ed., Sarah B. Cohen (Bloomington: Indiana University Press, 1983), 61.

3. Wallace Markfield, "The Yiddishization of American Humor," *Esquire*, October 1965, 114; see also Earl Rovit, "Jewish Humor and American Life," *American Scholar* 36:2 (Spring 1967): 237–44; and Joseph Dorinson, "Jewish Humor: Mechanism for Defense, Weapon for Cultural Affirmation," *The Journal of Psychohistory* 8:4 (Spring 1981): 447–65.

4. Sigmund Freud, *Jokes and Their Relation to the Unconscious*, translated and edited by James Strachey (New York: W. W. Norton, 1960), 33, 49–51, 55–56. 61–63, 111–35, 142; Theodore Reik, *Jewish Wit* (New York: Gamut

Press, 1962), 188–216, 221–22; and Albert Memmi, *The Liberation of a Jew*, trans. Judy Hyun (New York: Orion Press, 1966), 43–51.

5. Elliot Oring, "The People of the Joke," Unpublished Paper, October 1983.

6. I took this dichotomy from Mark Shechner and ran with it. For the source, don't go to Fortunoff's. Shechner sparkles in "Woody Allen: The Failure of the Therapeutic," in *From Hester Street to Hollywood: The Jewish-American Stage and Screen*, 232–44, and in "Dear Mr. Einstein: Jewish Comedy and the Contradictions in Culture," in *Jewish Wry: Essays on Jewish Humor*, ed. Sarah B. Cohen (Bloomington: Indiana University Press, 1987), 141–57.

7. Most of the biographical data comes from Martin Gottfried's judicious and definitive study *Nobody's Fool: The Lives of Danny Kaye* (New York: Simon & Schuster, 1994).

8. Joey Adams and Henry Tobias, *The Borscht Belt* (New York: Bentley, 1966), 6–7.

9. Stefan Kanfer, *A Summer World: The Attempt to Build a Jewish Eden in the Catskills, from the Days of the Ghetto to the Rise and Decline of the Borscht Belt* (New York: Farrar, Straus, Giroux, 1989), 160–61.

10. Gottfried, *Nobody's Fool*, 37–38.

11. Ibid., 39.

12. Ibid., 40.

13. Ibid., 18, 20–21, 43.

14. Ibid., 45.

15. Ibid., 48.

16. Ibid., 53.

17. *Time*, March 11, 1946, 64.

18. Ibid., 62.

19. Rosamond Gilder, "Hectic Holiday: Broadway in Review," *Theatre Arts* (1941–42): 7–8.

20. Neal Gabler, *An Empire of Their Own: How the Jews Invented Hollywood* (New York: Crown, 1988).

21. *Time*, March 11, 1946, 64; Gottfried, *Nobody's Fool*, 92–94.

22. Ibid.

23. Gottfried, *Nobody's Fool*, 103.

24. Ibid., 135–43.

25. John Belton, *American Cinema/American Culture* (New York: McGraw-Hill, 1994), 238–40.

26. Gottfried, *Nobody's Fool*, 144–46.

27. Ibid., 147–56.

28. Leonard Maltin, *The Great Movie Comedians: From Charlie Chaplin to Woody Allen* (New York: Harmony Books, 1982), 199.

29. Gottfried, *Nobody's Fool*, 166–69, 190, 192–95.

30. Ibid., 178.

31. Ibid., 196–97.

32. Ibid., 199.

33. Ibid., 219–20.

34. Maltin, *The Great Movie Comedians*, 202–05.

35. Gottfried, *Nobody's Fool*, 231–34.

36. Ibid., 325.

37. Raymond Durgnat, *The Crazy Mirror: Hollywood Comedy and the American Image* (London: Faber & Faber, 1969), 171–72.

38. Gottfried, *Nobody's Fool*, 330.

39. Ibid., 301.

40. *New York Times*, October 22, 1988, C28.

41. Sid Caesar, *Where Have I Been? An Autobiography*, with the assistance of Bill Davidson (New York: Crown, 1982), 3–22.

42. Sid Caesar, *Caesar's Hours: My Life in Comedy, with Love and Laughter*, with the assistance of Eddy Freifeld (New York: Public Affairs, 2003), 30–31.

43. Ibid., 32–33.

44. Ibid., 34.

45. Caesar, *Where Have I Been?*, 36–42; Kanfer, *Summer World*, 163–64, 225–27.

46. Caesar, *Caesar's Hour*, 29.

47. Caesar, *Where Have I Been?*, chapters 6–8.

48. Ibid., 64.

49. Ibid., 68.

50. Caesar, *Caesar's Hour*, 56.

51. Ted Sennett, *Your Show of Shows* (New York: Collier Books, 1977), 42.

52. Karin Adir, *The Great Clowns of American Television* (London: McFarland, 1988), 82–83.

53. Ibid., 83.

54. Caesar, *Where Have I Been?*, 103.

55. Ibid., 105.

56. Sennett, *Your Show of Shows*, 49.

57. Ibid., 55; Steve Allen, *Funny People* (New York: Stein & Day, 1981), 107–08.

58. Irving Howe, *World of Our Fathers*, with the assistance of Kenneth Libo (New York: Harcourt Brace Jovanovich, 1976), 569.

59. Caesar, *Where Have I Been?*, 114–16.

60. Sennett, *Your Show of Shows*, 120–52.

61. Kanfer, *Summer World*, 164–65.

62. See his article in *Next Year in Jerusalem*, ed. Douglas Villiers (London: Harrap, 1976); Kanfer, in *Summer World*, 165–66, also canvasses this subject.

63. Sennett, *Your Show of Shows*, 142.

64. Allen, *Funny People*, 106.

65. Ibid., 108.

66. Howe, *World of Our Fathers*, 570.

67. Ibid.

68. Caesar, *Where Have I Been?*, 169.

69. Caesar, *Caesar's Hours*, 291–94.

70. Ibid., 28–29.

71. Mervyn Rothstein and Peter Keepnews "Sid Caesar, Comedian of Comedians from TV's Early Days, Dies at 91," *New York Times*, February 12, 2014, A1.

Chapter Five

1. Kenneth Tynan, *Show People: Profiles in Entertainment* (New York: Simon & Schuster, 1979), 207–09, 213; Will Holtzman, *Seesaw: A Dual Biography of Anne Bancroft and Mel Brooks* (Garden City, NY: Doubleday, 1979), 6.

2. Maurice Yakower, *Method in Madness: The Comic Art of Mel Brooks* (New York: St. Martin's Press, 1981), 15–16.

3. Ibid., 17.

4. Tynan, *Show People*, 190.

5. Ibid., 191.

6. Yakower, *Method in Madness*, 52.

7. Sanford Pinsker, "Mel Brooks and the Cinema of Exhaustion," in *From Hester Street to Hollywood: The Jewish-American Stage & Screen*, ed. Sarah Blacher Cohen (Bloomington: Indiana University Press, 1986), 247.

8. Tynan, *Show People*, 253.

9. David Desser and Lester D. Friedman, *American-Jewish Filmmakers: Traditions & Trends* (Chicago: University of Illinois Press, 1993), 112–13; also consult Alan Cowell, "Germans and Hitler Jokes: He Who Laughs Last...," *New York Times*, September 9, 2001, WK, 5.

10. Mark Schechner, "Woody Allen: The Failure of the Therapeutic," in *From Hester Street to Hollywood: The Jewish American Stage and Screen*, ed. Sarah Blacher Cohen (Bloomington: Indiana University Press, 1986), 238.

11. Erik Erikson, *Life History and the Historical Moment* (New York: Norton, 1975), 18–22; also see Howard F. Stein, "Judaism and the Group Fantasy of Martyrdom," *The Journal of Psychohistory* 6:2 (Fall 1978): 164–65.

12. Gerald Mast, "Woody Allen: The Neurotic Jew as American Clown," in *Jewish Wry: Essays on Jewish Humor*, ed. Sarah. Blacher Cohen (Bloomington: Indiana University Press, 1987), 126.

13. Eric Lax, *On Being Funny: Woody Allen & Comedy* (New York: Charterhouse, 1975), 30–33.

14. Ibid., 13–17.

15. As quoted by Sam Roberts, "Arthur Gelb, an Editor Who Elevated the Times, Dies at 90," *New York Times*, May 21, 2014, A26.

16. Earl Wilson, *Show Business Laid Bare* (New York: New American Library, 1974),

246–47; Maurice Yacower, *Loser Take All: The Comic Art of Woody Allen* (New York: Frederick Ungar, 1976), 20; Gerald Nachman, *Seriously Funny: The Rebel Comedians of the 1950s and 1960s* (New York: Pantheon Books, 2003), 530; Richard Schickel, "The Basic Woody Allen Joke," *New York Times Magazine*, January 7, 1973, 33; many of these jokes are found on "Woody Allen: Stand-up Comic, 1964–1968," United Artists-LA849-J2, a wonderful two-record LP set.

17. Desser and Friedman, *American-Jewish Filmmakers*, 42, 44.

18. Ibid., 44–45.

19. Celestini Delayto, "The Narrator and the Narrative: The Evolution of Woody Allen's Comedies," in *The Films of Woody Allen: Critical Essays*, ed. Charles L. P. Silet (Lanham, MD: Scarecrow Press, 2006), 30.

20. Desser and Friedman, *American-Jewish Filmmakers*, 69.

21. Gerald Mast, "Woody Allen: The Neurotic Jew," in *Jewish Wry*, ed. Sarah Blacher Cohen, 135–37.

22. Ibid., 138.

23. Desser and Friedman, *American-Jewish Filmmakers*, 73.

24. Ibid., 76.

25. Ibid., 77.

26. Ibid., 79–82.

27. Ibid., 93–94.

28. Ibid.

29. Ibid., 94–96, 98–101.

30. Alan King, *Anybody Who Owns His Own Home Deserves It*, with the assistance of Kathryn Ryan (New York: Hearst Avon Books, 1962), 19.

31. Brian Hill, "Alan King, Comedic Royalty," http://www.oralcancerfoundation.org. people/alan_king.htm.

32. Alan King, *Name-Dropping: The Life and Lies of Alan King*, with the assistance of Chris Chase (New York: Hearst Avon Books, 1996), 26.

33. Hill, "Alan King."

34. King, *Name-Dropping*, 38.

35. Ibid., 110–11.

36. For an insightful analysis of this function, see Stephanie Koziski, "The Standup Comedian as Anthropologist: Intentional Cultural Critic," in *The Humor Prism in 20th Century America*, ed. Joseph Boskin (Detroit: Wayne State University Press, 1997), 86–114.

37. Bruce Weber, "Alan King: Comic with Chutzpah, Dies at 76," *New York Times*, May 10, 2004, B7.

38. James Barron, "Alan King's Love-Hate Relationship," *New York Times*, August 30, 1988, CY 1, 13.

39. Ibid.

40. Ibid.

41. King, *Anybody Who Owns His Own Home Deserves It*, 42–43.

42. Ibid., 43.

43. King, *Name-Dropping*, 128–33.

44. This genre is discussed in Dennis Carpenter and Joseph Dorinson, *Is Anyone Here a Sailor?* (Great Neck, NY: Brightlights Press, 1995), 105.

45. King, *Name-Dropping*, 139.

46. Ibid., 140–41; Desser and Friedman, *American-Jewish Filmmakers*, 193–95, discuss the same film but provide a different date, 1979 instead of 1980.

47. King, *Name-Dropping*, 101.

48. King told this joke at a Brooklyn College BCBC-sponsored event, which my wife and I attended.

49. King delivered this joke in one his last performances, at Kutcher's Country Club, where earlier that day I delivered a paper on "Alan King and Billy Crystal: Laughter in the Suburbs." In the best tradition of self-deprecating Jewish humor, he related a wisecrack made at his expense by comedienne Susie Estman during a Friars' roast in his honor. A version of my paper was later published in *The Scribner's Encyclopedia of American Lives*, eds. Arnold Markoe, Karen Markoe, and Kenneth T. Jackson (Farmington Hills, MI: Thomson Gale, 2007), 307–09.

50. King, *Name-Dropping*, 78.

Chapter Six

1. Shawn Levy, *King of Comedy: The Life and Art of Jerry Lewis* (New York: St. Martin's Press, 1996), 6.

2. Moss Hart, *Act One* (New York: Random House, 1959), as quoted in Stefan Kanfer, *A Summer World: The Attempt to Build a Jewish Eden in the Catskills, from the Days of the Ghetto to the Rise and Decline of the Borscht Belt* (New York: Farrar, Straus and Giroux, 1989), 99.

3. Frank Krutnik, *Inventing Jerry Lewis* (Washington: Smithsonian Press, 2000), 39; Levy, *King of Comedy*, 15.

4. As quoted in Kanfer, *A Summer World*, 191–92.

5. Nick Tosches, *Dino: Living High in the Dirty Business of Dreams* (New York: Doubleday, 1992), 56–93 describes the genesis of Martin and Lewis's teaming.

6. In his brilliant study, *Inventing Jerry Lewis*, Krutnik, on pp. 52–53, relates this pivotal moment in American comedy, but stops short of my contention that the encounter signals a major shift in comic sensibility with ethnics—in this case, Italian and Jew—playing dominant roles.

7. Ibid., 45.

8. Ed Sikov, *Laughing Hysterically: American Screen Comedy of the 1950s* (New York: Columbia University Press, 1994), 190.

9. Kenneth Tynan, *Show People: Profiles in Entertainment* (New York: Simon & Schuster, 1979), 213.

10. Elliot Finkel, the son of Feibish, related this coda to Harvey and Myrna Frommer; it is reprinted in their book *It Happened in the Catskills* (New York: Harcourt Brace Jovanovich, 1991), 72.

11. Levy, *King of Comedy*, 450–51.

12. *New York Times Film Reviews (1949–1958)*, 2361. The Crowther review appeared on September 29, 1949, 39.

13. Ibid.

14. HHT, "Living It Up," *New York Times Film Reviews* (July 24, 1954), 6.

15. Levy, *King of Comedy*, 340.

16. Ibid.

17. Ibid., 341.

18. Tynan, *Show People*, 233–34.

19. Levy, *King of Comedy*, 210–11.

20. Ibid., 213.

21. Ibid., 292–93.

22. Jerry Lewis, *The Total Film-Maker* (New York: Warner Paperback Library, 1973), 166.

23. Jerry Lewis, *Jerry Lewis—in Person!*, with the assistance of Herb Gluck (New York: Athenaeum, 1982), 233.

24. Lewis, *in Person!*, 182.

25. Levy, *King of Comedy*, 175–80.

26. John B. Cohen, ed., *The Essential Lenny Bruce* (New York: Ballantine Books, 1967); for Lewis's rejoinder see *Total Film-Maker*, 186.

27. http://www.jerrylewiscomedy.com/biography.htm.

28. Krutnik, *Inventing Jerry Lewis*, 185.

29. Tom Shales, "Send in the Clowns: Jerry Lewis's Labor Day of Love," *Washington Post*, August 30, 1997, D1, D5.

30. Krutnik, *Inventing Jerry Lewis*, 194.

31. *When Comedy Went to School*; see http://www.whencomedywenttoschool.com/.

Chapter Seven

1. Joseph Boskin, *Rebellious Laughter* (Syracuse: Syracuse University Press, 1997), 29–32; Lawrence J. Epstein, *The Haunted Smile: The Story of Jewish Comedians in America* (New York: Public Affairs, 2001), 161–62.

2. Boskin, *Rebellious Laughter*, 38–48.
3. Mel Watkins, *On the Reel Side: A History of African-American Comedy* (Chicago: Lawrence Hill Books, 1999), 480.
4. Gerald Nachman, *Seriously Funny: The Rebel Comedians of the 1950s and 1960s* (New York: Pantheon Books, 2003), 52–54.
5. Epstein, *The Haunted Smile*, 166–69.
6. *Time*, August 15, 1960, 42–44, 47–48.
7. Paul Krassner, *The Realist* 43 (September 1969): 19.
8. Nachman, *Seriously Funny*, 62.
9. Joseph Dorinson, "Jewish Humor," *The Journal of Psychohistory* 8:4 (Spring 1981): 452–54, 462.
10. For a brief biographical sketch, see Joseph Dorinson, "The Jew as Comic: Lenny Bruce, Mel Brooks, and Woody Allen," in *Jewish Humor*, ed. Avner Ziv (Tel-Aviv: Papyrus Publishing House, 1986), 30–34.
11. Nat Hentoff, "Where Liberals Fear To Thread," *Reporter* 22:13 (June 23, 1960): 51.
12. John Cohen, ed., *The Essential Lenny Bruce* (New York: Ballantine, 1967), 76.
13. Ibid., 45.
14. Watkins, *On the Reel Side*, 485.
15. Epstein, *The Haunted Smile*, 171.
16. Ibid., 172.
17. Ibid., 174.
18. "Talk of the Town," *New Yorker*, August 20, 1966, 25.
19. Watkins, *On the Reel Side*, 486.
20. Ibid., 497.
21. Lawrence W. Levine, *Black Culture and Black Consciousness* (New York: Oxford University Press, 1977) 345–46.
22. Tony Hendra, *Going Too Far* (Garden City, NY: Doubleday, 1987), 157–58.
23. Ibid., 159.
24. Watkins, *On the Reel Side*, 495; Dick Gregory, *Nigger: An Autobiography*, with the assistance of Robert Lipsyte (New York: Washington Square Press, 1986) 134–35.
25. Watkins, *On the Reel Side*, 496.
26. Nachman, *Seriously Funny*, 489.
27. Boskin, *Rebellious Laughter*, 228–30.

Chapter Eight

1. Richie Robertson, *Heine* (New York: Grove Press, 1988), 78–79.
2. Ibid., 80–81.
3. Ruth R. Wisse, *No Joke: Making Jewish Humor* (Princeton: Princeton University Press, 2013), 37.
4. Robertson, 80, 81.
5. Stefan Kanfer, *Stardust Lost: The Triumph, Tragedies, and Mishugas of the Yiddish Theater* (New York: Alfred A. Knopf, 2006), xxi.
6. Joel Shatsky, "Schlemiels and Schlimazels," in *Fools and Jesters in Literature, Art, and History*, ed. Vicki K. Janick (Westport CT: Greenwood Press, 1998), 388–89.
7. Sol Liptzin, *The Flowering of Yiddish Literature* (New York: Thomas Yoseloff, 1963), 23.
8. Ruth Adler, "Shalom Aleichem's 'On Account of a Hat': Universal and Jewish Applications" in Avner Ziv, editor, *Jewish Humor*, ed. Avner Ziv (Tel Aviv: Papyrus Press, 1986), 24–25. (Please note the varied spelling of Aleichem's first name. I prefer the basic Yiddish version in which the name, meaning "peace," is spelled Sholem; hence, my text reflects this preference.)
9. My aunt Feigel (Fanny) Dorinson's older brother Beryl Berkowtiz married Sholem Aleichem's daughter. When their daughter, Tamara Kahana Berkowitz, visited us in Brooklyn, my friend Dr. Henry Kellerman and I were trotted out to recite, in Yiddish, stories of the great Jewish writer, thus conferring highly regarded *koved* and *yichus* (pride and status) on our respective families.
10. As quoted in Peninna Shram's review.
11. Liptzin, *The Flowering of Yiddish Literature*, 94, 96.
12. A. E. Rivlin, "Tevye the Milkman—Intertwining Jewish Destiny and Humor," in *Jewish Humor*, 153.
13. Ibid.
14. Ibid., 153–55.
15. Ibid., 156.
16. Shlolem Aleichem's wish.
17. Shatsky, "Schlemiels and Schlimazels," 393; Nathan Ausubel, ed., *A Treasury of Jewish Folklore* (New York: Crown, 1949), 343.
18. Cynthia Ozick, "Judging the World," *New York Times*, March 16, 2014, BR, 1, 12.
19. James Atlas, *Bellow: A Biography* (New York: Random House, 2000), xi.
20. Philip Roth, "My Life as a Writer," interview with David Sandstrom, *New York Times* BR, March 16, 2014, 15.
21. Keith Opdahl, "The 'Mental Comedies' of Saul Bellow," in *From Hester Street to Hollywood: The Jewish-American Stage and Screen*, ed. Sarah Blacher Cohen (Bloomington: University of Indiana Press, 1983), 183–84.
22. Ibid., 186.
23. Sarah Blacher, *Comic Relief: Humor in Contemporary American Literature* (Urbana: University of Illinois Press, 1979), 8–9.
24. Ibid.
25. Atlas, *Bellow*, 41; also see Mark Schechner, "Dear Mr. Einstein: Jewish Comedy and

the Contradictions of Culture," in *Jewish Wry: Essays on Jewish Humor*, ed. Sarah Blacher Cohen (Bloomington: Indiana University Press, 1987), 149. Read the T. S. Eliot original for an approximate translation.

26. Ibid.; see Guttmann, 130–31.

27. Cohen, *Comic Relief*, 19.

28. Ibid., 220–21.

29. Atlas, *Bellow*, 342–43.

30. Norman Mailer, *Waiting for the End* (New York: Stein & Day, 1964), 97–98.

31. Atlas, *Bellow*, 343–44.

32. Robert Alter is quoted in *Bernard Malamud & the Critics*, eds. Leslie A. Field and Joyce W. Field (New York: New York University Press, 1970), xviii.

33. Theodore Solotaroff, "The Old and the New," in Field & Field, *Bernard Malamud*. 242–244; also see Ruth B. Mandel, "Ironic Affirmation" in the same book, 269, 273.

34. Marcus Klein, "The Sadness of Goodness," in *Bernard Malamud*, 256–57.

35. Ibid.

36. Claudia Roth Pierpont, *Roth Unbound: A Writer and His Books* (New York: Farrar, Straus & Giroux, 2013), 315–16.

37. Philip Roth, *The Facts: A Novelist's Autobiography* (New York: Penguin Books, 1988), 125–30.

38. Ibid., 131, 135–36.

39. Ibid., 137–38.

40. Jay L. Halio, *Philip Roth Revisited* (New York: Twayne Publishers, 1992), 6–7.

41. Ibid., 204.

42. Sheldon Grebstein, "Comic Anatomy of *Portnoy's Complaint*," in *Comic Relief*, 170–71.

43. Ibid., 159–62.

44. Halio, *Roth Revisited*, 2–3.

45. Hermione Lee, "'You Must Change Your Life': Mentors, Doubles and Literary Influences in the Search for Self," in *Philip Roth: Criticism & Interpretation*, ed. Harold Bloom (Philadelphia: Chelsea House, 2003), 77.

46. Philip Roth, *The Counterlife* (New York: Farrar, Straus, Giroux, 1987), 140.

47. Elaine Safer, "Tragedy and Farce in Roth's *The Human Stain*," in *Philip Roth*, 242.

48. Ibid., 243–45.

49. Roth, *The Facts*, 8, 9–10.

50. Roth, "My Life as a Writer," 15. Quoting this riff, Jody Rosen wrote a brilliant book on a variation of Roth's theme. See Jody Rosen, *"White Christmas": The Story of an American Song* (New York: Scribner, 2002).

51. Philip Roth, *Operation Shylock: A Confession* (New York: Simon & Schuster, 1993), 157.

52. Pierpont, *Roth Unbound*, 209, 212.

53. Ibid., 322–23.

54. Ibid.

55. Ibid., 235.

56. Bloom, *Roth*, 6.

57. Pierpont, *Roth*, 324–26.

58. Ibid., 365, supports my conclusion.

Chapter Nine

1. Mickey Katz, *Papa, Play for Me: The Autobiography of Mickey Katz As Told to Hannibal Coons*, foreword by Josh Kun (Middletown, CT: Wesleyan University Press, 2002), xix.

2. Ibid., xx–xxi.

3. Ibid., xxv–xxvii, 99.

4. Ibid., 15. My grandmother, who only spoke Yiddish, did likewise: referring to Ed Sullivan as *der Irisher* and her favorite wrestlers as *shtarkers* (strongmen).

5. Ibid., xxxii–xxxv.

6. Ibid., xxxiii.

7. Ibid., xx–xxii.

8. "Catskill Skits & Routines," *Sam Levenson Papers*, Brooklyn College Archives, Accession 92–061.

9. As related in a telephone conversation with Henry Foner, August 25, 2007.

10. Joey Adams and Henry Tobias, *The Borscht Belt* (New York: Bobbs-Merrill, 1966), 13–14.

11. Ibid., 14.

12. Stefan Kanter, *A Summer World: The Attempt to Build a Jewish Eden in the Catskills, from the Days of the Ghetto to the Rise and Decline of the Borscht Belt* (New York: Farrar, Straus & Giroux, 1989), 226.

13. Sam Levenson Archives, Brooklyn College, Series 12, Box 353.

14. Ibid.

15. Ibid. I found the document in the Levenson Archive, Box 353; see Louis Harap, "Is Sam Levenson Funny"? *Jewish Life*, 3:3 (January 1949): 17–20.

16. Brochure in Sam Levenson Archives.

17. Clipping in Levenson Archives of report by Robert Walsh in the *Washington Star*, September 4, 1952.

18. Clippings of *New York Daily News*, September 26, 1951, and September 27, 1952; *The Daily Mirror*, September 22, 1952, and *New York Times* articles in Levenson Archives. Also see Donald Weber, "Goldberg Variations: The Achievements of Gertrude Berg," in *Entertaining America: Jews, Movies, and Broadcasting*, eds. J. Hoberman and Jeffrey Shandler, with contributions by Maurice Berger, et al. (New York: Princeton: Princeton University Press and the Jewish Museum, 2003), 121–22.

19. Levenson Archives, Box 44.

20. Ibid., Box 52.

21. Ibid., Box 54.

22. Ibid., Box 54, 20.

23. The letters cited in this paragraph are found in the Levenson Archives. The one from Harvey Mindess is dated October 10, 1979; Nettie Silver's letter is dated June 2, 1980.

24. "Grandpa's Prayer for Peace," Levenson Archives, Accession No. 92–061, Box 42A.

25. Joe Franklin, *Joe Franklin's Encyclopedia of Comedians* (Secaucus, NJ: Citadel Press, 1979), 231; Phil Berger, *The Last Laugh* (New York: Ballantine Books, 1975), 85–88.

26. Jackie Mason, with Ken Gross, *Jackie Oy! Jackie Mason from Birth to Rebirth* (Boston: Little, Brown, 1988), 278.

27. Jan Garelik, "Jews versus Jew: Jackie Mason's Borscht Belt Minstrel Show," *The Boston Phoenix*, 29 October–5 November 1988, http://www/boston.phoenix.com/archive/theater/98/10/29Jackie_Mason.html.

Chapter Ten

1. Most of the biographical information on Red Buttons can be found in my sketch. See Joseph Dorinson, "Red Buttons," *Scribner Encyclopedia of American Lives* 14:37 (2009): 66–68.

2. Lawrence J. Epstein, *The Haunted Smile: The Story of Jewish Comedians in America* (New York: Public Affairs, 2001), 114.

3. Ibid., 132.

4. Joe Franklin, *Joe Franklin's Encyclopedia of Comedians* (Secaucus, NJ: Citadel Press, 1979), 83.

5. Many of these funny lines are found in http://scomedy.com/quotes/Red-Buttons.

6. Mervin Robinson, "Comedian Red Buttons Dies at 87," *New York Times*, July 14, 2006, provides salient information. Another incisive source is Steve Allen, *The Funny Men* (New York: Simon & Schuster, 1956), 91–104.

7. Tom Shales, "The Bright Appeal of Red Buttons," *Washington Post*, July 14, 2006, C1.

8. Robert Klein, *The Amorous Busboy of Decatur Avenue: A Child of the Fifties Looks Back* (New York: Simon & Schuster Touchstone, 2005), 3, 36; Klein, as narrator, makes the same observations in *When Comedy Went to School*, ttp://www.imdb.com/title/tt2167056/.

9. Ibid., 119–20; Richard Zoglin, *Comedy at the Edge: How Stand-up in the 1970s Changed America* (New York: Bloomsbury, 2008), 73–74.

10. Zoglin, 74–75; conversation with Sy Rose, former intermediate school colleague of Robert Klein.

11. Ibid., 74.

12. Ibid., 77.

13. Zoglin, *Comedy at the Edge*, 77–78.

14. Ibid., 77–78, 218.

15. Ibid., 80; Klein, 124–27.

16. Zoglin, *Comedy at the Edge*, 80–81.

17. Ibid., 220; Zoglin adds that Seinfeld liked Klein because he "was the first stand-up who sounded like his friends, not his parents' friends."

18. Rick Lyman, "In The Bronx with Billy Crystal; Facing Fifty with Memories of Mick," March 13, 1998, in *New York Times Biographical Service* Vol. 29, No. 3, 376–78.

19. Bryan Curtis, "Billy Crystal: The Comedian As Grief Counselor," *Slate*, June 1, 2005, http://slate.msn.com/id/2111085.

20. *Bravo*: "Billy Crystal Inside the Actors Studio," Bravotv.com.

21. Billy Crystal, with Dick Schaap, *Absolutely Mahvelous* (New York: G. P. Putnam's Sons, 1986), 20. Also see the more current autobiography, Billy Crystal, *Still Foolin' 'Em …* (New York: Henry Holt, 2013) *passim*.

22. Ibid., 33–42.

23. Ibid., 11.

24. Ibid., 9–14; also see http://www.geocities.com/jsmurfette/bcrystal.html.

25. Alan King, with Chris Chase, *Name-Dropping: The Life and Lies of Alan King* (New York: Scribner, 1996), 150–51.

26. Epstein, *The Haunted Smile*, 218–19.

27. "Alan King Quotes," http://www.brainyquote.com/quotes/authors/a/alan_king.html.

28. Curtis, *Slate*, 3.

29. Billy Crystal, "Why Did I Become a Comic? He Inspired Me," *New York Times*, February 15, 2014, C1, C6.

30. http /www.nme.com/filmandtv/news/billy-crystal-pays-tribute-to-robin-williams-at-the/349612.

31. Polarized perceptions of suburbia in American culture and their altered states are deftly captured by Samuel G. Freedman in his article, "Suburbia Outgrows Its Image in the Arts," *New York Times*, Section 2, Sunday, February 28, 1999, 1, 26–27.

Chapter Eleven

1. David Marc, *Comic Visions: Television Comedy & American Culture* (second edition) (Malden, MA: Blackwell Publishers, 1997), 10.

2. Ibid., 12; David Frye's quip comes from his album: *Richard Nixon: A Fantasy*, Buddah Records-1600 (1973).

3. Milt Josefsberg, *The Jack Benny Show*

(New Rochelle, NY: Arlington House Publishers, 1977), 43–44.

4. Jim Cox, *The Great Radio Sitcoms* (Jefferson, NC: McFarland, 2007), 159.

5. Ibid., 159–60.

6. Marc, *Comic Visions*, 36.

7. Cox, *The Great Radio Sitcoms*, 157.

8. Steve Allen, *The Funny Men* (New York: Simon & Schuster, 1956), 64; Benny's relationship with his writers is canvassed by Milt Josefsberg, one of his former writers, in his book *The Jack Benny Show*, 122–35.

9. Allen, *Funny Men*, 64–67; Cox, *The Great Radio Sitcoms*, 161.

10. Josefsberg, *The Jack Benny Show*, 109.

11. Ibid., 107–08.

12. Joseph Boskin, *Sambo: The Rise and Demise of an American Jester* (New York: Oxford University Press, 1986), 175–97; also see Epstein, *The Haunted Smile*, p. 61, for a spirited defense of Benny's use of ethnic humor and praise for desegregation of radio.

13. Epstein, *The Haunted Smile*, 59–60.

14. Ibid., 62–64.

15. Josefsberg, *The Jack Benny Show*, 316–18.

16. Ibid.

17. Allen, *Funny Men*, 74, 75.

18. Cox, *The Great Radio Sitcoms*, 167.

19. David Zurawik, *The Jews of Prime Time* (Hanover, NH: Brandeis University Press, 2002), 155.

20. Donald Weber, "Goldberg Variations: The Achievements of Gertrude Berg," in J. Hoberman & Jeffrey Shandler, *Entertaining America: Jews, Movies, and Broadcasting*, eds. J. Hoberman and Jeffrey Chandler (Princeton: Princeton University Press and the Jewish Museum, 2003), 113.

21. Ibid., 113–14.

22. Ibid., 114–15; Weber cites Gertrude Berg, "Why I Hate the Term 'Soap Opera.'" *Everywoman's* Magazine, February 1945, 28.

23. Weber, *Entertaining America*, 118–19.

24. Ibid., 121.

25. Zurovic, *The Jews of Prime Time*, 32–33.

26. Ibid.

27. Ibid., 33–35.

28. Victor S. Navasky, *Naming Names* (New York: Penguin Books, 1981), 268–70, 341.

29. Ibid., 42–45.

30. Joyce Antler, *You Never Call! You Never Write! A History of the Jewish Mother* (New York: Oxford University Press, 2007), 70.

31. Epstein, *Haunted Smile*, 73.

32. Ibid., 144–46.

33. Ibid., 266.

34. Ibid., 265.

35. Antler, *You Never Call!*, 181–83.

36. Marc, *Comic Visions*, 198–99.

37. Epstein, *The Haunted Smile*, 266; also see Suzanne Lavin, *Women in Comedy in Solo Performance* (New York: Routledge, 2004), pp. 53–69, for a positive assessment of Roseanne Barr as "negative exemplar" in Lawrence E. Mintz's paradigm of a comedian who rages against a Hobbesian world that is "nasty, brutish, and short." Lavin can be considered a true "Barrista."

38. Cynthia Crossen, "Funny Business," *Wall Street Journal* article, reprinted in the *Seattle Times* March 3, 1997, http://communi ty.seattletimes.nwsource.com/archive/?date= 19970303&slug=2526818.

39. Lewis Grossberger, "A World in Peril…" *Media Week* (January 12, 1988): 30, as cited in *Seinfeld, Master of its Domain: Revisiting Television's Greatest Sitcoms*, eds. David Lavery with Sarah Lewis Dunne (New York: Continuum, 2006), 40.

40. Jon Stratton, "*Seinfeld* Is a Jewish Sitcom" in Lavery and Dunne, 119.

41. Ibid., 120, 121.

42. Wallace Markfield, "The Yiddishization of American Humor," *Esquire*, October 1965, 114.

43. *Richard Zoglin, Comedy at the Edge: How Stand-up in the 1970s Changed America* (New York: Bloomsbury, 2008), 216–17.

44. Ibid., 218.

45. Ibid., 219, 222.

46. David Marc, "*Seinfeld*: A Show (Almost) about Nothing," in Lavery and Dunne, 23–24.

47. Ibid., 22.

48. Jerry Seinfeld, *Sein Language* (New York: Bantam Books, 1993), 51.

49. Stratton, *Seinfeld*, 128.

50. Marc, "*Seinfeld*," 25.

51. Bill Wyman, "*Seinfeld*," in Lavery and Dunne, 32–32.

52. Joann L. DiMattia, "Male Anxiety and the Buddy System," in Lavery and Dunne; also Seinfeld, *Sein Language*, 51.

53. Wyman, 38, cites Steven D. Stark, "A Tale of Two Sitcoms…" (New York: Free Press, 1997), 282–87.

54. Carla Johnson, "Lost in New York: The Schlemiel and the Schlimazel in *Seinfeld*," *Journal of Popular Film and Television*, 22:3 (1994): 116–24; and as partially cited in Lavery and Dunne, 43–44.

55. Wyman, "*Seinfeld*," 46; also see Stratton, *Seinfeld*, 127.

56. Ibid.

57. David Lavery and Marc Leverette, "Afterward: Re-Reading *Seinfeld* after *Curb Your Enthusiasm*," in Lavery & Dunne, 208–11.

58. Joanne Morreale, "Sitcoms Say Goodbye: The Cultural Spectacle of *Seinfeld*'s Last

Episode," *Journal of Popular Film and Television* 28:3 (Fall 2008): 108, as cited in Lavery and Dunne, 44.

59. Roy Rosenbaum, "Nothing Personal: Deprogramming the Cult of *Seinfeld*," in Lavery & Dunne, 36–37.

60. Zurawik, *The Jews of Prime Time*, 216–17.

Chapter Twelve

1. William Schecter, *A History of Negro Humor in America* (New York: Fleet Press, 1970), 128, offers a variant of the opening joke, with a Catholic replacing the Jew; Gershon Legman, *Rationale of the Dirty Joke: An Analysis of Sexual Humor* (New York: Grove Press, 1968), 9; Nathan Hurwitz, "Blacks and Jews in American Folklore," *Western Folklore* 33:4 (October 1974): 301–04, 306–09, 318–24.

2. Many of the jokes used in this chapter are found in a variety of sources. The wording, therefore, is rarely identical. I have tried to maintain the basic form without sacrificing either content or spirit. The Kuhn Loeb joke is from Hurwitz, "Blacks and Jews...," 172.

3. Irving Howe and Eliezer Greenberg, eds., *A Treasury of Yiddish Stories* (New York: Viking Press, 1965), 26.

4. For the "Snow White" joke and other jousting jests, see Joseph Boskin, "Black/Black Humor: the Renaissance of Laughter," in *A Celebration of Laughter*, ed. Werner Mendel (Los Angeles: Mara Books, 1970), 152–58; also consult Donald C. Simmons, "Protest Humor: Folkloristic reactions to Prejudice" *Journal of Psychiatry* 120 (December 1963): 567.

5. The first scholarly treatment in this genre is found in Antonin J. Obrdlik," "'Gallows Humor'—A Sociological Phenomenon," *American Journal of Sociology* 47:5 (March 1942): 709–16; also revisit Irving Kristol, "Is Jewish Humor Dead? The Rise and fall of the Jewish Joke," *Commentary* 12:5 (November 1951): 432–36.

6. Stephen J. Whitfield, "Laughter in the Dark: Notes of American Jewish Humor," *Midstream* 24:2 (February 1978): 51.

7. Rabbi H. R. Rabinowitz, *Kosher Humor* (Jerusalem: R. H. Hochen Press), 44–49; also see Steve Lipman, *Laughter in Hell: The Use of Humor during the Holocaust* (Northvale, NJ: Jason Aronson, 1991).

8. As quoted by Maria Popova, "Victor Frankl on the Human Search for Meaning," in *Brain Pickings: A Newsletter*; Lipman, "Laughter...," 11, 14–15.

9. William Novak and Moshe Waldoks,

ed., *The Big Book of Jewish Humor* (New York: Harper & Row, 1981), xx–xxii; also see Leo Rosten, *Hooray for Yiddish!* (New York: Simon & Schuster, 1984), 24–25.

10. Gil Osofsky, ed., *Puttin' on Ole Massa: The Slave Narratives of Henry Bibb, William Wells Brown, and Solomon Northrup* (New York: Harper & Row, 1969), 22–23. The "less turkey ... mo' nigger" retort comes from several sources, including Joseph Boskin, "Goodbye to Mr. Bones," *New York Times Magazine* (May 1, 1965): 85.

11. Norine Dresser, "The Metamorphosis of the Humor of the Black Man," *New York Folklore Quarterly* 26:3 (September 1970): 216–17.

12. Alan Lomax, *Folk Song U.S.A.: The 111 Best American Ballads* (New York: Duel, Sloan, & Pearce, 1947, 1962), 90.

13. Lawrence W. Levine, *Black Culture and Black Consciousness* (New York: Oxford University Press, 1978), 346–47 contains both clean and dirty "Dozens."

14. A. R. Radcliffe-Brown, "On Joking relationships," *Africa* 13 (1940), 195–210; Christopher Wilson, *Joke: Form, Content, Use and Function* (London: Academic Press, 1979), 88.

15. John Dollard, "The Dozens: Dialectic of Insult," in *Mother Wit from the laughing Barrel: Readings in the Interpretation of Afro-American Folklore*, ed. Alan Dundes (Englewood Cliffs: Prentice Hall, 1973), xiii, 279–80, 290; Roger Abrahams's thesis is advanced in two books: *Deep Down in the Jungle ... Negro Narrative Folklore from the Streets of Philadelphia* (Hatboro, PA: Folklore Associates, 1964), 49–59, and *Positively Black* (Englewood Cliffs: Prentice Hall, 1970), 41–42.

16. Sterling A. Brown, "Negro Character as Seen by White Authors," *Journal of Negro Education* 2 (April 1933), 180–201; Morris Goldman, "The Sociology of Negro Humor," unpublished dissertation, New School for Social research, 170; Phillip Sterling, ed., *The Intelligent White Reader's Guide to Negro Tales and Humor* (New York: Grosseto & Dunlap, 1965), 22.

17. Nathan I. Huggins, *Harlem Renaissance* (New York: Oxford University Press, 1971), 249–71, 274; Albert F. McLean, Jr., *American Vaudeville as Ritual* (Lexington: University of Kentucky Press, 1965), 24–26, 109, 114, 135–36; Robert Toll, *Blacking Up: The Minstrel Show in Nineteenth Century America* (New York: Oxford University Press, 1974), 228, 245, 254–56, 259, 262, 274.

18. Bernard Wolfe, "Uncle Remus and the Malevolent Rabbit," in *Mother Wit*, ed. Dundes, 527; Robert Bone, *Down Home: A History of*

Afro-American Short Fiction from Its Beginning to the End of the Harlem Renaissance (New York: G. P. Putnam's & Sons, 1975), 24–26, 27–29.

19. Jack Schiffman, *Uptown: The Story of Harlem's Apollo Theatre* (New York: Cowles Book, 1971), 124, 126; Bone, *Down Home*, 59, 60–61; Toll, *Blacking Up*, 247–48.

20. Ann Charters, *Nobody: The Story of Bert Williams* (New York: Macmillan, 1970), 15–19, 21–18, 72; Robert Toll, *On with the Show: The First Century of Show Business in America* (New York: Oxford University Press, 1976), 123.

21. Langston Hughes and Milton Meltzer, *Black Magic: A Pictorial History of the Negro in American Entertainment* (Englewood Cliffs: Prentice Hall, 1967), 58; William McFerrin Stowe, Jr., "Damned Funny: The Tragedy of Bert Williams," *Journal of Popular Culture* 10:1 (Summer 1976): 5–11; Charters, *Nobody*, 95–97.

22. Levine, *Black Culture*, 360–61; Charters, *Nobody*, 106; for the Jewish equivalent, see Nathan Ausabel, *A Treasury of Jewish Folklore* (New York: Crown Publishers, 1949), 442–43.

23. Charters, *Nobody*, 9, 135–37.

24. Mabel Roland, ed., *Bert Williams: Son of Laughter* (New York: English Crafters, 1923), 128.

25. Ibid., 182–83; Levine, *Black*, 361.

26. Charters, *Nobody*, 139.

27. As quoted in Nancy Levi Arnez and Clara B. Anthony, "Contemporary Negro Humor as Social Satire," *Phylon* 29:4 (Winter 1968): 339.

28. Ibid., 340. On celluloid portraiture of blacks, see Daniel J. Leab, *From Sambo to Superspade: The Black Experience in Motion Pictures* (Boston: Houghton Mifflin, 1976; Donald Bogle, *Toms, Coons, Mulattoes, Mammies and Bucks* (New York: Viking Press, 1973); Gary Null, *Black Hollywood: The Negro in Motion Pictures* (Secaucus: Citadel Press, 1975); Joseph Boskin, *Sambo: The Rise and Demise of an American Jester* (New York: Oxford University Press, 1986), especially chapter 7.

29. Robert Oberfirst, *Al Jolson: You Ain't Heard Nothin Yet!* (San Diego: A. S. Barnes, 1980), 22–24, 28–37, 79–81; William Cahn, *The Laugh Makers: A Pictorial History of American Comedians* (New York: G. P. Putnam's Sons, 1957), 126.

30. Stanley White, "The Burnt Cork Illusion of the 1920s in America: A Study in Nostalgia," *Journal of Popular Culture* 5:3 (Winter 1971), 531–43. The quote is found on p. 543. Also see Irving Howe, *World of Our Fathers* (New York: Harcourt, Brace & Jovanovich, 1976), 562–63; and Ronald Sanders, "The American Popular Song," in *Next Year in Jerusalem...*, ed. Douglas Villiers (New York: Viking Press, 1976), 197–202.

31. Theodore Reik, *Jewish Wit* (New York: Gamut Press, 1962), 85; Joey Adams and Henry Tobias, *The Borscht Belt* (New York: Bentley Publishing, 1966), 61–62; Albert F. McLean, Jr., *American Vaudeville as Ritual*, 144.

32. Alfred Kazin, *The Jew as American Writer*, in *Jewish American Literature*, ed. Abraham Chapman (New York: New American Library, 1974), 589–90; Sanders, "Popular Song," 197–93; Howe, *World*, 565–68.

33. Howe, *World*, 566.

34. Phillip Roth, *Portnoy's Complaint* (New York: Bantam, 1969), 164–65; How, *World*, 565–68.

35. Howe, *World*, 570.

36. Information from the above section issues from a variety of sources: Earl Rovit, "Jewish Humor & American Life," *American Scholar* 36:2 (Spring 1967): 237–45; Leslie Fiedler, *Waiting for the End* (New York: Stein & Day, 1964), 67–68; Howe, *World*, 569–71; Sig Altman, *The Comic Image of the Jew: Explorations of a Pop Culture Phenomenon* (Rutherford NJ: Fairleigh Dickinson University Press, 1971), 191–96, 199–205; Maurice Yacower, *Loser Take All: The Comic Art of Woody Allen* (New York: Frederick Ungar, 1979), 189, 191.

37. Redd Foxx and Norma Miller, *The Redd Foxx Encyclopedia of Black Humor* (Pasadena: Ward Ritchie, 1977), 235.

38. John Cohen, ed., *The Essential Lenny Bruce* (New York: Ballantine Books, 1967), 26–27.

39. Ibid., 41, 52–75, 133–39, 142, for Bruce's prime *shtick*. For Lenny's Jewish performance style, read Hentoff, "Yiddish Survivals," 692. Also see Robert Alter, "Defaming the Jews" *Commentary* 55:1 (January 1973): 80–81; and Walter Blair and Hamlin Hill, *America's Humor: From Poor Richard to Doonesbury* (New York: Oxford University Press, 1978), 516.

40. Yakower, *Loser*, 213.

41. Eric Lax, *On Being Funny: Woody Allen and Comedy* (New York: Charterhouse, 1975), 224–25.

42. Maurice Yakower, *Method in Madness: The Comic Art of Mel Brooks* (New York: St. Martin's Press, 1981), 6, 52.

43. *Newsweek*, May 3, 1982, 50; Mel Watkins, *On the Reel Side...* (New York: Simon & Schuster, 1994), 531–33; Richard Grenier, "Black Comedy," *Commentary* 73 (June 1982): 55–56; James McPherson, "The New Comic Style of Richard Pryor," *New York Times Magazine*, April 27, 1975, 22, 26, 32, 34, 42–43 provides important biographical data, including Pryor's actual birth date: December 1, 1940.

44. Mel Watkins, "Richard Pryor, Who Turned Humor of the Streets into Social Satire, Dies at 65," *New York Times*, December 12, 2005, A24; Richard Zoglin, *Comedy at the Edge: How Stand-up in the 1970s Changed America* (New York: Bloomsbury, 2008), 43–46.

45. Zoglin, *Comedy at the Edge*, 49.

46. *Newsweek*, 52.

47. Foxx and Miller, *The Redd Foxx Encyclopedia of Black Humor*, 209.

48. Elsie Griffin Williams, "The Comedy of Richard Pryor as Social Satire," *American Humor: An Interdisciplinary Newsletter* 4:2 (Fall 1977): 17–18; McPherson, "New Comic Style," 34, 42.

49. Zoglin, *Comedy at the Edge*, 61.

50. Ibid., 62.

51. Grenier, "Black Comedy," 58.

52. Zoglin, *Comedy at the Edge*, 62.

53. As cited by Albert Goldman, "The Comedy of Lenny Bruce," in *The Sense of the Sixties*, eds. Edward Quinn and Paul J. Dolan (New York: Free Press, 1968), 203, 205.

54. Griffin Williams, "Comedy of Richard Pryor," 18.

55. *Newsweek*, 54.

56. Joseph Boskin, "Protest Humor: Fighting Criticism with Laughter," *Bostonia* 54:5 (December 1980): 51, in which Boskin cites author Sharon Weinstein's apposite metaphor: "Fluid connection with … history."

57. Christopher Wilson, *Jokes, Form, Content, Use and Function* (London: Academic Press, 1979), 228–29.

58. The formula is derived from a French-speaking, African-Jewish author, Albert Memmi, *The Liberation of a Jew*, translated by Judy Hyun (New York: Orion Press, 1966), 53–54; a similar proverbial statement can be found in *Leo Rosten's Treasury of Jewish Quotations* (New York: McGraw-Hill, 1973), 7. It reads: "When you're hungry, sing; when you hurt, laugh."

59. As quoted in Bruno Bettelheim, "Reflections: Freud and the Soul," *New Yorker*, March 1, 1982, 92.

60. Ibid., 93; Saunders Redding in *Laughing*, 17–19; Joyce O. Hertzler, *Laughter: A Socio-Scientific Analysis* (New York: Exposition Press, 1970), 215–16.

Chapter Thirteen

1. Gene Lees, *Singers and the Song II* (New York: Oxford University Press, 1998), 46–48; Harold Myerson and Ernie Harburg, *Who Put the Rainbow in* The Wizard of Oz? *Yip Harburg, Lyricist* (Ann Arbor: Michigan University Press, 1993), 5–11. Until John Lahr's biography of Yip appears, this will remain the definitive study, one from which I cull lyrics, information, insights, and draw "grandish" inspiration. Rather than a squirrel by a fictional Yiddish name, Yip probably earned this moniker from his swift, darting movements: an energized figure in perpetual motion. See *Modern English-Yiddish, Yiddish-English Dictionary*, ed. Uriel Weinrich (New York: YIVO Institute for Jewish Research and McGraw-Hill, 1968), 307.

2. Deena Rosenberg, *Fascinating Rhythm: The Collaboration of George and Ira Gershwin* (New York: Dutton, 1991), 9–10.

3. Lees, *Singers and the Song II*, 48.

4. William Zinsser, *Easy to Remember …* (Boston: David R. Godine, 2001), 146.

5. Gary Giddins, *Bing Crosby: A Pocketful of Dreams, The Early Years 1903–1940*, (Boston: Little, Brown, 2001).

6. Meyerson and Harburg, 45–53; Lewis A. Erenberg, *Swingin' the Dream: Big Band Jazz and the Rebirth of American Culture* (Chicago: Chicago University Press, 1999), 22.

7. Undated clipping from the Harburg Papers, New York Public Library, *T-Mss 1990-002 Box 5, Folder 2.

8. Studs Terkel, *Hard Times: An Oral History of the Great Depression* (New York: Pantheon, 1970), 21.

9. Meyerson and Harburg, 106.

10. Ibid., 108–11.

11. Ibid., 122.

12. Lees, 50.

13. Ethan Mordden, *Beautiful Mornin': The Broadway Musical in the 1940s* (New York: Oxford University Press, 1999), 97.

14. Ibid., 98.

15. Ibid., 99.

16. Meyerson and Harburg, 196.

17. Ibid., 215.

18. Ibid., 222–23.

19. Ibid., 253.

20. Ibid., 256.

21. Ibid.

22. Ibid., 261.

23. Lees, 51.

24. John Cohen, ed., *The Essential Lenny Bruce* (New York: Ballantine Books, 1967), 75.

25. Burton Lane Interview, April 11, 1983, Harburg Papers, Box 24, Folder 23, 35–39.

26. Mordden, 168.

27. Meyerson & Harburg, 276; Lees, 51.

28. Ibid., 273; Victor Navasky, *Naming Names* (New York: Viking, 1980), 94.

29. Meyerson and Harburg, 273.

30. Ibid., 282; *Burlington Free Press*, November 4, 1970, 10.

31. Bernard Rosenberg and Ernest Gold-

stein, *Creators and Disturbers: Reminiscences by Jewish Intellectuals* (New York: Columbia University Press, 1982).

32. Ibid., 286.

33. Undated clipping, Harburg Papers, Box 1, Folder 7.

34. Rosenberg and Ernest Goldstein, 139.

35. Ibid.

36. John Lahr, "Profile: The Lemon-Drop Kid," *New Yorker*, September 30, 1996, 71.

37. Harburg Papers, Box 1, Folder 1; interview, Nick Markovich, executive director of the Harburg Foundation, March 14, 2003. Evidence of Yip's generosity can be found in his memorial service; see the Harburg Papers, Box 24, Folder 13.

38. Meyerson and Harburg, 303–05.

39. Ibid., 306–07; interview, Nick Markovich, executive director of the Harburg Foundation, March 14, 2003; Richard Gehr, "Resistance Hymns," *Village Voice* (5–11 March 5–11, 2003, 63. (I am indebted to Nick Markovich for calling my attention to this item and for providing a wealth of Harburg treasures.)

Chapter Fourteen

1. Robert Menchin, *101 Classic Jewish Jokes: Jewish Humor from Groucho Marx to Jerry Seinfeld* (Memphis, TN: Mustang Publishing, 1986), 6.

2. Salcia Landmann, "On Jewish Humor," *Jewish Journal of Sociology* 4 (1962): 193–204.

3. Lawrence E. Mintz, "Standup Comedy as Social and Cultural Mediation," in *What's So Funny? Humor in American Culture*, ed. Nancy Walker (Wilmington DE: Scholarly Resources, 1998), 193–204; Stephanie Kozisky Olson, "Standup Comedy" in *Humor in America: A Research Guide to Genres and Topics*, ed. Lawrence E. Mintz (Westport: CT: Greenwood Press, 1988), 109–22.

4. Myrna and Harvey Frommer, *It Happened in the Catskills* (New York: Harcourt, Brace, & Jovanovich, 1993), 133.

5. Michael Winerip, http://www.nytimes.com/1984/09/28/nyregion/catskill-resorts-bigger-and-seeking-younger-market.html.

6. Frommer and Frommer, 202–04.

7. Ibid., 207.

8. Michael Winerip, http://www.nytimes.com/1984/09/28/nyregion/catskill-resorts-bigger-and-seeking-younger-market.html.

9. Ibid.

10. Richard Zoglin, *Comedy at the Edge: How Stand-up in the 1970s Changed America* (New York: Bloomsbury, 2008), 185. Also see

Lawrence J. Epstein, *The Haunted Smile: The Story of Jewish Comedians in America* (New York: Public Affairs, 2001), 258.

11. Joan Rivers' biographical data was culled from several reliable sources, including her obituary. See Robert D. McFadden, "Joan Rivers, 1933–2014: A Comic Stiletto Quick to Skewer, Even Herself," *New York Times*, September 6, 2014, A1, B16; Jerry Adler, Pamela Abramson, and Susan Agrest, "Joan Rivers Gets Even with Laughs...," *Newsweek*, October 10, 1983, 58–60; Lawrence J. Epstein, *The Haunted Smile*, 253–60; "The Unkosher Comediennes," in *Jewish Wry: Essays on Jewish Humor*, ed. (and author) Susan Blacher Cohen (Bloomington, IN: Indiana University Press, 1987), 115–23; and Laurence Maslin and Michael Kantor, *Make 'Em Laugh: The Funny Business of America* (New York: Twelve Hatchette Book Group, 2008), 178–81.

12. Cohen, 117–18.

13. Ibid., 118.

14. Ibid., 121–22.

15. http://entertainment.suntimes.com/entertainment-news/joan-rivers-piece-work-roger-eberts-2010-review/.

16. Seth Mydans, "Comic's Wicked Wit Keeps Russians Tickled Pink," *New York Times*, October 11, 1984; http://www.nytimes.com/1984/10/11/world/comic-s-wicked-wit-keeps-russians-tickled-pink.html.

17. Harpo Marx, with Rowland Barber, *Harpo Speaks* (New York: Limelight Editions, 1985), 361.

18. Edward Fawcett, "No Faith in Progress..." *New York Times Book Review*, October 13, 2013, 15.

19. William Grimes, "Giving a Satirist of the Third Reich the Last Laugh," *New York Times*, June 7, 2014, C1, C4.

20. Stephen J. Whitfield, "Richard Nixon as a Comic Figure," in *American Humor*, ed. Arthur P. Dudden (New York: Oxford University Press, 1987), 149, 155.

21. Arthur P. Dudden, "The Record of Political Humor" in *American Humor*, 68.

22. As cited in Emil Draitser, "Soviet Underground Jokes," *The Journal of Popular Culture* 23:1 (Summer 1989): 123, 125.

23. http://www.spiegel.de/international/new-book-on-nazi-era-humor-did-you-hear-the-one-about-hitler-a-434399.html.

24. http://www.expatica.com/de/life-in-germany/blogs_photos/did-you-hear-the-one-about-hitler-goering-and-goebbels-33736_10350.html.

25. Ibid.

Bibliography

Abramovich, Ilana & Sean Galvin, eds. *Jews of Brooklyn*. Hanover, NH: Brandeis University Press, 2001.

Adams, Joey, and Henry Tobias. *The Borscht Belt*. New York: Bobbs-Merrill, 1966.

Adler, Bill. *Jewish Wit & Wisdom*. New York: Dell, 1969.

Aleichem, Sholem. *The Tevye Stories and Others*. Translated by Julius and Frances Butwin. New York: Pocket Books, 1965.

Allen, Steve. *The Funny Men*. New York: Simon & Schuster, 1956.

_____. *Funny People*. New York: Stein & Day, 1981.

Altman, Sig. *The Comic Image of the Jew: Explorations of a Pop Culture Phenomenon*. Rutherford, NJ: Fairleigh Dickinson University Press, 1971.

Anobile, Richard J., ed. *Why a Duck? Visual and Verbal Gems from the Marx Brothers Movies*. New York: Darien House, 1972.

Antler, Joyce. *You Never Call! You Never Write! A History of the Jewish Mother*. New York: Oxford University Press, 2007.

Atlas, James. *Bellow: A Biography*. New York: Random House, 2000.

Ausubel, Nathan, ed. *A Treasury of Jewish Folklore*. New York: Crown, 1948.

_____. *A Treasury of Jewish Humor*. New York: Paperback Library, 1998.

Berger, Joseph. "For Catskill Alumni, Yesterday's Summer Borscht and Knishes Return." *New York Times*, August 31, 2000.

Berger, Phil. *The Last Laugh*. New York: Ballantine Books, 1975.

Berle, Milton. *B. S. I Love You: Sixty Funny Years with the Famous and the Infamous*. New York: McGraw-Hill, 1988.

_____. *Milton Berle: An Autobiography*. With the assistance of Haskel Frankel. New York: Applause Books, 2002.

_____. *Milton Berle's Private Joke File*. Edited by Milt Rosen. New York: Crown Trade Paperbacks, 1989.

Bloom, Harold, ed. *Philip Roth: Criticism & Interpretation*. Philadelphia: Chelsea House, 2003.

Blythe, Cheryl, and Susan Sackett. *Say Goodnight, Gracie! The Story of George Burns & Gracie Allen*. Rocklin, CA: Prima, 1989.

Borns, Betsy. *Comic Lives: Inside the World of American Stand-up Comedy*. New York: Simon & Schuster (A Fireside Book), 1987.

Boskin, Joseph. "Goodbye, Mr. Bones." *New York Times Magazine*, May 1, 1966.

_____. *Rebellious Laughter: People's Humor in American Culture*. Syracuse: Syracuse University Press, 1997.

_____. *Sambo: The Rise and Demise of an American Jester*. New York: Oxford University Press, 1986.

_____, ed. *The Humor Prism in 20th Century America*. Detroit: Wayne State University Press, 1997.

_____, and Joseph Dorinson. "Ethnic Humor: Subversion and Survival." *American Quarterly* 37: 1 (Spring 1985): 81–97.

Brown, Phil. *Catskill Culture: A Mountain Rat's Memories of the Great Jewish Resort Area*. Philadelphia: Temple University Press, 1998.

Burns, George. *All My Best Friends*. With the assistance of David Fisher. New York: G. P. Putnam's Sons, 1989.

Caesar, Sid. *Caesar's Hours: My Life in Comedy with Love and Laughter*. With the assistance of Eddy Friedfeld. New York: Public Affairs, 2003.

_____. *Where Have I Been...?* With the assistance of Bill Davidson. New York: Crown, 1982.

Charyn, Jerome. *Movieland: Hollywood and the American Dream Culture*. New York: G. P. Putnam's Sons, 1989.

Cohen, John, ed. *The Essential Lenny Bruce*. New York: Ballantine, 1967.

Cohen, Sarah Blacher. *Comic Relief: Humor in Contemporary American Literature*. Urbana: University of Illinois Press, 1979.

_____. *Jewish Wry: Essays on Jewish Humor*. Bloomington: Indiana University Press, 1987.

_____. *Saul Bellow's Enigmatic Laughter*. Urbana: University of Illinois Press, 1974.

Cooper, Alan. *Philip Roth and the Jews*. Albany: State University of New York Press, 1996.

Crystal, Billy. *Still Foolin' 'Em: Where I've Been, Where I'm Going, and Where the Hell Are My Keys?* New York: Henry Holt, 2013.

Dargis, Manhola, and A. O. Scott. "The Woody Allen Genome." *New York Times*, January 3, 2014.

Dorinson, Joseph. "The Educational Alliance: An Institutional Study in Americanization and Acculturation." In *Immigration & Ethnicity*, edited by Michael D'Innocenzo and Joseph P. Sirefman. Westport, CT: Greenwood Press, 1992, 93–107.

_____. "From Soup to Nuts; Laughter in the Suburbs: Alan King and Billy Crystal." In *Nassau County: From Rural Hinterland to Suburban Metropolis*, edited by Joann P. Krieg and Natalie Naylor, 282–91. Interlaken, NY: Empire State Books, 2000.

_____. "The Jew as Comic." In *Jewish Humor*, edited by Ziv Avner Ziv, 29–42. Tel-Aviv: Papyrus Press, 1986.

_____. "Jewish Humor," *The Journal of Psychohistory* 8: 4 (Spring 1981): 447–464.

_____. "Lenny Bruce: A Jewish Humorist in Babylon." *Jewish Currents* 35: 2 (February 1981): 14–19, 31–32.

Draitser, Emil. *Forbidden Laughter*. Los Angeles: Almanac Publishing, 1978.

Dresser, David, and Lester D. Friedman. *American-Jewish Filmmakers: Traditions and Trends*. Urbana: University of Illinois Press, 1993.

Dudden, Arthur Power. *American Humor*. New York: Oxford University Press, 1987.

Epstein, Lawrence J. *The Haunted Smile: The Story of Jewish Comedians in America*. New York: Public Affairs, 2001.

_____. *Mixed Nuts: America's Love Affair with Comedy Teams*. New York: Public Affairs, 2004.

Field, Leslie, and W. Joyce, eds. *Bernard Malamud and the Critics*. New York: New York University Press, 1970.

Franklin, Joe. *Joe Franklin's Encyclopedia of Comedians*. Secaucus, NJ: Citadel Press, 1979.

Frommer, Myrna, and Harvey Frommer. *It Happened in the Catskills*. New York: Harcourt, Brace, Jovanovich, 1991.

Fry, William F. Jr., and Melanie Allen, eds. *Make 'Em Laugh: Life Studies of Comedy Writers*. Palo Alto, CA: Science & Behavior Books, 1975.

Gillota, David. *Ethnic Humor in Multiethnic America*. New Brunswick, NJ: Rutgers University Press, 2013.

Goldman, Herbert. *Banjo Eyes: Eddie Cantor and the Birth of Modern Stardom*. New York: Oxford University Press, 1997.

Gordon, Rae Beth. *Why the French Love Jerry Lewis: From Cabaret to Early Cinema*. Stanford, CA: Stanford University Press, 2001.

Green, Abel, and Joe Laurie, Jr. *Show Biz from Vaudeville to Video*. Port Washington, NY: Kennikat Press, 1951.

Gregory, Dick. *Nigger: An Autobiography*. With the assistance of Robert Lipsyte. New York: Washington Square Press, 1986.

Halberstam-Rubin, Anna. *Sholem Aleichem: The Writer as Social Historian.* New York: Peter Lang, 1989.

Halio, Jay L. *Philip Roth Revisited.* New York: Twayne, 1992.

Heller, Erich. *The Disinherited Mind: Essays in Modern German Literature and Thought.* Middlesex, Australia: Penguin Pelican Books, 1961.

Hendra, Tony. *Going Too Far.* Garden City, NY: Doubleday, 1987.

Hentoff, Nat. "Where Liberals Fear To Thread." *Reporter* 22:13 (June 23, 1960).

Hershinow, Sheldon. *Bernard Malamud.* New York: Frederick Ungar, 1980.

Hoberman, J., and Jeffrey Shandler, et al. *Entertaining America: Jews, Movies, and Broadcasting.* Princeton: Princeton University Press and the Jewish Museum, 1994.

Holtzman, Will. *Seesaw: A Dual Biography of Anne Bancroft & Mel Brooks.* Garden City, NY: Doubleday, 1979.

Howe, Irving, and Eliezer Greenber. *A Treasury of Yiddish Stories.* New York: Viking Press Compass Books, 1965.

Howe, Irving, with Kenneth Libo. *The World of Our Fathers.* New York: Harcourt, Brace, Jovanovich, 1976.

Janus, Samuel. "The Great Comedians: Personality and Other Factors." *The American Journal of Psychoanalysis.* 35: no. 2 (1975): 169–74.

Jenkins, Ron. *Subversive Laughter: The Liberating Power of Comedy.* New York: Macmillan, 1994.

Josefsberg, Milt. *The Jack Benny Show.* New Rochelle, NY: Arlington House, 1977.

Kanfer, Stefan. *Stardust Lost: The Triumph, Tragedy, and Mishugas of the Yiddish Theater.* New York: Alfred A. Knopf, 2006.

_____. *A Summer World: The Attempt to Build a Jewish Eden in the Catskills, from the Days of the Ghetto to the Rise and Decline of the Borscht Belt.* New York: Farrar, Straus, Giroux, 1991.

_____. "Vaudeville's Brief, Shining Moment." *City Journal* (Spring 2005); see http://www.city-journal.org/html/15_2_urbanites-vaudeville.html.

Katz, Mickey (as told to Hannibal Coons).

Papa Play for Me: The Autobiography of Mickey Katz. Middletown, CT: Wesleyan University Press, 1977.

King, Alan. *Alan King's Great Jewish Joke Book.* New York: Crown, 2002.

_____. *Name-Dropping: the Life and Lies of Alan King.* With the assistance of Chris Chase. New York: Scribner, 1996.

Klein, Robert. *The Amorous Busboy of Decatur Avenue: A Child of the Fifties Looks Back.* New York: Simon & Schuster Touchstone, 2005.

Kohen, Yael. *We Killed: The Rise of Women in American Comedy, a Very Oral History.* New York: Farrar, Straus, & Giroux, 2012.

Krassner, Paul. *The Realist.* 43 (September 1969).

Krutnik, Frank. *Inventing Jerry Lewis.* Washington, D.C.: Smithsonian Institution Press, 2000.

Laurie, Joe, Jr. *Vaudeville: From the Honky-Tonks to the Palace.* Port Washington, NY: Kennikat Press, 1972.

Lavery, David, with Sara Lewis Dunne, eds. *Seinfeld, Master of Its Domain: Revisiting Television's Greatest Sitcoms.* New York: Continuum, 2006.

Lavin, Suzanne. *Women and Comedy in Solo Performance: Phyllis Diller, Lily Tomlin, and Roseanne.* New York: Routledge, 2004.

Levenson, Sam. "The Dialect Comedian Should Vanish." *Commentary* (August 1953).

_____. *Everything but Money.* New York: Simon & Schuster, 1966.

Levine, Lawrence W. *Black Culture and Black Consciousness.* New York: Oxford University Press, 1977.

Levy, Shawn. *King of Comedy: The Life and Art of Jerry Lewis.* New York: St. Martin's Press, 1996.

Lewis, Jerry. *The Total Film-Maker.* New York: Warner Paperback Library, 1973.

Lipman, Steve. *Laughter in Hell: The Use of Humor during the Holocaust.* Northvale, NJ: Jason Aronson, 1991.

Louvish, Simon. *Monkey Business.* New York: St. Martin's Press Thomas Dunne's Books, 1999.

Marc, David. *Comic Visions: Television*

Comedy & American Culture (second edition). Malden, MA: Blackwell, 1997.

Marx, Arthur. *Life with Groucho.* New York: Popular Library, 1954.

Mason, Jackie. *Jackie Mason's "The World According to Me!"* New York: Simon & Schuster, 1987.

_____. *Jackie Oy! Jackie Mason from Birth to Rebirth.* With the assistance of Ken Gross. Boston: Little, Brown, 1988.

Mast, Gerald. *The Comic Mind: Comedy and the Movies.* Indianapolis: Bobbs-Merrill, 1973.

Meyerson, Harold, and Ernest Harburg. *Who Put the Rainbow in the Wizard of Oz?: Yip Harburg, Lyricist.* Ann Arbor: University of Michigan Press, 1993.

Mintz, Lawrence E. *Humor in America: A Research Guide to Genres and Topics.* Westport, CT: Greenwood Press, 1988.

Mostel, Kate, and Madeline Gilford. *170 Years of Show Business.* With the assistance of Zero Mostel and Jack Gilford. New York: Random House, 1978.

Nachman, Gerald. *Seriously Funny: The Rebel Comedians of the 1950s and 1960s.* New York: Pantheon Books, 2003.

Nilsen, Don L. F. "Humorous Contemporary Jewish-American Authors: An Overview of the Criticism," *Melus* 21:4 (Winter 1996): 71–101.

Parrish, James Robert, and William T. Leonard. *The Funsters.* New Rochelle, NY: Arlington House, 1979.

Pierpont, Claudia Roth. *Roth Unbound: A Writer and His Books.* New York: Farrar, Giroux, & Straus, 2013.

Richman, Irwin. *Borscht Belt Bungalows.* Philadelphia: Temple University Press, 1997.

Robbins, Michael W., ed. *Brooklyn: A State of Mind.* New York: Werkman Publishing, 2001.

Robertson, Ritchie. *Heine.* New York: Grove Press, 1988.

Rosen, Jody. *"White Christmas": The Story of an American Song.* New York: Scribner, 2002.

Rosenberg, Bernard, and Ernest Goldstein. *Creators and Disturbers: Reminiscences by Jewish Intellectuals of New York.* New York: Columbia University Press, 1982.

Rosten, Leo. *Hooray for Yiddish! A Book about English.* New York: Simon & Schuster, 1982.

_____. *The Joys of Yiddish.* New York: Pocket Books Kangaroo, 1968.

Roth, Philip. *Novels and Stories, 1959–1962.* New York: Random House, 2005.

_____. *Portnoy's Complaint.* New York: Random House, 1972.

Sahl, Mort. *Heartland.* New York: Harcourt Brace Jovanovich, 1976.

Samuel, Maurice. *In Praise of Yiddish.* New York: Cowles, 1971.

Sandrow, Nahma. *Vagabond Stars: A World of Yiddish Theater.* New York: Harper & Row, 1977.

Schechter, Joel. *Messiahs of 1933: How American Yiddish Theatre Survived Adversity through Satire.* Philadelphia: Temple University Press, 2008.

Silet, Charles L. P., ed. *The Films of Woody Allen: Critical Essays.* Lanham, MD: Scarecrow Press, 2006.

Slide, Anthony, ed. *Selected Vaudeville Criticism.* Metuchen, NJ: Scarecrow Press, 1988.

Smith, Janna Malamud. *My Father Is a Book: A Memoir of Bernard Malamud.* Boston: Houghton-Mifflin, 2006.

Smith, Ronald L. *Who's Who in Comedy.* New York: Oxford Facts on File, 1992.

Snyder, Robert W. *The Voice of the City: Vaudeville and Popular Culture in New York.* New York: Oxford University Press, 1989.

Stewart, D. Travis. *No Applause: Just Throw Money.* New York: Farrar, Straus, and Giroux, Faber and Faber, 2003.

Toll, Robert. *Blacking Up: the Minstrel Show in Nineteenth Century America.* New York: Oxford University Press, 1974.

Tracy, Kathleen. *Sacha Baron Cohen, The Unauthorized Biography: From Cambridge to Kazakhstan.* New York: St. Martin's Griffin, 2007.

Tynan, Kenneth. *Show People: Profiles in Entertainment.* New York: Simon & Schuster, 1979.

Walker, Nancy A., ed. *What's So Funny?*

Humor in American Culture. Wilmington, DE: Scholarly Resources, 1998.

Watkins, Mel. *On the Reel Side: A History of African-American Comedy*. Chicago: Lawrence Hill Books, 1999.

Winokur, Mark. *American Laughter: Immigrants, Ethnicity, and 1930s Hollywood Film Comedy*. New York: St. Martin's Press, 1996.

Yacower, Maurice. *Loser Take All: The Comic Art of Woody Allen*. New York: The Continuum Publishing Company, Frederick Ungar Book, 1991.

_____. *Method in Madness: The Comic Art of Mel Brooks*. New York: St. Martin's Press, 1981.

Zoglin, Richard. *Comedy at the Edge: How Stand-up in the 1970s Changed America*. New York: Bloomsbury, 2008.

Zurawik, David. *The Jews of Prime Time*. Hanover, NH: Brandeis University Press, 2002.

Index

Page numbers in bold italics indicate pages with illustrations.